LIBERTY, VIRTUE AND HAPPINESS
THE STORY OF ECONOMIC FREEDOM IN AMERICA

LIBERTY, VIRTUE AND HAPPINESS
THE STORY OF ECONOMIC FREEDOM IN AMERICA

EDWARD W. RYAN

FOREWORD BY WILLIAM E. SIMON

nova Science Publishers, Inc.
Huntington, NY

Senior Editors: Susan Boriotti and Donna Dennis
Coordinating Editor: Tatiana Shohov
Office Manager: Annette Hellinger
Graphics: Wanda Serrano
Book Production: Matthew Kozlowski, Jonathan Rose and Jennifer Vogt
Circulation: Cathy DeGregory, Ave Maria Gonzalez, Ron Hedges and Andre Tillman

Library of Congress Cataloging-in-Publication Data
Available Upon Request

ISBN 1-59033-040-4.

Copyright © 2001 by Nova Science Publishers, Inc.
227 Main Street, Suite 100
Huntington, New York 11743
Tele. 631-424-6682   Fax 631-425-5933
E Mail: Novascience@earthlink.net

All rights reserved. No part of this book may be reproduced, stored in a retrieval system or transmitted in any form or by any means: electronic, electrostatic, magnetic, tape, mechanical photocopying, recording or otherwise without permission from the publishers.

The authors and publisher have taken care in preparation of this book, but make no expressed or implied warranty of any kind and assume no responsibility for any errors or omissions. No liability is assumed for incidental or consequential damages in connection with or arising out of information contained in this book.

This publication is designed to provide accurate and authoritative information with regard to the subject matter covered herein. It is sold with the clear understanding that the publisher is not engaged in rendering legal or any other professional services. If legal or any other expert assistance is required, the services of a competent person should be sought. FROM A DECLARATION OF PARTICIPANTS JOINTLY ADOPTED BY A COMMITTEE OF THE AMERICAN BAR ASSOCIATION AND A COMMITTEE OF PUBLISHERS.

Printed in the United States of America

To Georgian, Jennifer, Sarah and Michael

"With the fall of communism and rise of capitalism around the globe, this book is a timely examination of the role economic freedom has played in our nation's success. Professor Ryan does a masterful job of demonstrating that all our other freedoms are entwined with our economic freedom. His insights into politics and markets bring a new perspective to our economic history. But rather than a purely academic discussion, it examines how we can enhance our society through insight into our failures as well as our successes. This highly readable account is a must for anyone who wants to understand the history of the United States."

Mary C. Farrell
Managing Director, Senior Investment Strategist
Paine Webber, Inc.; Regular Panelist:
Wall $treet Week With Louis Rukeyser

"Professor Ryan has taken us on an informative journey from the early years of our country's history where self-reliance was the byword to the age of dependency in our nation that exists today. It is a fascinating recapturing of how we got to where we are, and may make many yearn for the days when responsibility was a personal accomplishment and not a benefit expected from the state. He gives us a clear picture of the blessings we received from the economic freedoms of an unmanaged economy, and makes us painfully aware that the freedoms that we cherish, and which sprang from the moral beginnings of this "grand experiment," are in significant danger as the morality of this entire nation comes into question. Professor Ryan has produced a fascinating history of the economic events which developed this country and brought us to this crossroads."

Leopold Korins
President and CEO:
Security Traders Association and Former Chairman and
CEO: Pacific Stock Exchange

"America was an experiment testing a great idea: that individuals left free to pursue their own interests could build a prosperous nation and live in harmony. Professor Ryan brings the story of America to life, recounting the ideas, individuals, and events that have contributed to the successes, as well as the failures, of the American experiment in liberty. In so doing, Professor Ryan doesn't shy away from a cogent analysis of the challanges that lie ahead, particularly as we struggle to maintain virtue in an age of prosperity."

Roger R. Ream
President: The Fund for American Studies

"Professor Ryan does an outstanding job of explaining how entrepreneurship can advance the economic well-being of all. He emphasizes the importance of the often overlooked ingredients of value creation which make for success in a free market economy. Also, he provides an optimistic message and realistic encouragement to those who would frame public policy for the disadvantaged, not only in the United States, but in every nation."

Steve Mariotti: Founder and President
Michael J. Caslin: Chief Executive Officer
National Foundation For Teaching Entrepreneurship

CONTENTS

Foreword by Hon. William E. Simon		xi
Preface		xiii
About the Author		xv
1.	The Idea of Economic Freedom	1

PART ONE: THE QUEST FOR FREEDOM

2.	Economic Freedom in Colonial America	21
3.	The Great American War For Freedom and Independence	41
4.	1776-Political Freedom: The Declaration of Independence	63
5.	1776-Economic Freedom: Adam Smith and the Wealth of Nations	91
6.	Victory and its Aftermath	111
7.	The United States Constitution: Political Freedom	123
8.	The United States Constitution: Economic Freedom	139

PART TWO: FREE MARKETS, FREE PEOPLE, AND THE STATE

9.	Free Markets In Action: The People	155
10.	Free Markets In Action: The Results	183
11.	Economic Freedom and the State :I	211
12.	Economic Freedom and the State: II	231

PART THREE: ECONOMIC FREEDOM: HAPPINESS AND VIRTUE

13.	Economic Freedom: Happiness and Virtue I	253
14.	Economic Freedom: Happiness and Virtue II	277
15.	Conclusions	305
Index		293

FOREWORD

*Hon. William E. Simon**

Make no mistake about it, the United States of America is a nation where economic freedom and virtue are under siege. In the economic realm, government influences who may be hired, promoted, and fired; the wage to be paid; the technology to be employed; and the price to be charged for a good or a service. Government also determines who may enter an occupation or start up a business, and it monopolizes education and an assortment of public utilities. Financing the thousands of federal programs, rules, and regulations is a budget in which deficit is the norm.

And there is more. Just as economic freedom has come under attack, so too have virtue and the traditional institutions that promote it: those of a religious nature, the family, and the schools. These are the mediating institutions which teach the difference between right and wrong, which restrain human passions, and which foster virtuous behavior. Religion, however, has been drummed out of the public square. Liberalized laws and attitudes have made divorce commonplace and now it may be easier to dissolve a marriage than it is to fire someone for incompetence. Educational institutions where relativism and value clarification have replaced ideas of truth and of proper behavioral norms are also reluctant to impose disciplinary measures on unruly youngsters. In public grade schools and high schools, social issues, social promotion, and self-esteem replace hard work, and grades that are earned. In higher education, fads have undermined the fundamental nature of the curriculum, and transformed it from one rooted in Western Civilization and core knowledge into a smorgasbord of offerings, many of which are hostile to the United States and freedom.

Government programs that were intended to cure America's social ills have not only failed to do so, but in many cases, have made matters worse. The welfare state, which was intended to lift people out of poverty, has instead created an underclass of people dependent upon the government. Entitlement programs, such as Medicare and Medicaid, which were intended to care for the sick and the elderly, have created incentives for people not to save for their own long-term health security. As a result, the cost of these

---

* William E. Simon, Secretary of the Treasury under Presidents Nixon and Ford, is President of the John M. Olin Foundation. He is the author of two best selling books, *A Time for Truth* (1978) and *Time for Action* (1980).

programs continues to escalate beyond the system's ability to pay. And who is left to pick up the pieces? The hard working American taxpayer. Today, the average American must now work from January until June just to pay the costs of government.

And so, there is considerable reason for concern for the future. If nothing is done to stem our moral decline and to reform the entitlement and welfare states, we must be prepared to face several consequences: intractable poverty; a rise in marital instability; a rise in out of wedlock births; an uninformed and uneducated student population; alienation among the young; diminished civility; racial hostility; a rise in crime; an inefficient medical system; a troubled social security system; and a weakened national defense.

Professor Ryan has responded to these disturbing trends with his *Liberty, Virtue, and Happiness: The Story of Economic Freedom* in America. History is a great teacher, and his history of economic freedom explains how free markets and virtuous behavior not only bring prosperity but also protect our personal and civic liberties. He stresses the importance of the classical virtues of courage, temperance, justice, and wisdom; the religious values of faith, hope, and charity; and such commercial virtues as industry, frugality, honesty, and delayed gratification.

In short, Professor Ryan has given us an imaginative interdisciplinary study which offers a guide to reverse the dangerous trends brought forth by radical individualism and radical egalitarianism. His examination of history clearly shows the close relationship between freedom and virtue, and how each of these working together can produce a society characterized by personal responsibility, liberty, prosperity, and justice; a society which enables individuals to realize their dreams and to secure happiness. This is an important book and deserves the attention of those who would shape public policy in America and indeed throughout the world.

PREFACE

"Man", said Adam Smith, "is an anxious animal" and the late twentieth century has provided man with ample cause for anxiety. Poverty, financial insecurity, educational failures, environmental concerns, crime, drugs, violence, martial instability, culture wars, ethnic animosities, the decline of civility and the rise of the lawsuit -- all of these and more -- make this a troubled time, and surely give any thinking person cause for alarm.

Economic freedom which emphasizes voluntary exchange, private property, and a limited role for government is not only a vital source of material well-being, but it also acts as a guardian of our other freedoms. As such, this liberty needs to be a component of any study which seeks to determine the causes of and the solutions to the concerns of today.

Therefore, as we enter the third millennium, and as so many search for solutions to contemporary problems, wisdom suggests that we step back and examine the evolution of the idea and practice of economic freedom. A proper analysis of our problems really does demand an awareness of what took place in other eras. It requires an understanding of how ideas, attitudes and institutions developed, and of what we Americans were like as a people. It is an approach that enables us to learn about the causes of our successes and our failures.

This volume is unique in two ways. First, it provides an historical perspective which develops the vital relationship between economic freedom in America and other liberties, and it combines economics with history, political science, philosophy and theology. Along the way, it emphasizes the importance of classical, religious and commercial virtues in securing all of our freedoms, and it analyses the interconnections between liberty, virtue, wealth and happiness. This is a book that shows how we might successfully deal with many of our problems and how we might obtain a society where prosperity and true happiness reign.

Second, the book is addressed to the general reader – an individual usually ignored by professional economists. Understanding it does not require any formal training in economics, although those who have studied economics should find it rewarding. Its multidisciplinary approach allows it to be used as supplementary reading in courses in economics, political science, history, philosophy and theology.

The word America as it is used in this volume refers to North America during the colonial period and later it refers to the United States. Also, the words freedom and liberty are used interchangeably, and the word man usually is used in the generic sense to include both sexes.

My thanks go to Lawson Bowling, Robert Dilorenzo and William Perkins for their comments and suggestions, and to Frank Columbus for his faith in my work. Of course, any mistakes are my responsibility.

ABOUT THE AUTHOR

Edward W. Ryan is Ryan-Bacardi Professor of Economics at Manhattanville College. He is also the founder and director of the Manhattanville College Economic Freedom Institute which has as its mission the study of economic freedom in a scholarly manner. Professor Ryan is the author of *In The Words Of Adam Smith: The First Consumer Advocate*. A popular lecturer and the recipient of several teaching awards, he resides with his family in Scarsdale, New York.

CHAPTER 1

THE IDEA OF ECONOMIC FREEDOM

There is nothing in all the world greater than freedom. It is worth paying for; it is worth losing a job for; it is worth going to jail for. I would rather be a free pauper than a rich slave. I would rather die in abject poverty with my conviction than live in inordinate riches with lack of self-respect.

MARTIN LUTHER KING, Jr.[1]

GENERAL MEANING OF FREEDOM

Ah freedom. For centuries, men and women have, with remarkable fervor, advocated it and defended it. Many have expended emotion and bloodshed to secure freedom not only for themselves and loved ones but for others about whom they knew little or nothing.

In the American Civil War, each side claimed to be fighting on the side of liberty; it is the theme of speeches on public holidays; leaders of democratic nations extol the idea and even dictators provide it with lip service. Freedom for the individual has become the touchstone in the culture wars of the United States and the British historian Lord Acton has observed that from ancient to modern times, "Liberty next to religion, has been the motive of good deeds and the common pretext of crime." [2]

But just what is the meaning of this word about which such passion swirls? For some it is the condition of being able to act without restraint by a coercive authority. Others believe that freedom and equality are virtually synonymous, and there are those who claim that true freedom can exist only when material wants have been diminished. There are people who consider freedom to be a feeling or a spiritual state, defying definition and perhaps akin to the reply offered by the trumpeter--the Great Satchmo--Louis Armstrong who when queried about the meaning of jazz observed, "If you gotta ask, you ain't ever gonna know."

Historically, freedom (by any definition), has not always been a personal objective. Other values such as power, honor, glory, justice, hedonism and equality have often been the dominant goals.[3] Nonetheless, as Lord Acton has observed, concerns about freedom were expressed in biblical times by the Israelites and Jesus Christ; by philosophers and sages of antiquity, including Solon, Pericles, Plato, Aristotle, and Senaca; and in later eras by Saint Thomas Aquinas, Machiavelli, John Milton, John Calvin, John Locke, Adam Smith, Thomas Jefferson and a host of others.[4] But it is in 19th century England, in John Stuart Mill's *ON LIBERTY* that we find one of the best known and most forceful defenses of freedom. With this fascinating man and his influential book, we will begin our construction of the meaning of freedom.

A ONE WAY TICKET BACK HOME, PLEASE! This demand would be the nonnegotiable reaction of the vast majority (and not just a simple vast majority), of today's college students to the educational regimen thrust upon John Stuart Mill by his father James. The following passages from John Stuart's autobiography suggest the character of this regimen.

> I have no remembrance of the time when I began to learn Greek, I have been told that it was when I was three years old. My earliest recollection on the subject, is that of committing to memory what my father termed vocables, being lists of common Greek words, with their significance in English, which he later wrote out for me on cards. Of grammar, until some years later, I learnt no more than the inflexions of the nouns and verbs, but, after a course of vocables, proceeded at once to translation; and I faintly remember going through *AESOP'S FABLES,* the first Greek book which I read. The *ANABASIS*, which I remember better, was the second. I learnt no Latin until my eighth year. At that time I had read, under my father's tuition, a number of Greek prose authors, among whom I remember the whole of Herodotus, and of Xennophon's *CYROPAEDIA* and *MEMORIALS* of Socrates; some of the lives of the philosophers by Diogenes Laertius; part of Lucian, and Isocrates *ad Demonicum* and *Ad Nicolem*. I also read, in 1813, the first six dialogues (in the common arrangement) of Plato, from the *EUTHYPHRON* to the *THEOCTETUS* inclusive: which last dialog I venture to think, would have been better omitted, as it was totally impossible I should understand it. But my father, in all his teaching, demanded of me not only the utmost that I could do, but much that I could by no possibility have done.
>
> The only thing besides Greek, that I learnt as a lesson in this part of my childhood, was arithmetic: this also my father taught me: it was the task of the evenings, and I well remember its disagreeableness. But the lessons were only a part of the daily instruction I received. Much of it consisted in the books I read by myself, and my father's discourses to me, chiefly during our walks.
>
> In my eighth year I commenced Latin, in conjunction with a younger sister, to whom I taught it as I went on....
>
> In the same year in which I began Latin, I made my first commencement in the Greek poets with the *Iliad.* I never composed at all in Greek, even in prose, and but little in Latin. Not that my father could be indifferent to the value of this practice, in giving a thorough knowledge of these languages, but because there really was not time for it.[5]

Later in life (age twelve!), J. S. Mill studied logic and at thirteen, economics. With little time off and no friends, he survived these early years and went on to become the author of such classics as *PRINCIPLES OF POLITICAL ECONOMY; LOGIC;*

CONSIDERATIONS OF REPRESENTATIVE GOVERNMENT; UTILITARIANISM; and *ON LIBERTY.*

As a young man, Mill rebelled against Jeremy Bentham's utilitarianism, which was embraced by Mill's father and other "philosophical radicals." Bentham had advanced the idea that a good society could be formed through rigorous mental training, from which would emerge the completely rational man. The hoped for outcome of such undertakings would be a society characterized by "the greatest happiness for the greatest number."

At age twenty, Mill began to analyze this philosophy which he had accepted in his youth and promptly became the victim of mental depression. Out of this state emerged his belief that the "cultivation of reason" inherent in Bentham's rational utilitarianism needed to be balanced by the "cultivation of feelings" through interests which touched human passions and sensibilities. For Mill, happiness might be found not by choosing it as an end in itself, but rather as a by-product of activities undertaken for their own sake: advancing the arts; contemplating nature; improving mankind; activities which Mill considered exempt from the control of the reformer or legislator.[6]

Thus, we find Mill beginning to address the issue of authority versus liberty, and the extent to which society should have power over the individual. In *On Liberty*, published in 1859 when Mill was fifty-three years old, we find the most cogent expression of his mature thoughts on the subject of freedom, and here we find a working definition of freedom which will be useful as we go on to analyze freedom in the context of the American economy: "The only freedom which deserves the name is that of pursuing our own good in our own way, so long as we do not attempt to deprive others of theirs or impede their efforts to obtain it."[7] And yet, mindful of Bentham's notions of social engineering, which so depressed Mill as a young man: "...the only purpose for which power can be rightfully exercised over any member of a civilized community, against his will, is to prevent harm to others."[8]

With disdain for virtually all sanctions, including those of a social nature (the moral coercion of public opinion), *ON LIBERTY*, therefore, rejects the utilitarian idea that the reformer--legislator should interfere with individual freedom for one's own good, to make one happy. Rather, for Mill, freedom of thought, speech, and action are ends in themselves which public policy should foster and from which other goals, such as truth and morality (which government has the duty *not* to promote) would be fulfilled. Government might impose restraints only when harm to others was direct and perceptible.

Mill's ideas on liberty have not gone uncriticized. Among the many people antagonistic to his position, Matthew Arnold believed wisdom and virtue to be superior to liberty and individualism as social values. He thought the right of anyone to say whatever he likes was conducive to anarchy and subversive of culture."[9] After all, a not too burdensome limited conformity to societal standards and restraints has proven quite valuable in firming the social bond. It appears that what Mill called "one very simple principle" oversimplified a most complex subject. Furthermore, *On Liberty* unwittingly laid the basis for today's radical claims of absolute freedom in the moral/cultural system, and paved the way for morality and religion in the public realm to be considered adversarial to freedom.[10]

Undoubtedly, Mill would have been appalled by the radical individualism of the late 20th Century America, for in that same essay he has this to say: "A person who shows rashness, obstinacy, self-conceit-who cannot live within moderate means; who cannot restrain himself from hurtful indulgence; who pursues animal pleasures at the expense of those of feeling and intellect--must expect to be lowered in the opinion of others, and to have a less share of their favorable sentiments...."[11]

In addition, Mill believed that virtue was necessary to sustain a free society and should be developed in people during their youth. He thought that virtue could best be cultivated through voluntary institutions such as the family and schools.[12] It is important to understand that Mill was more optimistic about human nature than many of the philosophers and theologians that preceded or followed him, and he took it for granted that the virtues, traditions, and institutions embraced by the society of his day would continue to be embraced in the future.

He was no moral relativist and believed, for instance, that decency was superior to indecency, and sobriety superior to drunkenness. For Mill, there was such a thing as knowable truth; for him liberty was the best venue for securing it. However, it is quite interesting to observe that Mill was less enamoured with economic liberty. Although he accepted the classical position concerning the laws of production, he favored redistribution schemes such as the taxation of inheritances and landowners' income from rents. He also approved of the regulation of public utilities, and of government ventures to erect schools, harbors, and hospitals.

Obviously, debate regarding legitimate rights and obligations of individual, society and state continues and will continue as long as human thought prevails. However, Mill's work is considered a classic on liberty, and his influence is part of the European or Western tradition of liberty. Mill is the father of classic liberalism, in which freedom coexists with civic virtue, where civic virtue implies due regard for the common good.

IMPORTANCE OF FREEDOM

Unlike animals relying upon instinct, human beings possess the mental capacity to choose among alternatives and freedom allows them to exercise that capacity as alternatives present themselves. As the experience of contemplating and selecting among alternatives enlarges over time, analytical abilities develop. This process which fosters independent thought, action and personal growth leads inexorably to the conclusion that man's nature demands that he be free; a position diametrically opposed to the philosophy of determinism which perceives him to be but a puppet absolved from responsibility for his actions.

But free to do what? Which is to say that ethical considerations inhere in any discussion of freedom. A free person is morally responsible and accountable and worthy of praise or condemnation for his choices. As Lord Acton asserted, "Liberty is not the freedom to do what you wish; it is the freedom to do what you ought." Ideally, one's actions should have a positive influence on himself and others and help to generate truth, friendship, love, justice, prosperity, and peace.[13] If, however, an individual pursues a life devoted solely to acquisition of wealth and power, we have a situation where license rather than freedom obtains. In turn, this may well generate conditions whereby for the good of society, restraints on such licentious behavior may justly be imposed.

Freedom assumes many forms and, without doubt, these overlap and impinge upon one another. However, for purposes of simplicity, this discussion employs a tripartite classification: personal freedom, political or civic freedom, and economic freedom.

Personal freedom includes the freedoms of speech, worship, thought and association. Essentially, it means the liberty to live your life according to the dictates of your conscience as you strive to achieve various personal goals. Political or civic liberty embraces the right to vote for or against officials who might represent us in government and who would hold the responsibility of providing and administering just laws and institutions in order to secure the tranquility of society. Considerations of space preclude a more thorough treatment of personal and political liberty so that we can award more attention to our main subject--economic freedom. This branch of liberty, of tremendous importance to the average person throughout the world, is also the one which powerful, resolute, and eloquent and vociferous defenders of other aspects of freedom, frequently perceive with scorn. Let us turn to discussion of freedom's vital economic dimension.

ECONOMIC FREEDOM

In the beginning, Adam and Eve had everything. After their unfortunate experience with an apple offered by a talking snake, they faced the problem of scarcity, a problem that continues in varying degrees to the present day. Essentially, scarcity exists when all human wants cannot be satisfied, and the need to economize arises. Economics is the study of how scarce productive factors or resources--land, labor, and capital--can best be allocated to satisfy insatiable human wants. Arriving at our turn of the century standard of living in America required travel along a very long road.

Imagine living with malnutrition, inadequate shelter, high infant mortality rates, a brief lifespan, ubiquitous illiteracy, a shallow cultural existence, and an ever present threat of famine and plague. Most people throughout history have lived under such conditions, and while past public opinion is difficult to measure--not too many opinion polls in the good old days--one suspects that people did not appraise their lot in life with unrestrained joy, and surely, in the vocabulary of today, they failed to live up to their potential.

Escape from such misery necessitated economic growth, a process inseparable from the development of civilization. When each individual can produce only enough to take care of his own needs, life is grim. The task, therefore, is to organize the productive factors to generate a level of output exceeding survival requirements. When this happens, people with their tools, skill, and natural resources can produce things other than the basic necessities. Art, music, architecture, and the leisure time to enjoy them are the attributes of societies where production exceeds basic needs. Codes and standards of law, morality, and behavior, as well as institutions appropriate for their enforcement, also develop and insure social stability.

Essentially, three forms of economic organization present themselves: command, tradition, and free markets.

(A) COMMAND Under a command system, the king, emperor, dictator, commissar, planning board, or other individual or group directs the productive factors to predetermined objectives, often setting forth productive methods to be employed and determining the distribution of income. Authoritarian and totalitarian societies, such as the former Soviet Union, have made extensive use of this approach, but command tends to be grossly inefficient, and, by definition, displays little affection for economic freedom.

(B) TRADITION A variant of command, tradition relies on productive techniques and behavioral habits handed down over centuries. Generation after generation works the same land, employs the same tools and methods, consumes the same food, wears the same style of clothing etc. The dominant form of economic organization in Europe during the middle ages, tradition continues to be of great importance in many of today's less developed nations. Resistance to new products, new techniques, new ideas, "new" almost anything characterizes tradition dominated economies, as does minimal economic progress while inherent social pressure to conform (often backed by force), is less than compatible with economic freedom.

(C) FREE MARKETS Picture this. You own a time machine and decide to use this contraption to pluck someone out of the Middle Ages and transport him to a modern department store. Wow! Sure to attract the attention of this bewildered soul would be the incredible amount and variety of goods displayed. Perhaps equally amazing to him would be the fact that customers had not even ordered them in advance. How, then, does it come about that goods and services, so many and so varied in America, are produced and made available in approximately the amounts that people choose to purchase? The answer is to be found in the operation of a system of free markets.

Certain fundamental problems confront any society, whether of a Robinson Crusoe type or a technologically advanced one, such as the United States. People must choose what goods to produce and in what quantity to produce them. Second, they must decide upon the method of production, and third, they must determine the distribution of the resulting output.

Solving these three fundamental problems in a national economy requires millions of decisions, Take for example the subject of shoes. Should we produce shoes? If so, how many shoes, and in what styles, sizes, colors, and quantities.? What kinds and quantities of raw materials, capital and labor should we employ in our productive process? How should the shoes be distributed? Should equal or different quantities of shoes be produced for each family, each person, each age group, each sex, each member of a particular occupation? These are but a few of the questions about the production of shoes.

Although these decisions can be made under systems of command and tradition, a market economy (also known as capitalism) has shown itself to be the most successful mechanism by far.

A market economy is based on the tenets of economic freedom which, subject to the constraints of the proper functions of government, and in its pure form means the liberty to:

*enter any occupation
*start any business
*operate the enterprise in the manner one chooses
*produce any good or offer any service and charge any price
*conclude voluntary agreements with the owners of land, labor, and capital who themselves seek to obtain the most favorable terms of employment and who also possess the freedom to change to other business firms and move to other geographic areas
*sell a business or move it to another geographic area
*own, utilize (or not utilize), or improve upon one's property
*enter into any voluntary association to secure a legitimate end
*keep the wages interest, rents, and profits one has received.

On the subject of property, Richard Epstein puts these freedoms succinctly.

> Freedom of speech gives one the right to talk in ways that are unpleasant to others, without any justification for so doing. So too, private property gives the right to exclude others *without* the need for justification. Indeed, it is the ability to act at will and without need for justification within some domain which is the essence of freedom, be it of speech or property.[14]

In a market system, consumers spend money and in that sense "vote" for the continued production of the goods and services they desire. Entrepreneurs, undertaking uninsurable risks and in their search for profits, combine the productive resources of labor, land, and capital (the owners of which are in search of wages, rents, and interest payments), in enterprises that attempt to satisfy consumer needs and wants. Failure to do so successfully means bankruptcy. Competition among firms pressures them to combine the productive factors in the most efficient (least cost), manner, so that (in the long run), prices reflect costs, and monopoly profits erode. In this way, scarce resources are allocated among competing uses to produce the goods and services that people with limited incomes wish to obtain. King or queen, the consumer is sovereign.

In the market system, multiple markets develop for goods, services, and the factors of production. Such markets may be local, regional, national, or international, depending on the geographic range within which buyer and seller seek each other out. In addition, markets may be formal and located in a building such as the New York Stock Exchange, an employment office, or a supermarket, or they may be less structured and operate through telephone conversations, letters, or newspaper advertisements.

Markets exist so that voluntary exchange may take place between buyer and seller. Markets allow the forces of demand and supply to generate prices, which in turn, provide vital information to guide individual decisions: for consumers, as they try to maximize the benefits of their limited income; for entrepreneurs or business managers as they seek a least cost factor combination; and for resource owners as they seek to obtain the best deal for their services. Moreover, a circular nature inheres in this market process, as the incomes generated in the factor markets provide the basis for consumer spending in product markets. In turn, product markets produce revenue for business firms. Markets promote efficiency (getting the most with the least), and their self-adjusting nature facilitates changes in methods of production and consumer tastes, as well in as the correction of excesses.

Elements of tradition, command, and free markets co-exist in virtually all economic systems, so for analytical purposes, the important question lies in which of the three is the paramount force. Today, in the United States, we give presents at Christmas (tradition), the government imposes upon us a list of things we must do and must not do (command), but for most of the economy, free markets dominate.

ROLE OF THE STATE

The state is a politically defined and governed territory, and in a democracy its duties are carried out by a government chosen by the citizenry. Generally speaking, the role of the state is to protect against foreign invasion and to provide conditions of law and order so that members of society might conduct their legitimate activities without coercion and in an atmosphere of tranquility.

Economic freedom, like other kinds of freedom, is not an absolute, and government has several vital functions to perform. These include the definition and protection of property rights, enforcement of contracts, and the provision of means for modification of rights, adjudication of disputes, and enforcement of rules. Securing an efficient monetary system to facilitate exchange has long been considered a proper function of the sovereign. Insuring choice for participants in the market economy should lead government to pursue pro-competition policies so as to thwart the harmful effects of monopoly (higher prices, less production, and lower quality output when compared to competitive markets). When charitable endeavors prove inadequate, the state may provide assistance for the poor and those unable to care for themselves.

Finally, government may intervene where the market system fails to provide the "correct " amount of goods and services. For example, "public goods" such as national defense or a judicial system may not be forthcoming in desirable amounts from the private economy. In addition, private sector activities may generate external benefits or costs that spill over to third parties--those not directly involved in an economic transaction. For instance, manufacturers may cause pollution which effects the health of third party individuals, and the latter may not receive compensation for this external cost imposed upon them. In such a case, the government may develop policies to correct this resource misallocation so that manufacturing is accompanied by cleaner air. Education offers another illustration. To insure a proper resource allocation, the external benefits of education enjoyed by society (a literate nation, more informed participation in government etc.) should be added to the private benefits received by individuals. However, a market economy reflects only individual decisions, and therefore, the government may see to it that additional resources are directed to this sector.

Implementing the economic functions of government is easier said than done. My economic liberties might well conflict with yours, and external costs or benefits usually defy precise measurement. The extent to which different tasks are undertaken depends upon various national circumstances. To insure a smoothly functioning economy, it is important that these functions be performed efficiently, wisely, and with restraint, for if they are not, results may be worse than if intervention had never occurred.

IMPORTANCE OF ECONOMIC FREEDOM

Thus far, our discussion has emphasized the importance of free markets and a vital but restrained role for the state. It embodies the idea of what has been called negative freedom, that is, freedom "from" coercion or arbitrary impediments to action. This approach, however, has come under some criticism. Anatole France comments scathingly about the majestic equality of the law which forbids both rich and poor from sleeping under bridges, and in a similar vein, Harold Laski notes their respective freedoms to enter the Hotel Ritz. Marxists speak of "the freedom to starve" and deny the possibility of "real freedom" in the presence of a market system and the inequality it is sure to generate. Others, in less dramatic tones, stress "positive freedom" that is, the power or means to take advantage of conditions established via "negative freedom" so that realizing one's personal goals becomes more of a possibility.[15] Poverty, for instance, has been used as an example of a condition blocking the attainment of "positive freedom."

The relative merits of each approach have long been the subject of intense debate. Here, we consider negative freedom with appropriate societal standards and restraints to be the proper meaning of the word. Given negative freedom, the task is to establish an economic system in which virtue and prosperity reign and which enables people to realize positive freedom.

And this brings us back to the subject of a free market economy, which in the long history of humanity has stood head and shoulders above all other economic systems. By removing arbitrary obstacles to action (negative freedom), it has served as the mechanism which enabled people to utilize their talents and realize widely different personal goals (positive freedom). Further, it has led to national prosperity and has helped to preserve other liberties. While not without problems, free markets, have performed spectacularly. How all this came about is a long, complicated and fascinating story. However, the basics can be summed up rather briefly.

Free markets offer the incentive for action: to form a new business, introduce a new product, develop a new technique, learn a new skill, take a long-run perspective, sacrifice and save for a dream, finance a risky venture, or work hard for a promotion. Free markets lead one to conserve and to enhance the value of property, for as Aristotle noted, one provides better care for his own property than that which is held in common.

On this side of paradise, scarcity always will exist and people always will want more than is available. Thus, competition is inevitable. However, free markets generate prices which provide information on production costs, and on the relative values of goods and services, and thereby set the stage for people with mutual interests to enter into cooperative arrangements.[16]

From the acquisition of the basic ingredients to the formation of the final product, whether it be an automobile, a pencil, or a ham and cheese sandwich, multitudes of people necessarily become involved in the production process as goods and services are voluntarily exchanged over and over again. The word "voluntary" deserves emphasis because exchanges would not take place unless all parties expected to benefit. It is a form of cooperation--I will give this to you if you give that to me--and this cooperation may take place among people who do not like each other, or do not know each other, or who have never even heard of one another. This is a most important but not so obvious economic advantage to minorities subject to discrimination.

Free markets, truly are a combination of cooperation and competition, and they demand responsibility in the exercise of choice. Every decision entails a cost. The cost refers to what you give up by following a particular course of action; economists call it an "opportunity cost." For instance, my decision to take an evening class at the local college means that I forsake a sum of money and a block of time that could have been allocated to other uses. And so, as individuals contemplate choices, they are led to weigh the expected costs and benefits of alternatives and then to experience the pleasures or pains of good or bad decisions. This process, in which one bears the consequences of one's own decisions and learns from mistakes, fosters personal maturity and growth, thereby enhancing the ability to deal with economic as well as other issues including issues of an ethical nature. In contrast, those who have had their basic economic needs taken care of (rather badly to be sure), as in paternalistic welfare programs here or in the communist nations of eastern Europe, display little evidence of this ability. Moreover, the competitive element in free markets tends toward excellence, whereas government operations tend toward the mediocre and banal.[17]

Economic freedom, this vital component of a free society, intimately and inextricably relates to other liberties. Pope John Paul II has stated it clearly: "Economic freedom is an aspect of human freedom which cannot be separated from its other aspects and which must contribute to the full realization of people in order to conduct an authentic human community."[18]

The word "coercion" provides the focus for this bond among liberties. For the ability to coerce lies in power, the reduction of which enhances the viability of freedom. By definition, a free market economy, not only disperses power within itself, but, again by definition, limits the role of government, thereby reducing coercive power. If government officials could determine your occupation (as well as your wages and eligibility for promotion), or control your ability to start or maintain a business enterprise, would not they hold substantial power over you? Would not this power insidiously extend to matters of speech, of association, and of religious and political affiliation? Over two centuries ago, Alexander Hamilton provided the obvious answer: "In the general course of human nature, a power over a man's subsistence amounts to a power over his will."[19]

A society which accords high esteem to property rights and the other pillars of a free market system provides a bulwark which makes it all the more difficult for government to interfere with or to destroy economic liberties and thereby to add to its already formidable coercive powers. When custom and principles of law significantly diminish the ease with which property can be seized, the incentive to act tyrannically is also much diminished. All this is especially true when a free market has provided the populace real opportunities to improve its material position.

Free markets, by allowing individuals to meet their needs and wants through voluntary agreements (including those of a nonprofit nature), not only promote diversity but encourage it to flourish. Nobel Laureate Fredrich A. Hayek, notes that in the world where no one person or group is in command of all knowledge, the unforeseen and unpredictable receive the space which allows new ideas to alter circumstances and this process, generates even more new ideas which may further alter circumstances.[20] In contrast, by their very nature, government policies promote uniformity. Once a policy of the state has been enacted, all its citizens then have, for example, the same national defense, or the same rules of jurisprudence, or the same speed limit. We are not, of course, arguing that government should be abolished; we have already established that the vital involvement of the state is necessary to the prosperity of a society. Still, it bears repeating that in areas where people have very different views, the government tends to promote uniformity and to use its coercive powers to insure obedience.

From all this it follows that the more activities (economic and non-economic) are decided in the political arena, the less diversity will exist, the more minority viewpoints will be suppressed, and the more people will feel disgruntled about being forced to conform to policies of which they disapprove--especially when such policies prevent them from realizing their objectives. Government must rely upon its moral capital (patriotism, good citizenship, respect of neighbor), to succeed in performing even its basic functions. This capital dissipates when policies exceed these functions and fail to realize their objectives. A likely scenario as this process unfolds is a more troubled, less tranquil, and less cohesive society: one disillusioned with government and which accords less and less respect to traditional institutions; one whose citizens more and more perceive their opponents as demons.[21]

Unhappily, economic freedom does not absolutely guarantee its political counterpart. Great Britain ruled Hong Kong when the latter was said to be the epitome of free markets. Salazar's Portugal and (until recently), South Africa exemplify free market economies where political liberties have been wanting. And free markets, long dominant in the United States' economy, have coexisted with Negro slavery and the denial of the political franchise to women. Conversely, neither does political freedom insure the presence of economic freedom. Both India and Sweden have more of the former than the latter.

Thus we see that the relationship between economic and political liberty is not quite as clear cut as one might have imagined. Nonetheless, strong general conclusions can be drawn. In the rather grim economic history of humankind, free market economies have delivered more prosperity than has any other form of economic organization.[22] They have played an important role in generating political freedom (the collapse of totalitarian communism in Eastern Europe can be traced in good measure to its dismal economic performance), and they have served as a most important guardian for that and other forms of liberty.

THE VULNERABILITY OF A FREE MARKET ECONOMY

For all its strengths and virtues, the free market economy is a vulnerable system. Competitive markets allocate resources to the production of goods and services that people want. However, there are individuals who will find some of this output offensive and try to forbid it. Others will attempt to rig markets to their own advantage. Still others, well intentioned but ignorant of the complex nature of markets, believe they can improve the performance of the economy by restructuring it. Each of these beliefs or actions may lead to unwarranted government activity and thus diminish liberty.

Yes, freedom in general and economic freedom in particular have many enemies and some of them can be mortal. Among these most dangerous enemies, radical egalitarianism and radical individualism are prominent in the United States today. Our focus, for now, will be upon the former.

RADICAL EGALITARIANISM

Equality! A word most controversial to which virtually all nod or even scream approval. Of course, the reason for this near universal affirmation is that people impute many and often widely different meanings to it. Before the Enlightenment, equality was generally thought to be in the eyes of God. In the post-Enlightenment era, equality before the law and equality of opportunity became its connotation. Recently, the idea of equality of outcome has been much trumpeted. All of these perspectives upon equality continue to find their way into American discourse, but the two perspectives which cause the most controversy today are equality of opportunity and equality of outcome.

Perfect (or even near perfect) equality of opportunity for all members of society is the impossible dream, and any attempt to achieve it will be a nightmare. Each of us is unique in terms of our physical and mental endowments: family and society influence them: endowments and influences together profoundly effect our opportunities. State intervention to equalize all social influences upon its citizens is inseparable from radical loss of freedom.

This problem was addressed in the nineteenth century by Alexis de Tocqueville, a young French nobleman, who along with Gustave de Beaumont, came to America on a mission for the French government to learn about prison reform. For nine months they toured the country, studying not only their official assignment but that which lay closest to their hearts, the essence of democracy in action. Tocqueville's observations were published in 1835 (volume I), and 1840 (volume II), and his astute analysis has made *Democracy In America* a classic. The following passage pinpoints the elusiveness of perfect equality.

> ...men will never establish any equality with which they can be contented. Whatever efforts a people may make, they will never succeed in reducing all the conditions of society to a perfect level; and even if they unhappily attain that absolute and complete equality of position, the inequality of minds will still remain, which, coming directly from the hand of God, will forever escape the laws of man. However democratic, then, the

social state and the political constitution of a people may be, it is certain that every member of the community will always find out several points about him which overlook his own position; and we may foresee that his looks will be doggedly fixed in that direction. When inequality of conditions is the common law of society, the most marked inequalities do not strike the eye; when everything is nearly on the same level, the slightest are marked enough to hurt it. Hence the desire of equality always becomes more insatiable in proportion as equality is more complete.[23]

Although differing viewpoints on the meaning of equality are often presented in extreme, all-or-nothing language, room for moderation does, in fact, exist and the United States could well move to greater equality of opportunity, from which surely would follow greater (but by no means absolute), equality of outcomes. After all, as Aaron Wildavsky has observed, "...what makes America special is the deeply imbedded belief, accompanied by supporting relationships, that liberty and equality--the cultures of individualism and egalitarianism--are, (or can be), mutually reinforcing."[24] Advocates of free markets seek to promote this laudable goal through measures consistent with the cooperative/competitive, incentive/disincentive elements that inhere in this system. Alternatively, one can argue that a good deal of American poverty can be explained by public policies that have ignored, downplayed (and not infrequently held in contempt), the basic ingredients of a free market economy.

The attempt to establish greater equality of opportunity with the state directed policies favored by the radical egalitarians in their quest for a stringently defined equality of outcome and a classless society is fraught with dangers. A market economy tends to reward hard work, foresight, thrift, inventiveness, and entrepreneurship. Success comes from giving people what they want, and, inevitably, inequality of income results. However, wholesale transfers of income by the state, no matter what the timetable (yearly, monthly, weekly, daily), or other extreme redistributive policies would damage incentives, lower saving and investment, impede the formation of new firms, yield technological backwardness, and significantly impair if not destroy the efficiency attribute of a market economy. A significantly lower standard of living (including its diversity component) inevitably results.

Nor is that the end of the trouble, for tranquility and liberty would also join efficiency as victims of the thirst for equality. In the egalitarian society, envy--what J. S. Mill called "the most antisocial and evil of all passions"[25]--becomes ubiquitous. If I have a better suit than you do, a better stereo than you do, a better automobile than you do, then inevitably, in your eyes, I have behaved immorally to get them. Suspicion, always the close companion of envy will unite with the green-eyed monster to pit social groups against each other with seductive labels such as "unfair" and "greed." Among the casualties will be civility and tranquility.

Power to correct deviation from equality of material possessions (or any other disparity, for that matter) not only confers upon the state immense powers to control behavior (and not just economic behavior), but permits it--indeed requires it--to bid adieu to equality before the law. Remember also that democracy, the form of government most compatible with liberty, is a system that eschews violence for compromise and offers consent to the majority with appropriate safeguards for minority rights. However, if any government policy which fosters inequality is *de facto* held to be illegitimate, then the survival of democracy--and liberty--hardly seems likely.[26]

What of the classless society to which radical egalitarian policies are supposed to lead? By necessity, some ruling body, be it an individual or group, must have the power to decide what is fair and who gets what. This ruling body will occupy a position superior to the masses, and as has been amply demonstrated in various communist economies, that superiority includes not only power (with few checks placed upon it), but income, wealth, and prestige. George Orwell said it well: "all animals are equal, but some animals are more equal than others." Two major attempts to establish a radically egalitarian society within the last couple of hundred years--the French Revolution and the Russian Revolution--did not bring equality, but rather totalitarianism, hatred, deceit, murder and torture on the grand scale. As Lord Acton observed, "Power tends to corrupt and absolute power corrupts absolutely." Also appropriate are the warnings of both Alex de Tocqueville and Pope John Paul ll.

> There is, in fact, a manly and lawful passion for equality that incites men to wish all to be powerful and honored. This passion tends to elevate the humble to the rank of the great; but there exists also in the human heart a depraved taste for equality, which impels the weak to attempt to lower the powerful to their own level and reduces men to prefer equality in slavery to inequality with freedom.[27]

***

> Not only is it wrong from the ethical point of view to disregard human nature, which is made for freedom, but in practice it is impossible to do so. Where society is so organized as to reduce arbitrarily or even suppress the sphere in which freedom is legitimately exercised, the result is that life of society becomes progressively disorganized and goes into decline....The social order will be all the more stable, the more it...does not place in opposition personal interest and the interest of society as a whole, but rather seeks to bring them into a fruitful harmony. In fact, when self-interest is violently suppressed, it is replaced by a burdensome system of bureaucratic control which dries up the wellsprings of initiative and creativity. When people think they possess the secret of a perfect social organization which makes evil impossible, they also think that they can use any means, including violence and deceit, in order to bring that organization into being. Politics then becomes a "secular religion" which operates under the illusion of creating paradise in this world.[28]

History has shown us again and again how far radical egalitarian policies can fall short of their goals. When we recognize that in practice these policies often aim to control an economy, we can begin to appreciate the powerful connections between economics and freedom.

VIRTUE

When the people of a nation enjoy significant individual freedom, then the harmony and tranquility--and even the continued existence--of that nation depend upon the virtue of its citizens. Moral behavior based on principles of right and wrong constitutes virtue in general. Examples of virtue include the classical virtues of courage, prudence, temperance and justice; the religious virtues of faith, hope, and charity; and virtues of an economic nature, including industry, thrift, honesty, perseverance, and punctuality. Beyond the limits placed on behavior by government exercising its proper role, human beings must, on their own, conduct themselves morally. Here also, the appeal to authority is instructive:

> Montesquieu: The natural place of virtue is near to liberty; but it is not nearer to excessive liberty than to servitude."[29]

> Edmund Burke: "Liberty, too, must be limited in order to be possessed."[30]

> James Madison: "...liberty may be endangered by the abuse of liberty, as well as by the abuse of power..."[31]

> Fredrich Hayek: "It is a truth, which all the great apostles of freedom...have never tired of emphasizing, that freedom has never worked without deeply ingrained moral beliefs and that coercion can be reduced to a minimum only where individuals can be expected as a rule to conform voluntarily to certain principles."[32]

Thus far, we have established that the nature of man demands he be free; that economic freedom is an important aspect of liberty; and that moral behavior is essential to the preservation of freedom.

With emphasis placed on virtuous behavior, the following chapters present a history of economic freedom in America from the colonial era to the late 20th Century. They also explain and stress the importance of freedom and virtue in the human quest for happiness.

---

[1] Martin Luther King, Jr., *I Have A Dream* ed. Lotte Hoskins (New York: Grosset & Dunlap, 1968),P. 45.

[2] John E. E. Dalberg-Acton, *Selected Writings Of Lord Acton* vol.1, *Essays In The History Of Liberty*, ed. J. Rufus Fears, (Indianapolis:Liberty Fund, 1825), p,5.

[3] Orlando Patterson, *Freedom, vol.1, Freedom In The Making Of Western Culture* (New York: Basic Books, 1991), x.

[4] Dalberg - Acton, *Essays in the History of Liberty, Chap.1 and 2 passim.*

[5] John Stuart Mill, Autobiography, with a preface by Harold Laski (London: Oxford University Press, 1924), pp. 4-12.

[6] John Stuart Mill, *On Liberty*, ed. with an introduction by Gertrude Himmelfarb, (New York: Penguin Books, 1974), p.15

[7] John Stuart Mill, *On Liberty*, ed. with an introduction by Gertrude Himmelfarb, p. 72.

[8] Ibid., pp. 68.

[9] Mathew Arnold quoted by Gertrude Himmelfarb, ed. in *On Liberty*, p.43, 44.

[10] Gertrude Himmelfarb, Liberty, "One Very Simple Principle,"? in *The American Scholar,* Autumn 1993, pp.531-550.

[11] John Stuart Mill, *On Liberty*, p.144.

[12] On the importance of virtue for Mill see, Peter Berkowitz, Virtue and the Making of Modern Liberalism (New Jersey: Princeton University Press, 1999) pp.145-161.

[13] Mary T. Clark, *The Problem of Freedom* (Englewood Cliffs, New Jersey: Prentice -Hall, Inc., 1973), pp. 1-29 passim.

[14] Richard Epstein, *Takings: Private Property and the Power of Eminent Domain* (Cambridge, Harvard University Press, 1985), p. 66.

[15] Isiah Berlin, *Four Essays In Liberty* (New York: Oxford University Press, 1989), pp. 118-172 passim.

[16] James L Dotti and Dwight R. Lee, *The Market Economy: A Reader* (Los Angeles, Roxbury Publishing Company. 1991) p. 222.

[17] Milton Friedman and Rose Friedman, *Free To Choose* (New York: Harcourt Brace Jovanovich, 1980), pp. 9-37 passim.

[18] George Weigel, ed., *A New Worldly Order: John Paul III and Human Freedom* (Washington D. C. : Ethics and Public Policy Center, 1992), p. 26

[19] Alexander Hamilton, *The Federalist* No. 79, with an introduction and notes by Jacob E. Cooke (Middletown, Wesleyan University Press, 1982), p.531.

[20] Friedrich A. Hayek, *The Constitution of Liberty* (Chicago: University of Chicago Press, 1978), pp.22-28, passim.

[21] Dwight Lee, *The Market Economy: A Reader*, pp.230-233.

[22] In 1960, per capita income in Hong Kong was 28 % of that in Great Britain but had risen to 137 % of the latter by 1996. See Milton Friedman, "The Real Lesson Of Hong Kong," *National Review*, December 31, 1997.

[23] Alexis de Toqueville, *Democracy In America,* vol. II (New York: Vintage Books, 1957), pp.146,147.

[24] Aaron Wildavsky, *The Rise Of Radical Egalitarianism* (Washington, D.C., The American University Press, 1991), p.32.

[25] J. S. Mill quoted in Alexander H. Shand, *Free Market Morality* (New York, Routledge,1990), p.130.

[26] Arron Wildavsky, *The Rise Of Radical Egalitarianism*, p.229.

[27] Alexis de Toqueville, *Democracy In America*, vol. I (New York, Vintage Books, 1957). p. 56.

[28] George Weigel, ed. *A New Worldly Order: John Paul II and Human Freedom*, pp. 11-12.

[29] Gertrude Himmelfarb, "Liberty, One Very Simple Principle,"? p.546.

[30] E. Calvin Beisner, "Stewardship in a Free Society," in Michael Bauman, ed. *Morality And The Marketplace* (Hillsdale: Hillsdale College Press, 1940), p.23.

[31] James Madison, *The Federalist* No. 63, p.428.

[32] Fredrich A. Hayek, *The Constitution of Liberty*, p.62.

Part One

The Quest For Freedom

CHAPTER 2

ECONOMIC FREEDOM IN COLONIAL AMERICA

THE BEGINNING

While no one denies the gigantic impact of Christopher Columbus, he was not the first to "discover" America. The Norse, for instance, established a short lived colony as early as the 11th Century, and in the 6th Century, St. Brendon may have found his way from Ireland to this continent. But even earlier--thousands of years ago--people from Asia traveled across the Bering Strait and migrated throughout this vast territory, so that when Columbus arrived, millions of "Indians" already were present.

Since the earlier Norse venture, two major things had happened which made feasible the journeys of Columbus and other explorers of his era. First, the quality of ships as well as methods of navigation had much improved. But perhaps of greater importance were the changes in attitudes toward life that evolved in Europe during the late Middle Ages.

The term Middle Ages--measured roughly from the fall of Rome to the end of the fifteenth century--was used by Renaissance people who had come to appreciate the achievements of Greece and Rome. It was a time of considerable disorder in which the Roman Catholic Church, with a very influential voice in both economic and spiritual affairs, emerged as a rock of stability.

The medieval Catholic Church considered all human endeavor subsidiary to man's most important task: the salvation of his immortal soul, and human life a mere way station en route to eternal reward. Economic activity, albeit necessary for survival, was but another arena for personal moral behavior and a quest for riches but an impediment to salvation. Men of the Church debated the nature of the just price, and Rome threatened excommunication for those who charged interest. This latter state of affairs derived in part from Aristotle's conviction that money is barren and cannot beget money, and therefore the charging of interest is unnatural. It also stemmed from the harm that interest-bearing loans would inflict upon those rendered destitute by plagues, famines, and other worldly misfortunes.

Although there were probably many for whom the Church's admonitions fell on deaf ears, we do know that economic motivations as we define them today were not common in the Middle Ages, and if Church pronouncements were not accepted by everyone, at least they must have induced some guilt feelings. In any event, the dominant economic goal of medieval society was to hand down to the next generation what the present generation had inherited without either increase or diminution--hardly a strong motivating force for economic development.

During the Renaissance, however, more emphasis was given to worldly accomplishments and earthly pleasures. This change elicited a demand for the production and distribution of more and more goods and, as follows, more trade.

Europeans were especially taken with the spices (used as preservatives), jewels, rugs, and other luxury products of the Near East and Asia. However, European exports (textiles, metals, minerals) proved insufficient to pay for these imported goods and this, in turn, caused gold and silver to flow eastward to pay for the trade imbalances. Moreover, a round trip journey to these distant lands took a long time (often years), was very costly, and presented more hazards than a midnight ride on a New York City subway. The search began for a quicker and less expensive water route to the east.

Of course, economic reward was not the only motivation of these fifteenth century voyagers. The desire to spread Christianity and the enticements of exploration for its own sake also made their claims. Numerous journeys including those of Prince Henry the Navigator, Bartholomew Diaz, and Vasco de Gama appear quite glamorous in surviving narratives. In some respects they were, but they also were fraught with peril and perceived to be so. In some cases, these truly brave sailors would attend Church services in order to hear their *own* funeral masses.

Toward the end of the fifteenth century, August of 1492 to be more precise, Christopher Columbus, sponsored by the Spanish Crown, set sail on what he thought would be a voyage to Asia. Instead, on October 12, he landed on the island of San Salvador in the Bahamas.

When word of this reached Europe, other nations including Portugal, England, France, and the Netherlands, also sent ships to this "new world"--America (named after the Italian explorer Amerigo Vespucci), and for a long time there was no small amount of confusion and uncertainty over what had been found, where it was, and whose it was.

Columbus, for instance, thought he had landed on a Japanese island. The sixteenth century French Explorer Jacques Cartier and his accomplices were taken in by a Huron Indian chief who told them of a Kingdom of gold and silver mines, as well as of one legged men who did not eat and flew like bats. Cartier not only bought the story, but persuaded the chief to accompany him to France, where he told it again to King Francis I, who also swallowed it[1]. During the seventeenth century, the French explorer Jean Nicollet, believing that Chinese and Japanese dignitaries were engaged in commerce near the Great Lakes, sought to present himself to the Chinese Court. He arrived on the shore of Lake Michigan in a robe of Chinese damask, and with a pistol in each hand, he marched into an Indian settlement where today stands Green Bay Wisconsin.[2]

Spain, during the sixteenth century, established colonies in Central America, the mainland of South America (the Spanish Main), in Florida, and in the North American West. By the 17th Century, settlers had arrived from France, the Netherlands, and England. The 16th Century witnessed a few attempts to establish British settlements in

North America. Sir Humphrey Gilbert in 1533 engaged in a short lived effort to found a colony in Newfoundland, and Sir Walter Raleigh's efforts from 1585 to 1587 failed in what would become Roanoke, Virginia. However, not until 1607 did England establish its first permanent settlement at Jamestown.

ECONOMIC DEVELOPMENT

One suspects that anyone who ever has experienced the grip of real poverty surely must have envisioned a better life--which is to say a higher standard of living. For that matter, most people undoubtedly would probably like to improve their economic positions, and it appears that virtually all people throughout history have been able to imagine a nicer life for themselves. This fantasy can take many forms including better food, shelter, health, transportation, clothing, and amusements, as well as more time to relax or commune with nature, or to contemplate one's God. Although economic growth certainly brings some problems of its own, it also helps to make people's dreams come true.

A nation can develop economically in two basic ways. First, it may increase the quantity of its productive factors; land, labor, and capital. Second, it may effect productivity increases--that is, more output per input (a person who produced 10 widgets an hour yesterday produces 20 today). Factors which account for productivity gains may include: improvements in the quality of the factors of production, changes in how they are organized, entrepreneurship, and technological progress.

Whether economic growth derives from additions to the productive factors or to productivity advances, the key element in each avenue is the human one. For it is people with their strengths, skills, health, industry, and attitudes, who ultimately account for the wealth of a nation and who are most productive under conditions of economic freedom. With this principle in mind, let us look at the American colonists, why they emigrated, the work in which they were engaged, and what they accomplished.

(A) People

Starting with 105 settlers in Jamestown, the population of British North America, consisting of free individuals, indentured servants, and slaves, enlarged to approximately 2.5 million by the time of the Revolutionary War. Natural increase, rather than immigration, accounted for most of this growth.

Of those who did emigrate, economic, religious, and political reasons led them to leave Europe and sail to the new land. Among the economic inducements were the award of 50 acres of land (a headright), to each individual who could pay his way over, with an additional 50 acres to him for each additional person whose journey he financed. Land grants also were given to groups of colonists such as the Puritans.

Most individuals, however, could not afford the ocean voyage, and indentured servitude offered them their only means of securing passage. Lacking sufficient funds of his own, a potential immigrant usually represented something of a credit risk when it came to financing transportation costs. After all, he was headed to a distant land with himself as his sole collateral--an unsecured loan if ever there was one. To surmount this financial difficulty, he might contract to work a certain length of time (usually two to seven years) in America in exchange for transportation, along with room and board (but not a money wage) for the period of the indenture. The servant would be set free at the end of his indenture and receive "dues" which varied from colony to colony and might include land, clothing, tools, a gun, and sometimes money.

There were three categories of indentured labor. One type, prominent in the seventeenth century, occurred when an individual in Europe signed a contract with a planter, or the agent of a merchant, whereby he agreed to work in America for some remuneration. Markets for indentured servants developed overseas and a good deal of bargaining took place over the length of the indenture, the working conditions, and the dues receivable at the end of the indenture. Skilled labor, for instance, could usually obtain a shorter indenture than unskilled.

Toward the end of the seventeenth century, another sort of indentured servant appeared. This was the "free willer" or "redemptor." Planning to travel from the continent (especially Germany) to the New World, a family would have sold its possessions to finance the voyage, but at the port of embarkation the members of the family might find its funds to be insufficient. As a solution to this dilemma, they would give the captain of the vessel what money they possessed and contract to pay him the rest soon after arrival in America. The captain usually granted time to find work and earn what he was owed, but if the family failed to earn the balance (which was often the case), the captain would "redeem" his loss by selling the contract to someone who needed indentured servants. There were occasions when a group of such potential servants would be bought wholesale by "soul drivers" who would then march them from town to town, auctioning off whom he could at each stop, and often splitting up families in the process.

Convicts shipped from England for sale in America during the 17th and 18th Centuries represented the third category of indenture. During those times, hundreds of crimes were punishable by death, and a sympathetic judge might send a criminal to labor-hungry America instead of to his Maker.

The Colonial system of indentured servitude was not without its faults. The work was often very harsh, and some masters were cruel and tyrannical. Sometimes the European middlemen made misleading promises which were not always kept. Sometimes the sale of the contract meant that families were broken up. Sometimes, an employer could not be found for a potential servant, and that unfortunate soul might be forced to remain on the ship until one was discovered--or perhaps until he died. Sometimes the indentured convicts committed criminal acts.

The gradual enactment of laws designed to protect the servant, his property and rights, and to prevent the importation of convicts indicates these problems were not atypical. In assessing the indenture system, however, one must be aware that for many people, indentured servitude was the only way they could travel to the Colonies where they hoped to improve their lives. Today's economists consider indentured servitude a human capital investment--an investment in oneself, one's productivity, one's prosperity.

Also, remember, that at a time of tremendous labor shortage in the colonies, indentured servants (they could be bought and sold and even rented out), worked at a great many jobs both on the farm and in town shops--as laborers, carpenters, tailors, bricklayers, etc.--and even as overseers of slaves. In the seventeenth century they came predominately from England while the eighteenth century brought them from Ireland, Scotland, Germany, and other areas on the continent. Overall, indentured servants accounted for perhaps half of the immigration into America, and in some colonies, such as Pennsylvania, they represented up to three-quarters of the total.

Employing an indentured servant could be quite costly for the master who had to pay for the ocean voyage, provide support during the period of indenture, and assume the risk that the servant might die or run away. In fact, laws were enacted to control the movement of this valuable property and to prevent runaways.[3] Over time, with the cost of a trans-Atlantic voyage declining and real wages overseas rising, more and more people were able to pay for their own transportation and were less willing to be bound for a lengthy period. By the time of the American Revolution, the importance of indentured servitude had markedly declined, and other sources of labor were sought. Some Indians were enslaved, although that turned out to be an unsuccessful alternative. These native American males considered agricultural labor women's work; they detested supervised and disciplined labor; and their intimate knowledge of the terrain facilitated their escape. The colonists, especially planters, looked more and more to slavery in order to satisfy their labor needs.

Slaves from Africa were obtained by Europeans and Americans from the African slave traders who had initially captured these unfortunate souls. They were shipped to the Caribbean and South America and later to North America. The African slaves were sold by the Dutch in Virginia in 1619 and shortly thereafter, slaves could be found in other colonies. Initially, it appears that they worked as indentured servants, but soon had their status altered to that of slaves.

That the cost of buying and maintaining slaves had become less than similar costs for indentured servants helped to account for the growing number of colonial American slaves. At a pragmatic level we today find grotesque, a colonist's investment in African slaves was enhanced by other factors: the slaves identifying color made it extremely difficult for them to escape; and the growth in size of their families increased their masters supply of labor. In contrast to the indentured servant, for whom the legal system offered some potential protection, a slave was made by law the property of his master, a property that by 1664 was hereditary.

The first large scale importation of slaves stemmed from the failure of the English labor supply to meet the demand of the Chesapeake tobacco industry, and by the 1770's Blacks represented about twenty percent of the colonial population.[4] Most were located in the South where the climate permitted slaves to work more hours over the course of a year. And so they toiled in that region as unskilled labor requiring little supervision as they tended the plantation crops of rice, indigo, and tobacco. However, in the South and elsewhere, blacks, (both slave and free) were also employed as domestics, weavers, blacksmiths, carpenters, and in numerous other specialized occupations. An important component of the colonial labor supply and a significant contributor to the gross domestic product, slavery was for some of the colonists a disconcerting moral issue which became more disturbing as they began to advocate revolution to maintain their own freedoms.

The population growth in colonial America was due more to natural increase than to immigration of colonists and importation of slaves. With a higher birth rate and a lower death rate than in Europe, the population grew at an average of over three percent a year. By the middle of the 17th Century, most colonists in North America had been born here.

Economic analysis illuminates this phenomenon. Because labor was scarce and indentured servants as well as slaves were too expensive for many colonists, great advantages obtained in having many children (Nobel Laureate Theodore Schultz has referred to them as "poor man's capital"). From an economic standpoint, children were "investment goods"; they could perform numerous tasks on a farm and take care of their parents in the latters' old age.

In the very early settlements, high death rates had exceeded birth rates as colonists experienced tremendous handicaps and encountered new epidemic diseases. Over time, however, immunities to disease developed, agriculture became more productive, and death rates fell. On the average, American colonists ate as well as anyone on earth. In addition, most lived on or near the coast so that in the case of a crop failure or other shortage, food could be easily transported from elsewhere.

The North American slave population also experienced a natural increase, and thus the importation of slaves did not remain the most important source of slave labor. In fact, by 1680, blacks born in the Colonies comprised the majority of the slave population. This state of affairs stood in contrast to slavery conditions in the Caribbean Islands, where the slave death rate exceeded the birth rate (a natural decrease in economic--if not humanitarian--terms), and a continuous inflow of new slaves was needed to maintain the economy.

Slaves in North America had a higher standard of living than was true of their counterparts in the Caribbean Islands. Also, they worked in a healthier climate, were less subject to epidemic diseases, and therefore had a lower death rate.

(B) Migration To America

Throughout the great migrations in the 17th and 18th Centuries, immigrants, both singly and in groups, came to America in search of economic, religious, and political freedoms: of these, economic freedom was the prevailing incentive.

The first settlers at Jamestown, like other adventurers before them, hoped to become wealthy. Financed by a joint stock company--The VIRGINIA COMPANY OF LONDON--the profit motive dominated this venture in which settlers received orders to discover a passage to the Far East, find precious metals, produce goods which England had to import such as wine and silk, establish farms, send back lumber, trade with the Indians and convert them to Christianity.

In contrast, immigrants to the Plymouth Bay colony were searching for a place to practice religion without interference. These groups of Protestant separatists believed that the Bible rather than the king was the ultimate authority in both religious and secular matters. They had been persecuted for opposing the Anglican Church and had journeyed to Holland, which offered them welcome. But they encountered economic discrimination from the Dutch guilds and also became concerned as their children shed their traditions and adopted Dutch customs. When the opportunity to go to America under the English flag and worship God in their own way presented itself, these pilgrims quickly seized upon it.

The founders of the Massachusetts Bay colony came to America to establish a theocratic state based upon God's word as revealed in the Bible. These Puritans came intent upon simplifying the practices of the Church of England and abolishing its hierarchical structure. They hoped to establish, in the words of their leader John Winthrop "A Modal of Christian Charity" where "We shall be as a City upon a Hill, the eyes of all the people upon us."[5]

Catholics and others who were persecuted in Europe for their religious beliefs found a haven in Maryland, which upheld their freedom to worship.

The first arrivals were predominantly English while later colonists came from many different areas. One of these groups, the Scotch-Irish, has a history dating back to the seventeenth century when King James I, a Scotsman, decided to put down some rebellious Irish by moving Scottish and English settlers into northern Ireland. Later on, they, in turn, suffered religious and economic persecution from the English which induced them to sail to America.

Another large group of immigrants consisted of Germans fleeing from economic distress and religious and political persecutions in their native land. Many of them, along with the Scotch-Irish, located in Pennsylvania which had been founded by William Penn as a refuge for those so victimized. Many smaller groups also became part of the colonial mosaic. Huguenots came from France, Jews from Portugal, Spain, and Holland, while other nationalities, including the Swiss, Welsh, Irish, Swedes, and Dutch sought to find a better life in the new world.

(C) Work

Of the 105 colonists arriving in Virginia in 1607, only 38 survived that first year and similar odds awaited those who immediately followed them. In fact, about two-thirds of those who traveled to Virginia died during the first fifteen years of colonization.

Lack of appropriate tools and draft animals, epidemic disease, (particularly malaria), difficulty in adjusting to a new climate, and Indian attacks must be listed among the reasons for such a high death rate. In addition, many of the instructions given to the colonists by the VIRGINIA COMPANY OF LONDON were difficult if not impossible to fulfill. For these central planners, like those of the modern era, it all seemed so easy. However, orders from people living thousands of miles away in Europe who had little knowledge of conditions in America hardly contributed to colonial success.

But perhaps the most important problems were those of organization and incentives. The labors of the early Jamestown settlers were structured along military lines (a drumbeat, for instance, synchronized their daily march to work), and the total product was rationed equally among all members of the community. Predictably, in the absence of sufficient incentives, some of the men worked less earnestly than others, some did not work at all (free riders as economists say), innovations to increase total production failed to come forth, and output fell far short of its potential. In a land abundant with animals, birds, lumber, rivers, and fish, this early period became known as "The Starving Time."

Fortunately, the colonists were able to learn from their mistakes and make appropriate adjustments. Productivity improved, predictably enough, when in 1614, the system of community property began to be phased out, and each colonial family worked its own land as it saw fit, reaping the benefits or suffering the consequences. Harsh, to be sure, but beneficial to the community that now began to effect a rise in total output and general living conditions.

The Jamestown colony was also given a mighty assist with the discovery that tobacco could be sold as a cash crop. For tobacco, ("Benjamin Franklin said that if God had intended that man smoke he would have turned up his nose to provide an adequate draft"), could be shipped to England and the Continent to finance the import of much needed manufactured goods.[6] Introduced to John Rolfe by the Indian princess Pocahontas, this weed became a craze in Europe, where it not only provided an exhilarating experience, but was reputed to cure a variety of ills. It also became the crop that seduced Virginia into the acceptance of slavery.[7]

Farther north, the Plymouth Company had serious difficulties, some of which were of the members' own making. Although religious values united these Pilgrims, outsiders with valuable skills who might have made a positive contribution were denied entry to the community. Here, too, communal practices bore results similar to what had occurred at Jamestown. Eventually, the adoption of a system of private parcels and personal incentives wrought substantial changes for the better.

Later colonies managed to avoid some of the errors and agonies of their predecessors, although great effort remained essential for success in America.

The early settlers, faced with an abundance of natural resources and severe shortages of labor, money capital, and capital goods, made a rational decision--they concentrated their efforts on agricultural activity. Felling trees, preparing land for cultivation, raising livestock, and erecting houses, barns, and fences comprised the capital formation necessary to establish and enhance farm productivity. The trade-off of present sacrifice for greater future productivity inheres in capital formation and these colonists sacrificed much as they worked at subsistence level with basic implements to develop their land.

Small scale farming was the rule, although plantations could be found in the south, and regions varied in productivity and in the crops they emphasized. New England and the Middle Atlantic colonies (with the exception of New York where the Dutch feudal land holding system held sway) provided easy access to land. Settlers would be given parcels of land until a town was filled up, at which point, a new town would be opened up and the process repeated. New York took longer to settle because the relatively few people controlling the Dutch Patroon system made ownership of the land difficult for the common people.

England hindered the development of a manufacturing sector in the colonies. Already enjoying a lower cost structure, she proceeded to establish mercantile rules prohibiting much colonial production and trade. Shortages of money capital and skilled workers further thwarted growth in this area. On the other hand, manufacture in homes produced furniture, clothing, soap, candles and other domestic necessities, and small scale firms manufactured shoes, harnesses, rifles, axes, naval stores, and beer. Expert at shipbuilding, the colonists used high quality, low cost oak and pine to construct vessels for use in the colonies and for sale in England. While there was a shortage of the wood fuel needed for smelting in England, the virgin forests of North America provided wood fuel in abundance and the Colonists were able to produce a significant amount of iron.

The desire of the colonists for luxury and other products they could not manufacture domestically was intense, and the overriding financial problem (not enough colonial exports to support these imports), hardly dampened their ardor. Colonial expenditures by the British government and loans from the English met a part of this balance of payments deficit. However, these sources proved insufficient, and so, in spite of mercantile restrictions, the colonists rather ingeniously developed a complex trade network embracing North America, England, Southern Europe, the West Indies, and Africa. Ironically, their violation of mercantile rules provided the financial underpinning for the colonies to become markets for British wares.

(D) Accomplishments

Wealth consists of what is held to be valuable and for the colonists wealth included land, houses, barns and other structures, capital equipment, and livestock. Although the statistics on this subject are far from perfect, there is evidence that by the time of the American Revolution the average colonist probably had accumulated wealth superior to that of his counterpart in England or on the Continent. Generally, merchants, ship captains, and professionals stood at the top of an uneven distribution of these valuables, with farmers and shipowners occupying the middle, and seamen and laborers located at the bottom.

Over time, a vast accumulation of wealth had been amassed in the colonies and as a result, colonial per capita income approximated that of the high income nations of England and the Netherlands and indeed would exceed the per capita income of the vast majority of nations today. Moreover, and wonder of wonders, the average colonist not only was realizing a higher standard of living than his parents, but could anticipate his children doing even better.

Income also was unevenly distributed. At the bottom were slaves, and then indentured servants, although the latter when freed, might well move into a higher class. Real wages of unskilled labor hovered around the subsistence level and this was also true for those living in virtual isolation on the frontier.

In contrast, skilled workers, in short supply, fared quite well. Merchants tended to be better off, as did ships' captains, medical doctors, and lawyers. The colonial upper classes did achieve what any objective person would consider to be a high standard of living--lovely homes that were tastefully furnished, fashionable clothing, an abundance of food, and enough free time to cultivate artistic tastes.

Within virtually all occupations, however, substantial dispersion of income could be found. Some farmers eked out a subsistence on the frontier while others were owners of large plantations. Merchants ranged from the poorest peddlers to wealthy employers with many hired workers. When one considers real colonial income, one must not omit the natural blessings missing from urban America today; the clean air, pure water and unspoiled forests. Families were close-knit and religiously oriented, and they took care of their own including the aged, infirm and insane. Parents supervised the discipline and education of their offspring, and each family member (excluding the very young) bore responsibility for some aspect of farm output.[8]

Books that were primarily historical or religious, and poetry (mostly of a religious nature), were printed in the colonies. Both newspapers and pamphlets were important and available to the colonists. John Rittenhouse and Benjamin Franklin, among others, made scientific contributions. Members of an American Philosophical Society delivered learned papers. Construction of graceful and beautiful colonial homes and public buildings, such as meeting houses and churches, kept pace with the growing economy. Although limited in patronage, painting, especially of portraits, followed the schools of its European counterparts. Music, frowned upon in Puritan New England, nonetheless generally became an important element of colonial life. Professional musicians and makers of musical instruments established themselves in society and concerts and recitals of secular music augmented the singing of hymns which had once been the sole form of community music.

Educational achievements also warrant notice. The earliest attempt to establish a school system can be traced to the Massachusetts School Act of 1647 known as the Old Deluder Law. Enacted to stop Satan (that old deluder) in his attempts to prevent people from learning the scriptures, it stipulated that a person be hired to teach reading and writing in all communities that contained fifty families and to establish secondary schools in those with one hundred families. Town meetings levied fees in support of this program and similar policies could be found in other New England colonies. Rather than one system of education, the middle colonies relied upon various national and religious groups to provide education for their populace. The South offered less education than the other colonies.

Education in colonial America took many forms, including formal schools with teachers, instruction in the teacher's home, classes held in the fields and taught by a clergyman or the wife of a planter, and a craft system whereby a master would teach an apprentice a skill along with the elements of reading and writing. When it came to secondary education, there were Latin Grammar schools to prepare the young for college by stressing the classics, and academies with a more practical approach. Nor was higher education neglected. The following institutions have their origins in the colonial period:

Harvard College-1636
William and Mary-1693
The Collegiate School of Connecticut (Yale)-1701
University of Pennsylvania -1740
College of New Jersey (Princeton)-1746
Kings College (Columbia)-1754
Dartmouth College-1755

Rhode Island College (Brown)-1764
Queens College (Rutgers)-1766

With the exception of the University of Pennsylvania, all of the above were founded privately by religious groups. In England, King Charles I who held a degree granting monopoly, had eliminated Puritan elements from Oxford and Cambridge and, thus, did a need for a second Cambridge become apparent in America. To realize this goal, the colonist John Harvard donated books and money to the institution that bears his name--a college with a mission of training Puritan ministers. According to the Harvard Rules and Precepts, "The main end of the scholar's life and studies is the only foundation of all sound knowledge and harmony." Yale was also founded to train the clergy, while Dartmouth had for its objective the transmission of the Bible to the Indians.[9]

No one should doubt the importance of religion in colonial America. As de Toqueville noted, "In America it is religion which leads to enlightenment and the observance of divine laws which leads men to liberty."[10] Although religious prejudice, bigotry, and discrimination hardly disappeared, the colonists, exhibited a degree of religious tolerance significantly higher than could be found in Europe. Contributing to this was the large size of America and the multiplicity of competing religions which made monopoly by any religion difficult.

ECONOMIC FREEDOM

(A) Mercantilism

The colonization of North America took place during the era of mercantilism in a climate decidedly inhospitable to economic freedom. Mercantilism, the dominant economic school of thought in Western Europe during the 16th, 17th, and 18th Centuries, evolved as commerce, markets, money, and merchants replaced the self-sufficient agrarian feudalism of the Middle Ages. Nation states emerged and, with the discovery of America, were intent on establishing colonies and other spheres of influence.

The principal objective of mercantilism is to build up national economic power, and writers from various walks of life (whom today we call mercantilists) offered advice to the sovereign on how to realize this goal. The principle solution awarded government the role of directing the economy. While the ideas and practices of mercantilism varied from nation to nation, the essence of this philosophy consisted of this and a few basic ideas.

Gold and silver are of prime importance because their accumulation is thought to be the proper measure of national wealth. Today, we have better indicators of economic wellbeing (Gross Domestic Product and other National Income accounts), but during that era, precious metals were valuable in financing transactions, public projects, standing armies, and wars.

A nation can acquire the coveted treasure if it exports more goods than it imports and gold and silver are used to settle the deficit. The role of government was to make sure that this scenario took place, and thus, it imposed tariffs to keep out foreign products (often at the behest of business), encouraged domestic industries with monopolistic privileges and subsidies, established maximum prices, and (to elicit high quality output) issued detailed regulations on methods of manufacture. That people were required to eat fish on Friday (in Protestant England to boot) in order to build up the merchant marine (its ships and sailors were incorporated into the navy during time of war), provides some indication of the extent to which a state might be willing to engage in economic intervention.

Mercantile labor policy consisted of several parts. To meet the employment needs of agriculture, commerce, manufacturing, and the armed forces, a large labor force was desired and encouraged. France, for instance, offered tax exemptions to families with ten or more children: those offspring who had died in military service were counted while live offspring who were members of the clergy were not! Governments allocated labor among occupations, fixed wages, prohibited strikes, and discouraged idleness with a poor relief system that might most politely be described as harsh.

Colonies held an important place in the mercantile scheme of things. Denied the right to engage in most types of manufacturing, they served Europe as sources of raw material and as markets for the exports of the home country, whose vessels pretty much monopolized the carrying trade. To implement this colonial policy, England during the seventeenth century, began to enact a series of laws known as the Navigation Acts.

(B) British North America

Issued under a variety of circumstances, royal charters provided the legal basis (at least as far as Englishmen were concerned) for establishing colonies. The VIRGINIA COMPANY OF LONDON represented a joint stock venture intent on making a profit, while religion provided the motivating drive for the settlements in Plymouth and Massachusetts Bay. Roger Williams obtained a royal charter to secure religious freedom in Rhode Island, and as late as 1732, James Oglethorpe and John Percival were awarded a charter enabling Georgia to offer refuge to English debtors--and not so incidentally to serve as a buffer against Spanish Florida and French Louisiana. Maryland and Pennsylvania were "proprietary" colonies whose proprietors, Lord Baltimore and William Penn, respectively, received charters granting them broad governing powers. They, in turn, were to make their holdings safe havens for the persecuted. Charters not only gave their recipients a monopoly in certain economic activities, but also awarded settlers the same legal status as Englishmen.

The first example of representative self-government in the colonies occurred as early as 1619 (the same year that slaves first arrived), when the Governor of Virginia called together the first legislative assembly. This body, the Colonial Assembly of Virginia, consisted of a House of Burgesses (representatives), the Governor, and his council. But it was a year later, in 1620, that the Pilgrims were blown off course en route to Virginia, landed far north at Cape Cod, quarreled about rules of governance outside their charters patent, and agreed in the composition of the Mayflower Compact. This document was the first instrument of direct popular government in the New World. And William Penn's

Charter of Liberties, written in 1682 gave a constitution to Pennsylvania that embraced abundant religious, political, and economic freedoms.

By the time of the American Revolution, all of the colonies had representative legislatures of either one or two houses, and their laws, naturally enough, tended to follow the English pattern. While it is true that the Crown generally had--and used--the authority to appoint judges and governors directly responsible to it, and although Parliament did have the final word, it is also fact that the colonists possessed and exercised considerable power over their own affairs, and this was true for local areas where most government functions were performed as well as for higher level representative bodies.

Colonists arriving in America during the 17th century believed that human behavior should reflect societal values and saw nothing wrong in using government to achieve this end. The community initially established in Massachusetts, for instance, merged the material and the divine. Man might and should try to improve himself, but self-interest was subordinate to the common good, with the Gospel as foundation and guide for all aspects of living. As a result, state regulation of economic affairs was ubiquitous, as was the assumption of responsibility for the soul of one's neighbor ("holy watching").[11] Written on blue paper, there were the "blue laws" prohibiting blasphemous language, adultery, and intoxication, which was legally defined as, "where the same legs which carry a man into the house cannot bring him out again."[12] Also prohibited were certain modes of dress, (silk hoods, ribbons, and other luxury items denied to the poor), and various objectionable activities such as gambling. The Massachusetts Legislature even made Christmas a day of fast with a five shilling fine meted out to anyone discovered feasting.

While government influence in social and economic matters varied from colony to colony, in all of them, economic thought had an ethical dimension, and economic freedom was tempered by rules to restrain greed and protect the common good. This ethical brand of mercantilism was adhered to by the early settlers, lost its authority over the decades, but never totally disappeared. Although some public economic policy was misguided and inefficient, much of it promoted economic growth.

"The best investment is land," said Will Rogers, "because they ain't making any more of it." American colonists would have appreciated that sentiment, for so much did they love their land that it is difficult to overemphasize the importance of it to them. The prospect of having one's own land, something virtually impossible in the old world, was a major reason for emigration from Europe.

Working the land could provide a living and a bulwark against poverty. Possession of the land freed one from the arbitrariness, greed and power of the landlord, gave status, and for some of a speculative nature became the road to riches. It served as the foundation from which individual initiative could flourish and the basis for holding public office and the franchise to vote. Because of the widespread availability of land, as much as 80 percent of the free white male population met property qualifications in some colonies.[13]

However, property rights, although less encumbered than in England, were by no means absolute. The Old World system of primogeniture, wherein the entire estate of the deceased passed on to the eldest son, was the law in the South. This had come about because wealthy planters, who wished to realize the economies of large scale farms, used their influence in the legislature. Also, what Blackstone termed "offenses against public trade" such as usury were prohibited and sumptuary laws concerning morality might forbid the purchase of goods (playing cards for example) deemed injurious to the public welfare.

Other claims against property rights varied from colony to colony. Common grazing rights or common wood gathering rights might take precedence over property rights of ownership; rates charged by "public utilities" were subject to regulation; and eminent domain might justify the taking of property for the establishment of a road--and sometimes without compensation. Certain types of trees were owned de facto by the Crown, and in Maine and New Hampshire white pine trees used in the construction of sailing vessels were marked with a royal arrow to signify that they were within the king's domain. Mineral rights in some of the colonies were also property of the Crown. This derived from an English tradition that despite the grant of property to a subject, the Crown reserved rights to any swan located on said property or any whale to be found (the king owned the head and the queen the tail). And, of course, property could be taxed. This too derived from the English practice of "voluntary gift" giving, the gifts to be determined by the people's representatives and turned over to the appropriate public authority.[14]

Subject to such qualifications, allocation of land with secure title to individuals and groups of settlers became a major function of colonial government and it was one that was performed quite successfully.

Among other governmental functions (there were no legislative "programs" in those days), were the protection of property (including slaves), and the enforcement of contracts (including those with indentured servants). It was with property and contacts in mind that British Parliament, at the behest of British creditors who were paid by American debtors in depreciated notes, passed laws to restrain the colonies from issuing paper money. Governments also established courts to adjudicate disputes and punish crimes. And the latter included violations of religious codes (i.e. invectives against church, or cavorting around a maypole), for religion was a public matter. Although punishments embraced the death penalty, amputation of limbs, and whippings, these terrors sharply diminished during the 18th Century as colonial judges and juries became more lenient.[15] Initially, the colonists pretty much provided for their own defense although England assumed a larger role during the eighteenth century.

With idleness held in contempt, public relief to the truly poor was truly meager, albeit effective. What might loosely be called public policy toward the poor rested on private efforts and religion provided vital impetus for these endeavors.[16] Sermons often stressed the importance of compassion in pleasing God and, as John Wesley advised, "Put yourself in the place of every poor man and deal with him as you would God deal with you."[17] It was important for those offering help to get to know the character of individuals who sought assistance. In that way, aid could be effectively directed to the source of the problems.

With jobs plentiful in this expanding agricultural nation, unemployment was hardly a problem. Poverty, when it occurred, often stemmed from the early death of a spouse, or disabling accident, or fire. People frequently opened their homes and offered food, shelter, and care to the afflicted. Religion was an essential part of American compassion and poor people who had shown themselves to be unfaithful to God received instruction about God and His expectations for man along with charity.

For alcoholics or those with a disorderly temperament who refused work, towns might establish workhouses in which strict rules of conduct prevailed, and punishments including whippings were meted out to violators of such rules. Reform was intimately woven into charitable endeavors. Instructive are the words of the influential Puritan divine Cotton Mather:

> ...as for those who Indulge themselves in Idleness, the Express Command of God unto us, is, That we should let them starve.[18]

> Instead of exhorting you to augment your charity, I will rather utter an exhortation...that you not *abuse* your charity by misapplying it...Let us try to do good with as much application of mind as wicked men employ in doing evil.[19]

> Don't nourish 'em and harden 'em in that, but find employment for them. Find 'em work; set 'em to work; keep 'em to work....If there be any base houses, which threaten debauch and poison and confound the neighborhood--let your charity to your neighbors make you do all you can for the suppression of them[20]

Responsibility for one's self and one's community was an integral component of early American philosophy and theology. Most influential were the words of Saint Paul in his second letter to the Thessalonians.

> Our brothers, we command you in the name of our Lord Jesus Christ to keep away from all brothers who are living a lazy life and who do not follow the instructions that we gave them. You yourselves know very well that you should do just what we did. We were not lazy when we were with you. We did not accept anyone's support without paying for it. Instead, we worked and toiled; we kept working day and night so as not to be an expense to any of you. We did this, not because we do not have the right to demand our support; we did it to be an example for you to follow. While we were with you, we used to tell you, "Whoever refuses to work is not allowed to eat."
> We say this because we hear there are some people among you who live lazy lives and who do nothing except meddle in other people's business. In the name of the Lord Jesus Christ we command these people and warn them to lead orderly lives and work to earn their own living.
> But you, brothers, must not become tired of doing good. It may be that someone there will not obey the message we send you in this letter. If so, take note of him and have nothing to do with him so that he will be ashamed. But do not treat him as an enemy; instead warn him as a brother.
>
> (Paul: 2 Thessalonians 3:6-15)

As might be imagined, some other public policies proved unproductive. Various colonial governments placed ceilings on wages when labor was scarce and forbade craftsmen to leave areas where their skills were in short supply. Also, they tried to regulate the price, quantity, and quality of some products. Fortunately, the low level of taxation allotted to the enforcement of these barriers to freedom facilitated their evasion, and the frequency with which the laws were changed offers some indication that people did find ways to get around them.[21]

Usually, there were very few full time public employees and the private sector was often employed to achieve public objectives. If, for instance, government wanted the streets repaired, it simply told the appropriate private parties (under threat of sanction) to perform this chore. Charters and licenses were often used to induce private enterprise to undertake such projects as building a bridge or starting a college. In this regard, the government was more a facilitator than an owner and operator.[22]

To carry out its functions, government charged fees for some of its services, levied property, poll, and excise taxes, borrowed funds, and printed money. Sometimes, in-kind taxes requiring people to work on road construction, or other public projects were imposed. Used solely for colonial purposes, taxes overall remained quite low. Even in the larger colonies that spent more, such as New York (plus ça change, plus c'est la même chose) total peacetime expenditures did not reach 5000 pounds a year.[23] Loath to part with their funds, the colonists carefully monitored governmental activity, which itself was mostly local (New England town meetings exemplify this), and they had the power to thwart policies not to their liking. In some colonies, the royal governor depended on the colonial legislature not only for the revenue to implement policy, but for his own salary. The scope of government activity actually declined over time as the difficulties of regulating so many aspects of human behavior became increasingly evident. In economic terms, the costs exceeded the benefits.

SUMMARY

A motivated and courageous people, these American immigrants. They undertook dangerous journeys to a new world where primitive conditions awaited them. They and their offspring learned from often painful experience to discard old world practices ill-suited to American life. They willingly experimented, and adopted what worked. There was little titled nobility in America and over the years there developed some tendency to judge people more on the basis of ability than on parentage or social background. This is not to say that the influences of friendship or patronage were wholly absent, even on men of great talent. George Washington, Alexander Hamilton, and Benjamin Franklin, for instance, all enjoyed assistance in the development of their careers.[24] Nonetheless, self-made men and social mobility were ubiquitous in the colonies and generally speaking, life improved, and a positive attitude toward change prevailed.

In such a climate of enterprise and accomplishment, personal moral virtues shone with a luster they rarely had in the Old World. Benjamin Franklin was far from alone in his belief that material progress was good for the human spirit and led to happiness. His aphorisms, collected in *Poor Richard's Almanac* as "Father Abraham's Speech or The Way to Wealth" were popular throughout the Colonies, and they still strike a distinctly American chord today:

The Sleeping Fox catches no Poultry.
Lost Time is never found again.
Sloth makes all Things difficult, but Industry all easy.
Early to Bed and early to rise, makes a man healthy, wealthy and wise.
He that lives upon hope will die fasting.
There are no Gains, without Pains.
At the working Man's House Hunger looks in, but dares not enter.
Diligence is the Mother of Good Luck.
Little Strokes fell great Oakes.
The second Vice is Lying, the first is running in Debt....Lying rides upon Debt's back.
But poverty often deprives a Man of all Spirit and Virtue: Tis hard for an empty Bag to stand upright.[25]

Colonization took place during the age of mercantilism, but it was a mercantilism much less severe in the New World than in Europe, and the British Navigation Acts pretty much allowed settlers to do what they would have done had the Acts never existed. Many of the functions of colonial governments promoted economic growth. Ownership of land was widespread and there was little public interference with its use. There were often ways to circumvent unwise governmental policies and taxes, compared to England and Europe (not to mention those areas and the United States today), were held to low levels by the frugal colonists. Although at times misguided, public policy did not retard economic growth significantly and in many ways promoted it.

Americans were less enamoured with economic liberty in the early colonial period than at its later stages, but even then, failed to embrace it completely. The claims of interest groups (and not just income classes), seeking to feather their own nests often conflicted over public policy. Merchants, for instance, promoted legislation to keep out competing imports from other colonies. With economics, however, the case is not a matter of all or nothing but rather a matter of degree, and these generally self-governing colonists probably had more economic freedom than any other people in the world at that time.

In the picture drawn of the North American colonies, we have illustrated how economic and political freedoms were inextricably bound; how they reinforced each other; and how they sustained the enterprise and industriousness of the colonists. During a century and a half, the colonists wrought a spectacularly successful economy from the native abundance of their new homeland. The vital human source of this economic success was the initiative, pragmatism, hard work, and frugality of the people. Attempts by the British to take away their freedoms (and the colonists knew that their fruits would also disappear), gave rise to anxiety, ire, introspection, and ultimately to revolution.

---

[1] Samuel Eliot Morison, *The Oxford History of the American People* (New York: Oxford University Press,1965), pp. 40-41.

[2] Robert Royal, *1492 And All That* (Washington D.C.: Ethics And Public Policy Center, 1992), p.117.

[3] Gordon S. Wood, *The Radicalism of The American Revolution* (New York: Alfred A. Knopf, 1992),pp. 51-54.

[4] Bernard Bailyn, *The Peopling of British North America: An Introduction* (New York: Alfred A. Knopf, 1986), p.28.

[5] Benjamin Hart, *Faith and Freedom: The Christian Roots of American Liberty* (Dallas: Lewis and Stanley, 1990), p. 90.

[6] Shepard B. Clough, *The Economic Development of Western Civilization* (New York: McGraw-Hill Book Company, Inc., 1959) p.157.

[7] Benjamin Hart, *Faith and Freedom: The Christian Roots of American Liberty*, p.146.

[8] Good concise discussions of colonial wealth and output are provided in the following works:

Barry .W. Poulson, *Economic History of the United States* (New York: Macmillan publishing Co., Inc., 1981),pp.113-137.

Gary M. Walton and Hugh Rockoff, *History of the American Economy*, 6th ed., (New York: Harcourt Brace Jovanovich, Publishers, 1990), pp.97-104.

Robert C. Puth, *American Economic History*, 3rd ed., New York: The Dryden Press, 1993), pp.91-94.

[9] Benjamin Hart, *Faith and Freedom: The Christian Roots of American Liberty*, pp., 108-110 and 222-223.

[10] de Toqueville quoted in Benjamin Hart, *Faith and Freedom: The Christian Roots of American Liberty,* p.111.

[11] Oscar Handlin and Mary Handlin, *Liberty and Power 1600-1760* (New York: Harper & Row Publishers, 1986),pp.85-111.

[12] Ibid., p.100.

[13] Forest McDonald, *NOVUS ORDO SECLORUM; The Intellectual Origins of the Constitution*, (Lawrence: The University of Kansas Press, 1985), p.27.

[14] Ibid., pp. 9-37.

[15] Oscar and Mary Handlin, *Liberty and Power 1600-1760*, pp.216-221.

[16] Marvin Olasky, *The Tragedy Of American Compassion* (Washington, D..C.: Regnery Gateway, 1992), pp. 6-12.

[17] Ibid., p.8.

[18] Max Seville, *Seeds of Liberty* (New York: Alfred A. Knopf, 1948), p. 188.

[19] Marvin Olasky, *The Tragedy Of American Compassion*, p.9.

[20] Ibid., pp. 9,10.

[21] Robert C. Puth, *American Economic History*, 3rd ed., pp.95-97.

[22] Gordon S. Wood, *The Radicalism of The American Revolution*, pp.81,82.

[23] Barry W. Poulson, *Economic History of the United States*, pp. 103-105.

[24] Gordon S. Wood, *The Radicalism of The American Revolution*, pp.74-77.

[25] Daniel J. Boorstin, *An American Primer* (New York: Penguin Books, 1985), pp. 66-77.

CHAPTER 3

THE GREAT AMERICAN WAR FOR FREEDOM AND INDEPENDENCE

Imagine yourself back in the 1950s, in the midst of the Eisenhower presidency. You gaze into a crystal ball, and you foresee a state of affairs turbulent enough to overturn the nations traditional values. You foresee the seizure of universities, defiance of political, economic, and religious authority, race riots in major cities, coarse language and nudity featured in the local movie theatre, and women struggling for economic and social equality. Such soothsaying would have been accorded the same respect as a prophecy in 1763 that the American colonies would soon successfully revolt against Great Britain.

The colonists, as we saw in Chapter 2 had accomplished much by the mid 18th Century. They had established numerous educational and cultural institutions, and already made colonial contributions in music, literature, and architecture. A relatively tolerant religious atmosphere prevailed along with political and economic freedom and an already high standard of living which they expected to improve.

Significant benefits, moreover, flowed from Great Britain. Liberties of Englishmen had been extended to the colonies, and the armies and navies of the mother country protected the colonies from hostile nations as well as from pirates. For all these advantages, no direct taxes were paid. Colonial exports had access to British markets, and American mercantile restrictions were far less severe than those overseas. Under a policy of salutary neglect, the Navigation Acts (which were often ignored by the colonists) actually stimulated demand for construction and use of colonial ships. Against this background, the popular King George III, but 22 years old, ascended the throne in 1760.

Why, then, did the colonists revolt? The answer to this question is as fascinating as it is complicated. Let us begin with a narrative of the major events preceding the colonists' decision to declare for independence.

JAMES OTIS AND THE GENERAL WRITS OF ASSISTANCE

While it is difficult to pinpoint exactly when general animosity began, students of colonial history suggest that opposition to the use of general writs of assistance is an appropriate place to start.

Early on, the Navigation Acts had permitted issuance of blanket writs of assistance for the purpose of enforcing revenue laws. These documents allowed officials to enter homes, warehouses and other public buildings at any time in their search for smuggled goods. Although rarely used, they had expired along with King George II in 1760. Also in that year, William Pitt, the British Secretary of State, made known his determination to enforce the 1733 Sugar Act. This legislation, passed at the behest of British West Indian planters, had provided for a steep duty on molasses and sugar produced in the French or Spanish West Indies. However, the colonists could obtain these products (which were vital ingredients in the production of colonial rum), as well as Boston baked beans, shoofly pie, and apple pandowdy from other than British sources at much lower cost: thus, with much smuggling, they generally evaded the Sugar Act. Of this the officers of the Crown were well aware.

Leading the opposition to the renewal of these general search warrants--the writs of assistance--were the Boston merchants, who hired the lawyer James Otis to present their case in court. Otis did just that, and in February of 1761 he delivered a stirring oration before the Massachusetts Superior Court. While acknowledging the legality of the special writ which permitted search of a premise suspected of containing smuggled goods, Otis vigorously denounced general writs as tyrannical, illegal, and in violation of the constitution and of inalienable colonial rights. He further set forth the premise that Parliament lacked the right to override colonial authority without the latter's consent. Although the court decided against him, Otis publicized views not only about personal writs of assistance, but also about colonial relations with Britain, and many American colonists shared his thinking.

THE PARSONS' CAUSE

So dominant a crop was tobacco in Virginia that it often served as a medium of exchange; contracts might even stipulate payment in this crop. As with any other commodity, the forces of supply and demand determined its price, and in 1758, when a severe drought reduced supply, the price of tobacco rose to about three times its normal level. This meant that on the one hand, some debtors had to pay more for tobacco to satisfy their obligations and that some tobacco planters had to give their creditors quantities of tobacco more valuable than they had when credit initially was arranged.

This unhappy state of affairs led debtors to petition the colonial legislature for financial protection. The legislature responded with the Two Penny Act, which permitted contracts made in tobacco to be paid in currency at the rate of two pence a pound--a rate well below the market price of tobacco.

Now a statute enacted in 1748 had established an annual salary for Anglican clergymen of 12,280 pounds of tobacco. Because the Two Penny Act significantly reduced this real income, anger spewed forth, eventually sufficient to cause the dispatch of an ecclesiastic emissary to the British Privy Council. In August of 1759, the Privy Council upheld the clergy's position, whereupon some of the Anglican priests sued for back pay--in other words, the difference between the two pence per pound they had received and the actual market price of tobacco. They lost the first two court cases, but a third, tried in 1763, was decided in the favor of one Reverend James Maury. It was during this trial that the jury heard the rousing oratory of young Patrick Henry, hired by the county to present its defense--that is, to support governmental price fixing.

Patrick Henry, the son of a Virginia frontier farmer, had failed in a number of business ventures before receiving a license to practice law. In the court case of Reverend Maury, Henry deployed the oratory skills which would later make him an immortal voice in the annals of the American Revolution. He claimed to the jury that the Anglican clergy would, "...were their power equal to their will, snatch from the hearth of their honest parishioner his last hoecake, from the widow and her orphan children the last milch cow! the last bed, nay, the last blanket from the lying-in woman."[1]

He asserted that the Two Penny Act had been passed for the common good of the people of Virginia and (relying upon the philosophy of John Locke) maintained that British disallowance of colonial law broke the compact between the King and his subjects. The latter had pledged obedience to the former who, in turn, had agreed to protect his subjects. But no more, Patrick Henry went on, for the king "...from being the father of his people degenerated into a tyrant, and forfeits all rights to his subjects' obedience"[2]

His ringing summation led the jury to award Reverend Maury the grand sum of one penny in damages. Both Otis and Henry gave voice to what many colonists believed--that they should be free to govern themselves and that British attempts to violate this freedom were illegal, unconstitutional, tyrannical and worthy of resistance.

THE TREATY OF PARIS AND COLONIAL RELATIONS

Even in the early days of the settlements, there was friction between the French nation and the English colonies. King William's War in 1689, the first serious conflict between these groups, was followed by Queen Anne's War, and King George's War within the first half of the 18th Century, and between 1754 and 1763 the Seven Years War raged not only in America (where it was known as the French and Indian War), but also in Europe and as far away as India. This war culminated in the decisive defeat of France.

Under the terms of the 1763 Treaty of Paris, which formally brought hostilities to a close, both France and Spain recognized British supremacy in North America. England had emerged as the strongest of nations and its fleets sailed the globe. There was a hidden irony in the signing of the Treaty of Paris: it removed the threat Spain and France had posed to the colonies and thus reduced their need for British protection.

The complex relationship of Great Britain to the American colonies developed from no systematic plan. Rather, the colonial system evolved from shifting and accruing policies, laws, and decrees of government agencies; instruments which in turn reflected Britain's relations with other nations, as well as the influence of pressure groups such as merchants and manufacturers.

The Board of Trade was the British government agency designated to oversee administration of the colonies. Its functions included enforcing the Navigation Acts and monitoring colonial laws, economic conditions, and relations with the Indians. All well and good, except that the Treasury, the Admiralty, and the Parliament (among others) not only were involved, but often performed overlapping functions. By 1763, the North American portion of the British Empire was so large and unwieldy that the British decided to make colonial governance more coherent and efficient. Three areas warranted special attention.

First, the western part of America needed to implement a policy which determined how Indians should be treated and who had the right to claim what land. Second, the British focused upon enforcement of the Navigation Acts. After a period of "salutary neglect," the growing colonies had become increasingly important as a market for British exports. Simultaneously, they were now more competitive with British merchants and manufacturers for markets both within and outside the empire, and these British interest groups urged Parliament to address this economic threat. Related to this threat was England's increasing awareness that the ever growing, ever stronger colonies might become more and more difficult to rule despite the Crown's most foresighted legislation.[3]

And third, the Crown sought to make the colonies pay for some of the cost of their defense. Because of the expense of the Seven Years War, Britain's debt had expanded to about 130 million pounds and taxes had risen sharply. The very existence of such a debt perpetuated these burdensome taxes, the lion's share of which fell upon merchants and landlords--two groups with influence in Parliament. In addition, it was proposed that for defensive purposes, British troops be stationed around the periphery of the colonies. Therefore, it seemed appropriate to ask for colonial monetary assistance. After all, the British treasury had financed a war fought primarily by the British military whose soldiers would continue to provide for the colonial defense. Moreover, their level of real income surely enabled the colonies to help defray these costs.

In piecemeal fashion, ministries of George III developed policies to address these issues of Indian relations, trade, and remuneration for military protection. But King George's ministers were men who had never traveled to the colonies: they were ignorant of the character and opinions of the people, and the nature and priorities of the society. They enacted policies focused solely on interests of the Crown, and these policies provoked a revolution.

LORD GRENVILLE'S MINISTRY

(A) The Proclamation of 1763

Hostile encounters with the Indians frequently occurred as settlers, fur traders, and land speculators pushed westward. Conflicting claims over property rights were aggravated by vaguely defined colonial boundaries, which might extend to the Mississippi or perhaps even across the entire continent. Developing a coherent land policy to prevent more bloodshed and another costly war quickly became a major goal of the newly appointed (April, 1763) Prime Minister, Lord George Grenville. His efforts resulted in the Royal Proclamation of 1763, which extended British laws to territories acquired under the Treaty of Paris, prohibited colonial governors from making land grants beyond the Appalachian mountains, reserved large land holdings for Indians, and required colonists who had settled that reserved land, or were holding it for speculative purposes, to relinquish their claims and depart.

The proclamation, however, brought bitter resistance from numerous settlers and speculators. Not only did such luminaries as George Washington and Benjamin Franklin engage in speculative land actives, but as Bernard Bailyn has noted, "Land speculation was everyone's work and it affected everyone, for it was a natural and rational response to two fundamental facts of American life: the extraordinarily low ratio of people to arable land, and the strong likelihood that the ratio would change quickly and radically as the population grew."[4] These hopes, expressed by the slogan, "Buy by the acre and sell by the foot," led speculators to play an influential role in bringing people (often indentured servants) from Europe. Finally, colonial governments which often sold land to finance public expenditures, and thereby to hold down taxes, also expressed dissatisfaction with tenets of the Royal Proclamation.

(B) The Sugar Act of 1764

As we know, the Sugar Act of 1733 (passed at the behest of English business interests in the West Indies) had imposed a steep tariff on molasses and sugar imported into the American colonies from areas not under British control. However, enforcement of the act left something to be desired. Customs officials were amenable to bribes; colonial courts selected to enforce legislation tended to be sympathetic to the violators; and smuggling to avoid taxation continued.

In 1764, legislation known in England as the American Revenue Act, and in the colonies as the Sugar Act, passed Parliament. Twofold in purpose, it sought to end the smuggling which had been taking place in the West Indies, and to raise the revenue to defray the cost of military forces in the colonies.

Reasoning (rather badly, as things turned out) that the colonists would be happy to pay a lower tax, the act sharply reduced the tariff on molasses and sugar. However, it also raised duties on imports such as silk, wine, coffee, and indigo, and took away colonial eligibility for drawbacks (remittance of duties) which were received for foreign products imported through England. Finally, the act extended the list of enumerated products that colonies could export only to England and instituted measures to make the customs system more effective.

Lord Grenville's policies came into effect at a time when economic conditions were already depressed, and many colonists attributed the worsening of their financial woes to these new measures. Most of colonists' hostility was couched in economic rather than constitutional terms, although both were given voice at a Boston town meeting by James Otis, who spoke out against taxation without representation. The Massachusetts House of Representatives saw fit to establish a committee of correspondence to keep informed of the thinking in other colonies. Then in Boston, merchants started to boycott British luxury products, and this type of protest spread to other geographic areas.

(C) The Stamp Act of 1765

In March, 1765, Grenville introduced the Stamp Act and Parliament passed it by a large majority. Scheduled to go into effect during November, it required that official documents be written on specially stamped paper and stamps be affixed to all printed material including pamphlets, almanacs, newspapers, playing cards, liquor licenses, and school diplomas. Of course there was a fee for stamps and stamped paper, and although the act designated Americans to collect this tax revenue, responsibility for the Act's enforcement rested with Vice-Admiralty courts which tendered their rulings without trial by jury.

Fear that the Stamp Act signaled the end of trial by jury was not the only reaction of enraged colonists. Foreseeing that stamp fee revenues would be insufficient to cover British military expenses, they predicted that this tax would be but the first of many. Finally, they took the position that only colonial assemblies could levy taxes. The Stamp Act imposed the first direct British tax on the colonies, violated the colonists perceived right to self-government, and smacked of a plot to enslave them.

In speech and prose, vigorous opposition to the Act, spread throughout the colonials and became especially heated among legislators, lawyers, publishers, merchants, and other businessmen. In Virginia, Patrick Henry, recently elected to the House of Burgesses, introduced the "Virginia Resolves" with a stirring speech. "In former times," said Henry, "tarquin and Julius had their Brutus, Charles had his Cromwell, and he Did not Doubt but some good American would stand up, in favor of his country." Concluding with the words "if this be treason, make the most of it," he set forth the famous "Resolves" that as British subjects under the British constitution, Virginians had long possessed the right to govern their own affairs and therefore, held the sole right to levy taxes.[5] This news from Virginia quickly found its way into newspapers and discourse throughout the colonies, eliciting the cry, "No taxation without representation."

Colonists who referred to themselves as the Sons of Liberty, expressed their displeasure by sponsoring petitions, setting stamped paper afire, and meting out rough treatment to the opposition. These Sons of Liberty became a vital part of the storm of protest against British policy.

At the request of the Massachusetts House of Representatives, delegates from nine colonies assembled in New York during October of 1765 to discuss the colonies' position Among the delegates, many of whom met one another for the first time, were James Otis, from Massachusetts, John Dickinson from Pennsylvania, and Phillip Livingston from New York.

One of the major issues before this Stamp Act Congress was that of representation. Some, defending the British position, maintained that colonial interests were virtually represented in Parliament. Most others, inasmuch as no colonial delegates had ever been sent to Parliament held the idea of virtual representation to be unlikely if not absurd. James Otis observed that one could "as well prove that the British House of Commons in fact represent all the people of the globe as those in America," and Arthur Lee remarked that the idea of virtual representation "would, in the days of superstition be called witchcraft."[6]

Theoretically, colonial representation in Parliament might be one solution to this problem but in a system of proportional representation the colonists would be sadly outnumbered. And so, the delegates focused upon the exclusive right of the colonies to tax themselves and drew up resolutions to that effect, as well as a petition to the Crown. This effort to alter British policy was not immediately successful. However, the colonies had united for the first time to protect themselves against those who would take away their rights.

The Stamp Act was implemented in November. The colonists responded with rioting, destruction of property, and the hanging of public officials in effigy. New York initiated a boycott against the importation and consumption of British goods and other colonies followed suit. This bred fear among British merchants, manufacturers, and craftsmen: not only was America a most important market for their wares, but American colonists already owed them substantial sums of money which now might prove difficult to collect.

Although the British citizenry had trouble understanding the colonists' unwillingness to share the cost of their own defense, economics has a way of conquering ideology. Parliament was inundated with petitions for the repeal of the Stamp Act.

Unable to withstand the onslaught, the Grenville ministry fell and was replaced by that of the Marquis of Rockingham. This "Old Whig", consistent to the principles of the Glorious Revolution of 1688, looked with favor on the American position, pursued a more conciliatory policy and King George signed a bill repealing the Stamp Act in March, 1766.

Following this course was no smooth process. Landlords who had been shouldering a heavy tax burden and were incensed at the repeal, and many members of Parliament expressed anger over colonial defiance. Although a minority, including William Pitt who eloquently defended the colonial position, took an opposite stance, it failed to calm the opposition and Parliament, intent on asserting its authority, proceeded to pass the Declaratory Act on the same day that witnessed the repeal of the Stamp Act. The purpose of the former was to define clearly (or so it was thought at the time), the relationship of the colonies to the mother country, that is, Crown and Parliament would have complete legislative power over the colonies "in all cases whatsoever."

Across the Atlantic, its implications drowned out by the emotional impact of the Stamp Act repeal, this new legislation received little attention. Both sides in the controversy felt relief, the boycott quickly evaporated, and celebrations, toasts, ringing bells, and illuminated windows all became part of a most festive mood.

THE TOWNSHEND ACTS

Trivial political differences often accounted for the rise and fall of ministries in this era, and such was the case for the brief tenure of Rockingham. And so, in August 1766, the Crown called upon a colonial favorite, William Pitt, the Earl of Chatham, to form a new ministry. Unfortunately, Pitt soon became ill and his replacement, the weak Duke of Grafton, gave free reign to the Chancellor of the Exchequer, the brilliant but erratic Lord Townshend, who later was characterized by Edmund Burke as "a statesman who has left nothing but errors to account for his fame."[7]

Charged with the job of extracting money from the colonists, Townshend sought to capitalize on the distinction sometimes made between direct internal taxes and external taxes (customs duties). The colonists considered the former to be unconstitutional unless instituted by their own assemblies, but they acquiesced to the latter as part of England's right to regulate commerce. Actually, they objected to any British tax designed to raise general revenue. It was in this context that in June, 1767, Parliament passed a series of laws which became known collectively as the Townshend Acts. They would go into effect in November of that year.

A newly established American Board of Customs would enforce duties levied on lead, paint, glass, as well as tea from the East India Company. Designed to make tax collection more efficient, the board had authority to hire customs officials (whose salaries were linked to the amounts they collected), promulgate rules, issue writs of assistance, and form additional Vice-Admiralty courts. Revenue from these measures would be used to help defray the expense of the British military establishment in America, to cover the cost of administering the laws, and to provide salaries for governors, judges, and other officers of the Crown. Of course, the last provision made the income of these officials independent of the colonial assemblies. All of this was immediately perceived by the colonists as an unwarranted encroachment on their rights and liberties.

Another source of colonial distress revolved around the Quartering Act of 1765 which required colonies to provide shelter as well as food, beverages, and supplies for British troops. In December, 1766, the New York Assembly refused to appropriate funds sufficient to comply with the law and Lord Hillsborough, the Colonial Secretary, reacted by suspending the Assembly. With much alarm, colonists viewed this move as another precedent for future attempts to enforce unconstitutional laws.

These events served to resurrect the anxiety of those already suspicious of a plot to take away their property and liberty. The British seemed to be treating them as an angry parent who must discipline and bring under control his unruly children. While colonists had along accepted such family metaphors characterizing their relationship to England, the real subordination behind the metaphors had limits, and the British government was overstepping them.

Again, colonial opposition took several forms. John Dickinson, a wealthy lawyer and land owner and member of the Pennsylvania Assembly, became one of the most distinctive and influential pamphleteers of the time. Beginning in late 1767, he composed twelve *Letters From a Farmer in Pennsylvania to the Inhabitants of the British Colonies,* wherein he advocated a nonviolent solution to the controversies raging between England and the colonies. Published in colonial newspapers, the *Farmer's Letters* denied Parliament's right to impose taxes for the purpose of raising general revenue. Dickinson, whose reasoning and mild tone appealed to many colonists, proposed additional petitions to officials of the Crown, along with measures to reduce the consumption of British products.

More passionately than the moderate Dickinson, Boston agitator Samuel Adams successfully stirred anti-British emotions with newspaper articles and political maneuverings, while James Otis delivered speeches with similar themes. The Sons of Liberty, reactivated and true to form, hung opponents in effigy from the Liberty Tree, a large elm near the Boston Common.

A circular letter drafted by the Massachusetts Assembly in 1768 made the rounds of the colonies and received a warm reception. Moderate in tone, it took the position that Parliament (although supreme) ultimately derived its power from a constitution which guaranteed that taxation could be undertaken only with the consent of the people. The letter warned of British attempts to make royal officials independent of colonial control and solicited suggestions about how the colonies might cooperate against the British threat. By a vote of 92 to 17, the Massachusetts Assembly refused the order of Lord Hillsborough, the colonial secretary, to rescind the letter and Governor Bernard had it dismissed. The Sons of Liberty as well as others made much of the "fighting ninety-two," Paul Revere signed a punch bowl for the "Immortal 92," and these digits became a patriotic symbol for Massachusetts.[8]

In June of 1768, the sloop Liberty, owned by the wealthy merchant John Hancock, a major contributor to the colonial cause, was seized by the British under the charge of smuggling wine. However, both Hancock and the vessel were freed by a Boston mob which afterwards went on to intimidate the Governor.

Between 1768 and 1770, the Townshend Acts also provoked another non-importation movement. Merchants, shipowners, and planters, joined in the boycott of British goods. People relied upon homespun clothing, Yale students shunned imported wine, and Harvard men gave up tea. Although British imports did decrease, the effect of this mode of protest was somewhat less than had been true of protest against the Stamp Act. Hostility toward the Townshend duties was less severe, enforcement not as rigorous, and because of opposition to the strong-arm tactics of the Sons of Liberty, some of the merchants were less cooperative.

The most famous confrontation between the British and the colonists occurred in Boston which by 1770 had become a garrison town. British soldiers often misbehaved and many found this--and their very presence infuriating. The soldiers were shunned and at times harassed by the Bostonians. On March 5 of that year, rabble rousers threw snowballs at a British sentry who summoned the guard to his aid. They, too, were taunted and pelted, and when one of their number lost his temper, and fired into the crowd, others joined in. Five people died and a few more were wounded.

John Adams served as attorney for the defense of the British soldiers. A descendant of the early Pilgrims John and Pricilla Alden, John Adams (1735-1826), though of fragile health, went on to become the nation's longest living president. Born in Braintree Massachusetts, this ambitious young man was the first of his family to graduate from Harvard. In this era, class standing depended more on social standing rather than academic achievement. Adams, the son of a farmer, who also was a pillar of his community, found himself located slightly below the class average.

He married Abigail Smith, an early pioneer in the women's' movement. As the move toward independence gathered force, she strongly advocated a role for women in the affairs of state: "Remember the ladies and be more favorable to them than your ancestors. Do not put such unlimited power into the hands of the husbands. Remember, all men would be tyrants if they could. If particular care and attention is not paid to the ladies, we are determined to foment a rebellion, and will not hold ourselves bound by any laws in which we have no voice or representation."[9] Although not impressed with this desire "to repeal our masculine systems," John Adams did develop a very successful career which included membership in the Massachusetts legislature and the Continental Congress. He was also minister to the Netherlands and to England, Vice-President and the second President of the United States.

Adams believed that justice rather than vengeance should triumph. His able defense led to the acquittal of all but two of the soldiers who were convicted on the lesser charge of manslaughter and were branded on the thumbs and released. Coincidentally, Parliament repealed the Townshend duties on the same day as the "Boston Massacre" and when this good news reached America, tensions eroded and boycotts disintegrated.

LORD NORTH'S MINISTRY

The Duke of Grafton offered his resignation from the ministry in January, 1770, whereupon King George called Lord North to the post of Prime Minister. A man of even temperament who wished to pursue conciliatory policies, North thought it economically unwise to tax colonial imports. It was his proposal to repeal the Townshend duties that Parliament had accepted.

Termination of the boycott of European goods, a relaxation of customs regulations, and a strong European demand for American grain had brought prosperity and tranquility. Colonial leaders, including John Hancock, John Adams, and Benjamin Franklin, counseled acceptance of contemporary conditions and withdrew, at least temporarily, from conflict. Samuel Adams and his radical cohorts, however, sustained their hostility and formed a committee of correspondence in Boston which coordinated their revolutionary activities with those of similar committees in other towns and colonies. They focused their attention on the Crown's assumption of the salaries of governors and the judiciary, and the Gaspee affair.

In June 1772, the Gaspee, a British customs schooner used to prevent smuggling, ran ashore in Narragansett Bay off Rhode Island. The crews of such vessels were less than gracious while searching colonial vessels for contraband and they were hated by the colonists. News of the Gaspee mishap induced a group of patriots to board ship, set it on fire, and beat up the crew. Horrified British authorities announced that the culprits would be put on trial in England, and even though these guilty parties were never discovered, the threat of trial in another country violated the ever important colonial tradition of determining justice at home. Although the Gaspee affair fanned flames of the radical cause, its effect was minor compared to what was about to unfold.

From the time of Queen Elizabeth, the East India Company had held the monopoly of transporting tea to England, where it was subjected to high import and export taxes. For the colonists, this was the only legal source of tea. And the East India Company operated with all the inefficiency of most mercantile monopolies. Adam Smith pinpointed one of the sources of this efficiency.

> It is a very singular government in which every member of the administration wishes to get out of the country, and consequently to have done with the government, as soon as he can, and to whose interest, the day after he has left it and carried his whole fortune with him, it is perfectly indifferent though the whole country was swallowed up by an earthquake.[10]

The colonial boycott which was accompanied by an increase in smuggled Dutch tea further aggravated its troubles and to assist the floundering organization, Lord North proposed, and in May, 1773, Parliament passed the Regulatory Act. Known as the Tea Act in America, this legislation remitted the import tax paid by the East India Company when it brought tea to England if that same tea was exported to America. The Act also permitted the East India Company to carry the tea directly to the colonies where, as a monopoly, it could by-pass colonial importers and distribute the tea to retailers through its own agents in America. However, the company would still have to pay a small three pence a pound duty.

Able to circumvent both British and colonial middlemen, the East India Company now could sell its merchandise to retailers at a lower price--a price below even that charged by smugglers. Deliberately ignoring this consumer benefit, colonial merchants and their radical friends proceeded to attack these new measures with vigor. For if Britain could grant a monopoly on tea, they argued, might not it do the same for other commodities and eventually destroy colonial economic freedom?

In December, 1773, ships loaded with tea began to arrive at colonial ports where various contingents of the Sons of Liberty prepared to greet them. The cargo was unloaded in Charleston but kept in a warehouse while shipmasters in New York and Philadelphia became convinced that the wiser course led back to England. In Boston, however, when tea-bearing vessels sailed into her harbor, Samuel Adams called a convention of the Sons of Liberty at the Old South Meeting House, and when Governor Hutchinson refused their demand to send the cargo back to England, a group disguised as Indians boarded the ships and dumped tea valued at 15,000 pounds overboard. This act was met with less than unanimous approval among the colonists, many of whom (including Franklin who abhorred the destruction of property) maintained that there were less turbulent ways to negotiate terms with Parliament. Meanwhile, across the Atlantic, King George and Parliament agreed that the time had come to discipline the colonists; to remind them that they were servants of the Crown, and to quell further unseemly acts of rebellion. Led by Lord North, Parliament passed a series of laws which come to be known as the Coercive or Intolerable Acts.

In March, 1774, under the Boston Port Act--the first of these laws-- customs officials arrived in Salem and closed Boston harbor except to ships bringing essential supplies. These conditions were to prevail until the appropriate parties made restitution to the East India Company and to British officials who had suffered losses during the riots in Boston, and until the King deemed law and order restored. Complementing this scenario, were four regiments of British troops which arrived in Boston under the direction of General Gage, who now replaced Thomas Hutchinson as Governor of Massachusetts.

In May, a still smoldering Parliament issued more legislation. To protect royal officials from colonial law suits, the Administration of Justice Act allowed the transfer of trials to England for those charged with crimes while implementing British policy. Passed on the same day and striking at the heart of colonial self-government, the Massachusetts Regulatory Act, authorized the king to select members of the Council (the House would remain elective), and upper judiciary, and empowered the governor to appoint and remove the attorney general, lower level judges, sheriffs, and peace officers. Even town meetings and their agenda required the governor's approval.

Around the same time, but in this case designed to exercise greater control over the fur trade and thereby to avoid costly colonial--Indian conflicts, Parliament passed the Quebec Act. It's provisions included an extension of Canadian boundaries west to the Mississippi and south to the Ohio river. It also set aside substantial areas of other land for the Indians, allowed French Canadians to maintain their political institutions, secured religious freedom for Catholics, and provided more centralized British control. From the American point of view, this Act meant that some would be denied the riches which flowed from land speculation, while both Catholics and Indians--hardly colonial favorites--received advantages. Although the Quebec Act was less directly punitive than the Boston Port Act, many colonists found it infuriating and intolerable.

And finally, a Quartering Act, passed in June and applicable to all colonies, required local authorities to provide shelter for British troops on short notice, and if barracks were unavailable, to quarter soldiers in unoccupied buildings, taverns, and even houses. This series of Intolerable Laws, passed during a brief period in the heat of anger, became the gauntlet hurled down and a source of great tension.

THE FIRST CONTINENTAL CONGRESS

Some colonists responded to this challenge by sending supplies to the people of Massachusetts. Thomas Jefferson, James Wilson, and John Adams proposed a "dominion plan" in which America would become a dominion of Britain, with the King exercising control over foreign affairs (including war and trade) and allowing the colonies autonomy in other matters. (Later, in 1778 Lord North would propose something similar as a way of ending the war, but by then it would be too late.) The Virginia House of Burgesses, having been dissolved by the governor for condemning the Intolerable Acts, nonetheless passed a resolution that an attack on one colony was an attack on all, and along with the Massachusetts Assembly, called for a meeting of representatives of all the colonies.

On September 5, 1774, fifty-five delegates, representing all the colonies but Georgia (still under the tight control of the Crown), met in Carpenters Hall in Philadelphia. Composed of men with conservative, liberal, and radical beliefs, this Congress was indeed an illustrious body. From Massachusetts came John Adams and his cousin Samuel; New York sent Philip Livingston, James Duane, and John Jay; John Dickinson and James Galloway traveled from Pennsylvania; the Virginia delegation included George Washington, Patrick Henry, Peyton Randolph, and Richard Henry Lee; and representing Connecticut were Roger Sherman and Silas Deane. Among the other delegates were Thomas McKean and Ceasar Rodney from Delaware; John Sullivan from New Hampshire; Samuel Chase from Maryland; Stephen Hopkins from Rhode Island; Richard Caswell from North Carolina; and Edward and John Rutledge of South Carolina.

In an atmosphere of cordiality and public spirit, they set themselves to the formidable task of preserving their liberties. One interesting and favorably received idea came from James Galloway who advanced a plan of colonial government that included a president appointed by the Crown and a general council of colonists elected by their own assemblies. The council would have veto power over acts of British Parliament pertaining to the colonies, while the Parliament could reject measures enacted by the council. In the midst of a debate over this proposal came the news of the Suffolk Resolves. These resolutions, the product of a convention of towns in the Boston area, held the Intolerable Acts to be unconstitutional, counseled disobedience to them, directed taxes to be withheld from the Crown until it restored constitutional government, urged the cessation of trade with Britain, and advised colonists to arm themselves. To all of this did the Congress give its approval and went on to defeat the Galloway plan by one vote.

In keeping with how Englishmen of an earlier century had reacted when confronted with an abrogation of their constitutional rights, the Continental Congress on October 14 issued a Declaration of Rights and Grievances. While agreeing to the right of Britain to regulate external commerce, this document enumerated the numerous ways Parliament had violated colonial rights--rights of life, liberty, property, and self-government long rooted in colonial charters, the English constitution, and the laws of nature.

The Congress endorsed the Continental Association, a document in which they agreed to terminate imports from Britain and her possessions in December of that year and to cease exports to them by March of the following year. Local committees would enforce this with violations punishable by boycotts and unfavorable publicity. A most interesting and characteristically American aspect of the "Association" was its emphasis on morality and virtue. Advocating "frugality, economy, and industry," it counseled avoidance of dissipation and extravagance (including in the latter gaming, plays, consumption of imported tea or alcoholic beverages, and ostentatious funerals). Thus, Congress sought to reinforce the link between virtue and freedom in the minds of colonial Americans; to remind them of their Puritan heritage, and to lead them to contemplate the sort of people they were and what was important in this life.[11]

The First Continental Congress was brought to a close on October 26, 1774. and much took place in the weeks and months that followed. The Association plan went into effect while in England the King rejected Benjamin Franklin's suggestion that a body of inquiry be sent to America to make a first-hand determination of what the colonists really wanted. In January of 1775, the House of Lords listened to a stirring oration by William Pitt, the Earl of Chatham, who characterized the colonial manner as moderate and justified and then went on to note "...that for solidity of reasoning, force of sagacity, and wisdom of conclusion, under such complication of difficult circumstances, no nation or body of men can stand in preference to the general Congress at Philadelphia."[12] Pitt called for the withdrawal of British troops from the colonies and he forecast grave trouble if his words went unheeded--which, of course, they were.

A month later, the great parliamentarian Edmund Burke--who in his time spoke out against England's abuses of power in America, Ireland and India as well as the evils accompanying the French Revolution--pleaded eloquently for reconciliation with the colonies: "Terror is not always the effect of force and an armament is not a victory. If you do not succeed, you are without resource: for conciliation failing, force remains; but force failing, no further hope of reconciliation is left...."[13] Burke introduced a bill claiming the legitimacy of the Continental Congress and acquiescing to colonial demands. The bill went down to defeat.

The North ministry's only concession would exempt from taxation any colony raising its quota of funds for defense. Indicative of that ministry's lack of touch with reality was the monetary bribe it offered to Benjamin Franklin, in the hope that he might be induced to fix up everything in the colonies. However, the proposal so appalled this distinguished American that he, too, began to look more favorably on colonial independence.[14]

In March, Lord North proposed the New England Restraining Act, which denied the New England colonies fishing rights in the waters of Newfoundland and Nova Scotia and prohibited them from trading with any place but Britain, Ireland, and the British West Indies. Provisions of the Act were soon extended to other colonies. It was also in March that Patrick Henry, in the House of Burgesses, proclaimed in ringing tones: "There is no room for hope," and that "If we wish to be free, we must fight! An appeal to arms and to the God of Hosts is all that is left us!...Is life so dear, or peace so sweet as to be purchased at the price of chains and slavery? Forbid it Almighty God! I know not what course others may take, but as for me, give me liberty or give me death!"[15]

Concerned with the surrounding dangers, General Gage fortified the area known as Boston Neck and ordered the Massachusetts Assembly to be dissolved. That body, however, moved to Salem, then to Concord, and finally to Cambridge where, under the leadership of John Hancock, it continued to perform governmental functions. A treasurer was appointed along with a Committee of Safety which engaged in espionage, built up a store of arms, and drilled the militia of minutemen.

On April 14, 1775, General Gage received a letter from the colonial secretary, endorsed by the king, ordering him to enforce the Intolerable Acts and to terminate the buildup of colonial strength. Four days later, dispatched in the secrecy of night, a contingent of British troops headed for the military stores at Concord. Patriots, however, had discovered what was happening and gave the alert.

Paul Revere, an artisan, agitator, and patriot if there ever was one, upheld the colonial concept of liberty that was common at his time: personal liberty, personal responsibility, and collective rights (how different from today's emphasis on radical individualism and entitlement). Following his well-thought out plan, he hung lamps in the steeple of the North Church to indicate troop movements over Back Bay--"one if by land, two if by sea"--and then along with other messengers--"ready to ride and spread the alarm"--galloped off into the countryside to deliver the Lexington Alarm.[16]

As the sun rose on Lexington on April 19, arriving British troops encountered militiamen gathering on the village common. While they were trying to disperse them, shots were fired and eight Americans were left dead and ten wounded. The British troops continued their march to Concord where they destroyed munitions and set ablaze the courthouse. A less felicitous return journey lay ahead of them. More and more militiamen fired at them along their way, and the British might have been wiped out entirely if reinforcements had not joined them at Lexington. Even so, harassment continued until they reached Charleston. By the end of these first battles, there were 366 casualties including the deaths of 49 colonists and 73 British.

News of these events spread rapidly through the colonies, England, and Europe. The great revolutionary war had begun. Indicative of its impact and still worth recalling are the words of Ralph Waldo Emerson's *Concord Hymn* that were sung at the completion of the battle monument on July 4, 1837:

> By the rude bridge that arched the flood,
> Their flag to April's breeze unfurled,
> Here once the embattled farmers stood
> And fired the shot heard round the world.[17]

THE SECOND CONTINENTAL CONGRESS

The Continental Congress reconvened on May 10, 1775. Many who had attended the earlier session were present, along with the notable addition of Benjamin Franklin, John Hancock, and Thomas Jefferson. For this august body, much was on the agenda: declaration of war; call for the raising of an army; and appointment of George Washington as its commander.

Born a Virginian in 1732, this tall, powerful, and deeply respected man approached life with seriousness and a high degree of integrity. Although part of the Virginia gentry, Washington was born into a not very well-to do family (as a teenager he was unable to attend a dance because he could not afford to buy oats for his horse). With but a rudimentary education (experience was to be his teacher--and a superb one it turned out to be), he learned the skills of the surveyor. He fought bravely in the French and Indian war, where on two occasions his horse was shot out from under him and with distinction in the Virginia Militia achieving the rank of colonel and regimental commander. He became a member of the House of Burgesses, and a delegate to the First and Second Continental Congress.

The Congress also voted to form a navy, establish diplomatic relations with other nations, develop means to finance the war, and take control of Indian affairs. Initially, this Congress regarded itself as an advisory body to the colonies, but gradually assumed more functions as the need for centralized authority became apparent.

Although fighting had begun, Congress was far from declaring for independence. Instead, it adopted a Declaration of the Causes and Necessity for Taking Arms. Drawn up by Jefferson and Dickenson, this document insisted that the purpose of raising a military force was neither to separate nor to establish independence, but rather to resist British aggression and tyranny inspired by ministers of the king who were giving his majesty such poor advice.

Congress then adopted John Dickinson's "Olive Branch Petition" to King George, which affirmed colonial devotion to the Crown, deplored the current events, and expressed desire for restoration of harmony. It begged for the king's intervention to terminate the Coercive Acts. But the Crown, unreceptive and adamant, declared the colonies to be in "an open and avowed rebellion," and ordered the insurrection suppressed and justice meted out to the traitors. Edmund Burke, among others, attempted reconciliation but a royal proclamation, issued in December, 1775 and scheduled to take effect by March 1, 1776, declared all trade and commerce with the colonies terminated.

Throughout this period of political and diplomatic maneuvering, things in the military arena were less than serene. Ethan Allen and his Green Mountain Boys had seized Ticonderoga in May, and colonists gave a good account of themselves at the Battle of Bunker Hill in the following month. The British, in turn, burned Portland, Maine and defeated an expedition of Americans against Quebec. Blood had been shed, and passions already deeply aroused received another jolt with the news that Britain had recruited German mercenaries.

The American flag was first raised on the flagship *Alfred* by John Paul Jones on December 3, 1775, and George Washington performed a similar feat with this new patriotic symbol near Boston on the following New Year's Day. Its thirteen stripes represented the thirteen colonies with the British Union Jack (replaced with stars in the following June) in the upper left corner.[18]

COMMON SENSE

Opinions on these events, vigorously presented in conventions, orations, and sermons, also found expression in print--newspapers, broadsides, almanacs, and pamphlets. Of the latter, the most influential was Thomas Paines' *COMMON SENSE*. This Quaker author, a former schoolmaster, corset-maker, and failure in these and other previous endeavors, migrated from England to America with a letter of introduction from Ben Franklin (and his contempt for authority unimpaired). A journalist, par excellence, Paine also served in the American army, later migrated to France where he almost was guillotined, returned to America, and died in 1809 in the Greenwich Village section of

New York City. His famous pamphlet is our concern, and through it he stirred the colonial desire for a complete separation from England.

The very idea of a king, was repugnant to Paine, and in *Common Sense* he attacked the institution of monarchy with an unprecedented ferocity:

> Of more worth is one honest man to society and in the sight of God, than all the crowned ruffians that ever lived.[19]

> One of the strongest natural proofs of the folly of hereditary right in kings, is that nature disapproves it, otherwise she would not so frequently turn it into ridicule by giving mankind an ass for a lion.[20]

There were colonists who inveighed against specific British actions but continued to maintain their loyalty: Paine was not one of them. He thought reconciliation with England was virtually impossible; but even if it were obtained, the danger of Parliamentary interference with colonial rights and freedoms would be ever present.

> Every thing that is right or natural pleads for separation. The blood of the slain, the weeping voice of nature cries, "TIS TIME TO PART. Even the distance at which the Almighty hath placed England and America, is a strong and natural proof, that the authority of the one, over the other, was never the design of Heaven.[21]

> Though I would carefully avoid giving unnecessary offence, yet I am inclined to believe, that all those who espouse the doctrine of reconciliation, may be included within the following descriptions. Interested men, who are not to be trusted; weak men who cannot see; prejudiced men who will not see; and a certain set of moderate men, who think better of the European world than it deserves; and this last class by an ill-judged deliberation, will be the cause of more calamities to this continent than all the other three.[22]

> Men of passive tempers look somewhat lightly over the offences of Britain, and still hoping for the best, are apt to call out, 'Come we shall be friends again for all this.' But examine the passions and feelings on mankind. Bring the doctrine of reconciliation to the touchstone of nature, and then tell me, whether you can hereafter love, honor, and faithfully serve the power that carried fire and sword into your land? If you cannot do all these, then are you only deceiving yourselves, and by your delay bringing ruin upon posterity. Your future connection with Britain, whom you can neither love nor honour, will be forced and unnatural, and being formed only on the plan of present convenience, will in a little time fall into a relapse more wretched than the first. But if you say, you can still pass the violations over, then I ask, Hath your house been burnt? Hath your property been destroyed before your face? Are your wife and children destitute of a bed to lie on, or bread to live on? Have you lost a parent or child by their hands, and yourself the ruined and wretched survivor? If you have not, then are you not a judge of those who have. But if you have, and can still shake hands with the murderers, then are you unworthy the name of husband, father, friend, or lover, and whatever may be your rank, or title in life, you have the heart of a coward, and the spirit of a sycophant.[23]

> As to government matters, it is not in the power of Britain to do this continent justice: The business of it will soon be too weighty, and intricate, to be managed with any tolerable degree of convenience, by a power, so distant from us, and so very ignorant of us; for if they cannot conquer us, they cannot govern us. To be always running three or

four thousand miles with a tale or a petition, waiting four of five months for an answer, which when obtained requires five or six more to explain it in, will in a few years be looked upon as folly and childishness-There was a time when it was proper, and there is a proper time for it to cease.

Small islands not capable of protecting themselves, are the proper objects for kingdoms to take under their care; but there is something very absurd, in supposing a continent to be perpetually governed by an island. In no instance hath nature made the satellite larger than its primary planet, and as England and America, with respect to each other, reverses the common order of nature, it is evident they belong to different systems: England to Europe, America to itself.[24]

For no nation in a state of foreign dependence, limited in its commerce, and cramped and fettered in its legislative powers, can ever arrive at any material eminence. America doth not yet know what opulence is; and although the progress which she hath made stands unparalleled in the history of other nations it is but childhood, compared with what she would be capable of arriving at, had she, as she ought to have, the legislative power in her own hands.[25]

...virtue, as I have already remarked, is not hereditary, neither is it perpetual. Should an independency be brought about...we have every opportunity and every encouragement before us, to form the noblest, purest constitution on the face of the earth. We have it in our power to begin the world over again. A situation, similar to the present, hath not happened since the days of Noah until now. The birth-day of a new world is at hand, and a race of men perhaps as numerous as all Europe contains, are to receive their portion of freedom from the event of a few months. The Reflection is awful-and in this point of view, How trifling, how ridiculous, do the little, paltry cavellings, of a few weak or interested men appear, when weighed against the business of a world.[26]

First published in Philadelphia and then in other cities, *COMMON SENSE* sold over one hundred thousand copies in a few months (Paine used some of the profits to purchase clothing for the American troops), and went far (one American said it burst like Jove in Thunder), to crystallize American sentiment.

Meetings, conventions, declarations, petitions, acts of vengeance, pitched battles, prose, poetry, and oratory, all had combined to make reconciliation increasingly difficult and to accelerate the movement toward independence.

---

[1] Bernard Bailyn, *The Ideological Origins of the American Revolution* (Cambridge: The Belknap Press of Harvard University Press, 1967), p. 253.

[2] Ibid., p.253.

[3] This thesis is developed in Theodore Draper, *A Struggle for Power* (New York: Times Books 1996).

[4] Bernard Bailyn, *The Peopling of British North America: An Introduction*, p.66.

[5] Robert Middlekauff, *The Glorious Cause* (New York: Oxford University Press, 1982), pp. 80-83 and
Arthur M. Schlesinger, jr., general editor, *The Almanac of American History* (New York: G.P. Putnams's Sons, 1983), p.101.

[6] Bernard Bailyn, *The Ideological Origins of the American Revolution*, p. 168.

[7] Benjamin Hart, *Faith and Freedom : The Christain Roots of American Liberty*, p.248.

[8] Samuel Eliot Morison, *The Oxford History of the American People* p. 193.

[9] William A. DeGregorio, *The Complete Book of U.S. Presidents* (New York: Dember Books,1984), p.24.

[10] Adam Smith, *An Inquiry Into The Nature And Causes of The Wealth of Nations*, ed. with an introduction by Edward Cannan and an introduction by Max Lerner (New York: The Modern Library, Random House, Inc. 1937), p.605.

[11] Robert Middlekauff, *The Glorious Cause*, p.249.

[12] Benjamin Hart, *Faith and Freedom: The Christian Roots of American Liberty*, p. 265.

[13] Ibid., p.265.

[14] Samuel Eliot Morison, *The Oxford History of the American People*, p. 210.

[15] Benjamin Hart, *Faith and Freedom : The Christian Roots of American Liberty*, p. 266.

[16] David Hackett Fischer, "Myths of the Midnight Rider," *The New York Times*, April 18,1994.

[17] *The Complete Essays And Other Writings of Ralph Waldo Emerson*, edited with a Biographical Introduction by Brooks Atkinson with a Foreword by Tremainie McDowell (New York: The Modern Library, Random House, 1950), p. 783.

[18] Samuel Eliot Morison, *The Oxford History of the American People*, p.219.

[19] Thomas Paine, *Common Sense*, edited with an introduction by Isaac Kramnick (New York: The Penguin American Library, 1985), p. 81.

[20] Ibid., p. 76.

[21] Ibid., p.87.

[22] Ibid., p.88.

[23] Ibid., pp. 88,89.

[24] Ibid., pp. 90,91.

[25] Ibid., p. 115.

[26] Ibid., p. 120.

CHAPTER 4

1776-POLITICAL FREEDOM: THE DECLARATION OF INDEPENDENCE

THE VIEW FROM AMERICA

"Hey, Hey, Ho, Ho Ho, Western Civ. Has To Go." During the 1980's, this chant of the campus radicals rang out at numerous institutions of higher learning in America. Nor was this singsong--along with other more substantial efforts--in vain. For in that same decade, denigration of western ideas and institutions had become such a force that many colleges and universities would no longer require many of the great classics of the West or the history of its civilization to be parts of the curriculum. "Eurocentric", "Phallocentric", "Hierarchical", "Rational" were among the invectives levied against any study of the western past and the greatest contributors to its civilization--the "dead white males." These radical individualists and radical egalitarians of the eighties considered most things to be relative and all cultures equal--with the exception of the West, which was perceived to be down at the bottom. It mattered not much if one knew little (or anything) about the western past. One is reminded of the proclamation of Henry Ford: "History is bunk!" at least history as presented through the efforts of traditional scholarship.

Fortunately, eighteenth century Americans held a different perspective, and because of it, a body of colonial thought developed which provided a basis--the intellectual foundation--for reactions to the British policies that we have charted. Not only colonial leaders such as Thomas Jefferson and John Adams but numerous others drawn from the occupations of lawyer, merchant, planter, and clergyman, articulated principles of political and economic freedom. In vivid contrast to the typical American student of the 1990's, they were usually knowledgeable about western history and political philosophy.

HISTORY

Educated colonists knew in varying degrees, about the rise and fall of ancient civilizations and were familiar with the classics of antiquity. Some knew little, others much, and sometimes quotations from the ancients were used to dress up lines of reasoning. In any event, many did know about Athens and Sparta, and especially were they aware of Roman history from the first century B.C. to the formation of an empire in the second century A.D. They had read, among others, Plutarch, Cicero, Cato, Virgil and Tacitus, authors who focused on morality, patriotism, and justice and who related the decline of these virtues to the corruption and oppression characteristic of the latter period. Colonial revolutionaries found an analogy between British-American relations in the 1760's and 1770's and the decline of Rome.[1] Americans also possessed a sense of British history, and for the purpose of background, it is appropriate to present (in a rather abbreviated form) the major contours of this knowledge.

The colonists knew that the despot, King John, who exacted arbitrary financial sums and who exhibited more than his share of cruelty, had also, in 1215, submitted to the Nobles at Runnymede and sealed the Magna Carta. This document, although feudal in nature (emphasizing the mutual rights of lord and vassal), called a ruler to account, limited sovereignty, guaranteed religious liberties, indicated procedures governing those arrested, and laid the basis for trial by jury.

Centuries of experience had made Englishmen cognizant of the perils of concentrated power. King Richard II (deposed in 1399), for instance, believed "the laws were in his mouth" and proceeded to violate his coronation oath as well as the Magna Carta. And although Henry Tudor, victorious in the final battle of the War of the Roses at Bosworth, fashioned England (as King Henry VII) into an economically and politically stronger nation, he also accumulated dangerous authority for himself and influence over Parliament by appointing nobles loyal to the Crown, by refusing to call the legislature into session, and by establishing prerogative courts (in contrast to the ordinary common law courts), in which those displeasing to the monarch could be made to testify against themselves through intimidation or even torture.

Successive reigns under both the Houses of Tudor and Stuart were witness to great struggles over religion and the relative power of Church, Parliament, and Crown. Henry VIII undertook a schismatic break with Rome (thereby making his rule absolute), his daughter Mary restored Catholicism (slaughtering Protestants with considerable gusto), while still another daughter, Elizabeth, brought back Protestantism to the Anglican Church.

The ascendancy of James I, the first monarch of the House of Stuart, to the throne of England began a most turbulent seventeenth century. This potentate, a descendent of Henry VII whose daughter Margaret had married King James IV of Scotland, had become a firm believer in absolute rule and found it exceedingly irksome to have his power restricted either by Parliament, common law, or the Magna Carta. Faced with an ever expanding need for funds, he circumvented a hostile Parliament by imposing high tariffs and by selling monopolistic privileges and titles. When Parliament complained, he jailed some of its members and had that legislative body dissolved. It was during his reign that Puritans saw fit to depart on the Mayflower.

His son and successor, Charles I, another advocate of absolute monarchy, continued to exhibit what seemed to be a royal trait--serious financial problems. After dissolving Parliament on two occasions, a third Parliament granted him money but only with the quid pro quo that he sign its Petition of Right, in which he agreed that his rule would conform to the law and that he would refrain from levying unauthorized taxes, placing soldiers in private homes, declaring marital law in time of peace, and permitting arbitrary arrest and imprisonment. Conflict, nonetheless, continued. At one point Charles I dissolved a Parliament and ruled without it for eleven years. He dissolved another Parliament after it met for only three weeks (called the short Parliament), imposed unauthorized taxes, staffed common law courts with loyalists to the Crown, strengthened prerogative courts and incarcerated opponents.

Still another Parliament, coming into session in 1640 and lasting twenty years (aptly called the Long Parliament), was able to seize considerable power and abolish prerogative courts, do away with various taxes, annul the power of the Crown to dissolve the legislature, and pass a law requiring that body to meet at least every three years.

Intrigue and political and religious conflict, however, refused to disappear and the machinations of this most untrustworthy king led to civil war and eventually to Cromwell's signature on his death warrant. Amid groans from the crowd assembled at Whitehall, the head of Charles I was severed from its body by the executioner's axe on January 30, 1649.

Oliver Cromwell, leader of the New Model army now stood as head of state. Under his rule, Parliament passed the first Navigation Act, and the army brought rebellious Irish and Scots under control. This stern and forceful man who harbored an intense dislike for democracy, dissolved Parliament, experimented with different forms of government, and became a virtual dictator. Upon Oliver's death, his son Richard (Tumbledown Dick) assumed the helm. That he was less than able in this role paved the way for the restoration.

Sports, plays and music (not to mention gambling and swearing)--all had been prohibited under the moral code of Cromwell's Puritan Commonwealth, and more than a few welcomed the more relaxed social climate that accompanied the reign of the new king. Charles II, son of the decapitated ruler and a rather popular and extravagant monarch, set the moral tone when he appeared in public accompanied by his numerous dogs and a bevy of mistresses. Less manipulative than his predecessors, his reign saw Parliament grow stronger and internal economic controls loosen. The Navigation Acts expanded and colonies became increasingly important.

However, all was not serene. The major controversy of the era focused upon religion and the fear that it might generate another civil war. Although Anglicanism occupied the prime position in England, both Charles and his brother James were brought up in France by their Catholic mother in exile, and each looked with favor on the religion of Rome. With intrigue and rumors of popish plots the order of the day, an Exclusion Bill, designed to keep Catholics from the throne was introduced but failed to pass Parliament. Eventually, two political parties emerged. Composed of landowners, merchants, the more liberal Anglicans, and some dissenters, the Whig party advocated a strong Parliament and gave support to the bill. Alternatively, the Tory party, harboring Anglicans of a conservative bent, favored the continuation of hereditary monarchy. As a matter of principle, Charles held to the latter position and following his death the conflict came to a head.

A tendency toward despotism only partially explains the brevity of the reign of King James II the brother and successor of Charles II. Another major contributor to his downfall was the attempt to restore Catholicism. Suspending laws that discriminated against Catholics, and awarding them high positions in government, the army, and universities annoyed both Tories and Whigs. But the crucial episode revolved around his political successor.

James II had two married daughters, Mary and Anne, by his first wife and each daughter was a Protestant. However, in 1688, his second wife Mary who was a Catholic gave birth to a son named James who also was a Catholic and this meant that the next in the line of succession would be of the Roman faith. As leaders of both major political parties conspired to prevent this from happening, a group of prominent Englishmen invited Mary's husband, the Dutch ruler William of Orange to England. The warm welcome at his arrival in 1688 induced James II to leave for France, and in 1689, Parliament gave William III and Mary II the crown to rule as joint sovereigns. The attempt by Catholics to reinstate him met defeat on Irish soil in the 1690 battle of the Boyne.

This was the Glorious Revolution. Glorious because Parliament, by its ability to put aside an hereditary monarch without a civil war, and award the Crown to someone else, had established itself as supreme. Glorious also because it issued The Declaration of Rights in 1689 which became law in a Bill of Rights in that same year. According to this document the sovereign, who must be Anglican, was prohibited from interfering with free discussion in Parliament, with the conduct of free elections, or with the free speech of the English people. In addition, juries were to be impartial and bail not excessive. The Crown could be petitioned to redress grievances, and was prohibited from suspending laws, imposing taxes, or maintaining an army without permission of the Parliament. Also, a 1689 Toleration Act, while placing many restrictions on Catholics and excluding those not of the Anglican faith from public affairs, did allow freedom of worship to other Protestant sects.

Several years later Parliament passed the Act of Settlement (1701) which stipulated the manner by which the successors of William III would be chosen. Although the provisions of this law were rather complex, it essentially insured Protestant succession and laid the groundwork for George Lewis, Elector of Hanover to become King of Great Britain (George I) in 1714.

American colonists were aware of this historic struggle for freedom and civil rights, and since it covered every permutation of power, it enabled them to understand the arbitrariness and abuse of power and the need for eternal vigilance. Knowledge of historical events, however, by no means exhausted their intellectual arsenal as many had more than a passing acquaintance with western political thought.

POLITICAL PHILOSOPHY

Essentially concerned with man's attempts to adapt to conditions on this planet and thereby make survival and advancement possible, political philosophy focuses upon the customs, practices, and institutions that bind humans together and includes elements of economics, sociology anthropology, psychology, law, religion, and ethics. Among the questions that it poses and seeks to answer are these: Is government necessary? What is the best form of this collective endeavor? What is the proper role for the individual, the family, the state and religious and other institutions of society.

The great philosophers of antiquity, Plato and Aristotle for example, wrestled with such problems, as did Dante, Machiavelli, St. Thomas Aquinas and other Church Fathers, as well as various religious reformers. In the Middle Ages and during the Renaissance, men searched through the works of the ancients for knowledge and wisdom, and the Protestant reformers familiarized themselves with the Scriptures and practices of the early Christians. However by the seventeenth century a belief gained currency that human reason could, without looking back into the past, discover truths and universal laws that were grounded in the regularity of nature and from which would flow substantial progress on this earth. The ideas generated during it culminated in the eighteenth century Enlightenment. In this Age of Reason, two political philosophers stand out: Thomas Hobbes and John Locke.

Thomas Hobbes (1588-1679), the son of an English clergyman was born prematurely as a result of his mother's fear of invasion by the Spanish Armada (or so it is said). In his long life he witnessed many unsettling events including the overthrow of Charles I, the English Civil War, and his own exile to the continent.

He developed his political ideas in works written between 1640 and 1651, which reflect those chaotic times. Hobbes considered the reigns of Henry VIII and Elizabeth successful and he became a supporter of absolute monarchy and the Stuarts. Hobbe's science of politics stressed the importance of written laws and his clarity of thought made him the most important English philosopher since Bacon and one of the greats in the history of political philosophy.

His most important literary effort and the one for which he is best known is *Leviathan,* in which the leviathan of the title is the state, a giant that oversees human activity. In this work, Hobbes demonstrates that self-preservation is the basic psychological principle dictating all human behavior, and that human behavior is a perpetual struggle for security. The quest for security, in turn, elicits a desire for power which also is interminable because every means of protection that one obtains also needs to be defended.

Hobbes rejects Aristotle's portrayal of man as a political animal who naturally gravitates into forming a society. He also dismisses the laws of the Church Fathers which embody the ideas of right and wrong. The philosophy of Hobbes is materialistic in the sense that he focuses not on the moral conditions of civilized life but rather on the controlling causes of behavior. He posits a "state of nature" in which man is pictured as selfish, egoistic, always trying to gratify some desire, concerned only about his own power and security, and interested in others only to the extent that they might effect his goals. Because of unequal human endowments of strength and guile, insecurity dictates the continuous warfare of everyone against everyone. No rights or wrongs or property rights in this "state of nature"--a state anathema to civilization.

> In such condition, there is no place for Industry; because the fruit thereof is uncertain: and consequently no Culture of the Earth, no Navigation, nor use of the commodities that may be imported by Sea; no commodious Building; no Instruments of moving, and removing such things as require much force; no knowledge of the face of the Earth, no account of Time; no Arts; no Letters; no Society; and which is worst of all continual fear, and danger of violent death; And the life of man, solitary, poor, nasty, brutish, and Short.[2]

Hobbes also maintains that man possesses a degree of reason which leads him to desire peace. Toward this end, he forms society and enters a compact wherein each person surrenders some of his liberty and agrees to abide by certain rules. Due to antisocial tendencies, man might well violate the agreed upon accord unless threatened by punishment and for this reason an important part of the covenant empowers the sovereign to enforce its terms and penalize transgressors. Hobbes believes it is the sovereign who makes a society out of a multitude of people and that to carry out his functions, all governmental power--virtually absolute power--should be lodged in him. Such a system is a means to an end, with obedience to the monarch forthcoming neither out of reverence or for reasons of morality, but simply to further the cause of self-interest.

According to Hobbes, the people themselves enter into a covenant rather than the people and the sovereign. The latter is appointed by the people for their protection, and although his powers border on the absolute, the people retain some rights. Thus, a subject cannot be ordered to kill himself or to refrain from protecting himself from those who would cause him injury. The people in Hobbes' system are free in those areas their ruler sees fit to disregard; buying and selling, entering contracts, and choosing what to eat and where to live. Moreover, the covenant remains valid only as long as the ruler protects the people, and if he fails to meet this condition, they may rebel and establish a new sovereign in his place.

Hobbes considers any government to be better than anarchy, but he favors an absolute form because diffusion of powers would invite conflict, and even civil war. Believing the masses to be influenced and easily misled by the words of agitators, he views democracy as an unstable system. As for the role of religion, Hobbes (a deist) believes in one sovereign, which meant that the church would occupy a position subordinate to the state.

In *Leviathan*, Hobbes raises important issues of human behavior. Critics of Hobbes have argued that humans are not always selfish, as he claims, but sometimes act with altruistic motives. True enough, but how often do men act altruistic and are there ways to promote man's impulse toward altruism? Another area where Hobbes has been taken to task is the near absolute authority of the sovereign in his system. Critics argue that he endows a ruler really with more authority then he needs to mediate disputes and protect life and property. They also question the wisdom of concentrating so much power in one person. Questions of human virtue, the amount of liberty that need be surrendered to obtain tranquility, and the best form of government are addressed by those who come after Hobbes: these questions are major concerns of American colonists.

Between Hobbes and Locke, a variety of lesser personages are influential in seventeenth century political thought. However, it is the philosophy of John Locke which dominates and it is to this most influential man to whom we now turn.

John Locke (1632-1704), the great moral and political philosopher, and an economist to boot, received both bachelor's and master's degrees from Oxford and then stayed on there to do some teaching. This renaissance man studied medicine and although he never took a degree in it, knew enough to be selected as the personal physician to the Earl of Shaftesbury and at one point performed an operation which saved his employer's life. His intellectual proclivities led him to a serious interest in philosophy, a deep appreciation of scientific method, and membership in the Royal Society. He became actively involved in political affairs (at one time the English government labeled him a traitor), and escorted the future Queen Mary to England after James II had been replaced by William III. Locke also served in various government posts including Commissioner on the Board of Trade and Plantations where he offered much practical and well-received advice.

It is his work as an author, however, that most concerns us. In his pamphlets on economics, he employed systematic analysis of such subjects as the determination of value, the circular nature of economic activity, and relative prices. He also explained the folly of government regulation of prices and interest rates. Although his embrace of laissez-faire was not total, he did stress the desirability of limited government, which was contrary to the positions of most other writers in the mercantile era.[3] His fame, however, rests on other efforts, including *An Essay on Human Understanding, Letter Concerning Toleration* and the *Two Treatises on Government* in which he develops his political ideas. The *First Treatise* attacks Filmer's defense of the divine right of kings, and is of little importance in the history of political thought. It is the *Second Treatise* which insured his prestige as a political philosopher.

In the *Second Treatise*, the concept of a state of nature is used to develop the essential nature of government. Originally, according to Locke, all men are in a state of nature which in contrast to the one described by Hobbes, is generally peaceful, and men have "...perfect Freedom to order their Actions, and dispose of their Possessions, and Persons as they see fit, within the bounds of the Law on Nature, without asking leave or depending upon the will of any other Man."[4] A Law of Nature, representing the will of God, guides human behavior, and, according to this Law, men "...being all equal and independent, no one ought to harm another in his Life, Health, Liberty, or Possessions."[5] If violations of the law occur, then "...everyone has a right to punish the transgressors of that Law to such a Degree, as may hinder its Violations."[6] In addition, an injured party has the right to seek reparations.

Problems, however, are bound to emerge in the process of carrying out such punishments. Each man tends to favor his own cause and therefore the need arises for someone to settle disputes impartially. Moreover, the actual force needed to apprehend and punish a transgressor may be lacking, and finally, with each person acting as his own judge, punishment for the same crime might display considerable variation. It is to come to grips with these difficulties that men form a society and establish government. To appreciate the role of this government requires an understanding of Locke's theory of property.

In the state of nature, economic activity exists before the formation of government. Although property is initially held in common, man has a right to the needs of subsistence, which, by applying his labor to the soil, he acquires and makes his property. Because God wants man to survive and provides the means to do so, the right to property (in existence before society), is held to be a natural law. Moreover, private property enhances labor productivity to the benefit of both individual and society: "To which let me add, that he who appropriates land to himself by his labor, does not less but increase the common stock of mankind."[7]

An abundance of resources characterizes the original state of nature, and their use by one person does not adversely affect another. Economic activity (which preceeds political), however, changes this relationship. As an economy develops, men work, produce, exchange, fashion tools, enter into voluntary contracts, and accumulate property. Perishable goods in excess of current needs are traded for durable goods, and eventually, money--the most durable good and a facilitator of wealth--comes into existence. Of course, some people are more industrious than others and as population grows amidst the institution of private property, economic inequalities become more pronounced and disputes more numerous. It is for this reason that a civil society is formed which in turn establishes a government.

> If man in the State of Nature be so free, as has been said; If he be absolute Lord of his own Person and Possessions, equal to the greatest, and subject to no Body, why will he part with his Freedom? Why will he give up this Empire, and subject himself to the Dominion and Control of any other Power? To which 'tis obvious to Answer, that though in the state of Nature he hath such a right, yet the Enjoyment of it is very uncertain, and constantly exposed to the Invasion of others. For all being Kings as much as he, every Man his Equal, and the enjoyment of the property he has in this state is very unsafe, very insecure. This makes him willing to quit a Condition, which however free, is full of fears and continual dangers: And 'tis not without reason, that he seeks out, and is willing to join in Society with others who are already united, or have a mind to unite for the mutual Preservation of their Lives, Liberties and Estates, which I call by the general Name, Property.[8]

To form a society, men voluntarily enter a contract wherein they relinquish power, equality, and liberty and agree to act as one body--as a "Commonwealth"--which holds the ultimate power to enact laws and punish violators (those "at war" with society). Government refers to the particular bodies or structures established by society to protect life, liberty, and property, to interpret the natural law, to enact legislation, and, thereby, make effective, the intrinsic moral code.

Although Locke believes that the form of government should be up to the people, he favors a constitutional monarchy in which Executive, Legislative, and Federative branches would check each other and avoid undue concentration of power. The executive, appointed by the elected party in power, would enforce the laws, a legislature make the laws, and the federative branch negotiate with foreign powers. The legislature which Locke believes is the most important sector should be guided by the following rules:

> First, They are to govern by promulgated establish'd Laws, not to be varied in particular Cases, but to have one Rule for Rich and Poor, for the Favourite at Court, and the Country Man at Plough.
> Secondly, These Laws also ought to be designed for no other end ultimately but the good of the People.
> Thirdly, they must not raise taxes on the property of the people, without the Consent of the People, given by themselves or their Deputies. And this properly concerns only such Governments where the Legislative is always in being, or at least where the People have not reserev'd any part of the Legislative to Deputies, to be from time to time chosen by themselves.
> Fourthly, The Legislative neither must nor can transfer the power of making laws to any Body else, or place it any where but where the People have.[9]

Toward the end of the Second Treatise, Locke speaks of rebellion. Both executive and legislature need some leeway to perform their functions, and therefore man has a right to rebel only when other redress of grievances fails and only in extremity, including substantial evidence of tyranny and "a long train of Abuses."[10]

For example, the executive (and this was the branch about which Locke and later the Americans are most concerned), might neglect his duties, or overturn a law, or prevent the legislature from meeting, or even deliver the nation over to a foreign power. In such circumstances, the power of sovereignty reverts to the people, who not only may rebel but have a duty to rebel (lest they fall back to the problems besetting them in the state of nature), and form a new government. Note here that men do not revert to a state of nature, but keep the structure of society, including its economic structure, thereby precluding expropriation and redistribution of property.

The Second Treatise has antecedents among the medieval philosophers such as Hooker and Halifax, who believe that government should be for the common good, that rulers are responsible to their subjects, and that power has traditional and moral limits. Locke places these ideas in the context of recent English history. He embraces natural law, but interprets it so that private property and individual rights and liberties have a higher status than in the medieval tradition. The latter emphasizes the common good, and Locke did also, but he develops a closer connection between the common good and individual rights.

Locke also demonstrates the important linkage of economics and government. According to Locke, economic development leads to the formation of government, a major purpose of which is to protect property rights (broadly construed), which themselves provide the basis for man's self-improvement and the common good. A sound, functioning economy enhances individual and national welfare and is more important than the capricious will of a sovereign.

Hardly a radical philosopher, Locke considers self-government to be consistent with the institutions of crown, nobility, and church, with his "social compact" providing an alternative to the morally bankrupt "divine right of kings." The views of this well-liked, decent person of great charm and modesty were popular during the eighteenth century

Enlightenment, especially among Whigs, the American colonists, and the French. Voltaire, Montesquieu, Rousseau and other Frenchmen felt his influence and his ideas appeared in the 1789 Declaration of the Rights of Man.

Americans were enamored with Locke's thoughts on human rights, the separation of powers, and the emphasis on property. The Second Treatise helped to lay the philosophical basis for the American rebellion and democracy. Some phrases of the Declaration of Independence were taken almost verbatim from Locke and his ideas shaped the writing of the United States Constitution, including its Bill of Rights.

John Locke loved liberty ("Where-ever Law ends Tyranny begins"),[11] and upheld the dignity of man ("The end of Government is the good of Mankind"),[12] and the wisdom of the majority, (although the framers of the U.S. Constitution would have some questions about the latter). Unlike Hobbes, Locke believes that men are created equal in a state of nature, hold inalienable rights, and can live together in peace without the need for an absolute authority. He further held that in a democracy, unwise laws can be altered and the stability of the community insured. It is not without cause that Locke became known as America's Philosopher.

CONSIDERATIONS OF LAW

Of particular importance to the colonists was the law. Not only did it embody principles of justice, but could help to explain history and shed light on the meaning of current events. Especially were the colonists taken with the concept of "natural law" which they thought should inform the positive laws of mankind: statutory laws (legal enactment's) and common laws (laws following precedents in the form of court decisions which are common throughout the realm). Natural law concerns itself with the nature of things, their essence when ephemeral aspects are stripped away, in other words the metaphysical dimension of reality. The nature of man as a species, the nature of lower classes of animal life, the nature of government, and the nature of the universe, with its orderliness and unique patterns of regularity, are all the proper domain of natural law.

Upholders of natural law doctrine generally consider manifest patterns of nature to be universally applicable and intimately related to the Divine plan.[13] Historically, the Roman authority Marcus Tullius Cicero believed the natural law to be God's law, as did Thomas Aquinas, who thought human reason capable of comprehending the nature of things.[14] Natural law concepts were invoked in the Middle Ages to delineate the proper or natural roles of the state and religion, thereby serving as impediments to absolutist tendencies of a monarch. John Locke's *Second Treatise* examines the nature of government and is filled with natural law ideas.

Now, on the subject of law, the great 17th Century English authority Sir Edward Coke stood out. His *Institutes,* a magnificent study and interpretation of English common law, was widely quoted and significantly influenced the thinking of Thomas Jefferson, Patrick Henry, John Adams, John Dickinson, and James Otis, among others. Coke had served as the first Lord Chief Justice of England and in this capacity he upheld the supremacy of the law over the edicts of the monarch, thereby defying both James I and

Charles I. It was Coke's belief that the common law should reflect natural law and Americans, of course, had incorporated and adopted the English common law system and believed it should control Parliament.[15]

Americans further believed that certain natural and therefore inalienable rights were part of the natural law framework: the right to life, to property, to the fruits of one's toil, to a trial by jury, and to a list of other liberties including those of movement, speech, the press and representative government. All freedoms and rights to be enjoyed responsibly by human beings within the just boundaries established by society and the state.[16]

CONSIDERATIONS OF RELIGION

The sacred also played and has always played an important role in mankind's history. In the ancient societies of Egypt, Sumeria, the Roman Empire and even Athenian Democracy, it is the state that matters and its leaders who mediate with the deities of their respective theologies. The ordinary individual counts for little in this arrangement. In contrast, the later monotheistic Judaic/Christian tradition upholds the intrinsic worth of the individual, the respect each is due, and the limits to which one person may compel another. Each person has a personal relationship with God in this tradition and no longer is the King required to mediate. Rather, the role of the monarch is secular in nature. He too, is subject to a higher law.[17]

Religious leaders throughout European history often found themselves at odds with secular authorities. The deadly altercation between Thomas Becket and Henry II, and that between Sir Thomas More and Henry VIII stand out, but there also were numerous others. American colonial leaders were aware of such conflicts and were familiar with teachings on the proper role of the state.

Also, the Great Awakening in the early 18th Century, with its emphasis on individual experience, had generated a personal evangelicalism which affected all religious groups (the Anglicans hated it). Not only did religion become more voluntary and diverse, but Christian colonists developed an enthusiasm for political liberty and a monumental distrust of the tyrannies associated with the combined powers of church and state.[18]

Adding to this religious dimension was an idea that had begun to evolve as far back as the early settlers; that the colonists were a chosen people and the Divine plan influenced, indeed, dictated America's development. Although that plan had yet to be made perfectly clear, contemporary colonial difficulties were thought to be a vital component and perhaps even represented a turning point in history. Note the religious underpinnings of the American revolution and how in this regard it so vividly contrasts with the anticlericalism of its French counterpart.

The colonists would build their case for freedom on a foundation of thought about such historic, philosophical, and religious issues as we have been considering in these pages. And as tensions between England and the colonies came to a head, these Americans developed a rhetoric of rebellion and freedom in which the will of God, the laws of Nature, and the rights of man fused together and inspired the Revolution. There have been few events in the history of nations so lucidly supported and nobly argued as was the colonist's break from England to claim independence. It is worthwhile to pause and consider examples of how they deployed their rhetoric to forward their cause.

> Jonathan Mayhew, the pastor of the West Church in Boston: "...no government is to be submitted to at the expense of that which is the sole end of government: the common good and safety of society.... For a nation thus abused to arise unanimously, and to resist their prince, even to dethrone him, is not criminal, but a reasonable way of vindicating their liberties and their rights; it is making use of the means, and the only means, which God has put into their power, for mutual and self-defense..."[19]

> James Otis: Government, "has an ever-lasting foundation in the unchangeable will of God, the author of nature, whose laws never vary.... There can be no prescription old enough to supercede the law of nature, and the grant of God almighty, who has given all men a natural right to be free..." [20]

> John Adams: "Let the pulpit resound with the doctrine and sentiments of religious liberty. Let us hear of the dignity of {man's nature}, and the noble rank he holds among works of God...Let it be known that British liberties are not the grants of princes and parliaments..."[21]

> John Dickerson: On American freedoms "We claim them from a higher source, from the King of Kings and Lord of all the earth. They are not annexed to us by parchments and seals. They are created in us by the decree of Providence which established the laws of our nature...they are founded in the immutable maxims of reason and justice."[22]

> Alexander Hamilton: The sacred rights of mankind are not to be rummaged for among parchments and musty records. They are written, as with a sunbeam, in the whole volume of human nature, by the Hand of the Divinity itself, and can never be erased or obscured by mortal power."[23]

> John Jay: "we are...entitled by the bounty of an indulgent Creator to freedom,"[24]

CONSIDERATIONS OF POWER AND VIRTUE

Americans, like their brethren across the ocean, loved the English Constitution and considered it their own. Not a written document (and therefore different from what was to become its counterpart in the United States), this constitution consists of a collection of documents (such as the Magna Carta and the Bill of Rights), acts of Parliament and of institutions and customs that evolved over centuries. In effect, it designates the rights of the citizenry and provides for a limited or republican monarchy. Its success rests upon checks and balances of three social orders--royalty, the nobility, and the common people.[25]

Monarchy stands for authority, unity, and order and is held to be the natural form for royalty. It implies hierarchy, social and economic inequality, power and thus dependency.

Motivated by honor, ambition, pride, and the prospect of immortality, aristocracy (the proper form for nobility), offers not just public service but patronage and leadership in war, government and the arts, and brings impartiality when disputants cry for mediation. In other words, aristocrats make things happen and to fulfill their responsibilities they need to be independent. They must possess wealth in order to be free--free from want, free from the fickleness of the market, free from the caprice of others in a world characterized by dependencies.[26]

As for the common people, the upper classes considered them to be unthinking, ignorant, and fit only to be ruled, and meant to live, die, and be forgotten. They were referred to by what they did--cooper, cordwainer, blacksmith, laborer. Even those engaged in such middle class professions as merchant, lawyer, doctor, or banker enjoying higher incomes and living standards were lumped into this general category of "commoner" and were accorded little prestige.

This labeling by occupation--that is, how they were occupied--indicated an inability to secure leisure and thus, serve the public. At best, they exhibited such virtues as frugality and industry which helped them to realize personal aspirations. However, the superior virtues of disinterestedness and the willingness to sacrifice for the national welfare were thought to remain foreign to them. They were meant to produce goods and services, unlike the aristocracy whose expenditures on their luxurious lifestyle not only gave evidence of social position but provided employment for the lesser folk.

Fear of poverty was thought to be the main force keeping the common people at work and idleness was positively correlated with trouble. In an era of dependency (the word itself implied no will of one's own), the common people depended upon market work for sustenance and the most dependent--women, servants, and children were excluded from public life. Nonetheless, the Parliament offered something in the way of democracy which enabled the commoners, or at least some of them, and the aristocracy, to participate in the affairs of government.[27]

Each of the branches had its rights and duties but each standing alone held the capacity to be oppressive. However, the simultaneous existence of all, as was the case with the British constitution, insured proper safeguards. The three branches shared the task of providing for the nation's general welfare, and while far from perfect, this constitution was widely considered the best in the world. For Great Britain was the exception to the absolutism that prevailed on the continent and blessings of liberty and happiness gushed forth. As he who would shortly become King George III noted: "The pride, the glory of Britain, and the direct end of its constitution is political liberty."[28] John Adams called it, "the most perfect combination of human powers in society which finite wisdom has yet contrived and reduced to practice for the preservation of liberty and the production of happiness."[29] Even though thousands of miles away, troubled in many ways by their relations with England, the Americans felt themselves to be under the protection of this constitution.

There was, however, potential and grave danger that the balance might be upset. Liberty had been seriously jeopardized more than once--most recently by the Stuarts-- and although the Glorious Revolution had successfully wrested sovereignty from the Crown and placed it in Parliament, eternal vigilance against an unbalance of power had become a necessary condition of freedom.

Critical English writers (who seemed to have had more influence in America then in their native land), attacked what they perceived to be defects in the political system: lack of adult male suffrage; insufficient freedom of the press; and government control over religion. They worried about the abuses of power and lamented the decay of virtue.

The problems of power and virtue were very much on the minds of the Americans. The state's power, of the utmost importance to colonists and considered legitimate where men had surrendered some of their freedoms to government in order to promote the common good (à la Locke), had the inherent characteristic of expanding beyond its proper boundaries until it overwhelmed liberty.[30] Andrew Hamilton, the defense attorney in the 1735 trial of John Peter Zenger, explained it this way:

> Power may be justly compared to a great river; while kept within its bounds, it is both beautiful and useful, but when it overflows its banks, it is then too impetuous to be stemmed; it bears down all before it, and brings destruction and desolation wherever it comes. If, then, this be the nature of power, let us at least do our duty, and, like wise men who value freedom, use our utmost care to support liberty, the only bulwark against lawless power, which, in all ages, had sacrificed to its wild lust and boundless ambition the blood of the best men that ever lived. [31]

Americans understood that ruling powers in general possessed great capabilities-"like elephants in war."[32] Moreover, they understood the weakness of human nature (a view expressed later in the Federalist papers and in the design of the U.S. Constitution). Virtue, therefore, was a necessary condition of freedom. As John Adams observed: "Liberty can no more exist without virtue and independence than the body can live and move without a soul."[33]

America had been settled by individuals who longed for more freedom, a purer freedom--than they had known in their native lands. Alexis de Tocqueville wrote tellingly of this disparity:

> If, after having cast a rapid glance over the state of American society in 1650, we turn to the condition of Europe, and more especially to that of the Continent, at the same period, we cannot fail to be struck with astonishment. On the continent of Europe at the beginning of the seventeenth century absolute monarchy had everywhere triumphed over the ruins of the oligarchical and feudal liberties of the Middle Ages. Never perhaps were the ideas of right more completely overlooked than in the midst of the splendor and literature of Europe; never were the principles of true freedom less widely circulated; and at that very time those principles which were scorned or unknown by the nations of Europe were proclaimed in the deserts of the New World and were accepted as the future creed of a great people.[34]

Success had rewarded the colonists' quest for freedom, and the picture the colonists drew of themselves, shared by many abroad, was that of a virtuous people leading a simple life, with little corruption (as in a state of nature), governed by elected representatives, defended by a militia, and enjoying the economic, civic, intellectual, educational, religious, and artistic blessings of liberty. By 1776, this portrait had emerged of a people not only defending themselves but the hopes and liberties of mankind. The old idea that America was to play a vital role in history remained strong and vigorous.

The colonial view of England, however, was of a remarkably different landscape. For England displayed luxury, self-aggrandizement, vice, licentiousness, pagan revelry, cynicism, lack of respect for law and religion, and a general decline in virtue. Power-hungry executive ministers corrupted and manipulated Parliament (which had become much too powerful), by exchanging money, appointments, and promises for votes to raise taxes; they incurred unconscionable debts to finance standing armies and subsidize luxury goods, and other extravagances. Lest the ministers take back their rewards, recipients of them had become increasingly servile, thereby undermining constitutional checks and balances and making conditions in England inimical to freedom.

Exemplifying this illicit power-hungry government was the repeated denial to Jack Wilkes of a seat in the House of Commons, to which he had been duly elected. Wilkes, the publisher of a radical newspaper, *Number 45 North Britain*, had railed against general writs of assistance and other aspects of English colonial policy. A staunch defender of private property, he was a colonial favorite, and his cause became part of the iconography of colonial revolt. So taken with his efforts were the Sons of Liberty, that they sent him two turtles one weighing 45 and the other 47 pounds. The number forty-five symbolized Wilkes' newspaper, and the sum of the turtles' weights, the "Immortal 92" of Massachusetts. Paul Revere engraved "Wilkes and Liberty," "No. 45," and other slogans on the silver punch bowl he made and dedicated to the ninety-two assembly members. The South Carolina legislature agreed to pay 1500 pounds to assist Wilkes with his indebtedness.[35]

During these tense prerevolutionary days, the colonists' increasing readiness to defy British interference derived in part from their knowledge of Parliamentary corruption and in part from their fear of its incursions into their own affairs. They had only to remember the Stamp Act and its consequences, or to consider encroachments on their judiciary bodies, the institution of general writs of assistance, and the standing army stationed in Boston to find ample cause for increasing their vigilance. And compounding these insults were the unconstitutional adjournment of colonial legislatures, the unwarranted power lodged in the executive, the forced quartering of troops, the land taken from industrious colonists and awarded to Indians and "papist" provinces, and legislation designed to cripple Massachusetts. Ironically, Parliament was pursuing policies toward the colonies similar to those it had tried to prevent the Monarchy from undertaking in previous centuries.[36]

All these actions on England's part offered more than enough evidence of a systematic plan to enslave the colonies. Why this web of intrigue? In a word, greed. English lust for power, wealth, and position had exhausted the tax base at home, and the colonists knew they looked to England like a fertile source of new revenue.[37]

PRECURSORS TO INDEPENDENCE

By 1776, America was a land without a repressive established church, or a titled nobility, or the social extremes of great wealth and seething poverty and the discontent usually associated with revolutions.[38] Yet as we have seen, the colonists were defining themselves in terms of their own social and governmental achievements, and in terms of the differences from polarized British society and corrupt British government. In the light of the relatively egalitarian character of America, the colonists began to believe that they might establish a successful republic.

This concept of equality warrants closer examination. Although poverty surely existed in America, it was less ubiquitous (reaching perhaps 10 percent of the population and often of a temporary nature), than poverty in England (where about 50 percent of the people depended on charity).[39] Also, the American upper classes did not possess wealth comparable to their counterparts in England, nor did they spend as much on luxuries. Only on the Southern plantations, based as they were on slavery, was there what might be called a leisure class in classic British terms.[40]

Inequality in the colonies manifested itself in different and intricate ways, including hierarchical social arrangements suggesting different stations in life. For instance, college students, as a mark of deference, were expected to remove their hats at varying distances depending upon the status of the approaching person: ten rods for the president, eight for a professor, and five for a tutor; seating at church was based on age and wealth; and there were designations, such as "Mister" (wives often called their husbands Mister) and "Esquire," that attached to social or occupational positions; and guidebooks explained when to remove one's hat, how to bow and how to give different people their proper respect.[41]

Nonetheless, economic inequality and social distinctions throughout the colonial era remained significantly less rigid and extreme than their counterparts overseas. Equality was a vital idea in colonial America, but it came nowhere close to the radical egalitarianism preached in the late twentieth century. "Equality did not mean that everyone was in fact the same, but only that ordinary people were closer in wealth and property to those above them and felt freer from aristocratic patronage and control than did common people elsewhere in the Western world."[42] And British visitors noted that "...an idea of equality...seems generally to prevail, and the inferior order of people pay but little external respect to those who occupy superior stations."[43] This idea of social equality had an inherent corollary in colonial thought: no person is inherently better than another. It followed that America was the land of opportunity for everyone--a truth rumored throughout the Old World and manifest to those who came to the new. No wonder America had become known as "the best poor man's country in the world."[44]

It must be emphasized that eighteenth century philosophy of Enlightenment had made profound impressions on the colonial mentality. Sir Isaac Newton's law of gravitation was universally applicable, could be expressed rather simply, and had been discovered through human intelligence. These qualities stimulated students of science, history, government, and economics to search for natural, universal laws in their own fields. That human reason could discover natural, rational laws fed colonial optimism that their society might do away with the arbitrary and unnecessary impediment to progress which might be imposed by state and church.

Those who conceived and articulated Enlightenment ideas, tended in the eighteenth century to be atheists or deists (the latter believing God created the universe and then stepped out of the picture; the former not believing in God at all). As might be expected, these postures led to some hostility to organized religion and the supernatural. Man was thought to be perfectible through human reason alone. As Alexander Pope put it, "Know then thyself, presume not God to scan. The proper study of Mankind is Man." Many thinkers in the age of enlightenment believed that through reason alone, humankind could banish war and other worldly evils and create societies characterized by progress, equality, benevolence, and even love of neighbor.

John Locke in his *Essay Concerning Human Understanding* had advanced the idea that all knowledge came from information impressed upon the senses and he developed this further in *Some Thoughts On Education*. Here he asserted that the mind of a child is a tabula rasa--a clean slate--waiting for education to be imposed upon it--an education to make him an autonomous human being.

Well aware of Locke's ideas, leaders of the American Revolution believed they could create a new world, one where the obsequiousness fawning, and flattery employed to obtain favors in monarchical societies based on kinship, patronage, and hierarchical dependencies, would be replaced by one in which people were treated as equals with authentic politeness, and were judged upon merit. Thomas Jefferson, for instance, believed that through education some of the common people would acquire the traits of republicanism and form a "natural aristocracy." He thought those enlightened ones would serve with distinction in the armed forces, the judiciary, the professions, and the government and that their social demeanor would be marked by natural grace, politeness, and taste.[45] After all, most of the founding fathers came from less than aristocratic backgrounds, worked hard to educate and improve themselves, and, having embraced the ideas of the Enlightenment, sought by their words and deeds (along with the classical postures of disinterest and gentility) to promote the common good. It should be noted that such virtuous behavior would go far to secure that which was often most coveted--honor and fame.[46]

Challenge to authority constituted another of the Enlightenment's dimensions.[47] As the eighteenth century unfolded, people became less willing to accept traditional roles and duties; less willing to defer to their superiors and more willing to accept the tenets of republicanism (the ideology of the Enlightenment) which, of course, included civic virtue. But this social assault was not the sort we are used to today in describing revolutions. The great antagonists of the American Revolution were not poor vs. rich, workers vs. employers, or even democrats vs. aristocrats. They were patriots vs. courtiers-categories appropriate to the monarchical world in which the colonists had been reared. Courtiers were persons whose position or rank came artificially from above--from hereditary or personal connections that ultimately flowed from the Crown or court. Courtiers, said John Adams, were those who applied themselves "to the Passions and Prejudices, the Follies and Vices of Great Men in order to obtain their Smiles, Esteem, and Patronage and consequently their favors and Preferments." Patriots, on the other hand, were those who not only loved their country but were free of dependent connections and influence; their position or rank came naturally from their talent and from recognition by the people. "A real patriot," declared one American in 1776, was "the most illustrious character in human life. Is not the interest and happiness of his fellow creatures his care?"[48]

INDEPENDENCE

Although the move toward independence seemed to be gathering steam, many Americans strongly disagreed about the desirability of complete separation. Even in January of 1776, only about a third of the delegates to the Continental Congress held independence as a goal. This reluctance had several sources: affection for England, apprehension about bloodshed, the possibility of defeat, and fear of the unknown--of what the new America would be like. Well aware that petty politics had been the downfall of previous republics, the colonists worried that a repeat performance might lead to a takeover by foreign governments. However, the King's proclamation declaring American patriots to be in rebellion, his hiring of mercenaries, the fighting itself, especially Lord Dunmore's burning of Norfolk, Virginia, along with the influence of Paine's *Common Sense* made dominance by the radicals virtually inevitable and delegates to Congress began to receive instructions supporting independence.

Vital in this movement was the work of the Virginia Convention (a new name for the House of Burgesses). In May of 1776, it instructed its delegates to declare for independence, and in June it adopted the Declaration of Rights (drafted primarily by George Mason), and a constitution for the now independent Commonwealth of Virginia. On June 7, Richard Henry Lee, "the Cicero of America," representing that state's delegation moved for the Independence resolutions in Congress.

> That these United colonies are, and of right ought to be, Independent states, that they are absolved from all allegiance to the British Crown, and that all political connection between them and the State of Great Britain is, and ought to be, totally dissolved.
> That it is expedient forthwith to take the most efficient measures for forming foreign alliances.
> That a plan of confederation be prepared and transmitted to the representative Colonies for consideration and approbation.[49]

Because some of the state delegations had yet to receive orders, these resolutions were debated but not voted upon. Congress then appointed a committee composed of Thomas Jefferson, John Adams, Robert Livingston, Roger Sherman, and Benjamin Franklin to begin work on a declaration of independence for use at the appropriate time.

Thomas Jefferson had become known as the anonymous author of *A Summary View of the Rights of British America*, which was an attack on the authority of Parliament over the colonies. Because of his "peculiar felicity of expression,"[50] the committee selected Jefferson (at age thirty-three) to draft the document.

Early in life Jefferson (1743-1826) had developed an appreciation of the classics and as a serious student at the College of William and Mary, he learned the joys of intellectual excitement, read broadly, and went on to become a knowledgeable lawyer. This tall man with reddish hair and freckles possessed immense curiosity and had an extraordinary variety of interests, among which may be listed architecture (he designed Monticello), farming, animal husbandry, engineering, botany, and books. His inventions include the dumbwaiter, beds that folded into the wall, the swivel chair and a more efficient plow. He founded the University of Virginia and introduced elective courses. President John F. Kennedy once designated a group of Nobel Prize winners dining at the White House as the largest assembly of talent gathered there since Thomas Jefferson dined alone.

It is in the political arena, however, that he is best known. Sensitive in disposition and lacking oratorical skills (hardly the characteristics of a successful politician), he was a member of the Virginia House of Delegates, Governor of Virginia, member of the Continental Congress, Minister to France, Secretary of State, Vice-President, and twice President of the United States, and, of course, the author of the Declaration of Independence. Later in life, this lover of liberty ("Rebellion to tyrants is obedience to God" was his lifelong slogan and appeared on his seal), explained what he had tried to accomplish as he drafted the Declaration of Independence:

> ...Not to find out new principles, or new arguments, never before thought of, not merely to say things which had never been said before; but to place before mankind the common sense of the subject, in terms so plain and firm as to command their assent, and to justify ourselves in the independent stand we are compelled to take. Neither aiming at originality of principle or sentiment, nor yet copied from any particular and previous writing, it was intended to be an expression of the American mind, and to give to that expression the proper tone and spirit called for by the occasion.[51]

Upon completion of the draft, John Adams, Benjamin Franklin and Jefferson himself, as well as Congress made several deletions and additions. Struck from the document, (at the insistence of the representatives from South Carolina and Georgia), were Jefferson's bitter condemnation of King George III for permitting the slave trade and slavery. Added were a couple of references to God. The document was presented to Congress on June 28, but before Congress considered it, that body accepted Richard Henry Lee's resolutions on July 2: this, of course, was the actual declaration of independence.

The official document which we call the Declaration of Independence was adopted by Congress and signed by its President and Secretary John Hancock, and Charles Thompson respectively, on July 4, 1776. Copies were sent out to the army and the states and amidst cheers, parades, and ringing bells, it was read to the public on July 8, at Independence Hall. The Liberty Bell, cast to celebrate William Penn's Charter of Privileges in 1751, tolled on that festive day. The bell bore the inscription "Proclaim Liberty throughout the land unto the inhabitants thereof."

Two interesting sidelights. On that same fourth of July, Lord North conferred an honorary degree on the former Governor of Massachusetts Bay, Thomas Hutchinson, at Oxford University. And July 4, 1826, the fiftieth anniversary of the document, witnessed the death of John Adams and Thomas Jefferson, the only two Presidents who had signed it.

Beginning with the words, "When in the course of human events...", the Declaration of Independence asserts the necessity of dissolving the bonds between Britain and America, and explains that, "...a decent respect to the opinions of mankind requires that they should declare the causes which impel them to separation." The second paragraph presents the documents most famous words: "We hold these truths to be self-evident: that all men are created equal; that they are endowed by their Creator with certain inalienable rights; that among these are Life, Liberty, and the pursuit of Happiness; that to secure these rights, governments are instituted among men, deriving their just powers from the consent of the governed..."

Next, the document develops the idea that people have a right to change government when it fails to adhere to these principles. This, however, should not be undertaken for "light and transient causes...But when a long train of abuses and usurpations, pursuing invariably the same object, evinces a design to reduce them under absolute despotism, it is their right, it is their duty, to throw off such government, and to provide new guards for their future security."

The next section contains a rather lengthy list of grievances, directed mostly at the King and notes that the British people have failed to heed requests for justice.

Then comes the final paragraph:

We, therefore, the representatives of the United States of America, in General Congress assembled, appealing to the Supreme Judge of the world for the rectitude of our intentions, do, in the name and by the authority of the good people of these colonies, solemnly publish and declare,

The words of Richard Henry Lee's Independence Resolution are repeated:

that these United Colonies are, and of right ought to be, Free And Independent States; that they are absolved from all allegiance to the British crown, and that all political connection between them and the state of Great Britain is, and ought to be, totally dissolved;

The document then continues:

and that, as free and independent states, they have full power to levy war, conclude peace, contract alliances, establish commerce, and do all other acts and things which independent states may of right do.

The "Declaration" solemnly concludes with these momentous words:

And for the support of this Declaration, with a firm reliance on the protection of Divine Providence, we mutually pledge to each other our lives, our fortunes, and our sacred honor.[52]

Certain aspects of this inspirational document warrant further attention. Most controversial has been the meaning of the words, "all men are created equal..." Many, if not most Americans probably have taken this to mean equality in the eyes of God. Others have come to a different understanding. Garry Wills contends that Locke had little influence on Jefferson and that equality for him was found not in mind or in body, or before God, but rather in the moral sensibility--which sets humans beings apart from other sentient beings--their humanity. Moreover, this moral sense has a strong egalitarian component to which, Wills contends, Jefferson subscribed.

> To say that men are equal in their exercise of this faculty is to define them as essentially equal, for the moral sense is what makes man accountable to himself and others, self-governing and consenting to social obligation. This separate faculty, equal in all, makes difference in other capacities comparably minor, unable to reach the heights of self-regulation.[53]

Other authorities believe that Locke had much influence on Jefferson, and that Jefferson's concept of equality derives from the social contract theory in Locke's *Second Treatise Of Government*. Man leaves the perfect freedom of his original state of nature and forms a society in which some freedom is surrendered for the equal and inalienable rights that comprise political liberty: this, in Jefferson's terms, is the intended meaning of equality in the Declaration of Independence.[54]

Although it is difficult to know with certainty the precise meaning that Jefferson intended, the latter interpretation or something quite akin to it appears to have the support of most historians. The Declaration of Independence is very much a spiritual document and reflects natural law as Jefferson grounds his case for independence of the American people on "the separate and equal station to which the Laws of Nature and of Nature's God entitle them..." He believed in social mobility and opportunity but he never believed all men to be equal in mind or body and never did he advocate any leveling scheme to secure equality. His assault on primogeniture, however, proved to be beneficial in that regard as did his efforts in education as well as those directed to insure democracy in the west.

Also note that the idea of equality in 1776 certainly had a different connotation than the "equality of results egalitarianism" entertained by some Americans two hundred years later. The words of Lincoln are instructive on the earlier meaning.

> The authors of that notable instrument...did not intend to declare all men equal in all respects. They did not mean to say all were created equal in color, size, intellect, moral development, or social capacity. They defined with tolerable distinctness, in what respects they did consider all men created equal-equal in 'certain inalienable rights, among which are life, liberty, and the pursuit of happiness.'[55]

A slaveholder himself, Jefferson condemned slavery as morally wrong. At one time he advanced a plan to terminate it to the Virginia legislature. Later, he began to see slavery to be closely bound with property rights and henceforth proceeded against it with great caution.[56]

The author of the Declaration of Independence was against wholesale manumission believing that freed slaves would face great hostility in Virginia. He believed that the manumitted slaves' own memories of injustice and the inevitable new provocations they would suffer would lead to race war and genocide.[57]

He did favor education of blacks, followed by mass deportation to a separate colony where they could practice self-rule. He believed that in the meantime they should be treated with kindness, and in this regard, Jefferson seems to have practiced what he preached.[58] He freed only a few of his own slaves and he did nothing to abolish this institution when he served as Governor of Virginia or President of the United States. Jefferson believed blacks to be the equal of whites in the moral sense, but inferior in beauty and in the ability to reason. He thought it impossible that they could live together as equals.[59] Yet his great concern over this moral issue lies behind this statement, "I tremble for my country when I reflect that God is just."[60]

Others, including such luminaries as James Madison, and George Mason shared Jefferson's anguish. Manifest was a concern that slavery would corrupt those who practiced it: for they who so casually took away other people's freedom showed little regard for their own; for freedom could not survive in such an atmosphere; for God would not offer protection.[61]

However, most Americans did not seem to exhibit much concern. Accounting for this posture is the fact that Western nations as well as Africa had accepted slavery: it was a basic institution in the classic republics of Greece and Rome, and Aristotle, reflecting upon the institutions of his era, had pronounced slavery natural. Even John Locke found slavery justifiable when someone, "...forfeited his own Life, By some Act that deserves Death; he, to whom he has forfeited it, may (when he has him in his Power) delay to take it, and make use of him to his own Service, and he does him no injury by it."[62] Moreover, many Americans had experienced some deprivation of freedom in the form of indentured servitude and slavery itself had become an established way of doing things. Finally, in an age when most of humankind toiled at the poverty level, slaves in America were perceived to be in a superior condition (in terms of work load and leisure time) to the average European peasant. Most Americans in 1776 were not very interested in extending these inalienable rights, worth fighting and dying for, to slaves. Their prime effort was to secure independence, and anything else, especially manumission, was secondary in comparison[63]

The reason why Jefferson substituted the word "happiness" (life, liberty, and the pursuit of happiness) for Locke's word 'property' has also been open to dispute, although it does not appear to be a matter of great significance. According to his biographer Dumas Malone, "Locke presupposed the pursuit of happiness and Jefferson always assumed as basic, the right of an individual to hold property."[64] Surely each would consider property a natural right and a means to an end rather than an end in itself. Perhaps, Jefferson substituted happiness because it appeared all-encompassing.[65]

This elegantly written document, the Declaration of Independence, expresses fundamental American principles, and since they were written, its words have been an inspiration to patriots and a threat to tyranny. Ponder the thoughts of Abraham Lincoln:

> All honor to Jefferson-to the man, who in the concrete pressure of a struggle for national independence by a single people, had the coolness, forecaste [sic], and sagacity to introduce into a merely revolutionary document an abstract truth, applicable to all men

and all times, and so to embalm it there that to-day and in all coming days it shall be a rebuke and a stumbling-block to the very harbingers of reappearing tyranny and oppression.[66]

The ideas proclaimed in the Declaration of Independence induced many Americans to wage war and sacrifice both property and life and also won the support of liberals in Europe. In England, quite understandably, the Declaration was received critically, while the French embraced it with enthusiasm. Lafayette ("the hero of two worlds") placed a copy of it in his library and kept a spot next to it for a similar French document of the future.

With the hope of reconciliation ended, colonists were forced to choose between the patriot and loyalist positions and to do so without assurance of the outcome. Many in America and overseas believed that this radical attack on the status quo would end in disaster. However, there also were many with strong faith that a better world than was ever known would be constructed; one where status comes from achievement instead of accident of birth; where power is severely restricted; and where human aspirations would flourish.[67]

---

[1] Bernard Bailyn, *The Ideological Origins of the American Revolution* (Cambridge: The Belknap Press of Harvard University Press, 1967), PP. 22-54 passim.

[2] Thomas Hobbes, *Leviathan*, with an introduction by A. D. Lindsay (New York: E. P. Button and Company, Inc. 1950), p. 104.

[3] For an analysis of Locke's contributions to economic thought, see Karen Inversion Vaughan, *John Locke: Economist and Social Scientist* (Chicago: The University of Chicago Press, 1980).

[4] John Locke, *Two Treatises Of Government*, with an introduction by Peter Laslett (New York: New American Library, A Mentor Book 1963), p. 309.

[5] Ibid., p. 311.

[6] Ibid., p. 312.

[7] Ibid., p. 336.

[8] Ibid., p. 395.

[9] Ibid., p. 409.

[10] Ibid., p. 463.

[11] Ibid., p. 448.

[12] Ibid., p.466.

[13] Clarence B. Carson, *Basic American Government* (Wadley Alabama: American Textbook Committee, 1993), pp. 54, 172-176.

[14] Ibid., pp.84-86,97-99.

[15] M. Stanton Evans, *The Theme Is Freedom* (Washington, D.C: Regnnery Publishing,Inc.,1994), pp.79-86. and 233.

[16] Clarence B. Carson, *Basic Government,* pp. 172-176.

[17] M. Stanton Evans, *The Theme Is Freedom,* pp. 131-148.

[18] Paul Johnson, *The Almost Chosen People* (San Francisco: Laissez Faire BooksAudio, 1995).

[19] Clarence B. Carson, *Basic Government,* pp.177,178.

[20] M. Stanton Evans, *The Theme Is Freedom,* p.238.

[21] Ibid., p.239

[22] Ibid., p.239.

[23] Ibid., p.239.

[24] Ibid., p.239.
[25] Ibid., pp. 66-79.
[26] Gordon S. Wood, The Radicalism of *The American Revolution* (New York: Alfred A. Knopf, 1992), pp. 27,28.
[27] Ibid., pp. 22,23, 33, 34, 56,107.
[28] Ibid., p.14.
[29] Bernard Bailyn, *The Ideological Origins of The American Revolution*, p. 67.
[30] Ibid., pp. 55-93.
[31] Diane Ravitch, *The American Reader* (New York: Harper Collins Publishers,1990),pp.7-9.
[32] Gordon S. Wood, *The Radicalism of The American Revolution*, p.108.
[33] Bernard Bailyn, *The Ideological Origins of The American Revolution*, p. 135.
[34] Alexis de Touqeville, *Democracy In America*, vol.1,(New York: Vintage Books, 1957), p.43.
[35] Samuel Eliot Morison, *The Oxford History of The American People* (New York: Oxford University Press,1965), p.193. Also see Bernard Bailyn, *The Ideological Origins of the American Revolution*, pp.110-112.
[36] M. Stanton Evans, *The Theme Is Freedom*, pp.224,225.
[37] Bernard Bailyn, *The Ideological Origins of The American Revolution*, pp.94-143 passim.
[38] Gordon S. Wood, *The Radicalism of The American Revolution*, p.169.
[39] Ibid., p. 122.
[40] Ibid., p. 115.
[41] Ibid., pp. 20,21.
[42] Ibid., p. 171.
[43] Ibid., p. 171.
[44] Ibid., p. 172.
[45] Ibid., pp. 180, 194, 218, 229, 233, 234, 236.
[46] Ibid., pp. 196-212.
[47] Ibid., pp. 145,146.
[48] Ibid., pp. 175,176.
[49] Samuel Elliot Morrison, *The Oxford History of the American People*, p. 221.
[50] M. Stanton Evans, *The Theme Is Freedom,* p.231.
[51] Dumas Malone, *Jefferson The Virginian* (Boston: Little, Brown and Company 1948), p.220. That Jefferson sought to make this document the embodiment of the American mind is developed by Pauline Maier, *American Scripture* (New York: Alfred A. Knopf, 1997).
[52] Samuel Eliot Morrison, *The Oxford History of the American People*, pp.219-223.
[53] Gary Wills, *Inventing America: Jefferson's Declaration of Independence* (New York: Random house, Vintage Book. 1979), p. 211. Also see, Oscar Handlin and Mary Handlin, *Liberty in Expansion* (New York: Harper & Row Publishers, 1989), pp.375-389.
[54] Ann Stuart Diamond, *Decent, Even Though Democratic*, in *How Democratic Is The Constitution?* ed. Robert A. Goldwin and William A. Schambra (Washington: American Enterprise Institute for Public Policy Research, 1980), p.23.
[55] Ibid., p.23.
[56] Joseph Dorfman, *The Economic Mind In American Civilization 1606-1865* vol. 1, (New York: Ausustus M. Kelly, Publishers, 1966), p.435.
[57] Robert Middlekauff, *The Glorious Cause* (New York: Oxford University Press, 1982), pp. 331,332.
[58] There is inconclusive evidence that Jefferson fathered children by his slave Sally Hemings. See "Review & Outlook-Founding Fatherhood," *The Wall Street Journal*, February 26,1999.

[59] David K. Shipler, *Jefferson Is America-And America Is Jefferson*, New York Times, April 12, 1993.

[60] Forest McDonald, *Novus Ordo Seclorum, The Intellectual Origins of the Constitution* (Lawrence: University Press of Kansas, 1985),p.55.

[61] Bernard Bailyn, *The Ideological Origins of the American Revolution*, pp.232-246.

[62] John Locke, *Two Treatises Of Government*, with an introduction by Peter Laslett, p.325.

[63] Forest McDonald, *Novus Ordo Seclorum, The Intellectual Origins of the Constitution*, pp. 50-55. Also see Robert Middlekauff, *The Glorious Cause*, pp.556-558.

[64] Dumas Malone, *Jefferson The Virginian*, p.227.

[65] Thomas M. Neis, "Ethics and the Marketplace" in Michael Bauman,ed., *Morality And The Marketplace* (Hillsdale: Hillsdale College Press, 1994), p63.

[66] Dumas Malone, *Jefferson The Virginian*, p.226.

[67] Bernard Bailyn, *The Ideological Origins of the American Revolution*, pp.318, 319.

CHAPTER 5

1776-ECONOMIC FREEDOM: ADAM SMITH AND THE WEALTH OF NATIONS

Having brought the reader to the very brink of the American Revolution, we now digress from the course of events for one chapter. The intention is to arm the reader with a powerful analytic tool: a grounding in the economic thought of Adam Smith. Often called the father of modern economics, Smith gave clarity, shape and coherence to economic forces which effect the character and fate of societies and which hitherto had been little understood. This pioneer in the field of economics published his seminal work *An Inquiry Into The Nature And Causes Of The Wealth Of Nations* (*The Wealth Of Nations*) in the same year the colonists declared their independence.[1] A discussion of Smith's ideas will gain for us clarity into pre and post Revolutionary conditions and events in America. Let us consider the background to this work before we analyze it.

Over the centuries, theologians, philosophers, statesmen, and businessmen had expounded on various aspects of the economy but attention to ways of raising the standard of living of the average person was lacking, to put it mildly, and for many, such a goal was suspect. Two principal reasons account for this posture.

First, the Christian tradition holds wealth and luxury to be dangers on the path to the salvation of man's immortal soul. This Christian perspective which emphasizes such virtues as love, abstinence, and humility, and simultaneously denigrates commercial activities was central to the lives of many colonists. The Puritan, for instance, led an ascetic life, aspects of which were self-discipline and fruitful labor. Although this Puritan work ethic resulted in material rewards, they were but incidental to the salvation of the soul.

A second realm of thought was republicanism in its classical form; what might be called civic republicanism, and its elements of citizen participation in the affairs of the nation, self-sacrifice, and devotion to the common good. It was thought that one needed considerable property to pursue these civic virtues, for this would allow the independence and leisure to be a virtuous citizen seeking honor and glory for himself and his country. Such a social model thus required a landed aristocracy--an aristocracy hardly appropriate for the person who by necessity engaged in vulgar commercial activities where self-interest and its partners, avarice and corruption, held sway and mitigated against political virtue. Thus, the concept of civic republicanism while popular among the upper classes, consigned economic thought and activity to low esteem. One more point. Common people, treated with disdain, were thought simply to be born, live, breed, and die. They should be continuously employed at low wages to prevent idleness and dissipation.[2]

In the context of these ideas philosophers and theologians focused on the role of self-interest and its relationship to the common good. The subject, of course, had long been of interest to them and especially was this true since the time of Hobbes in the seventeenth century.

Hobbes himself noted that he and fear were born twins. The political turmoil surrounding him forced a flight to France and he was witness to the fire and plague that devastated London. As we have already seen, Hobbes was adamant about restraining man's self-interest and while an advocate of private property, he believed that the interests of the state should come first and would thus limit economic freedom. In fact, too large an accumulation of personal property was worrisome to him, because it represented a threat to the Leviathan. Although economic activity was subservient to government, it, for Hobbes, would generate more economic progress than a state of nature.[3]

Many writers sought to rebut the ides of Hobbes, especially his position on the relationship between self-interest and public welfare. They tried to fathom man's place in creation, the role of reason, the role of instinct, and the extent to which there is harmony in the world. They also sought to explain the importance of virtue and the question of how to make people more virtuous. Richard Cumberland, Anthony Ashley Cooper (the third Earl of Shaftesbury), Joseph Butler, Alexander Pope, Bernard Mandeville, Hugo Grotius, Francis Hutchinson, Henry St. John (Lord Bolingbroke), Joseph Priestly, Voltaire, and David Hume are among the important writers in this post-Hobbesian quest.[4]

By the eighteenth century, some were visualizing economic activity not just in the personal terms of the Puritan, or the negative terms of Hobbes, but as something endowed with broader implications for society. They noted positive aspects of the relationship between economic progress and civilization. Some philosophers of the Enlightenment even thought that human potential might be realized through a division of labor, and if man could effect this division, the outcome would likely be harmony between self-interest and social good.[5] Happiness seemed to wait at the end of the tunnel, and it is in this time of philosophical optimism that Adam Smith lived and wrote.

ADAM SMITH

Born in Kirkaldy, Scotland, Adam Smith (1723-1790) was the son of a customs official who died just before his son's birth. An able student in grammar school and, indeed, throughout his life, Adam entered the University of Glasgow at age fourteen and came under the influence of Professor Francis Hutchinson, an important figure in the Scottish Enlightenment.

Hutchinson rejected the position of such writers as Hobbes and Mandeville who believed that all motives can be reduced to self-interest. He thought self-interest is vital and beneficial because the work of the world must be done: self-interest serves society and makes it tick. However, he also posited a more important force, an innate moral sense through which man approves and reacts positively--benevolently--toward virtuous activities and condemns those which are evil. This moral force exists along with but is superior to self-love. The ideas of Hutchinson would later be reflected in Smith's writings.[6]

Smith's success at Glasgow was rewarded with a scholarship to Balliol College at Oxford where he was discriminated against as a Scotsman and was disappointed by a faculty not inclined to do much teaching. Nonetheless, this was a time of great learning for him: he read widely, especially in the classics. Eventually he decided that a life in the clergy was not for him and he returned to Scotland.

Back in Kirkaldy, Smith continued his scholarly activities and was invited to give a series of lectures on English literature in Edinburgh. These were very well received, and when a vacancy occurred in 1751 at the University of Glasgow, Smith assumed the title of Professor of Logic and lectured on logic as well as rhetoric and belles letters. He was awarded the Chair of Moral Philosophy and now his lectures encompassed theology, ethics, justice, and political economy. This experience provided the foundation for his lifelong project of designing institutions to control human passions and to elevate human character and enhance the well-being of society. This intellectual journey led him to examine not only the economy but government, family, religion, and the law. It was with this background and in this context that Smith produced his first book, *The Theory Of Moral Sentiments*.[7]

THE THEORY OF MORAL SENTIMENTS

Initially published in 1759 (like *The Wealth Of Nations* it too is beautifully written), *The Theory of Moral Sentiments* concerns itself with the process through which man modifies his egoistic passions and becomes benevolent. Prior to Smith, a person's conscience was thought to be derived from reason and/or a sense of morality usually relating to the deity.[8] Rejecting this view, Smith advances the theory that one's conscience evolves as a result of a desire to win the approval of others and because of an ability to think of oneself in the place of someone else.

Smith believes that we are naturally egoistic and tend to put our own welfare before that of others. Nonetheless, we do concern ourselves with the mental state of others--with their joys and woes. In other words, the feelings of others affect us. This "sympathy" comes about because we experience pleasure when we share the emotions of others and they experience pleasure when they share ours. We possess the ability to see others as others see us. and we learn to evaluate our actions as we think others evaluate them. While we are less interested in others than in ourselves, we naturally want their approval and praise. We develop the ability to adjust and to moderate such emotions as happiness, grief, and disappointment, to the level that others find appropriate for our situation. This learning process, which takes place through human interaction in society leads us to exercise control (the basis of other virtues) of our egoistic passions. In this manner do social norms develop with regard to such matters as justice, truth, chastity, and fidelity.

Reinforcement of this process comes from the felt presence of an external standard--one's conscience--which Smith calls "the impartial spectator" that judges our actions in an unbiased manner. Smith notes that man wants the approbation of others to be authentically deserved (after all, praise can be based on deception). Further, the desire to be praiseworthy can be fulfilled, even when others fail to offer fulfillment, by acting according to the norms of the "impartial spectator."

> But though man has... been rendered the immediate judge of mankind, he has been rendered so only in the first instance; and an appeal lies from his sentence to a much higher tribunal, to the tribunal of their own consciences, to that of the supposed impartial and well informed spectator, to that of the man within the breast, the great judge and arbiter of their conduct. The jurisdictions of those two tribunals are founded upon principles which, though in some respects resembling and akin, are, however, in reality different and distinct. The jurisdiction of the man without, is founded altogether in the desire of actual praise, and in the aversion to actual blame. The jurisdiction of the man within, is founded altogether in the desire of praise-worthiness, and in the aversion to blame-worthiness; in the desire of possessing those qualities, and performing those actions which we love and admire in other people; and in the dread of possessing those qualities and performing those actions, which we hate and despise in other people.[9]

> What so great happiness as to be beloved, and to know that we deserve to be loved? What so great misery as to hated, and to know that we deserve to be hated?...Man naturally desires, not only to be loved, but to be lovely...[10]

> Let us suppose that the great empire of China, with all its myriads of inhabitants, was suddenly swallowed up by an earthquake, and let us consider how a man of humanity in Europe, who had no sort of connection with that part of the world, would be affected upon receiving intelligence of this dreadful calamity. He would, I imagine, first of all, express very strongly his sorrow for the misfortune of that unhappy people, he would make many melancholy reflections upon the precariousness of human life, and the vanity of all the labors of man, which could thus be annihilated in a moment. He would too, perhaps, if he was a man of speculation, enter into many reasonings concerning the effects which this disaster might produce upon the commerce of Europe, and the trade and business of the world in general. And when all this fine philosophy was over, when all these humane sentiments had been once fairly expressed, he would pursue his business or his pleasure, take his repose or his diversion, with the same ease and tranquility, as if no such accident had happened. The most frivolous disaster which could befall himself would occasion a more real disturbance. If he was to lose his little finger to-morrow, he would not sleep tonight; but, provided he never saw them, he will snore with the most profound security over the ruin of a hundred million brethren, and the destruction of that immense multitude seems plainly an object less interesting to him, than this paltry misfortune of his own. To prevent, therefore, this paltry misfortune to himself, would a man of humanity be willing to sacrifice the lives of a hundred millions of his breathen, provided he had never seen them? Human nature startles with horror at the thought, and the world, in its greatest depravity and corruption, never produced such a villain as could be capable of entertaining it. But what makes this difference? When our passive feelings are almost always so sordid and so selfish, how comes it that our active principles should often be so generous and so noble? When we are always so much more deeply affected by

> whatever concerns ourselves, than by whatever concerns other men; what is it which prompts the generous, upon all occasions, and the mean upon many, to sacrifice their own interests to the greater interests of others? It is not the soft power of humanity, it is not that feeble spark of benevolence which Nature has lighted up in the human heart, that is thus capable of counteracting the strongest impulses of self-love. It is a stronger power, a more forcible motive, which exerts itself upon such occasions. It is reason, principle, conscience, the inhabitant of the breast, the man within, the great judge and arbiter of our conduct. It is he who, whenever we are about to act so as to affect the happiness of others, calls to us, with a voice capable of astonishing the most presumptuous of our passions, that we are but one of the multitude, in no respect better than any other in it; and when we prefer ourselves so shamefully and so blindly to others, we become the proper objects of resentment, abhorrence, and execration. It is from him only that we learn the real littleness of ourselves, and of whatever relates to ourselves. and the natural misrepresentations of self-love can be corrected only by the eye of this impartial spectator. It is he who shows us the propriety of generosity and the deformity of injustice; the propriety of resigning the greatest interests of our own, for the yet greater interests of others, and the deformity of doing the smallest injury to another, in order to obtain the greatest benefit to ourselves. It is not the love of our neighbor, it is not the love of mankind, which upon many occasions prompts us to the practice of those divine virtues. It is a stronger love, a more powerful affection, which generally takes place upon such occasions; the love of what is honorable and noble, of the grandeur, and dignity, and superiority of our own characters.[11]

According to Smith, God has so arranged our minds that pleasure flows from virtuous behavior and guilt from the immoral. The truly wise man is led to a love of virtue and an abhorrence of vice. His conscience is a more important guide than public opinion. "To a real wise man the judicious and well--weighed approbation of a single wise man, gives more heartfelt satisfaction than all the noisy applause of ten thousand ignorant though enthusiastic admirers."[12] Moreover, a well-developed conscience leads us to act with justice and is the major source of benevolence. "The wise and virtuous man is at all times willing that his own private interest should be sacrificed to the public interest of his own particular order or society."[13] Note the contrast between this deistic stance and the modern position that views altruism as mere egoism in disguise.[14]

Ever the keen observer of the human condition and thus, ever the realist, Smith knew that only some people developed superior consciences. He believed that most people never reach the highest level of conscience where virtue is sought for its own sake. Instead, the majority tend to adapt their behavior primarily to win the approval of society.

> We desire both to be respectable and to be respected. We dread both to be contemptible and to be contemned. But, upon coming into this world, we soon find that wisdom and virtue are by no means the sole objects of respect; nor vice and folly, of contempt. We frequently see the respectful attentions of the world more strongly directed towards the rich and the great, than towards the wise and the virtuous. We see frequently the vices and follies of the powerful much less despised than the poverty and weakness of the innocent. To deserve, to acquire, and to enjoy the respect and admiration of mankind, are the great objects of ambition and emulation. Two different roads are presented to us, equally leading to the attainment of this so much desired object; the one, by the study of wisdom and the practice of virtue; the other, by the acquisition of wealth and greatness. Two different characters are presented to our emulation; the one of proud ambition and ostentatious avidity; the other, of humble modesty and equitable justice. Two different

models, two different pictures, are held out to us, according to which we may fashion our own character and behavior; the one more gaudy and glittering in its coloring; the other more correct and exquisitely beautiful in its outline: the one forcing itself upon the notice of every wondering eye; the other, attracting the attention of scarce any body but the most studious and careful observer. They are the wise and virtuous chiefly, a select, though I am afraid, but a small party, who are the real and steady admirers of wisdom and virtue. The great mob of mankind are the admirers and worshippers, and, what may seem more extraordinary, most frequently the disinterested admirers and worshippers, of wealth and greatness.[15]

The moral learning process that Smith delineates diminishes the need for government to control society, for the morally enlightened individual is in command of self. However, the ability to exercise this self-control, and to hold benevolent thoughts and to engage in altruism depends on the extent to which one has developed these traits. The primary social forces that account for this moral development are institutions such as the family, the school, the religious organization, and the market. A most important role for government, then, is to establish the framework within which social institutions can operate effectively.

The Theory Of Moral Sentiments won fame for Smith both in Britain and Europe. Especially taken with this work was the statesman Charles Townshend, who saw fit to offer him a sizeable sum of money as well as a pension if he would serve as a tutor to his stepson, the Duke of Buccleuch. Smith accepted Townshend's offer. Part of his tutorial obligation entailed escorting the young Duke to the Continent. There Smith met Voltaire and became acquainted with the Physiocrats, a group of French economists who believed the road to progress lay in minimal government interference. It was while abroad that Smith began writing his work on economics and he continued this labor when he returned to Scotland. Finally, in 1776, he published *The Wealth Of Nations*. It was an immediate success. Two years later Smith was made a commissioner of customs and in 1787 the University of Glasgow bestowed upon him the honorary position of Rector. He continued to enjoy his books, his social clubs, and his friends. This much beloved man died at age sixty-seven on July 17, 1790.

THE WEALTH OF NATIONS

Smith, of course, lived in the era of mercantilism, a system that when compared to feudalism, had accomplished much of an economic nature. In England and on the Continent, national authorities replaced petty fiefdoms, taxes on goods and numerous tolls that impeded their movement were reduced, uniform weights, measures, and coins were introduced and bridges, canals, roads, as well as a multiplicity of national monuments were constructed. However, special interests dominated the system and ubiquitous poverty, monopolistic practices, and impediments to innovation impaired its effectiveness. Also, at this point in history people had little sophisticated knowledge of how wealth is created. Trade, for instance, was thought to be what today we call a zero-sum game. Part of Smith's purpose for writing *The Wealth Of Nations* was to attack this system that had outlived its usefulness. The other motive was to advise the legislator on how to create wealth by fostering economic growth so the average citizen as well as the wealthier class might have a decent standard of living. Smith calls this broad distribution of wealth "universal opulence."

Contrary to the tenets of mercantilism, Smith maintains that real output--and not precious metals--constituted the wealth of a nation. His scheme for increasing real output has many dimensions and we can begin to understand it by taking another look at his conception of human nature.

Smith believes that man comes equipped with, a "...propensity to truck, barter, and exchange one thing for another."[16] This is unique to humanity, for "Nobody ever saw a dog make a fair and deliberate exchange of one bone for another with another dog."[17] Self-interest, according to Smith, is man's dominant motive: "It is not from the benevolence of the butcher, the brewer, or the baker, that we expect our dinner, but from their regard to their own interest. We address ourselves, not to their humanity but to their self-love, and never talk to them of our own necessities but of their advantages."[18]

This tendency to engage in exchange expresses itself through the operation of markets. Markets, through the combination of the forces of supply and demand, generate prices which coordinate vast quantities of information, and allocate scarce resources among competing uses. Markets work to eliminate surpluses and shortages of goods, services, and the productive factors, and deliver to people (given their incomes) what they want.

Markets also tend to promote the division of labor which is a vital source of improved productivity. Specialization increases the dexterity of the workman, allows him to save time that would be spent in going from one task to another, and leads to the discovery of improvements in the machinery with which he is coupled. Writing at the beginning of the industrial revolution, however, Smith failed to foresee the tremendous productivity gains that would result from improved technology and capital accumulation. For him, most productivity advances could be traced to the labor sector.

There is no doubt that mercantilist policies retarded growth. Progress, nonetheless, was evident in wealthier societies because they possessed more elaborate markets, and a relatively sophisticated degree of specialization:

> Every workman has a great quantity of his own work to dispose of beyond what he himself has occasion for; and every other workman being exactly in the same situation, he is enabled to exchange a great quantity of his own goods for a great quantity, or, what comes to the same thing, for the price of a great quantity of theirs. He supplies them abundantly with what they have occasion for, and a general plenty diffuses itself through all the different ranks of society.[19]

The following observation relates to "... the most common artificer or day--laborer in a civilized and thriving country..."

> Compared, indeed, with the more extravagant luxury of the great, his accommodation must no doubt appear extremely simple and easy; and yet it may be true, perhaps, that the accommodation of an European prince does not always so much exceed that of an industrious and frugal peasant, as the accommodation of the latter exceeds that of many

an African king the absolute master of the lives and liberties of ten thousand naked savages.[20]

Smith considers the benefits of free trade to extend to international markets and views as harmful attempts by government to protect domestic manufacturers through trade barriers or subsidies. "It is the maxim of every prudent master of a family, never to attempt to make at home what it will cost him more to make than to buy...What is prudence in the conduct of every private family, can scarce be folly in that of a great kingdom."[21]

His support of free trade, though staunch, is not total and he allows for two exceptions. National defense represents one category, and Smith looks with favor on those aspects of the Navigation Acts that enlarge the number of sailors and vessels. Secondly, where the domestic product is subject to a tax, its foreign counterpart should also bear that burden when imported. Where protective tariffs are already in place, he suggests that they be removed gradually so as to forestall undue unemployment. He also notes that the removal of artificial barriers to free commerce within domestic markets would make it much easier for workers to find new sources of employment.

Adam Smith's antagonism toward monopoly stems from the belief that it reduces supply, charges an above competitive price, and "...is a great enemy to good management...." Moreover his animosity embraces both private and public monopoly. As such, the state should not favor one group over another:

> To hurt in any degree the interest of any one order of citizens, for no other purpose but to promote that of some other, is evidently contrary to that justice and equality of treatment which the sovereign owes to all the different orders of his subjects.[22]

Thus, we see that competition is the essential ingredient in the economic system that Smith develops. Not only does it allocate scarce resources among competing uses, but it insures that prices reflect costs, affords consumers choice, and impedes exploitation. Moreover, competition harnesses and channels the drive of self-interest into socially desirable endeavors and leads to a harmony of interests.

> Every individual is continually exerting himself to find out the most advantageous employment for whatever capital he can command. It is his own advantage, indeed, and not that of the society which he has in view. But the study of his own advantage naturally, or rather necessarily leads him to prefer that employment which is most advantageous to the society.[23]

> ...every individual necessarily labors to render the annual revenue of the society as great as he can. He generally, indeed, neither intends to promote the public interest, nor knows how much he is promoting it. By preferring the support of domestic to that of foreign industry, he intends only his own security; and by directing that industry in such a manner as its produce may be of the greatest value, he intends only his own gain, and he is in this, as in many other cases, led by an invisible hand to promote an end which was no part of his intention. Nor is it always the worse for the society that it was no part of it. By pursuing his own interest he frequently promotes that of the society more effectively than when he really intends to promote it. I have never known much good done by those who

affected to trade for the public good. It is an affectation, indeed, not very common among merchants, and very few words need be employed in dissuading them from it.[24]

"The invisible hand," a metaphor for competition, promotes the harmony of interests characteristic of a free market economy. In other words, survival is insured in such a system if one produces what others wish to purchase. And, contrary to the maxims prevalent at that time, the harmony of interests included the international sphere.

> Commerce, which ought naturally to be, among nations, as among individuals, a bond of union and friendship, has become the most fertile source of discord and animosity.[25]

> The wealth of a neighboring nation, however, though dangerous in war and politics, is certainly advantageous in trade. In a state of hostility it may enable our enemies to maintain fleets and armies superior to our own; but in a state of peace and commerce it must likewise enable them to exchange with us to a greater value, and to afford a better market, either for the immediate produce of our own industry, or for whatever is purchased with that produce...A nation that would enrich itself by foreign trade, is certainly most likely to do so when its neighbors are all rich, industrious, and commercial nations.[26]

When a foreign nation restricts its imports, Smith would not be averse to the home nation retaliating by erecting similar barriers. He would, however, proceed with caution and undertake such a policy only if the probability of success seemed high. A strategy failing to induce the offending nation to lower its barriers should be abandoned. Otherwise, with import restrictions in place, domestic producers of the product would enjoy a degree of monopoly power that allows them to raise prices and thereby burden the citizenry at large: "...it seems a bad method of compensating the injury done to certain classes of our people, to do another injury ourselves, not only to those classes, but to all other classes of them."[27]

Smith considers the quality of business decisions made by self-interested men operating in a self-adjusting free market economy to be far superior to business decisions rendered by politicians.

> What is the species of domestic industry which his capital can employ and of which the produce is likely to be of greatest value, every individual, it is evident can, in his local situation, judge much better than any statesman or lawgiver can do for him. The statesman, who should attempt to direct private people in what manner they ought to employ their capitals, would not only load himself with a most unnecessary attention, but assume an authority which could safely be trusted, not only to no single person, but to no council or senate whatever, and which would no-where be so dangerous as in the hands of a man who had folly and presumption enough to fancy himself fit to exercise it.[28]

> It is the highest impertinence and presumption, therefore, in kings and ministers, to pretend to watch over the economy of private people, and to restrain their expense, either by sumptuary laws, or by prohibiting the importation of foreign luxuries. They are themselves always, and without exception, the greatest spendthrifts in the society. Let them look well after their own expense, and they may safely trust private people with theirs. If their own extravagance does not ruin the state, that of their subjects never will.[29]

Although Smith believes the colonization process extends the market for British goods and thereby promotes the division of labor, the monopoly privileges enjoyed by British merchants doing business in America are, nonetheless, harmful to the British economy.

> To found a great empire for the sole purpose of raising up a people of customers, may at first sight appear a project fit only for a nation of shop-keepers. It is, however, a project altogether unfit for a nation of shopkeepers. Such statesmen, and such statesmen only, are capable of fancying that they will find some advantage in employing the blood and treasure of their fellow-citizens, to found and maintain such an empire. Say to a shopkeeper, Buy me a good estate, and I shall always buy my clothes at your shop, even though I should pay somewhat dearer than what I can have them for at other shops; and you will not find him very forward to embrace your proposal. But should any other person buy you such an estate, the shopkeeper would be much obliged to your benefactor if he would enjoin you to buy all your clothes at his shop. England purchased for some of her subjects, who found themselves uneasy at home, a great estate in a distant country.[30]

> It cannot be very difficult to determine who have been the contrivers of this whole mercantile system; not the consumers, we may believe, whose interest has been entirely neglected; but the producers, whose interest has been so carefully attended to; and among this latter class our merchants and manufacturers have been by far the principal architects.[31]

Smith considers it appropriate to ask the colonists to contribute to their own defense. However, if they refuse to contribute, he does not believe it to be an issue over which a war should be waged. Smith is not very optimistic about a British triumph over the Americans and suggests that the former should voluntarily give up its possessions.

> If any of the provinces of the British empire cannot be made to contribute towards the support of the whole empire, it is surely time that Great Britain should free herself from the expense of defending those provinces in time of war, and of supporting any part of their civil or military establishments in time of peace, and endeavor to accommodate her future views and designs to the real mediocrity of her circumstances.[32]

Adam Smith believes that the vital, albeit restricted, role of government is to protect the individual and his property from foreign invasion and from domestic oppression and injustices. It should also accept some responsibility for certain public projects--harbors, roads, education etc.--which might not otherwise come to fruition due to a weakness in the profit motive. Local government, thought Smith, is best suited to undertake these public projects.

When it came to financing government expenditures, Smith supports the employment of a user's fee--that is, a financial charge on those who most directly benefit from the good or service--a payment for the use of a turnpike, for instance. Beyond that, however, he offers general maxims of taxation that still appear in textbooks on economics.

I   The subjects of every state ought to contribute towards the support of the government, as nearly as possible, in proportion to their respective abilities;

that is, in proportion to the revenue which they respectively enjoy under the protection of the state....

II The tax which each individual is bound to pay ought to be certain, and not arbitrary. The time of payment, the manner of payment, the quantity to be paid, ought all to be clear and plain to the contributor, and to every other person....The uncertainty of taxation encourages the insolence and favors the corruption of an order of men who are naturally unpopular, even when they are neither insolent nor corrupt....

III Every tax ought to be levied at the time, or in the manner, in which it is most likely to be convenient for the contributor to pay.

IV Every tax ought to be so contrived as both to take out and to keep out of the pockets of the people as little as possible, over and above what it brings into the public treasury of the state.[33]

Smith's suspicions of government extends, naturally enough, into the area of finance: "There is no art which one government sooner learns of another, than that of draining money from the pockets of the people."[34] And anticipating twentieth century supply-side economics, he thinks that high tax rates were counterproductive.

> The high duties which have been imposed upon the importation of many different sorts of goods in order to discourage their consumption in Great Britain, have in many cases served only to encourage smuggling; and in all cases have reduced the revenue of the customs below what more moderate duties would have afforded. The saying of Dr. Swift, that in the arithmetic of the customs two and two, instead of making four, make some times only one, holds perfectly true with regard to such heavy duties....[35]

Much concerned about the size of Britain's national debt, Smith considers it detrimental to the health of its economy, and is well aware of the propensity of politicians to borrow rather than tax:

> To relieve the present exigency is always the object which principally interests those immediately concerned in the administration of public affairs. The future liberation of the public revenue, they leave to the care of posterity.[36]

Smith observes that income inequality is often traced to occupational wage differentials and public policy. The former are due to:

> ...first, the agreeableness or disagreeableness of the employment themselves; secondly, the easiness and cheapness, or the difficulty and expense of learning them; thirdly, the constancy or inconstancy of employment in them; fourthly, the small or great trust which must be reposed in those who exercise them; and fifthly, the probability or improbability of success in them.[37]

Public policy often accentuates income inequality by restricting entry in some occupations, by subsidizing others, and by restricting the mobility of labor and capital. Imposing artificial barriers of entry for some occupations allows guild members to receive above competitive wages, but--of greater importance--deprives outsiders from earning a living in these occupations.

> The property which every man has in his own labour, as it is the original foundation of all other property, so it is the most sacred and inviolable. The patrimony of a poor man lies in the strength and dexterity of his hands; and to hinder him from employing this strength and dexterity in what manner he thinks proper without injury to his neighbor, is a plain violation of this most sacred property. It is a manifest encroachment upon the just liberty both of the workman, and of those who might be disposed to employ him. As it hinders the one from working at what he thinks proper, so it hinders the others from employing whom they think proper. To judge whether he is fit to be employed, may surely be trusted to the discretion of the employers whose interest it so much concerns. The affected anxiety of the law-giver lest they should employ an improper person, is evidently as impertinent as it is oppressive.[38]

Well-intentioned public subsidies of occupations such as the clergy and teachers, "That unprosperous race of men commonly called men of letters...," serve to depress their wages. He notes that "... the usual reward of the eminent teacher bears no proportion to that of the lawyer or physician; because the trade of the one is crowded with indigent people who have been brought up to it at the public expense...."[39]

Smith attacks public policies which obstruct the movement of labor, not only from one occupation to another within the same town, but of the same occupation in a different town. Also under his assault are the English poor laws, which impede the movement of workmen to other communities in search of better economic opportunities.

That Adam Smith is often portrayed as an apologist for business interests constitutes a gross distortion of his position. Workers, for instance, receive much better treatment in *The Wealth Of Nations* than do employers, whom Smith tends to look upon harshly.

> Masters are always and every where in a sort of tacit, but constant and uniform combination not to raise the wages of labour above their actual rate.[40]

> The liberal reward of labour, as it encourages the propagation, so it increases the industry of the common people. The wages of labour are the encouragement of industry, which, like every other quality, improves in proportion to the encouragement it receives. A plentiful subsistence increases the bodily strength of the laborer, and the comfortable hope of bettering his condition, and of ending his days perhaps in ease and plenty, animates him to exert that strength to the utmost. Where wages are high, accordingly, we shall always find the workman more active, diligent, and expeditious, than where they are low.... If masters would always listen to the dictates of reason and humanity, they have frequently occasion rather to moderate, than to animate the application of many of their workman. It will be found, I believe, in every sort of trade, that the man who works so moderately, as to be able to work constantly, not only preserves his health the longest, but, in the course of the year, executes the greatest quantity of work.[41]

> Our merchants and master-manufacturers complain much of the bad effects of high wages in raising the price, and thereby lessening the sale of their goods both at home and abroad. They say nothing concerning the bad effects of high profits. They are silent with regard to the pernicious effects of their own gains. They complain only of those of other people.[42]

> People of the same trade seldom meet together even for merriment and diversion, but the conversation ends in a conspiracy against the public, or in some contrivance to raise prices.[43]

> The interest of the dealers, however, in any particular branch of trade or manufactures, is always in some respects different from, and even opposite to, that of the public. To widen the market and to narrow the competition, is always the interest of the dealers. To widen the market may frequently be agreeable enough to the interest of the public; but to narrow the competition must always be against it, and can serve only to enable the dealers, by raising their profits above what they naturally would be, to levy, for their own benefit, an absurd tax upon the rest of their fellow-citizens. The proposal of any new law or regulation of commerce which comes from this order, ought always to be listened to with great precaution, and ought never to be adopted till after having been long and carefully examined, not only with the most scrupulous, but with the most suspicious attention. It comes from an order of men, whose interest is never exactly the same with that of the public, who have generally an interest to deceive and even to oppress the public, and who accordingly have, upon many occasions, both deceived and oppressed it.[44]

Smith, however, should not be considered a defender of any particular social or economic class, as he decried monopoly of any sort. Remember that for people to act as consumers, goods and services must be available for sale, and people must have the income to purchase them. Smith's focus is on economic growth, which generates more goods and services as well as higher real incomes. Here, then, we find a true consumer advocate:[45]

> Consumption is the sole end and purpose of all production; and the interest of the producer ought to be attended to, only so far as it may be necessary for promoting that of the consumer. The maxim is so perfectly self-evident, that it would be absurd to attempt to prove it. But in the mercantile system, the interest of the consumer is almost constantly sacrificed to that of the producer; and it seems to consider production, and not consumption, as the ultimate end and object of all industry and commerce.[46]

Smith believed people to be quite similar at birth and held environmental conditions primarily responsible for the skills that they developed and the incomes they enjoyed.

> The difference of natural talents in different men is, in reality, much less than we are aware of; and the very different genius which appears to distinguish men of different professions, when grown up to maturity, is not upon many occasions so much the cause as the effect of the division of labour. The difference between the most dissimilar characters, between a philosopher and a common street porter, for example, seems to arise not so much from nature, as from habit, custom, and education. When they came into the world, and for the first six or eight years of their existence, they were perhaps, very much alike, and neither their parents nor playfellows could perceive any remarkable difference. About that age, or soon after, they come to be employed in very different occupations. The difference of talents comes then to be taken notice of, and widens by degrees, till at last the vanity of the philosopher is willing to acknowledge scarce any resemblance.[47]

> By nature a philosopher is not in genius and disposition half so different from a street porter, as a mastiff is from a greyhound, or a greyhound from a spaniel, or this last from a shepherd's dog.[48]

Under Smith's "system of natural liberty," obstructive public barriers to economic freedom would be eliminated, and individual initiative allowed to flourish in a market economy that, via competition, harnessed self-interest for the common good. And this would lead to the "universal opulence" (one might say to more equality) that he sought.

Adam Smith's inquiry into the nature of things economic proved an immediate success. *The Wealth Of Nations* was translated into several languages, found a wide audience among the intelligentsia in Europe and America, and proved influential in the formulation of national economic policy. It was included in the libraries of Alexander Hamilton, James Madison, John Adams, and Thomas Jefferson, who called it the best book on political economy in existence.

Adam Smith wrote at a time when the systematic study of economics was in its infancy. While many of the ideas contained in *The Wealth Of Nations* were not original, he possessed the unique ability to organize, interpret, and present concepts in a manner vastly superior to the attempts of his predecessors. His study of the vital parts of the overall economy became the foundation for subsequent scholarship. The appellation awarded to him of father of modern economic is deserved.

While each of Smith's works had a different focus, *The Theory Of Moral Sentiments* and *The Wealth Of Nations* should be looked upon as complements rather than substitutes and they bear more than a passing relationship to one another. Adam Smith, a preeminent moral philosopher of his day, was, naturally enough, concerned with moral excellence, and he set for his life's work the goal of establishing a more decent society. This objective runs like a thread throughout his works.[49]

Addressed to the educated, *The Theory Of Moral Sentiments* seeks to explain the learning of self-control so that egoistic human passions can be channeled into virtuous behavior. Smith believes that "Happiness consists in tranquility and enjoyment,"[50] and that in a virtuous society, people practice benevolence, treat each other politely, and live harmoniously. That virtue leads to happiness made its attainment a most desirable objective.

In *The Wealth Of Nations*, it is the market which controls man's passions, and allocates the energy with which they are pursued into cooperative activities that redound to the benefit of society. Thus the market system fosters the virtues of honesty, order, frugality, punctuality, and moderation as well as the ability to defer gratification, and to behave decently toward others. And of course such personal attributes tend to promote pleasant social relationships.

In a commercial society, success depends more on industry, ability, and merit than on the fawning and flattery so prevalent in Smith's time when royalty and aristocracy dominate societal relations. Contrary to the tradition of his era, Smith attributes respectability to the merchant.[51] Also in contrast to the zero-sum game mentality characteristic of mercantilist thought, Smith's system offers the aforementioned universal opulence: *both* parties to free market transactions might gain from them and economic well-being would ultimately increase throughout society. This in turn allows more and more people to engage in benevolent behavior, for as Smith observed, "If our own misery pinches us very severely, we have no leisure to attend to that of our neighbor."[52]

An intriguing and important aspect of Smith's thought concerns both the motivations for and the unintended results of human actions. Of the latter--those consequences so undesigned and unforeseen in an original plan of action--we have already considered: how high customs duties, instead of raising revenue, caused more smuggling; how well intentioned occupational subsidies depressed wages; how self-interest and greed--abetted by the "invisible hand"--promoted healthy economic development even as it fulfilled selfish desires. As for the motivations behind human actions, Smith was a shrewd and often penetrating observer of the many ways avarice informed decisions and actions in the marketplace. We conclude this chapter with three substantial quotations from *The Theory Of Moral Sentiments*: they will give the reader a sense of the charm of Smith's style and his penetration below the surface of commercial dealing to the passions that drive and shape it.

In this first passage, Smith considers the situation of the laborer and then of the rich man, and discusses why it might be that mankind longs for wealth.

> For to what purpose is all the toil and bustle of this world? what is the end of avarice and ambition, of the pursuit of wealth, of power, and preeminence? Is it to supply the necessities of nature? The wages of the meanest laborer can supply them. We see that they afford him food and clothing, the comfort of a house, and of a family. If we examined his economy with rigour, we should find that he spends a great part of them upon conveniences, which may be regarded as superfluities, and that, upon extraordinary occasion, he can give something even to vanity and distinction. What then is the cause of our aversion to his situation, and why should those who have been educated to the higher ranks of life, regard it as worse than death, to be reduced to live, even without labour, upon the same simple fare with him, to dwell under the same lowly roof, and to be clothed in the same humble attire? Do they imagine that their stomach is better, or their sleep sounder in a palace than in a cottage? The contrary has been so often observed, and, indeed, is so very obvious, though it had never been observed, that there is nobody ignorant of it. From whence, then, arises that emulation which runs through all the different ranks of men, and what are the advantages which we propose by that great purpose of human life which we call bettering our condition? To be observed, to be attended to, to be taken notice of with sympathy, complacency, and approbation, are all the advantages which we can propose to derive from it. It is the vanity not the ease or the pleasure, which interests us. But vanity is always founded upon the belief of our being the object of attention and approbation. The rich man glories in his riches, because he feels that they naturally draw upon him the attention of the world, and that mankind are disposed to go along with him in all those agreeable emotions with which the advantages of his situation so readily inspire him. At the thought of this, his heart seems to swell and dilate itself within him, and he is fonder of his wealth, upon this account, than for all the other advantages it procures him. The poor man, on the contrary, is ashamed of his poverty. He feels that it either places him out of the sight of mankind, or, that if they take any notice of him, they have, however, scarce any fellow-feeling with the misery and distress which he suffers. He is mortified upon both accounts; for though to be overlooked, and to be disapproved of, are things entirely different, yet as obscurity covers us from the daylight of honor and approbation, to feel that we are taken no notice of, necessarily damps the most agreeable hope, and disappoints the most ardent desire, of human nature. The poor man goes out and comes in unheeded, and when in the midst of a crowd is in the same obscurity as if shut up in his own hovel. Those humble cares and painful attentions which occupy those in his situation, afford no amusement to the dissipated and the gay. They turn away their eyes from him, or if the extremity of his distress forces them to look a him, it is only to spurn so disagreeable an object from

among them. The fortunate and the proud wonder at the insolence of human wretchedness, that it should dare to present itself before them, and with the loathsome aspect of its misery presume to disturb the serenity of their happiness. The man of rank and distinction, on the contrary, is observed by all the world. Every body is eager to look at him, and to conceive, at least by sympathy, that joy and exultation with which his circumstances naturally inspire him. His actions are the objects of the public care. Scarce a word, scarce a gesture, can fall from him that is altogether neglected. In a great assembly he is the person upon whom all direct their eyes; it is upon him that their passions seem all to wait with expectation, in order to receive the movement and direction which he shall impress upon them; and if his behavior is not altogether absurd, he has, every moment, an opportunity of interesting mankind, and of rendering himself the object of the observation and fellow-feeling of every body about him. It is this, which, notwithstanding the restraint it imposes, notwithstanding the loss of liberty with which it is attended, render greatness the object of envy and compensate, in the opinion on mankind, all that toil, all the anxiety, all those mortifications which must be undergone in the pursuit of it; and what is of yet more consequence, all the leisure, all the ease, all that careless security, which are forfeited for ever by the acquisition.[53]

In the next passage, Smith's darkest appraisal of the quest for wealth, power and status shows mankind the tragic victim of its own cravings--and even of their hard earned realization.

The poor man's son, whom heaven in its anger has visited with ambition, when he begins to look around him, admires the condition of the rich. He finds the cottage of his father too small for his accommodation, and fancies he should be lodged more at his ease in a palace. He is displeased with being obliged to walk a-foot, or to endure the fatigue of riding on horseback. He sees his superiors carried about in machines, and imagines that in one of these he could travel with less inconveniency. He feels himself naturally indolent, and willing to serve himself with his own hands as little as possible; and judges, that a numerous retinue of servants would save him from a great deal of trouble. He thinks if he had attained all these, he would sit still contentedly, and be quiet, enjoying himself in the thought of the happiness and tranquility of his situation. He is enchanted with the distant idea of this felicity. It appears in his fancy like the life of some superior rank of beings, and, in order to arrive at it, he devotes himself for ever to the pursuit of wealth and greatness. To obtain the conveniences which these afford, he submits in the first year, nay in the first month of his application, to more fatigue of body and more uneasiness of mind than he could have suffered through the whole of his life from the want of them. He studies to distinguish himself in some laborious profession. With the most unrelenting industry he labours night and day to acquire talents superior to all his competitors. He endeavors next to bring those talents into public view, and with equal assiduity solicits every opportunity of employment. For this purpose he makes his court to all mankind; he serves those whom he hates, and is obsequious to those whom he despises. Through the whole of his life he pursues the idea of a certain artificial and elegant repose which he may never arrive at, for which he sacrifices a real tranquility that is at all times in his power, and which, if in the extremity of old age he should at last attain to it he will find to be in no respect preferable to the humble security and contentment which he had abandoned for it. It is then, in the last dregs of life, his body wasted with toil and diseases, his mind galled and ruffled by the memory of a thousand injuries and disappointments which he imagines he has met with from the injustice of his enemies, or from the perfidy and ingratitude of his friends, that he begins at last to find that wealth and greatness are mere trinkets of frivolous utility, no more adapted for procuring ease of body or tranquility of mind than the tweezer-cases of the lover of toys; and like them too, more troublesome to the person who carries them about with him than all the advantages they can afford him are commodious...But in the languor of disease and the weariness of old age, the pleasures of the vain and empty distinctions of greatness disappear. To one, in this situation, they are no longer capable of recommending those toilsome pursuits in which they had formerly engaged him. In his heart he curses ambition, and vainly regrets the ease and the indolence of youth, pleasures which are fled for ever, and which he has foolishly sacrificed for what, when he has got it, can afford him no real satisfaction. In this miserable aspect does greatness appear to every man when reduced either by spleen or disease to observe with attention his own situation, and to consider what it is that is really wanting to his happiness. Power and riches appear then to be, what they are, enormous and operose machines contrived to produce a few trifling conveniencies to the body, consisting of springs the most nice and delicate, which must be kept in order with the most anxious attention, and which in spite of all our care are ready every moment to burst into pieces, and to crush in their ruins their unfortunate possessor. They are immense fabrics, which it requires the labour of a life to raise, which threaten every moment to overwhelm the person that dwells in them, and which while they stand, though they may save him from some smaller inconveniences, can protect him from none of the severer inclemencies of the season. They keep off the summer shower, not the winter storm, but leave him always as much, and sometimes more exposed than before, to anxiety, to fear, and to sorrow; to diseases, to danger, and to death.[54]

And so we see that in Smith's eyes power and riches ultimately betray the very people who work so hard to acquire them. Happily, however, this grim assessment is counterbalanced by the positive (albeit unintended), aspects of human "toil and bustle" when we consider them in the context of "the machine of economy."

We are then charmed with the beauty of that accommodation which reigns in the palaces and economy of the great; and admire how every thing is adapted to promote their ease, to prevent their wants, to gratify their wishes, and to amuse and entertain their most frivolous desires. If we consider the real satisfaction which all these things are capable of affording, by itself and separated from the beauty of that arrangement which is fitted to promote it, it will always appear in the highest degree contemptible and trifling. But we rarely view it in our imagination with the order, the regular and harmonious movement of the system, the machine or economy by means of which it is produced. The pleasures of wealth and greatness, when considered in this complex view, strike the imagination as something grand and beautiful and noble, of which the attainment is well worth all the toil and anxiety which we are so apt to bestow upon it.

And it is well that nature imposes upon us in this manner. It is this deception which rouses and keeps in continual motion the industry of mankind. It is this which first prompted them to cultivate the ground, to build houses, to found cities and commonwealths, and to invent and improve all the sciences and arts, which enable and embellish human life; which have entirely changed the whole face of the globe, have turned rude forests of nature into agreeable and fertile plains, and made the trackless and barren ocean a new fund of subsistence, and the great high road of communication to the different nations of the earth. The earth by these labors of mankind has been obliged to redouble her natural fertility, and to maintain a greater multitude of inhabitants.[55]

We may note that Adam Smith not only examined the institutions that made for a virtuous and prosperous society, but through the force of his arguments and the exquisite quality of his prose sought to convince that "small company" of wise and virtuous men-- the hero, the statesman, and the legislator--to promote and defend his ideas--ideas that will reappear explicitly or implicitly throughout this volume. Now, with the analysis of these classic eighteenth century documents on political and economic freedom behind us, it is time to return to the battle for independence and freedom.

---

[1] Adam Smith, *An Inquiry Into The Nature And Causes Of The Wealth Of Nations*, ed. with an introduction by Edwin Cannan, and an introduction by Max Lerner (New York: The Modern Library, Random House Inc., 1937).
[2] Jerry Z. Muller, *Adam Smith In His Time And Ours* (New York: The Free Press, Macmillan Inc., 1993), pp.39-60. passim.
[3] Milton L. Myers, *The Soul Of Economic Man* (Chicago: The University of Chicago Press, 1983), pp. 28-34.
[4] Ibid., pp. 37-89 passim.
[5] Ibid., pp. 78-89.
[6] Ibid., pp. 68-69.
[7] Adam Smith, *The Theory Of Moral Sentiments*, ed. by D. D. Raphael and A. L. Macfie (Indianapolis: Liberty Classics, 1976).
[8] Jerry Z. Muller, *Adam Smith In His Time And Ours*, p. 100.
[9] Adam Smith, *The Theory Of Moral Sentiments*, pp. 130-131.
[10] Ibid., p. 113.
[11] Ibid., pp. 136-137.
[12] Ibid., p. 253.
[13] Ibid., p.235.
[14] Jerry Z. Muller, *Adam Smith In His Time And Ours*, pp. 203-204.
[15] Adam Smith, *The Theory Of Moral Sentiments*, p. 62.
[16] Adam Smith, *The Wealth Of Nations*, p.13.
[17] Ibid., p. 13.
[18] Ibid., pp. 13-14.
[19] Ibid., p. 11.
[20] Ibid., pp. 11-12.
[21] Ibid., p.424.
[22] Ibid., p. 618.
[23] Ibid., p. 421.
[24] Ibid., p. 423.
[25] Ibid. p. 460.
[26] Ibid., p. 461.
[27] Ibid. p. 435.
[28] Ibid., p. 423.
[29] Ibid. p. 329.
[30] Ibid. pp. 579-580.
[31] Ibid., p.626.
[32] Ibid., p. 900.
[33] Ibid., pp. 777-778.
[34] Ibid., p. 813.
[35] Ibid., p. 832.
[36] Ibid., pp. 867-868.
[37] Ibid., p. 100.
[38] Ibid., pp. 121-122.
[39] Ibid., pp. 131-132.
[40] Ibid., pp. 66-67.

⁴¹Ibid., pp. 81-82.
⁴²Ibid., p.98.
⁴³Ibid., p. 128.
⁴⁴Ibid., p. 250.
⁴⁵For an interpretation of Adam Smith as a champion of the consumer, see Edward W. Ryan, *In The Words Of Adam Smith: The First Consumer Advocate* (Sun Lakes, Arizona: Thomas Horton and Daughters,1990).
⁴⁶Adam Smith, *The Wealth Of Nations*. p.625.
⁴⁷Ibid., p. 15-16.
⁴⁸Ibid., p. 16.
⁴⁹An analysis of this theme is developed in Jerry Z. Muller's book, *Adam Smith In His Time And Ours*.
⁵⁰Adam Smith, *The Theory Of Moral Sentiments*, p. 149.
⁵¹Jerry Z. Muller, Adam Smith In His Time And Ours, pp. 131-139.
⁵²Adam Smith, *The Theory Of Moral Sentiments,* p. 205.
⁵³Ibid., pp. 50-51.
⁵⁴Ibid., pp. 181-183.
⁵⁵Ibid., pp. 183-184.

CHAPTER 6

VICTORY AND ITS AFTERMATH

A SUCCESSFUL REVOLUTION

It was a long, difficult, costly, and bloody struggle from the first shots fired at Lexington until the defeat of General Cornwallis at Yorktown in 1781.

Compared to the rebels, Britain possessed superior manufacturing abilities, greater wealth, a larger population, along with a unified government, the best navy in the world, and a well-trained army already in existence. How, then, did the Americans win? One factor was the relative lack of competence among the British generals and others directing the British war effort. Foreign assistance to the colonies, especially from France, was another vital ingredient. By far and away, the most important contribution to victory was from the people--from the civilians who provided support, and from the soldiers and their generals--all those who fought bravely, learned from their mistakes in true American fashion, and refused to give up under exceedingly trying circumstances.

Although approximately two million Americans inhabited the rebellious colonies when the hostilities began, not all were available for military service. Concentrated in the upper classes (government officials, members of the Anglican church, wealthy merchants, well-to-do planters), perhaps a third remained loyal to the Crown and not only failed to offer support, but often actively assisted the British. And there were many non-loyalists who were not enthusiastic over the idea of independence from Britain and assumed a neutral position. Of those on the patriot side, non-combatant women and children represented over a half and some militarily eligible men were needed to produce food and other necessary commodities. As a result, the largest number of American troops at any one time numbered about 20,000, and usually there were fewer than that. Over the course of the entire war, about 200,000 men performed in the armed forces.[1]

Soldiers served in state militias and in the Continental army. Bounties to encourage enlistment were often accompanied by conscription, although one could hire a replacement. Many hesitated to serve far from home for any length of time, and the difficulty of maintaining a sufficient quantity of troops continued throughout the war. Disciplinary problems also impeded the war effort. These young, freedom-loving warriors of a fiercely independent mind tended to balk at the regimen of training, and unlike their European counterparts, they wanted to know why they were being told to do something. They have been described as "exceedingly dirty and nasty people" who marched improperly and wore their hats incorrectly. Such was the stench of the encampment at Valley Forge, that General Anthony Wayne considered going into battle preferable to making an inspection.[2] Dissension was not unknown, and at times Washington had trouble getting his troops to stand and fight.[3]

Early in the war, colossal economic problems arose. Insufficient financial resources and poor organization (Alexander Hamilton, Washington's aid-de-camp, noted the "imbecility" of government)[4] meant that troops had inadequate food and clothing and needed medical supplies--sometimes tragically so.[5] In 1776, George Washington's soldiers endured a terrible, bitter winter. Scanty provisions and Congress' failure to pay the men their wages (even back then, Congress proved less than able in economics and management) understandably made for low morale, and many returned home when their enlistment expired. It was in this setting that Thomas Paine, now a military aide, provided inspiration in yet another pamphlet, *Crisis*.

> These are the times that try men's souls. The summer soldier and the sunshine patriot will, in this crisis, shrink from the service of his country; but he that stands it now, deserves the love and thanks of man and woman.[6]

A more horrendous event awaited American troops in the following bitter winter at Valley Forge, where the earth served as flooring for ineffective shelters, where some men lacked even shirts, where food consisted of firecakes (baked flour that had been mixed with water), where the soap supply ran out, and where footsteps in the snow left traces of blood. George Washington's tribute to his men is instructive:

> To see men without clothes to cover their nakedness, without blankets to lay on, without shoes, by which their marches might be traced by the blood from their feet, and almost as often without provisions as with; marching through frost and snow, and at Christmas taking up their winter quarters within a day's march of the enemy, without a house to cover them till they could be built, and submitting to it without a murmur is a mark of patience and obedience which in my opinion can scarce be paralleled.[7]

Deprivation throughout the conflict had the accompaniment of terror in battle--of cannon, gunshot and bayonet, wounds, of dismemberment, amputation, the agonies and screams of pain, and of death.

Yet the Americans, judging their efforts over the entire span of the war, generally fought quite well. A multiplicity of factors account for this performance. Some fought out of fear--fear of the enemy, or of punishment, or of being branded a coward, or tried for treason. Even those not directly involved in combat--Congress and other revolutionary leaders--probably experienced trepidation as English law allowed those judged as traitors to be partially strangled, drawn, and quartered.

On a positive note, many troops undoubtedly believed that defending their freedoms, accomplishments, loved ones and possessions was a righteous--perhaps even a sacred cause. John Adams felt that they had been "sent into life at a time when the greatest lawgivers of antiquity would have wished to live."[8] Appeals were made to the soldiers' patriotism, honor, and courage--the elements of the eighteenth century's definition of manhood. In the turmoil of fighting, officer leadership often played a crucial role and the close personal and physical relationship among comrades on a relatively small field of battle enabled men to give and receive support from one another; and some felt that divine Providence would protect them.[9]

On October 19, 1781, the British General Cornwallis, sealed off from help by a sea blockade and opposed by a vastly superior American army, surrendered his forces to Washington at Yorktown, Virginia. Then, in a moving display of military ceremony, "One by one, the British regiments, after laying down their arms, marched back to camp between two lines, one of American soldiers, the other of French, while the military bands played a series of melancholy tunes, including the one which all recognized as *The World Turned Upside Down*."[10]

The war ended after the major defeat at Yorktown as it became apparent to the British that the costs of continuing hostilities would exceed the benefits. Negotiations began with John Jay, a lover of freedom and an active opponent of slavery, brilliantly leading the American delegation. Less renowned than many other founding fathers, John Jay nonetheless had a very exemplary career during .which he served as delegate to the First and the Second Continental Congresses, as the first Chief Justice of the United States Supreme Court, and as Governor of New York. He also played a vital role in securing the adoption of the United States Constitution. Eventually, a treaty of peace granting independence was signed with Great Britain on September 3, 1783, in the city of Paris, and on December 4 of that year, Washington offered a farewell address to his troops at Fraunces Tavern in Manhattan, New York.

> "With heart full of love and gratitude, I now take my leave of you. I most devoutly wish that your later days be as prosperous and as happy as your former ones have been glorious and honorable."[11]

A few weeks later, Congress offered a tribute to the General in a public ceremony which an eyewitness describes:

> It was a solemn and affecting spectacle....The spectators all wept, and there was hardly a member of Congress who did not drop tears. The General's hand which held the address shook as he read it. When he spoke of the officers who had composed his family, and recommended those who had continued in it to the present moment to the favorable notice of Congress he was obliged to support the paper with both hands. But when he commended the interests of his dearest country to almighty God...his voice faltered and sunk, and the whole house felt his agitations. After the pause which was necessary for him to recover himself, he proceeded to say in the most penetrating manner, "having now finished the work assigned to me I retire from the great theatre of action, and bidding an affectionate farewell to this august body under whose orders I have so long acted I here offer my commission and take leave of all the employments of public life." So saying he drew out from his bosom his commission and delivered it up to the president of Congress. He then returned to his station, when the president read the reply that had been prepared.[12]

STATE GOVERNMENTS

Even before the Declaration of Independence, colonies had begun to transform themselves and establish new governments. In contrast to the English, Americans insisted upon written constitutions. After all, colonists had a history of using royal charters as buffers against the Crown's unwarranted intrusion into their internal affairs. That, and fear of an overly powerful state, led them to set forth explicitly and with some precision the rights of the citizenry, safeguards to these rights, and the duties and limits of government.

A typical constitution provided for a bill of rights, an executive, a legislature, and a judiciary, and although a plan of checks and balances was not apparent, there was, in fact, a separation of powers. These documents placed severe limitations on the power of the executive so that a governor usually could not control the legislature, veto legislation, or establish courts. The governor shared the appointments to executive or judicial areas with the legislature. Subject to annual elections (often by the legislatures themselves), governors also could be impeached.

Power to levy taxes and form alliances belonged to the legislatures, and for these bodies, great emphasis was placed on annual elections and residence requirements. All states but Pennsylvania, Georgia, and Vermont established both a lower house and an upper house. It was intended that the latter be composed of people of stature and wisdom who would guard against well-intentioned (and not so well-intentioned) but unwise actions of the populace. French intellectuals were particularly taken by the Pennsylvania constitution with its highly democratic provisions and unicameral legislature. They deemed it "rational", for with the people as rulers, an upper house and other checks are rendered superfluous.[13]

Development of state constitutions by these earnest Americans was an important epoch in constitutional history and the quest for self-rule. These documents, derived from both the English system and from American experience before and during the revolutionary era, offered a republican form of government, albeit one in which not all could participate. A passage from Forrest McDonald sheds some light on the reasons for barriers to participation.

> "Women were excluded because "nature has made them fittest for domestic cares" and unfitted them for "the great business of life, and the hardy enterprises of war, as well as the arduous cares of state." Children, servants, and the propertyless were excluded because they were "too little acquainted with public affairs to form a right judgement, and too dependent upon other men to have a will of their own."[14]

Nonetheless, these constitutions embodied many ideas of the Enlightenment along with those of previous epochs, and were studied and debated here and abroad. The analysis that went into their formation became useful later, when it was time to design a national constitution.

THE ARTICLES OF CONFEDERATION

With independence declared, the need for a permanent central government was obvious. The Second Continental Congress appointed a committee, led by John Dickinson, which quickly developed a plan called the Articles of Confederation. For over a year, Congressmen, who were busy enough overseeing the war, debated these articles and on November 15, 1777, reached an agreement. The revised articles were then sent to the states under the proviso that each state must ratify the document before it went into effect. Because of conflicts over the claims of some states to the western lands, ratification was not completed until March 1781. The new Congress of the Confederation assumed office in November of that year with John Hanson chosen to chair congressional meetings.

The Articles of Confederation numbered thirteen. The first proclaimed the name of the confederacy to be The United States of America. Intended to preserve individual liberties and restrain central government, Article Two declared that each state was to retain "...its sovereignty, freedom, and independence, and every power, jurisdiction, and right which is not by this confederation expressly delegated to the United States, in Congress assembled."

Congress was the most important body established by the Articles, and although each state possessed one vote, each could send from two to seven delegates to that national body. The approval of nine states was required on matters deemed to be most important-- the power to declare and conduct war, to appoint a commander-in-chief, to conclude treaties, to coin money, and to borrow money. A simple majority vote was deemed sufficient to regulate Indian affairs, to develop a postal system, and to establish a national system of weights and measures.

Congress also carried out executive functions through appointed committees. When Congress was in recess, a committee composed of one delegate from each state could use the congressional powers on matters of lesser importance. Although the Articles did not create a national judiciary, Congress had the authority to set up courts to try piracy cases and to establish committees for resolution of disputes among the states.

One potentially troublesome aspect of the Articles stemmed from the denial to Congress of any power to enforce its decisions. In addition, the ability to negotiate change--a basic condition for any successful government--was virtually negated by the requirement that an amendment to the Articles receive unanimous approval of the thirteen states. Nonetheless, the citizenry warmly greeted the adoption of this document.

Not only did the Articles legitimatize the work of the Second Continental Congress, but there was widespread hope that they might created a "perpetual union." Indicative of this aspiration is the Great Seal which was adopted in 1782, and continues in use today. Its eagle (symbolic of imperial Rome) holds an olive branch in one talon and a sheaf of arrows in the other. E Pluribus Unum is inscribed in the ribbon it holds in its beak. On the other side of the seal is a stone pyramid to indicate permanence and on top of that is the eye of Divine Providence. There are also two Latin mottoes suggested in the poetry of Virgil: ANNUIT COEPTIS which means "he has favored our undertakings;" and NOVUS ORDO SECLORUM. "A New Cycle of Centuries." Trained in the classics,

American leaders hoped they were inaugurating a new heaven-born generation predicted by the Latin poet.[15]

The successful conclusion of the American Revolution represents a major triumph of government under the Articles of Confederation. Also, of great consequence, national land policies--the Ordinances of 1785 and 1787--provided for the relatively orderly settlement of western territories. Allowing new sovereign states to be formed and political liberties extended facilitated the mobility of capital and labor. During the few years of the Article's existence, an energetic and rapidly growing population sought out new domestic and foreign markets, formed voluntary societies to promote manufacturing, and established a variety of new enterprises. Victory, however, did not insure prosperity and these accomplishments tended to be overshadowed by problems most profound.

PROBLEMS OF THE NEW UNION

First of all, British mercantilism now worked against the United States. No longer the recipient of bounties, American exports became subject to the import restrictions of England as well as of other nations, and it would take time to develop new markets. The seriousness of this problem, however, was dwarfed by other immediate concerns.

The Revolutionary War (and this is true of any military conflict) entailed a reallocation of land, labor, and capital from civilian to military use. Ideally, the financial wherewithal for such an effort should come from an imposition of taxes which would cause the demand for private goods to decline and provide government with the funds to obtain the resources needed to wage war. Tax revenues, however, proved woefully inadequate and the authorities resorted to other measures. To describe as gigantic the financial problems of this fledgling nation (both during the war and in its aftermath) is to indulge in understatement.

Who could levy taxes? Under what circumstances might they be collected? These were highly charged subjects. Jealous of their sovereignty, the states, under the Articles of Confederation, had denied the right of taxation to the central government. The latter could only requisition funds on the basis of the estimated value of each state's land and improvements thereon. Following the requisition, it was up to the states to impose the taxes to meet it. As things turned out, determining the value of land and improvements was difficult indeed. States never came up with all the money requested, and the central government held no power to force them to do so. England, one may recall, had experienced similar difficulties but a short time before.

During the war, the central government sometimes could not, at times, pay the Continental Army soldiers their wages, and some of them had threatened to mutiny. Congress tried--with little success--to regulate prices and profits and even resorted to forcibly requisitioning supplies--a move met with fierce and sometimes violent resistance. Some suggested that Washington should take his army and reform these civilian governments, but he refused to succumb to these and other improper pressures. As Jefferson recalled, "The moderation and virtue of a single character prevented this revolution from being closed, as most others have been, by a subversion of the liberty it was intended to establish."[16] Congress also resorted to borrowing, but its inability to pay even the interest due on existing debts limited its domestic and foreign sources of credit, especially with the outcome of the war uncertain.

To meet all these problems, the Continental Congress and the states themselves printed up tremendous amounts of money--over 226 million dollars worth by Congress alone between the years 1775 and 1779. This issuance of paper currency took place during a time when the production of civilian goods was declining, and this combination caused an inflation of no small magnitude. In fact, prices by 1781 had risen 135 times over their value in 1775.[17] This not only resulted in an expropriation of property but interfered with economic intercourse, especially debtor/creditor relationships. As Oscar and Mary Handlin have slyly observed, "Creditors desperately sought a measure of protection against rapacious debtors who pursued them with payments in worthless paper."[18]

During the 1780's, both the states and the central government had so overissued currencies that their values were greatly depressed--often to the point of virtual worthlessness. In addition, tender laws were removed and this resulted in the withdrawal of these currencies from circulation. This and the shortage of specie caused commodity prices to adjust downward which in turn brought hardship to debtors and some businesses. Also around this time, some states began to impose taxes in order to pay off their war bonds. Taken together, these events caused much consternation within the nation.

The case of Massachusetts, while not quite typical in its outcome, nonetheless, illustrates some of the problems and dangers of economic and political life under the Articles. To pay off its bonds, Massachusetts had levied taxes on real estate and these taxes fell most heavily on farmers. Because deflation had depressed commodity prices, the farmers now had to sell more of their crops to obtain any given amount of money, including, of course, the money owed to the government.

In essence, taxes were to be excised from farmers who tended to reside in the western part of the state and the monies were to be transferred to bondholders more apt to be of a merchant class gathered on the eastern seaboard. To rub a little salt in the wound, some bondholders would receive more purchasing power then they had lent while the farmers would face debtors prison or loss of their property.

By 1786, many of the debtors were so incensed by the state of these affairs that they refused to pay their taxes and mobs in some cities prevented courts from sitting. In January of 1787, under the leadership of Daniel Shays, a former captain in the Continental Army, about two thousand of these rebels marched on Springfield in order to seize its arsenal and prevent the courts from collecting debts. Although the state militia put down this insurrection, many found Shays' Rebellion deeply disturbing. What if the militia had been unable to stop it? The central government was most unlikely to offer help, and a weak central government unable to provide law and order worried many thinking people throughout the nation.[19] Shays, moreover, had more than a few sympathizers, many of whom were elected to office in the following year and promptly began passing laws to provide relief for debtors.

Men of property were anxious and Torries delighted. When it came to matters of debt and its repudiation, Thomas Jefferson assumed a consistently conservative stance and certainly did not condone the actions of Shays and his followers. Nonetheless, Jefferson hesitated to see them punished harshly, because "The people are the only censors of their governors: and even their errors will tend to keep these to the true principles of their institution. To punish these errors too severely would be to suppress the only safeguard of the public liberty."[20] And in a letter to Abigail Adams: "The spirit of resistance to government is so valuable on certain occasions, that I wish it to be always kept alive. It will often be exercised when wrong, but better so than not to be exercised at all. I like a little rebellion now and then. It is like a storm in the Atmosphere."[21] To those in Europe who perceived America to be in a state of anarchy, Jefferson offered a spirited reply. He pointed out that one rebellion in a century and a half is not a very bad record and asked "... what country can preserve its liberties if their rulers are not warned from time to time that their people preserve the spirit of resistance?...The tree of liberty must be refreshed from time to time with the blood of patriots and tyrants."[22]

Serious problems also developed in the area of international diplomacy. England had refused to abide by provisions of the Treaty of Paris, which required the removal of its troops from military posts near the Great Lakes. The British noted with some truth that America was not fully living up to its own treaty obligations either. In fact, the states had made it difficult for Tories to recover prewar debts and refused to return Tory property confiscated during the war. In addition, Spain continued to stir up trouble in the southwest, and pirates off the coast of Africa had seized American ships and enslaved their crews.

The central government, sad to say, could do little to remedy these problems. Less than eight hundred soldiers comprised the nation's army, its navy was nonexistent, and Congress lacked funds to ransom kidnapped vessels and their crews. States could not be compelled to honor treaty obligations with Britain, nor could British troops be forced from American soil. Even if additional treaties were negotiated with other nations, Congress did not possess the power to insure that states would honor their terms. Congress itself frequently could not obtain even a quorum to conduct its business. With cause did many nations view the future of the United States as bleak.

The conduct of the state legislatures also left something to be desired. Many differed in character from when they were established. Office holders were now more numerous, more rural, more political, and less educated and they made for legislatures of countless interests all clamoring for advantage. The continuous enactment, amendment, and repeal of laws by state legislatures led James Madison to observe that more legislation had been passed in the ten years since independence then during the entire colonial period.

Legislatures often overreached their authorities and assumed executive and judicial functions. Jury trials were declared invalid, newspapers were destroyed, and laws were enacted in contradiction to state constitutions. Further consternation arose with the issuance of excessive amounts of paper money and the passage of laws assisting debtors. At the behest of politically powerful farmers, Rhode Island first allowed paper money to be printed and then after its value depreciated, made the refusal of creditors to accept it a felony. And for a second offence, one could lose his rights as a citizen. When the court declared these policies unconstitutional, its judges were dismissed by the legislature. Under such conditions, merchants began to take their businesses elsewhere. In fact, the ubiquitous use of government to foster business activities of dubious ethical standards led this state to become known as "Rogues Island."[23]

Although some states had begun to address these problems through constitutional revisions, many citizens continued to find legislatures most untrustworthy. As Thomas Jefferson remarked about the Virginia legislature:

> All the powers of government, legislative, executive, and judiciary, result to the legislative body. The concentrating these in the same hands is precisely the definition of despotic government. It will be no alleviation that these powers will be exercised by a plurality of hands, and not by a single one. 173 despots would surely be as oppressive as one.... An *elective despotism* was not the government we fought for; but one which should not only be founded on free principles, but in which the powers of government should be so divided and balanced among several bodies of magistracy, as that no one could transcend their legal limits, without being effectively checked and restrained by the others."[24]

Legislative office holders, moreover, tended to represent only their own districts and appeared little interested in the common good. An absence of public spirit had helped insure the downfall of other republics in history, and this unhappy trait seemed increasingly common in America.

Last, but assuredly not least, were problems between the states themselves, and of particular importance were problems of tariffs. With the unhappy experience of the British Navigation Acts still fresh in memory, the Articles of Confederation had denied power to the central government to regulate either domestic or foreign commerce. States, not Congress, had the power to tax imports, with each state free to establish its own rates. Often one state would treat another as if it were a foreign nation. Connecticut, for instance, levied duties on goods imported from England that were lower than duties imposed on the produce of Massachusetts. Pennsylvania discriminated against Delaware; New York against New Jersey. This type of commercial warfare not only diminished trade, it but also seriously undermined the ability of the central government to negotiate foreign treaties.

To deal with such interstate trade problems, James Madison, Governor of Virginia, proposed a national convention, and in September, 1786, a group of delegates from five of the states met in Annapolis, Maryland. They quickly perceived a variety of serious problems to be inextricably bound up with what they had come to discuss and forwarded a report to Congress requesting another convention. At the instigation of Alexander Hamilton, Congress thereupon called for another convention to meet on May 2, 1787, "for the sole and express purpose of revising the Articles of Confederation," and to "render the federal constitution adequate to the exigencies of government, and the preservation of the Union."[25] Philadelphia, because of its central location, became the site of what turned out to be a surpassingly significant event.

[1] Robert Middlekauff, *The Glorious Cause* (New York: Oxford University Press, 1982), pp. 549-555.
[2] Oscar Handlin and Mary Handlin, *Liberty in Expansion 1760-1850* (New York: Harper & Row Publishers, 1989), p.260.
[3] Ibid., pp. 334-336,464,468.
[4] Forest Mc Donald, *Novus Ordo Seclorum: The Intellectual Origins of the Constitution* (Lawrence: University of Kansas Press, 1985), p.2.
[5] Robert Middlekauff, *The Glorious Cause*, pp. 512-519.
[6] Thomas Paine quoted in Samuel Eliot Morison, *The Oxford History of The American People* (New York: Oxford University Press, 1965), pp.244,245.
[7] William A. Gregorio, *The Complete Book of Presidents* (New York: Dembner Books, 1984), p.6.
[8] Oscar Handlin and Mary Handlin, *Liberty in Expansion 1760-1850* (New York: Harper & Row, Publishers, 1989), p.109.
[9] Robert MIddlekauff, *The Glorious Cause*, pp. 496-510.
[10] Samuel Eliot Morison, *The Oxford History of The American People*, p.265.
[11] George Washington quoted in Benjamin Hart, *Faith and Freedom* (Dallas: Lewis and Stanley, 1988), p. 299.
[12] Samuel Eliot Morison, *The Oxford History of The American People*, p. 269.
[13] Ibid., pp. 270-276.
[14] Forest McDonald, *Novus Ordo Seclorum: The Intellectual Origins of the Constitution*, p. 161.
[15] Samuel Eliot Morison, *The Oxford History of The American People*, pp.280,281.
[16] James Thomas Flexner, "George Washington-What a Guy!," *The New York Times*, April 29,1989.
[17] Barry W. Poulson, *Economic History Of The United States* (New York: Macmillan publishing Co., Inc., 1981), pp.105-109.
[18] Oscar Handlin and Mary Flugg Handlin, *Commonwealth,* rev. ed. (Cambridge: Harvard University Press, the Belknap Press, 1969), p. 23.
[19] James Thomas Flexner, *Washington: The Indispensable Man* (Boston: Little, Brown and Company, 1974), p.200.
[20] Thomas Jefferson to Edward Carrington in *Thomas Jefferson* (New York: The Library Of America,1984), p.880.
[21] Thomas Jefferson to Abigail Adams in *Thomas Jefferson* (New York: The Library Of America, 1984), pp. 889,890.
[22] Thomas Jefferson to William S. Smith in *Thomas Jefferson* (New York: The Library Of America,1984), p.911.
[23] Forest McDonald, *Novus Ordo Seclorum: The Intellectual Origins of the Constitution*, pp. 175,176.
[24] Thomas Jefferson, *Notes on the State of Virginia* in *Thomas Jefferson* (New York: The Library Of America, 1984), p.245.
[25] Samuel Eliot Morison, *The Oxford History of The American People*, p.305.

CHAPTER 7

THE UNITED STATES CONSTITUTION: POLITICAL FREEDOM

THE CONSTITUTIONAL CONVENTION

When America declared independence, its leaders certainly did not envision a strong central government for the new nation. After all, the revolution was being fought against a powerful central government far removed from the people, and if anyone in 1776 had proposed the constitutional structure established in 1787, he probably would have been called a monarchist. Experience under the Articles of Confederation, however, had elicited a substantially different attitude.

On May 25, 1787, fifty-five delegates representing all states but Rhode Island, began to carry out the work of the Convention. Among this group of delegates characterized by Jefferson as an "assembly of demigods," forty-six were American born. Samuel Eliot Morison notes that "Practically every American who had useful ideas on political science was there except John Adams and Thomas Jefferson on foreign missions and John Jay, busy with foreign relations of the Confederation.[1]

Characteristic of most of the delegates was their commitment to a stronger national government. Madison thought it would provide the basis for law and order; Hamilton viewed it as a necessity for improving commerce; Franklin and Washington saw it as a prerequisite for diplomatic and economic success.

American leaders of more provincial outlook were wont to absent themselves from the convention because they correctly perceived the gathering to be one of nationalists (Patrick Henry "smelt a rat"[2]), which they had small interest in legitimizing. Further, they knew that amending the Articles of Confederation required approval of all the states, so there seemed to be little at stake in staying home--or so they thought. Luther Martin of Maryland, Elbridge Gerry of Massachusetts, and George Mason of Virginia shared this philosophy but attended the convention anyway and remained throughout its proceedings. Others departed after a short time when they realized what was going on.

The Convention selected George Washington as its president. Like the famed Roman general Cincinnatus who returned to his farm after enjoying military successes, Washington, to the amazement of many, had also retired from public life. His voluntary relinquishment of power was a moral act of high order and was considered so in his time.[3] As Madison wrote in a letter to Jefferson about this patriot. "To forsake the honorable retreat to which he had retired and risk the reputation he had so deservedly acquired, manifested a zeal for the public interest that could, after so many and illustrious services, scarcely have been expected of him."[4] And with these words did Washington set the tone of the Convention:

> If, to please the people, we offer what we ourselves disapprove, how can we afterward defend our work? Let us raise a standard to which the wise and honest can repair; the event is in the hands of God.[5]

Meetings were held in rooms guarded by sentries and inaccessible to the public. Delegates swore to keep the proceedings secret lest tensions and pressures build outside the rooms and disrupt their work. William Jackson maintained an outline of the closed proceedings, and James Madison set down a more thorough account. The latter work, published posthumously in 1840 remains a vital document of the Convention's activities.

It quickly became apparent to many of the delegates that simply revising the Articles of Confederation--the task to which they had been charged by Congress--would not be sufficient to deal with the new nation's problems. Thereupon, they embarked on the greater project of creating a different legal foundation and a new government. On September 17, 1787, thirty-nine of the forty-two delegates still in attendance approved the Constitution. Thereupon, copies of the final draft, written by Gouverneur Morris were sent to each of the states for ratification.

THE UNITED STATES CONSTITUTION

Unlike many national constitutions written since 1787, the U.S. Constitution is brief enough to carry in one's pocket. Its contents--a preamble and seven articles--are summarized below.

The Preamble to the Constitution of the United States of America explains the purposes and goals of the document, the rationale for legislative enactments and the exercise of government power. Most Americans are familiar with its words.

> We The People of the United States, in Order to form a more perfect Union, establish Justice, insure domestic Tranquility, provide for the common defense, promote the general Welfare, and secure the Blessings of Liberty to ourselves and our Posterity, do ordain and establish this Constitution for the United States of America.

Article I Virtually half of the Constitution is devoted to the legislature, the subject of this article. Specific issues include eligibility to hold office; the powers of Congress; activities prohibited to this bicameral body; and the powers denied to the states.

Article II treats the executive branch of the federal government which consists of a President, a Vice-President and other officials. This article sets forth eligibility requirements; conditions for election; the powers and duties of the executive branch (which are broader and more substantial than under the Articles of Confederation), and procedures for removing executive officials from office.

Article III establishes a judiciary and explains its powers and jurisdiction, as well as the conditions under which judges hold office.

Article IV presents the rights of the states and their citizens, along with the criteria for admission of new states into the union.

Article V explains how the Constitution may be amended.

Article VI upholds the validity of debts contracted under the Articles of Confederation. It also proclaims that the Constitution and laws of the United States made in pursuance thereof, "shall be the Supreme law of the Land," which judges are bound to obey, the constitutions or laws of the states notwithstanding. Finally, this article prohibits a religious test as a requirement for holding public office.

Article VII states that, "The Ratifications of Conventions of nine States shall be sufficient for the Establishment of this Constitution between the States ratifying the Same".

Thirty-nine delegates--a great majority-- signed the document, and each state had at least one representative signature. Thereafter, state conventions were held with delegates elected by the people for the purpose of determining whether or not each state would ratify the Constitution. Intense debate spread throughout the country and found its way into public addresses, articles, and even poetry. As the controversy gathered steam, two parties, the Federalist and the Anti-Federalist, emerged and proceeded to engage in an historically great and robust debate.

Federalists wanted a complex commercial republic with a strong central government that would not impinge upon liberty. As such, the new constitution received their strong support. Notable on the Federalist side were essays published in newspapers under the anonymous signature Publius, a man instrumental in establishing republicanism in the government of ancient Rome. Writers of political essays in the eighteenth century sometimes employed pseudonyms, often taken from Plutarch, with the intention of conveying their stance to readers.[6] Actually written rather hastily by Alexander Hamilton, James Madison, and John Jay, they were later collected into a book, *The Federalist*, which has become recognized as an important contribution to the theory of government and one of the great documents of American history. Thomas Jefferson called it the "best commentary on the principles of government which was ever written."[7]

Anti-Federalists including George Mason, Richard Henry Lee, and Patrick Henry (it "Squints toward monarchy")[8] led the charge against ratification of the Constitution. Some also used the nom de plume device--Cato, Brutus, and Cassius--when signing. Overall, the anti-Federalists tended to be more simple, less sophisticated folk who would have preferred several small sovereign republics to a strong central government. In their thinking they relied more heavily upon civic virtue than did the Federalists. Also, they feared the proposed constitution would elicit an excess of devotion to commerce and competition, which in turn would generate extremes of wealth and poverty. These people sought order and equality in life; they looked favorably on a government that would promote public morality and even religion. According to Anti-Federalists, the Federalists, were using commerce as a substitute for morals.

It was clear from the beginning that under the Constitution, the people of the United States would enjoy inalienable rights, and the central government would possess powers. Both the Federalists and the Anti-Federalists wanted the Constitution to defend citizen rights, but the Anti-Federalist found it deficient in this regard. Specifically, they believed the executive branch would be too powerful, members of the House of Representatives too few, and the authority of states too weak. Afraid that by ratifying the Constitution the people would surrender their power to a privileged few, they accused Federalists of sympathizing with the aristocracy, and lest monarchy and tyranny result, they demanded more elections, more direct elections, and a bill of rights. Intrinsic to this attitude was the fear that the real interests of the common people would be neglected while the very different objectives of the aristocracy were promoted. Moreover, they felt that solutions to foreign and domestic problems could be provided by simply amending the Articles of Confederation. The Anti-Federalist position is, perhaps, best represented by Richard Henry Lee's, *Letters from the Federal Farmer to the Republican.*

On December 7, 1787, Delaware became the first state to ratify the Constitution, and Pennsylvania and New Jersey voted in its favor before the year ended. Georgia, Connecticut, Massachusetts, Maryland, and South Carolina followed suit in 1788, and in June of that year, the vote of New Hampshire, the ninth state to take an affirmative position, made it possible to put the document into effect. Virginia and New York also voted for ratification later in 1788, and the national government had already begun to operate before North Carolina and Rhode Island gave approval in 1789 and 1790, respectively.

Not everyone, however, participated in the ratification process. States determined who could vote and excluded children, women, most blacks, and white males who failed to meet franchise requirements because of insufficient property holdings. While twentieth century Americans find adult suffrage restrictions appalling, one should remember that rule by king and aristocracy was the eighteenth century norm. The United States in 1787 provided the most extensive franchise in the world, and what the framers of the Constitution set forth in terms of government structure was truly unique.

The two men considered most responsible for the development and adoption of the Constitution were George Washington and James Madison. The former, the father of his country and a man with whom many Americans identified, presided over the convention, made use of his remarkable ability to bring together the diverse ideas of very different people, and gave the document his endorsement. He thought it "little short of a miracle" that so many different delegates from such diverse states could join in forming this new governmental structure. The latter, James Madison (Thomas Jefferson called him "the greatest man in the world") possessed a strong sense of morality and purpose as well as a deliberative nature. Short, slight, and shy, and was sometimes referred to as "Little Jimmy--no bigger than half a cake of soap."[9] Treasury Secretary Albert Gallatin described him as "...slow in taking his ground, but firm when the storm rises."[10] This scholarly graduate of the College of New Jersey who later became Secretary of State, twice the President of the United States, and Rector of the University of Virginia, arrived in Philadelphia with a plan to strengthen the national government while simultaneously providing safeguards against tyrannical tendencies. Madison worked assiduously to secure these ideals and became known as the father of the U.S. Constitution.

There is one more person who should be remembered as influential in the making of this constitution, and that is Benjamin Franklin (1706-1790). Born in Boston, he moved, to Philadelphia at age seventeen to get away from his brother under whom he had served as a printer's apprentice. He started a newspaper, the *Pennsylvania Gazette*, and then published *Poor Richard's Almanac*, an immensely popular collection of aphorisms. Despite a formal education that ended when he was ten, Franklin helped to improve Philadelphia's streets, founded a philosophical society, a hospital, a library, a fire insurance company, as well as the academy that evolved into the University of Pennsylvania. He invented an efficient home heating stove, bifocal spectacles, and the lightening rod. His observations on electricity, climate, medicine, and botany won him widespread acclamation from scientific communities.

This most colorful individual served as deputy postmaster general for North America and journeyed to England as an agent for several American colonies. Eventually he promoted independence (much to the consternation of his son William, who just happened to be the Royal Governor of New Jersey), became a member of the Continental Congress, and then ambassador to France, where he captivated the populace with his charm and rustic colonial dress, led that nation to an alliance with the colonies, and successfully negotiated loans from it. When news of his death reached Europe, the French National Assembly declared a period of national mourning. He also set forth some economic ideas which will wait for presentation until the following chapter. At this point our concern is with his activities during the Constitutional Convention.

Benjamin Franklin led the Pennsylvania delegation to the Constitutional Convention and although advanced age had dealt him some infirmities, he managed to travel to and from meetings in a sedan chair. Because he was unable to stand on his feet for very long, some of his speeches were read to the delegates by James Wilson. Nonetheless, Franklin summoned the energy to entertain delegates with tea and conversation under the tree by his house near Independence Hall. He advanced some ideas that were respectfully rejected and supported some that met with general approval. But it is his role as master conciliator that merits our attention.

At the time of the Constitutional Convention, Benjamin Franklin was thought to be the wisest man in America. And this high esteem extended across the ocean. The philosopher David Hume, for instance, called him, "the first philosopher and indeed the first great man of letters for whom we are beholden to America."[11] Moreover, this regard for his wisdom was mixed with a strong dose of affection. Thus, when Franklin spoke, people listened. And speak he did at this convention. At one point, when delegates' exchanges became rancorous, Franklin, hardly renowned for his piety, proposed that "henceforth, Prayers imploring the assistance of Heaven and its blessings on our Deliberations, be held in this assembly every morning" and observed that without God's aid, "we shall succeed in this Building no better than the Builders of Babel."[12] Although the motion met with defeat (the delegates could not decide on the proper mode of prayer and not being on expense accounts, could not have afforded a chaplain even if they had reached an agreement), Franklin succeeded in reducing acrimony and paved the way for

"The Great Compromise" which accorded each state equal representation in the Senate and proportionate representation in the House.

When the final draft of the Constitution was approved, Franklin addressed the delegates in the hope that all would sign the document despite the fact that some had misgivings. It is a speech (read by Wilson) that remains a classic, not only for its persuasiveness but because it epitomizes the historically famous ability of Americans to compromise:

> ...when you assemble a number of Men to have the advantage of their advanced Wisdom, you inevitably assemble with those Men all their Prejudices, their Passions, their errors of Opinion, their local Interests, and their selfish Views. From such an Assembly can a perfect Production be expected? It therefore astonishes me, Sir, to find this system approaching so near to Perfection as it does; and I think it will astonish our Enemies, who are waiting with Confidence to hear that our Councils are confounded like those of The Builders of Babel, and that our States are on the Point of Separation, only to meet hereafter for the Purpose of cutting one anothers Throats. Thus, I consent to this Constitution because I expect no better, and because I am not sure that it is not the best. The Opinions I have had of its Errors, I sacrifice to the Public Good.[13]

After these words, all but three of the delegates signed the document. Franklin's address was printed and widely distributed because of its importance during the ratification debates.

One more Franklin story; this one related by James Madison.

> Whilst the last members were signing it, Doctor Franklin looking towards the Presidents chair, at the back of which a rising sun happened to be painted, observed to a few members near him, that painters had found it difficult to distinguish in their art a rising from a setting sun. I have, said he, often and often in the course of the session, and the vicissitudes of my hopes and fears as to its issue, looked at that behind the President without being able to tell whether it was rising or setting: But now at length I have the happiness to know that it is a rising and not a setting sun.[14]

In January, 1789, after the New Hampshire ratification, Congress chose Presidential electors, and they made their choices in February. George Washington and his first administration took office in March. The first federal republic in history had begun. The unprecedented nature of these processes and events has been captured by de Tocqueville:

> It is new in the history of society to see a great people turn a calm and scrutinizing eye upon itself when apprised by the legislature that the wheels of its government are stopped, to see it carefully examine the extent of the evil, and patiently wait two whole years until a remedy is discovered, to which it voluntarily submitted without its costing a tear or a drop of blood from mankind.[15]

The emergence of a bill of rights provides an interesting postscript to this discussion. Anti-Federalists were not the only ones concerned by an absence of the written guarantees which such a bill might offer. Jefferson, for instance, favored a bill of rights and believed it might be used to remind future generations about their rights. On the other hand, many of the framers (including Hamilton) who saw little sense in stating "that things shall not be done which there is no power to do," thought it unnecessary.[16] After all, most of the state constitutions contained a bill of rights; checks and balances had been woven into the Constitution; and Congress, with its powers enumerated, lacked the power to legislate against inalienable rights. Also, there was fear that such a bill would imply that rights unspecified in it would not warrant protection.

The struggle between these opposing forces became so intense that in the midst of the ratification process, to insure the Constitution's adoption, a bill of rights was promised--a promise, wonder of wonders, that was kept. From a large number of proposed amendments, twelve were submitted to the first Congress and ten were adopted. These first ten amendments, referred to as the Bill of Rights, are an integral part of the Constitution; a part designed by the states to restrain the powers of the federal government. One should also note that these rights were not considered as grants from the government, but were held to be "natural" and therefore "inalienable."

POWER AND HUMAN NATURE

Although some of the men who framed the Constitution were enamoured with enlightenment ideas, they also knew their Adam Smith, and they saw man as far from perfect, with the possibility of reaching perfection remote indeed. To these framers, self-interest dominates human nature, and the Constitution reflects this perspective. The Scottish philosopher and historian David Hume, who died the same year the colonists declared for independence, wrote an essay, *On the Independence in Parliament,* which also informed the thinking of the Constitution's creators:

> that, in contriving any system of government, and fixing the several checks and controls of the constitution, every man ought to be supposed a knave, and to have no other end, in all his actions, than private interest. By this interest we must govern him, and, by means of it, make him, notwithstanding his insatiable avarice and ambition, co-operate to public good.[17]

Not surprisingly, this theme is developed by James Madison in *The Federalist* No. 51:

> But what is government itself but the greatest of all reflections on human nature? If men were angels, no government would be necessary. If angels were to govern men, neither external nor internal controls on government would be necessary. In framing a government which is to be administered by men over men, the great difficulty lies in this: You must first enable the government to control the governed; and in the next place, oblige it to control itself. A dependence on the people is no doubt the primary control on the government; but experience has taught mankind the necessity of auxiliary precautions.[18]

Alexander Hamilton expresses a similar sentiment in *The Federalist* No. 15:

> Why has government been instituted at all? Because the passions of men will not conform to the dictates of reason and justice, without constraint.... Power controlled or

abridged is almost always the rival and enemy of that power by which it is controlled or abridged. This simple proposition will teach us how little reason there is to expect, that the persons, entrusted with the administration of the affairs of the particular members of a confederacy, will at all times be ready, with perfect good humor, and an unbiased regard to the public weal, to execute the resolutions or decrees of the general authority. The reverse of this results from the constitution of human nature.[19]

Man, however should not be considered totally egoistic. According to Madison in *The Federalist* No. 55:

> As there is a degree of depravity in mankind which requires a certain degree of circumspection and distrust: So there are other qualities in human nature, which justify a certain portion of esteem and confidence. Republican government presupposes the existence of these qualities in a higher degree than any other form.[20]

And then Hamilton in *The Federalist* No. 76:

> The institution of delegated power implies that there is a portion of virtue and honor among mankind, which may be a reasonable foundation of confidence.[21]

Madison as well as others believed that among the passions by which men are driven, those of a more lofty or more noble and heroic nature--honor, fame, love of country--might be included. They hoped that men imbued with public spirit would become the dominant breed of those who held public office. In fact, some of the framers, including Washington and Madison wished to establish a national university through which a desire to serve a much beloved country would be instilled among its finest young men.[22]

But despite these hopes for public spirited government officials, the framers recognized that self-aggrandizement is inherent to human nature. They saw how this truth bred problems associated with delegation of power. In addition, they had witnessed power's abuse by Britain as well as by the newly formed states, and they understood that the very nature of government is to force people to do things they generally would not do on their own--to pay taxes or to join the army, for example--and that enforcement is based on power. Therefore, because government is staffed by human beings, a danger presents itself: that a lust for power and wealth may be placed before the common good.

How then, to prevent a person or group with government power from seizing control of the new central government and imposing tyranny? How to control power and prevent the harm from its unwarranted exercise? How to establish a government that would be stable, yet open to change while preserving freedom? In answer to these questions, the framers created a constitutional system wherein certain rights were held inalienable, and which provided for an extended compound federal republic that separated, checked and balanced different branches of government and made those who would govern responsible to the governed.

Montesquieu in *The Spirit of the Laws,* warns of the dangers to liberty when one or even two branches of government exercise executive, legislative, and judicial powers and the framers took his words to heart. An American President may veto laws of Congress, and the Senate may reject his appointments or a treaty negotiated by the executive office. If the President or another federal official is thought to have committed a crime, he may be formally accused (impeached) by the House of Representatives and tried in the Senate. The United States Supreme Court may find state or federal legislation inconsistent with the Constitution and declare it null and void. This process of judicial review is not explicitly mentioned in the Constitution but evolved from interpretations of it as the 'Supreme law of the Land" (words lifted from the Magna Carta). Judicial review helps to determine the residence of power--with the Congress, the President, the judiciary, the state, or the people freely acting on their own.

When interpreting the Constitution, Supreme Court justices have relied upon the wording of that document, the intentions of the framers, the intentions of Congress when the law was enacted, and their own deliberations concerning Constitutional meaning. The Supreme Court lacks the military and financial resources to enforce its decisions directly. Its power is one of moral authority and the framers surely never intended it to assume an "activist" posture. Worth noting in this matter are Alexander Hamilton's observations in *The Federalist* No. 78:

> Whoever attentively considers the different departments of power must perceive, that in a government in which they are separated from each other, the judiciary, from the nature of its functions, will always be the least dangerous to the political rights of the constitution; because it will be least in a capacity to annoy or injure them. The executive not only dispenses the honors, but holds the sword of the community. The legislature not only commands the purse, but prescribes the rules by which the duties and rights of every citizen are to be regulated. The judiciary on the contrary has no influence over either the sword or the purse, no direction either of the strength or of the wealth of the society, and can take no active resolution whatever. It may truly be said to have neither Force nor Will, but merely judgment; and must ultimately depend upon the aid of the executive arm even for the efficacy of its judgements.
>
> This simple view of the matter suggests several important consequences. It proves incontestably that the judiciary is beyond comparison the weakest of the three departments of power; that it can never attack with success either of the other two; and that all possible care is requisite to enable it to defend itself against their attacks. It equally proves, that though individual oppression may now and then proceed from courts of justice, the general liberty of the people can never be endangered from that quarter: I mean, so long as the judiciary remains truly distinct from both the legislative and executive. For I agree that "there in no liberty, if the power of judging be not separated from the legislative and executive powers."[23]

The Constitution is not the product of common law which flows from court decisions and custom, and thus, should not be changed by common law. Instead, it is a type of statutory law but on a higher level: in fact, it is the highest law of the land. Different Supreme Courts have rendered disparate interpretations of particular issues thereby denying absolute finality to any one decision. One should note that other branches of the federal government as well as the states and their subdivisions also have the right to interpret the Constitution in matters appropriate to their constitutionally legitimate spheres of responsibility. Of course, the people possess the right to amend the constitution itself, and this rather than usurpation is the proper way to alter these spheres of responsibility. As George Washington asserted in his Farewell Address:

> If in the opinion of the people the distribution or modification of the constitutional powers be in any particular wrong, let it be corrected by an amendment in the way which the Constitution designates. But let there be no change by usurpation; for though this in one instance may be the instrument of good, it is the customary weapon by which free governments are destroyed.[24]

Well aware of the dangers of democracy, the framers particularly feared its deterioration into mob rule. "The vote" had provided the death warrant, for both Jesus and Socrates, and the worst of tyrannies was thought to be the tyranny of the majority. Checks and balances, therefore, were thought to impede any group from imposing its will on the nation through hastily conceived legislation that reflects some passionately held idea of the moment. Beyond the presidential veto (which Congress can reconsider and override with a two-thirds vote), each legislative body can prevent the other from bringing a law into existence. Senators serve six year terms which insulate them from fashionable, albeit ephemeral pressures, and judges of the Supreme Court (as well as other federal judges) receive lifetime tenure as protection from reaction to unpopular decisions. Enacting a constitutional amendment has proven to be far from easy.

The problem of "an excess of democracy" which may result from too much power is also addressed through the system of federation. The nation is governed by two basic units--federal and state--and each possesses certain powers denied to the other. That each unit depends somewhat on the other serves to check their respective powers. James Madison put it succinctly in *The Federalist* No. 51:

> In the compound republic of America, the power surrendered by the people, is first divided between two distinct governments, and then the portion allotted to each, subdivided among distinct and separate departments. Hence a double security arises to the rights of the people. The different governments will control each other; at the same time that each will be controlled by itself.[25]

The framers believed that government should be responsible to the people, with citizens the rulers served by public officials. And so beyond the checks and balances, the President and members of Congress must be elected either directly or indirectly for specified terms, and if they choose to continue in office, they must stand for re-election.

Failure of the small republics of antiquity can be traced to their adherence to an idea of how man ought to be. As we have seen, the framers of the Constitution accepted man as he is, and the checks and balances to control human avarice include division of the republic into states. Within this structure, so many different interests--"factions" to use Madison's word--over a vast geographical area tend to offset each other. In economic terms, the various interest groups would find it prohibitively costly to form the alliance necessary to realize their special interest goals.

In *The Federalist* No. 10, James Madison expands on the subject of factions:

> By a faction I understand a number of citizens, whether amounting to a majority or a minority of the whole, who are united and actuated by some common impulse of passion, or of interest, adverse to the rights of other citizens, or to the permanent and aggregate interest of the community.

There are two methods of curing the mischief's of faction: the one, by removing its causes; the other, by controlling its effects.

There are again two methods of removing the causes of faction: the one by destroying the liberty which is essential to its existence; the other, by giving to every citizen the same opinions, the same passions, and the same interests.

It could never be more truly said than of the first remedy, that it is worse than the disease. Liberty is to faction, what air is to fire, an aliment without which it instantly expires. But it could not be a less folly to abolish liberty, which is essential to political life, because it nourishes faction, than it would be to wish the annihilation of air, which is essential to animal life, because it imparts to fire its destructive agency.

The second expedient is as impracticable, as the first would be unwise. As long as the reason of man continues fallible, and he is at liberty to exercise it, different opinions will be formed. As long as the connection subsists between his reason and his self-love, his opinions and his passions will have a reciprocal influence on each other; and the former will be objects to which the latter will attach themselves....

The latent causes of faction are thus sown in the nature of man; and we see them every where brought into different degrees of activity, according to the different circumstances of civil society. A zeal for different opinions concerning religion, concerning Government and many other points, as well of speculation as of practice; an attachment to different leaders ambitiously contending for pre-eminence and power; or to persons of other descriptions whose fortunes have been interesting to the human passions, have in turn divided mankind into parties, inflamed them with mutual animosity, and rendered them much more disposed to vex and oppress each other, than to co-operate for their common good. So strong is this propensity of mankind to fall into mutual animosities, that where no substantial occasion presents itself, the most frivolous and fanciful distinctions have been sufficient to kindle their unfriendly passions, and excite their most violent conflicts. But the most common and durable source of factions has been the various and unequal distribution of property. Those who hold, and those who are without property, have ever formed distinct interests in society. Those who are creditors, and those who are debtors, fall under a like discrimination. A landed interest, a manufacturing interest, a mercantile interest, a monied interest, with many lesser interests, grow up of necessity in civilized nations, and divide them into different classes, actuated by different sentiments and views. The regulation of these various and interfering interests forms the principal task of modern Legislation, and involves the spirit of party and faction in the necessary and ordinary operations of Government....

It is in vain to say, that enlightened statesmen will be able to adjust these clashing interests, and render them all subservient to the public good. Enlightened statesmen will not always be at the helm: Nor, in many cases, can such an adjustment be made at all, without taking into view indirect and remote considerations, which will rarely prevail over the immediate interest which one party may find in disregarding the rights of another or the good of the whole.[26]

Having discussed the difficulty of controlling the causes of faction, Madison then discusses the control of its effects. He notes that"...neither moral nor religious motives can be relied on as an adequate..."[27] And a pure democracy also fails to provide effective control.

...a pure Democracy, by which I mean a Society, consisting of a small number of citizens, who assemble and administer the Government in person, can admit of no cure for the mischief's of faction. A common passion or interest will, in almost every case, be felt by a majority of the whole; a communication and concert results from the form of Government itself; and there is nothing to check the inducements to sacrifice the weaker party, or an obnoxious individual. Hence it is, that such Democracies have ever been spectacles of turbulence and contention; have ever been found incompatible with personal security, or the rights of property; and have in general been as short in their lives, as they have been violent in their deaths. Theoretic politicians, who have patronized this species of Government, have erroneously supposed, that by reducing mankind to a perfect equality in their political rights, they would, at the same time, be perfectly equalized and assimilated in their possessions, their opinions, and their passions.[28]

Madison places his faith in a republican form of government and develops David Hume's idea that such a government, wherein the citizenry delegates individuals to represent them, might be more successful in a large republic. With many states joined together it becomes more difficult for various factions to achieve their ends.

> The smaller the society, the fewer probably will be the distinct parties and interests composing it; the fewer the distinct parties and interest, the more frequently will a majority be found of the same party; and the smaller the number of individuals composing the majority, and the smaller the compass within which they are placed, the more easily will they concert and execute their plans of oppression. Extend the sphere, and you take in a greater variety of parties and interests; you make it less probable that a majority of the whole will have a common motive to invade the rights of other citizens; or if such a common motive exists, it will be more difficult for all who feel it to discover their own strength, and to act in unison with each other. Besides other impediments, it may be remarked, that where there is a consciousness of unjust or dishonorable purposes, communication is always checked by distrust, in proportion to the number whose concurrence is necessary....
>
> The influence of factious leaders may kindle a flame within their particular States, but will be unable to spread a general conflagration through the other States: a religious sect, may degenerate into a political faction in a part of the Confederacy; but the variety of sects dispersed over the entire face of it must secure the national Councils against any danger from that source: a rage for paper money, for an abolition of debts, for an equal division of property, or for any other improper or wicked project, will be less apt to pervade the whole body of the Union, than a particular member of it; in the same proportion as such a malady is more likely to taint a particular county or district than an entire State.[29]

The framers, aware that self-interest would scarcely be absent among politicians, nevertheless believed it would flow toward the political arena rather than the economic. Fame as a legislator or a political leader, they reasoned, would push aside a quest for material riches. Some politicians might be corrupt, but as faction countered faction in the private sector, so too in the public. Moreover, once elected, a national legislator would gain a perspective extending beyond purely local interests. Perhaps even more important, the framers considered it likely that the typical representative would be of an aristocratic character--well above the ordinary man.

Madison, in *The Federalist* No. 10, refers to those apt to be elected as, "...a chosen body of citizens, whose wisdom may best discern the true interest of their country, and whose patriotism and love of justice, will be likely to sacrifice it to temporary or partial consideration."[30] A major reason for the selection of such people is because in a large republic, "...it will be more difficult for unworthy candidates to practice with success, the vicious arts, by which elections are too often carried:..."[31] It is interesting to note here that Madison had lost a campaign for the Virginia Assembly by refusing to abide by the custom of providing alcoholic beverages for his constituents. Be that as it may, he goes on to add, "...and the suffrages of the people being more free, will be more likely to center on men who possess the most attractive merit, and the most diffusive and established characters."[32]

In summary, we have seen how the framers who feared a strong central government and who took human nature on its own terms, tried to provide stability, allow for change, and preserve liberty. As James Madison wrote in *The Federalist* No. 62, "A good government implies two things; first, fidelity to the object of government, which is the happiness of the people; secondly, a knowledge of the means by which that object can be best attained."[33] Their means was the creation of a Republic, wherein the powers of government are derived from the people who vote for those who would represent them in the affairs of state. On the central level, a mixed government includes Monarchical (the Executive), Aristocratic (the Senate), and Democratic (the House of Representatives) elements.[34] The powers of the different sectors are separated as the framers believed that an extended republic with horizontal and vertical checks and balances would provide a framework in which disparate interest groups would neutralize one another. It is important to note that the Constitution is a document that not only provides the foundation for political liberty but serves as the cornerstone for economic freedom as well. Next, we examine its economic dimensions.

---

[1] Samuel Eliot Morison, *The Oxford History of The American People* (New York: Oxford University Press, 1965), p.305.
[2] Catherine Drinker Bowen, *Miracle at Philadelphia*, with a Foreword by Warren E. Burger (Little, Brown and Company, 1986), P. 18.
[3] Gordon S. Wood, *The Radicalism of the American Revolution*, (New York: Alfred A. Knopf,1992), pp.205,206.
[4] James Thomas Flexner, *Washington The Indispensable Man* (Boston: Little Brown and Company, 1974), p.203.
[5] Ibid., p. 205.
[6] Forest McDonald, *Novus Ordo Seclorum: The Intellectual Origins of the Constitution* (Lawrence: University Press of Kansas, 1985), pp. 66-69.
[7] Dumas Malone, *Jefferson and The Rights of Man* (Boston: Little, Brown and Company, 1951), p. 170.
[8] Samuel Eliot Morison, *The Oxford History of The American People*, p. 315.
[9] Clarence B. Carson, *Basic American Government* (Wadley Alabama: American Textbook Committee,1993) p. 205.
[10] William A. Degregorio, *The Complete Book of U.S. Presidents* (New York: Dembner Books, 1984), p.55.
[11] Michael Zukerman, "And In The Center Ring...," *The Pennsylvania Gazette* (Philadelphia: The General Alumni Society of the University of Pennsylvania, May, 1993), p. 20.
[12] Daniel J. Boorstin, ed. *An American Primer* (New York: A Meridian Classic, Penguin Books, 1985), p.95.
[13] Ibid.,p.97.
[14] Clarence B. Carson, *Basic American Government*, p.211.

[15] Alexis de Tocqueville, *Democracy In America*, vol. 1 (New York: Vintage Books, 1957), pp. 117,118.
[16] Forest McDonald, *Novus Ordo Seclorum: The Intellectual Origins of the Constitution*, p. 269.
[17] Ibid., p. 188.
[18] Jacob E. Cooke, ed., *The Federalist* (Middletown: Wesleyan University Press, 1961), p. 349.
[19] Ibid., pp. 96,97.
[20] Ibid., p. 378.
[21] Ibid., p. 514.
[22] Forest McDonald, *Novus Ordo Seclorum: The Intellectual Origins of the Constitution*, pp. 189-191.
[23] Jacob E. Cooke, ed., The Federalist, pp. 522,523.
[24] Daniel J. Boorstin, ed., *An American Primer*, p.221.
[25] Jacob E. Cooke, *The Federalist*, p. 351.
[26] Ibid., pp. 57-60.
[27] Ibid., p. 61.
[28] Ibid., pp. 61,62.
[29] Ibid., pp. 63-65.
[30] Ibid., p. 62.
[31] Ibid., p. 63.
[32] Ibid., p. 63.
[33] Jacob E. Cooke, *The Federalist*, p.419.
[34] Clarence B. Carson, *Basic American Government*, pp. 30-33.

CHAPTER 8

THE UNITED STATES CONSTITUTION: ECONOMIC FREEDOM

Economics and politics were inseparably intertwined in 1789 and remain in a similar state today. The United States Constitution, ostensibly a political document, contains enough clauses of either direct or indirect economic relevance to classify it as an economic document as well. This chapter discusses the economic aspects of the Constitution as well as economic ideas prevalent at the time of its framing and adoption.

A FREE ENTERPRISE SYSTEM

Protection of private property and the enforcement of contracts (voluntary exchanges through which one obtained property) provide the basis of a free enterprise economy, and in late eighteenth century America, they were accorded the utmost respect. The Declaration and Resolves of the Continental Congress had stated that people were entitled to "life, liberty, and property;" abuses of the rights of property, including taxation without representation and the mandatory quartering of soldiers, helped precipitate the revolution; "liberty, property and no stamps" became one of the first slogans of the revolution; those favoring the Constitution's adoption gave the protection of property as a major reason for their support; and one need only recall the anti-federalist fight for additional safeguards which resulted in the Fifth Amendment.

Sir William Blackstone and Lord Edward Coke, the great legal authorities known to the Constitution's framers, along with John Locke, had placed great emphasis upon the positive aspects of private property. James Madison, in a letter to Jefferson concerning the proposed Constitution, asserted that, "A reform, therefore, which does not make provision for private rights, must be materially defective."[1] That same author, after noting in *The Federalist* No. 10 that not all people possess similar abilities or faculties when it came to acquiring property proclaimed, "The protection of these faculties is the first object of government."[2] And as we have already seen, the purpose of establishing an extended republic was to thwart the danger of "... a rage for paper money, for an abolition of debts, for an equal division of property, or for any other improper or wicked project..."[3] Later, in *The Federalist* No. 54 Madison observed that, "Government is instituted no less for the protection of the property, than of the persons of individuals."[4] A few years later, Madison significantly broadened the meaning he attached to property.

> In its larger and juster meaning, {property} embraces every thing to which a man may attach a value and have a right; and *which leaves to every one else the like advantage.*
> In the former sense, a man's hand, or merchandise, or money is called his property.
> In the latter sense, a man has property in his opinions and the free communication of them.
> He has a property of peculiar value in his religious opinions and in the profession and practice dictated by them.
> He has property very dear to him in the safety and liberty of his person.
> He has an equal property in the free use of his faculties and free choice of the objects on which to employ them. In a word, as a man is said to have a right to his property, he may be equally said to have a property in his rights.[5]

Madison went on to explain the constitutional responsibilities which flow from this concept of property:

> Government is instituted to protect property of every sort; as well that which lies in the various rights of individuals, as that which the term particularly express. This being the end of government, that alone is a *just* government, which *impartially* secures to every man whatever is his *own*....That is not a just government, nor is property secure under it, where the property which a man has in his personal safety and personal liberty, is violated by arbitrary seizures of one class of citizens for the service of the rest....That is not a just government, nor is property secure under it, where arbitrary restriction, exemptions, and monopolies deny to part of its citizens that free use of their faculties, and free choice of their occupations, which not only constitute their property in the general sense of the word; but are the means of acquiring property strictly so called....If there be a government then which prides itself on maintaining the inviolability of property; which provides that none shall be taken *directly* even for public use without indemnification to the owner, and yet *directly* violates the property which individuals have in their faculties; nay more, which *indirectly* violates their property in their actual possessions, in the labor that acquires their daily subsistence, and in the hallowed remnant of time which ought to relieve their fatigues and soothe their cares, the inference will have been anticipated, that such a government is not a pattern for the United States. If the United States mean to obtain or deserve the full praise due to wise and just governments, they will equally respect the rights of property, and the property in rights: they will rival the government that most sacredly guards the former; and by repelling its example in violating the latter, will make themselves a pattern to that and all other governments.[6]

Indicative of the high regard in which Thomas Jefferson held private property is his assertion that "...the true foundation of republican government, is the equal right of every citizen, in his person and in his property."[7] Also, his second inaugural address gives support to "...that state of property, equal or unequal, which results to every man from his own industry, or that of his fathers."[8] And in a letter to Dupont de Nemours, he pronounced the basis of property to be "...in our natural wants, in the means with which we are endowed to satisfy these wants, and the right to what we acquire by those means without violating similar rights of other sensible beings."[9] Jefferson believed that property--broadly conceived to include not only the tangible but skills as well--gives one independence and independence provides the basis for public spirit. As he asserted in his *Notes on the State of Virginia*, "Dependence begets subservience and venality, suffocates the germ of virtue, and prepares fit tools for the designs of ambition."[10] In another letter, he wrote the following:

> To take from one, because it is thought his own industry and that of his fathers has acquired too much, in order to spare to others, who, or whose fathers have not exercised equal industry and skills, is to violate arbitrarily the first principle of association, "the guarantee to everyone of a free exercise of his industry and the fruits acquired by it."[11]

Samuel Adams also entertained, strong feelings about property rights:

> ...if property is necessary for the support of savage life, it is by no means less so in civil society. The utopian schemes of leveling, and a community of goods, are as visionary and impracticable as those which vest all property in the Crown are arbitrary, despotic, and in our government unconstitutional.[12]

And in the words of John Adams:

> The moment the idea is admitted into society that property is not as sacred as the laws of God and there is not a force of law and public justice to protect it, anarchy and tyranny commence. IF THOU SHALT NOT COVET, and THOU SHALT NOT STEAL, were not commandments of Heaven, they must be made inviolable precepts of every society before it can be made civilized or made free.[13]

Neither poor nor rich, the 'demi-gods' who framed the Constitution owned property at a time when such ownership was relatively easy to come by. In the belief that owners of property would be likely to protect its rights, individual state constitutions imposed property qualifications for suffrage and office holding. However, the national constitution mandated no property qualifications for those who would govern the new republic and left the matter of suffrage up to the states.

It should come as no surprise that the U. S. Constitution establishes the legal basis for a free enterprise system. With regard to private property, the Fifth Amendment requires the federal government to provide due process when private property is taken, and such a taking must be justly compensated and restricted to public use. Most state constitutions have similar clauses. Moreover, the Third Amendment places strict limits on the government's right to quarter troops on private property, while the Fourth Amendment safeguards people and their property against "unreasonable searches and seizures." Contracts also occupy a lofty position. Article 1, section 10, clause 1 (1-10-1) prohibits states from passing legislation impairing contractual obligations.

Property and contract enforcement (not to mention life) receive protection via a judiciary system sanctioned by Article Three. External dangers (and internal during time of civil strife) may be countered with military efforts directed by the President acting in his capacity of Commander-in-Chief under Article Two and authorized by Congress under the war powers clauses of Article One.

The above provisions allow individuals to enter into voluntary exchanges at lower costs (economists call these transaction costs) than would be the case if the government failed to perform such functions. Of course the rights of property are not absolute. This was true in colonial times as well as in the post-Constitutional history of this nation simply because the government must have the power to tax and regulate in order to carry out its legitimate functions.

There is a sad and tragic aspect to the Constitution's emphasis on property, and this is the case of slavery which was very much alive in 1787. While it is true that by the 1780's many states north of Maryland had been quite successful in their efforts to gradually free the slaves, and the Northwest Ordinance had made slavery illegal in the new territories, the Constitution did allow the right of property in this matter to take precedence over the right to liberty. Although the Constitution does not use the word "slave," it nonetheless makes clear that for purposes of apportionment such "persons" will count as three-fifths of free persons. This number represents a compromise between southerners and northerners: the southerners wanted representation in Congress based on property holdings including slaves, which would give them more votes, and the northerners wanted the slave population excluded.

In order to ensure the entrance of southern states into the Union (North Carolina, South Carolina, and Georgia would have refused to join without protection for slavery), Article 1 Section 9, which James Mason called the "the fatal section,"[14] allowed the importation of slaves for another twenty years and established a maximum tax of ten dollars on any slave imported. Also, the clause "No Capitation, or other direct, tax shall be laid, unless in Proportion to the Census or Enumeration herein directed to be taken," in effect, eliminated manumission via taxation levied solely on slaves. Finally, according to Article 4, Section 2, "No person held to Service or Labour in one State, under the Laws thereof, escaping into another, shall, in Consequence of any Law or Regulation therein, be discharged from such Service or Labour, but shall be delivered up on Claim of the Party to whom such Service of Labour may be due." And this, then, was the terrible price to maintain a union under the new Constitution.

Not all southerners came to the defense of slavery. Because of this institution, George Mason of Virginia said he would "sooner chop off his right hand than put it to the Constitution,"[15] and Luther Martin of Maryland found slavery to be "inconsistent with the principles of the Revolution."[16]

ECONOMIC ROLE OF GOVERNMENT

All supporters of the Constitution's adoption favored a stronger central government than existed under the Articles of Confederation. Some, Madison and Hamilton for instance, wished it to be stronger than did others, but all wanted its powers and conduct restricted in varying degrees. Of course, limited government is a basic component of a free enterprise economy. Following are the thoughts of Hamilton, Washington, Madison, and Jefferson.

The major interests of Alexander Hamilton (1755-1804), lie not in economic matters but in the military (as a fourteen year old he wished for war so that he might gain honor and glory).[17] Of an aristocratic nature, (a posture reinforced by his marriage into the socially prominent Schuyler family), he admired the British government and believed that people of financial means knew what was best for a nation while those without property tended to be captivated by short run passions. Fearing an "excess of democracy" he favored a strong central government at the Constitutional Convention and advocated life tenure for both the executive and one of the legislative branches. This approach would impede any radicalism from the other branch which he would subject to election every three years. On all this he was turned down.

When it came to economic matters, Alexander Hamilton, the first Secretary of the United States Treasury, upheld the sanctity of contracts, urged full payment of the public debt, and convinced that a strong economy made for national power, labored for policies that contained some mercantile characteristics. His proposals included a national bank, direct subsidies to business, and import duties to protect infant American manufacturing industries.[18]

While advocating a more activist role for government than other framers of the Constitution, he thought that the vertical and horizontal checks and balances would be sufficient to thwart despotism. Moreover, Hamilton viewed his program as providing the necessary economic and financial stability to safeguard the republican principles of the new nation.

Although George Washington was favorably disposed toward agrarianism, (like Jefferson he believed that agricultural pursuits should dominate the nation), he lent support to some of Hamilton's ideas because Hamilton's mercantile system did not require slaves. Never (unlike Jefferson) did Washington hold slaves as inferior and always the humane master he eventually set all his slaves free: he was the only founding father from Virginia to do so.[19] He also wondered about the desirability of having American staples processed in other countries. He thought manufacturing should be encouraged, and in a symbolic gesture to the textile industry, wore at his inauguration a suit made of cloth woven domestically.[20]

Convinced that the chaotic conditions which had prevailed under the Articles of Confederation as well as the failures of ancient republics could be traced to a lack of strong central authority, James Madison sought a more powerful central government: one that possessed control over both domestic and foreign affairs and that could veto state legislation. He believed free commerce benefited society and while surely allowing for government intervention in the public interest, Madison took a narrow interpretation of the general welfare clause of the Constitution and thought the specific powers set forth in Section 8 of that document limited Congressional activity.[21]

Thomas Jefferson opposed paper money, advocated full payment of public debts, and wanted the national government to have power over state commerce as well as the ability to borrow and tax. Like Madison, he believed the general welfare clause to be applicable only to the specific powers enumerated in the Constitution and assailed Hamilton's business subsidies because they would tax the many to benefit the few and would dangerously augment government power.[22]

Repelled by extremes of wealth and poverty but not against inequality itself, Jefferson opposed the use of taxation to redistribute wealth although he did support import duties because they fell more heavily on the rich. He successfully fought primogeniture in his native Virginia, "...in the interests of encouraging an "aristocracy of virtue and talent"[23] and thereby minimizing inequality. He thought government activity should prevent people from harming one another, a function which would allow individual enterprise to flourish and provide opportunity for more and more people.

Jefferson's views of government can be summed up in the words of his first inaugural address, in which he referred to "...a wise and frugal Government, which shall restrain men from injuring one another, shall leave them otherwise free to regulate their own pursuits of industry and improvement, and shall not take from the mouth of labor the bread it has earned."[24] This theme is echoed in letter sent from Paris to his friend James Madison: "I am not a friend to a very energetic government....It is always oppressive. It places the government more at ease, at the expense of the people..."[25]

The Constitution reflects this fear of powerful government. Beyond the checks and balances discussed in Chapter 7, restraints on government are found in several places in the Constitution. So that attempts to extract taxes meet with popular approval, revenue bills must originate in the House of Representatives--Article One, Section Seven, Clause One (1-7-1). Tax revenues may only be used to "...provide for the Common Defence and General Welfare of the United States..." (1-8-1); the executive branch may not spend money without congressional authorization; an accounting of receipts and expenditures must be published (1-9-7); and because "...all Duties, Imposts and Excises shall be uniform throughout the United States," an income tax was denied (1-8-1).

All of the above, of course, must be within the bounds of the Constitution which under Article Six, Clause Two "...shall be the supreme Law of the Land..." Further circumscribing the power of government is the Ninth Amendment: "The enumeration in the Constitution, of certain rights, shall not be construed to deny or disparage others retained by the people," and the Tenth Amendment (framed by Richard Henry Lee): "The powers not delegated to the United States by the Constitution nor prohibited by it to the States, are reserved to the States respectively, or to the people." This is to say that the authority of the federal government is limited to specific areas, and that the states or the people can do what is not expressly forbidden to them. James Madison's observations in Federalist paper No. 45 leave little doubt that states were meant to have a vital role in this republic:

> The powers delegated by the proposed Constitution to the Federal Government, are few and defined. Those which are to remain in the State Governments are numerous and indefinite. The former will be exercised principally on external objects, as war, peace, negotiation, and foreign commerce; with which last the power of taxation will be for the most part connected. The powers reserved to the several States will extend to all the objects, which. in the ordinary course of affairs, concern the lives, liberties and properties of the people; and the internal order, improvement, and prosperity of the State.

> The operations of the Federal Government will be most extensive and important in times of war and danger, those of the State Governments, in times of peace and security.[26]

ECONOMIC DEVELOPMENT

While religion, civic virtue, or tradition have been the bases of other governments in various forms, the founders of this federal republic based much of our system of government on economic intercourse. Of course they understood the dangers in this, but most believed, like Madison, that economic interests tended to be less zealous than those interests based on religion or politics. As Doctor Samuel Johnson noted, "There are few ways in which a man can be more innocently employed than in getting money."[27] Alexis de Toqueville harbored a comparable point of view.

> I know of nothing more opposite to revolutionary attitudes than commercial ones. Commerce is naturally adverse to all the violent passions; it loves to temporize, takes delight in compromise, and studiously avoids irritation. It is patient, insinuating, flexible, and never has recourse to extreme measures until obliged by the most absolute necessity. Commerce renders men independent of one another, gives them a lofty notion of their personal importance, leads them to seek to conduct their own affairs, and teaches how to conduct them well; it therefore prepares men for freedom, but preserves them from revolutions.[28]

A century and a half later Lord Keynes expressed a similar sentiment when he wrote, "It is better that a man should tyrannise over his bank balance than over his fellow citizens...."[29]

There also was a general belief that economic development would confer substantial benefits upon society. Below are the thoughts of Hamilton, Jefferson, and Franklin.

The Federalist No. 12 contains Alexander Hamilton's favorable views toward economic activity:

> The prosperity of commerce is now perceived and acknowledged by all enlightened statesmen to be the most useful as well as the most productive source of national wealth, and has accordingly become a primary object of their political cares. By multiplying the means of gratification, by promoting the introduction and circulation of the precious metals, those darling objects of human avarice and enterprise, it serves to vivify and invigorate the channels of industry and to make them flow with greater activity and copiousness. The assiduous mechanic, and the industrious manufacturer, all orders of men look forward with eager expectation and growing alacrity to the pleasing reward of their toils.[30]

Born in the West Indies out of wedlock ("the bastard brat of a Scots peddler," John Adams once called him[31]), Hamilton came to America at age seventeen, studied at King's College, and served with distinction on Washington's staff during the Revolutionary War. He also was a member of Congress and the New York Legislature, as well as a delegate to the Constitutional Convention. Arriving in this country as a virtual pauper, he had risen to prominence in the atmosphere of freedom. As such, he desired an economic meritocracy with little power attached to inheritance and social position. He believed that his system would encourage hard work and industry while penalizing idleness. He foresaw that economic growth might well be accompanied by increasing disparities of personal wealth which was not in keeping with republican principles: nonetheless, for Hamilton the national benefits attaching to economic development outweighed financial inequalities.[32] Also, he thought that under conditions of freedom, American blacks would prove to be the intellectual and social equal of whites.[33]

In economic matters, the heart of Thomas Jefferson was bound to agriculture. He harbored the values of the British Old Whigs, those gentlemen farmers who had championed the Glorious Revolution. He saw an inextricable link between agricultural virtue and political virtue, and as a member of the Virginia gentry, looked askance at what he considered the luxurious and decadent behavior of business classes.[34]

Jefferson wanted a nation dominated by small, owner occupied farms that would have income sufficient to make people free from the fickleness of manufacturers and to thereby maintain a country of sturdy, independent, well-informed yeoman farmers. In his *Notes on the State of Virginia*, he asserts that, "...the proportion which the aggregate of other classes of citizens bears in any state to that of its husbandmen, is the proportion of its unsound to its healthy parts."[35]

Although wary of merchants whom he believed were too often greedy and lacking in civic virtue, he considered commerce an important source of wealth and thought it should be allowed to develop freely. Jefferson believed that manufacturing was not only useful, but made for a more interesting society. He disliked large factories, which he associated with pauper employees who had lost their independence. His condemnations of industrialization and urbanization undoubtedly reflected his experience with the wretchedness accompanying the factory system and the conditions he found in the cities of Europe. While apprehensively admitting its necessity, he disdained the world of finance. Jefferson struggled within himself, favoring the agrarian life and its values, but aware that commerce, manufacturing, and banking would bring wealth to the nation and its citizenry.[36]

Not surprisingly, Benjamin Franklin displayed a vivid interest in matters economic. Beyond his personal financial endeavors (he was a successful land speculator and his keen business sense enabled him to retire in his early forties), he attacked British mercantile restrictions, railed against government price controls, and to stimulate economic activity, supported the judicious issuance of paper money as a supplement for scarce specie. His analysis of colonialism in the West Indies led him to a cost-benefit approach from which he concluded that the costs to European nations exceeded the benefits. He accepted the mercantile tenet that it is necessity which forces people to labor. His belief that hard work fostered affluence led him to denounce the English poor laws, which compelled the upper income groups to subsidize the lower, and which he thought were responsible for diminished incentives, idleness, and dissipation. A staunch foe of slavery, he published papers against it, was president of the Pennsylvania Society for Promoting the Abolition of Slavery, and in his final public endeavor he petitioned Congress for its abolition.[37]

While living abroad he met a number of distinguished personages including Adam Smith, David Hume, and the Physiocrats. The doctrine of the latter seems to have dominated his views on economic development.

> There seem to be but three ways for a nation to acquire wealth. The first is by *war*, as the Romans did, in plundering their conquered neighbors. This is *robbery*. The second by *commerce*, which is generally *cheating*. The third by *agriculture*, the only *honest way*, wherein man receives a real increase of the seed thrown into the ground, in a kind of continual miracle, wrought by the hand of God in his favour, as a reward for his innocent life and his virtuous industry.[38]

These passages suggest that there was less than unanimous agreement among delegates to the Convention about which sector of the economy should receive the emphasis. Nonetheless, there was general agreement that economic development was important and that the defects in the Articles of Confederation needed to be cured. In that remedial process, beyond what already has been mentioned, several other clauses which facilitate economic growth also became part of the Constitution.

The Constitution provides for a large free trade area within the United States which permits a greater degree of specialization and more competition: both factors promote efficiency. The liberties as well as the movement of the citizenry among states are guaranteed in (4-2-1). Under the commerce clause (1-8-3), Congress has the ultimate authority to regulate commerce among the states. Further, "No Preference shall be given by any Regulation of Commerce or Revenue to the Ports of one State over those of another: nor shall Vessels bound to, or from, one State, be obliged to enter, clear, or pay Duties in another" (1-9-6). Congress also possesses the power to establish uniform rules on bankruptcy (1-8-4), to coin money, impose a uniform value on it, regulate its relationship to foreign money, fix weights and measures (1-8-5), and punish counterfeiters (1-8-6). In fact, states are explicitly forbidden to coin money or "make any Thing but gold and silver Coin a Tender in Payment of Debts" (1-10-1).

In external affairs, a tax on goods to be exported to foreign nations is prohibited (1-9-5), and the commerce clause extends congressional authority over trade between the United States and foreign nations.

The Constitution also offers more direct stimulation to the economy. To foster communication, Congress may authorize construction of post offices and roads (1-8-7), and to assist science and art by encouraging discovery and invention, it may offer protections such as patents and copyrights for limited periods of time (1-8-8). The First Amendment, by protecting the press and freedom of speech, encourages the discussion and dissemination of new ideas. Guaranteeing the right to peaceful assembly allows people to form associations to carry out various economic, social, and political programs. This amendment also safeguards the right to petition government thereby providing an orderly way to bring about legislative changes--economic or otherwise.

Finally, we note that the Constitution not only explicitly enables the federal government "...to make all laws which shall be necessary and proper..." to execute its limited and enumerated powers (1-8-18), but establishes the financial basis to do so: Congress is given the power to levy and collect taxes (1-8-1), and to borrow money (1-8-

2). To enhance the credit standing of the new nation, Article Six accepts as valid the debts incurred under the Articles of Confederation.

One more point. An amendment takes precedence over anything in the Constitution to which it refers. For example, although the commerce clause confers regulatory power on the central government, the Fifth Amendment stipulates boundaries within which it may be exercised.

CONCLUSIONS

Eager to have a strong economy which would allow America to become powerful, influential, and less vulnerable to foreign control, the framers of the Constitution developed an instrument of governance which, without doubt, laid the basis for economic development.

However, along with other Americans of this era they could not foresee the free market capitalism or vigorous economic growth that emerged in the nineteenth century. From the Constitution itself, which permitted both slavery and indentured servitude, we know that labor markets were less that perfectly free. State governments often regulated prices and marketing practices, exhibited downright hostility toward banking, and encouraged an assortment of mercantile projects, all with rather general popular approval. Much of the citizenry perceived economic development as a zero-sum game rather than as a process of expanding mutually advantageous voluntary exchanges.[39] Remember also, that the science of economics was in its infancy, and the premises and foundations for economic growth as we understand them were not clear to the framers or to the citizenry. Nor, for many in the United States, are they today!

Undoubtedly, a commercial republic would foster the virtues of industry, prudence, self-reliance, moderation, compromise, temperance, and frugality. It would allow talents that would be hidden at the bottom of the hierarchical ladder in traditional societies to be observed and to flourish on the higher rungs. Cognizant, however, that the pursuit of material gain would also tend to promote avarice, the framers thought that unwarranted self-interest could be harnessed by the checks built into the extended, compound republic.

However, the framers, along with other Americans were aware that the constitutional checks by themselves would not be sufficient to insure the national welfare. They knew that commercial virtues and religious virtues and the classical virtues of courage, temperance, justice, and wisdom were also necessary. As Madison, who wanted a stronger central government than he was able to obtain, observed "No theoretical checks--no form of government, can render us secure. To suppose that any form of government will secure liberty or happiness without any virtue in the people is a chimerical ideal."[40] And according to John Adams, "Our Constitution was designed only for a moral and religious people. It is wholly inadequate for the government of any other."[41] For this republic to survive, virtue was a necessity. Monarchies relied upon fear, patronage, and family while republics were held together with virtue, patriotism, and self-sacrifice.[42]

The idea that a people possessed enough virtue and intelligence to govern not only themselves but to secure liberty, stability, and prosperity met with derision from many abroad. After all, past attempts at self-government had failed in small nations and had never even been tried in a large one. However, the Constitution of the United States rather than providing a utopian blueprint of what should be, is really a most permissive document. Instead of telling people what to do, it allows the pursuit of private interests. The economic role of government is to act as a referee and to enforce the rules of the game. This provides the basis for the emergence of a free market economy in which self-reliance takes precedence over heredity, and through which a variety of talents can flourish. It encourages the creation (rather than the distribution) of wealth. In the terms that we have been using--negative freedom is established as the road to positive freedom.

Thomas Jefferson, believed that too much power was concentrated in the federal government. Nonetheless, "the sage of Charlottesville" thought this Constitution "...unquestionably the wisest yet ever presented to man."[43] In 1789, Benjamin Franklin perhaps best expressed the guarded optimism prevalent at the time: "Our Constitution is in actual Operation; everything appears to promise that it will last; but in this world nothing is certain but death and taxes." However, in the following century, the British Prime Minister William Gladstone was able to proclaim it "the most wonderful work ever struck off at a given time by the brain and purpose of man."[44]

---

[1] Bernard H. Siegan, *Economic Liberties and the Constitution* (Chicago: University of Chicago Press, 1980), p. 31.
[2] Jacob E. Cooke, ed., *The Federalist* (Middletown: Wesleyan University Press, 1961), p. 58.
[3] Ibid., p. 65.
[4] Ibid., p. 370.
[5] Ellen Frankel Paul and Howard Dickman ed., *Liberty, Property, and the Foundation of the American Constitution* (New York: State University of New York Press, 1989), p.11.
[6] Ibid., p. 12.
[7] Catherine Drinker Bowen, *Miracle at Philadelphia*, with a Foreword by Warren E. Burger, (Boston: An Atlantic Monthly Press Book, Little Brown and Company, 1986), p. 73.
[8] Merrill D. Peterson, ed., *Thomas Jefferson* (New York: The Library Of America, 1984), p.522.
[9] Ibid., p. 1387.
[10] Ibid., pp. 290-291.
[11] Robert A. Goldwin and William A. Schambra, ed., *How Capitalistic Is The Constitution* (Washington D.C.:American Enterprise Institute for Public Policy Research, 1982), p.16.
[12] Benjamin Hart, *Faith And Freedom* (Dallas: Lewis and Stanley, 1988), p.318.
[13] Ibid., p.319.
[14] Morton White, *Philosophy, The Federalist, and the Constitution* (New York: Oxford University Press, 1987), p.170.
[15] Mort Gerberg, *The U.S. Constitution For Everyone* (New York: Perigee Books, The Putnam Publishing Group, 1987), p.21.
[16] Ibid., p. 21.
[17] Gordon S. Wood, *The Radicalism of The American Revolution* (New York: Alfred A. Knopf. 1992), p.40.
[18] Joseph Dorfman, *The Economic Mind In American Civilization*, 1606-1865, vol. 1, (New York: Augustus M. Kelley, Publishers, 1966), pp. 404-417. Also see Donald F. Swanson and

Andrew P. Trout, "Alexander Hamilton's Invisible Hand," *Policy Review*, Winter 1992, pp. 86, 87.

[19] James Thomas Flexner, *Washington: The Indispensible Man* (Boston: Little, Brown and Company, 1974) pp. 385-394.

[20] Ibid., pp. 213, 214.

[21] Mortimer J. Adler, *We Hold These Truths: Understanding the Ideas and Ideals of the Constitution*, with a Foreword by Richard A. Blackmun (New York: Macmillan Publishing Company, 1987), pp. 117-119.

[22] Joseph Dorfman, *The Economic Mind In American Civilization*, 1606-1865, vol. 1, pp. 433-437.

[23] Gordon S. Wood, *The Radicalism of The American Revolution*, p.182.

[24] Merrill D. Peterson, ed., *Jefferson*, p.494.

[25] Catherine Drinker Bowen, *Miracle at Philadelphia*, p.105.

[26] Jacob E, Cooke, ed., *The Federalist*, p.313.

[27] Dwight R, Lee," Celebrating the Economic System that Makes Diversity Worth Celebrating," in *The Intercollegiate Review*, Spring, 1994.

[28] Alexis de Toqueville, *Democracy In America*, vol. 2 (New York: Vintage Books, 1957), p.268.

[29] John Maynard Keynes, *The General Theory Of Employment, Interest, and Money*. (New York: Harcourt Brace Jovanovich, Publishers, 1953), p.374.

[30] Ibid., pp. 73, 74.

[31] Walter Berns, "On Hamilton and Proper Government," *The Public Interest*, (Washington D.C.: National Affairs Inc. Fall 1992), p.110.

[32] Joseph Dorfman, *The Economic Mind In American Civilization*, 1606-1865, vol. 1, pp. 404-417.

[33] Forrest McDonald, *Novus Ordo Seclorum: The Intellectual Origins of the Constitution* (Lawrence: University Press of Kansas, 1985), pp. 53.54.

[34] James Thomas Flexner, *Washington The Indispensible Man*, pp. 242,243.

[35] Merrill D. Peterson, ed., *Thomas Jefferson* (New York: The Library Of America, 1984), 291.

[36] Joseph Dorfman, *The Economic Mind In American Civilization*, 1606-1865, vol. 1. pp. 433- 437.

[37] Ibid., pp. 178-195.

[38] Jacob Oser and William C. Blanchfield, *The Evolution Of Economic Thought*, 3rd. ed. (New York: Harcourt Brace Jovanovich, Inc., 1975), p.339.

[39] Forrest McDonald, "The Constitution and Hamiltonian Capitalism" in *How Capitalistic Is The Constitution*, ed. Robert A. Goldwin and William A. Schambra (Washington D. C., American Enterprise Institute for Policy Research, 1982), pp. 49-74.

[40] Gertrude Himmelfarb, "Liberty One Very Simple Principle?", *The American Scholar*, Autumn 1993, p.546.

[41] Peter Marshall, "Recovering the Original Vision" in Michael Bauman, ed., *Morality And The Marketplace* (Hillsdale: Hillsdale College Press, 1994), p.119.

[42] Gordon S. Wood, *The Radicalism of the American Revolution*, p.105.

[43] Dumas Malone, *Jefferson and the Rights of Man* (Boston: Little, Brown and Company, 1951), p. 178.

[44] Benjamin Hart, *Faith & Freedom* (Dallas: Lewis and Stanley, 1988),p.329.

Part Two

Free Markets, Free People, and the State

CHAPTER 9

FREE MARKETS IN ACTION: THE PEOPLE

What a piece of work is a man! How noble in reason, how infinite in faculties, in form and moving how express and admirable, in action how like an angel, in apprehension how like a god! The beauty of the world, the paragon of animals!
                                                                    Hamlet: Act II Scene II

It certainly was not planned to turn out the way that it did. Indeed, one would have had to possess incredible powers of clairvoyance to predict the evolution path of the American economy, because from the time of George Washington, free markets and not a centrally directed master plan have dominated the economic system. This means that people generally have been free to exercise choice and to bear the consequences of their decisions, and it is this wealth creating process that has made America an economic powerhouse.

In this chapter, we will focus initially upon population size and then will explore other aspects of the human element in a free market system.

THE HUMAN FACTOR I: POPULATION SIZE

Numbering close to 4 million in 1790, the United States population approximated 270 million by 1998. With the legal importation of slaves terminated in 1808, the major sources of population growth consisted of natural increase and immigration.

(A) Natural Increase

A natural increase in a nation's population implies more births than deaths--a continuum through U. S. population history. Of course rates of natural increase have fluctuated with changes in these two variables. Estimated to be about 55 per thousand of population at the beginning of the nineteenth century, the birth rate declined to roughly 30 per thousand a hundred years later and by the 1980's had dropped to around 15 per thousand. Improvements in such factors as sanitation, medical treatment, diet, clothing, and shelter, have led to a reduction in mortality rates over time. Our concern, however, will be with fertility. The supply and demand (cost-benefit) tools of the economist can be used to explain why people decide to adjust family size to changing economic conditions.[1]

Children may be wanted (demanded) for the benefits they yield and may therefore be looked upon as consumption goods, investment goods, or both. Of course children are different from all other economic goods. Parents become more emotionally attached to a child than to their other possessions, and unlike other goods, they cannot see the child before it is acquired--that is, born. Nor can they legally sell it. Finally, as any parent knows, a child has a mind of its own.

As a consumer durable good, a child may (*may* is key) act as a companion, give pleasure, award love and respect as he or she grows and matures, and be a source of prestige (my son/daughter-the doctor). Viewing the child as an investment good: parents allocate their scarce resources of time and money to produce (the economist's word) and rear it with the expectation of positive returns--not unlike a business decision to purchase an investment good, such as a machine. Hoped for benefits might include contributions to family income and care of parents in their old age. All this exemplifies what economists call a human capital investment.

In the low income agricultural society of early nineteenth century America, people chose to have many children (the average woman bore about four times as many children as the average today), for both consumption and investment reasons. The latter was especially important because with a sparse population and abundant natural resources, many children were needed to work the farm and eventually to look after their parents. In addition, many people died young. Given all these factors, the decision to have large families was a highly rational one.

Over the course of the nineteenth century, birth rates and family size declined, a trend that has continued until today. Industrialization brought forth more cities, larger cities, and a diminution in the relative importance of agriculture. Urban society provided fewer economic opportunities for the young and the investment motive for having children suffered further reduction with compulsory schooling laws and child labor legislation as well as the development of securities markets, insurance plans, and various public and private retirement programs.

Technology, especially in the twentieth century, gave rise to numerous consumption substitutes for children (jet travel, stereos, TV's, VCR's etc.), and increasing average real wages meant that people could avail themselves of these alternatives. And so they did. Parents also allocated more resources to the cultivation of their own tastes and to raising fewer but "higher quality" (more education, dance lessons etc.) children. Moreover, technology developed inexpensive and effective methods of contraception, thereby reducing the number of unintended births.

Supply (cost) considerations also have contributed to declining fertility rates. The costs of having and rearing children (including prenatal care, birth, visits to doctors, food, shelter, clothing, education, entertainment) have risen enormously in the twentieth century. Costs also include--and this is of prime importance--the opportunity cost of the mother who stays home to care for her children--that is, the loss of her monetary earnings if she worked for pay. This cost, rising with the long term increase in national average real wages, directly correlates with levels of the mother's education. The cost to the college educated woman who stays at home with her children for twenty years will run into the hundreds of thousands of dollars.

Demography--the science of vital population statistics--constitutes an exceptionally complicated field of study that includes cultural, religious, moral, and economic ingredients along with a host of others. The analytical tools of the economist (although incomplete by themselves) have been employed fruitfully to explain phenomena in this science and have provided conclusions consistent with the facts. To wit: Americans in the early nineteenth century acted rationally in choosing to have large families and when conditions changed later on, economic logic propelled them to a different response.

(B) Immigration

President George Washington believed that rather than entwining itself with European conflicts, America might better serve humanity by allowing those experiencing hardship to come freely to these shores and thereby secure a more prosperous existence. And come they did, for augmenting America's natural increase--and eventually contributing to it themselves--were the millions who emigrated.

Between 1800 and 1920, over 30 million people came to the United States. At first rather insignificant, immigration picked up during the 1820's and thereafter became more substantial. In the 1840's and 1850's, crop failure and political turmoil in northwestern Europe were prime factors in the migration of over 4.3 million to America. A decline, naturally enough, accompanied the American Civil War, but the inflow rose rapidly as the nation industrialized in the second half of the nineteenth century. The first decade of the twentieth century witnessed an historic peak when almost 9 million people came to America.

After 1920, restrictive legislation, wars, and depression served to reduce the numbers of immigrants. In recent times legal immigration has risen substantially, with somewhere between 700,000 and 1,000,000 persons admitted annually. However, illegal entry raises these figures. It includes not only people who enter the country illegally, but also visitors and students who were admitted legally but then stayed on in violation of their visas. The nature of illegal entry makes hard data difficult to obtain, (no one really knows for sure), but the Immigration and Naturalization Service has estimated it to be around 5 million. The number of foreign-born residents in the United States is approximately 27 million and constitutes about 10 percent of the population. Comparable in size to the 1901-1910 decade, immigration (both legal and illegal), continues to be important and may account for over a third of the growth of the U.S. labor force.[2]

"Fellow immigrants" chided President Franklin Roosevelt to a gathering of the Daughters of the American Revolution." Although Roosevelt employed humor to a group with claims to deep colonial roots, the point was well made: all U. S. citizens (other than Native American Indians) can trace their national heritage to other countries, whether their ancestors immigrated in the seventeenth century or they just arrived here.

People from the British Isles and Germany constituted the major portion of immigrants in the first half of the nineteenth century; in the second half, southern and eastern Europeans gained predominance. Favoritism toward European countries characterized U.S. immigration policies until the 1960's when new legislation evened out national immigration quotas. This permitted easier access for previously underrepresented groups such as Asians.

> "Give me your tired, your poor,
> Your huddled masses yearning to breathe free
> The wretched refuse of your teeming shore.
> Send these, the homeless, tempest-lost to me,
> I lift my lamp beside the golden door!"

With these words, inscribed at the base of the Statue of Liberty, did the immigrant Zionist poet Emma Lazarus reflect upon the inhospitable conditions of her native Russia. These sentiments greeted all immigrants as their ships sailed into New York harbor, but most found far less hospitable welcomes once they disembarked in this land of promise and plenty. The established population feared that the frequently poor newcomers would take away jobs, diminish wages, and in general reduce opportunities in the work world. These fears generated hostility and its corollary, discrimination. The newcomers' differences in religion, culture, and ethnic background made them easy targets for angry prejudice. It is interesting that legislation did not reflect this state of affairs: between 1789 and the early 1880's there were virtually no exclusionary federal immigration policies. As for the states, some restricted immigration, and others encouraged. it.

In 1882, the national government began to enact immigration laws which excluded particular groups of people--lunatics, criminals, prostitutes and the Chinese are examples--The new laws also provided for the deportation of those caught violating the rules of entry. By the 1920's a mood of isolationism and protectionism characterized the nation. Organized labor, which feared that new arrivals would be difficult to organize and would depress wages, lobbied intensively for restrictive immigration policies. Beginning in 1921, new laws established quotas based on national origin (and these laws particularly were directed against southern and eastern Europe). The virtually open door policy had begun to close.

By 1965, a Harris Poll found the American citizenry opposed a change in current immigration policy by a two to one margin.[3] Nonetheless, Congress (while promising that immigration numbers would not rise), passed the Immigration and Nationality Act. This new policy reflected the idea of equality as expressed in the Civil Rights Act of that same year and did indeed provide more of a global balance. It permitted unlimited immigration of immediate family members of American citizens as well as a limited immigration for other reasons. Family reunification, broadly defined, receives the highest priority and accounts for the lion's share. Possession of the skill to fill a labor shortage (well documented and approved by the United States Department of Labor), is another category. Since the passage of this act, about eighty-five percent of immigrants have come from third world nations especially from South America (and from there, particularly Mexico) and Asia.

Almost twenty years later, the 1986 Immigration Reform and Control Act sought more effective controls over illegal entry by imposing sanctions against employers who hire illegal aliens. This Act also provides amnesty for those illegal aliens who entered the United States prior to 1982 and who have resided here continuously since their arrival.

Then, the Immigration Act of 1990 approximately tripled the annual number of visas (to about 140,000) that could be issued to individuals possessing various skills including that of "investor." It increased the number of visas for countries with recent low immigration rates, particularly Ireland. The Act also continued to stress family unification. Although the historic path followed by U. S. immigration policy has not been exactly a bee line, the policies have rested upon various restrictions, including quotas, for much of the twentieth century. Many more people, however, wish to enter this country than the law permits. As in the nineteenth century, immigration remains a controversial subject: some, especially business firms, want more of it and others, especially organized labor, demand less. (Samuel Gompers a founder of the American Federation of Labor in 1886 and an immigrant himself, fought to restrict entry into America.) Economic analysis helps to shed light on some of the various assertions surrounding this topic.

Why do so many people voluntarily come to America? The human capital model that economists use to answer this question basically revolves around the benefit/cost relationship perceived by potential immigrants.[4] Although they hope for the political and religious freedoms lacking in their countries of origin, their dominant goal is economic freedom--the opportunity to obtain a higher wage and standard of living than is possible at home. This incentive was and is especially important to the young immigrants who stand to receive these benefits over a longer time span. Evidence of the dominance of the economic motive derives from observing the generally strong direct relationship between immigration and economic conditions in the United States relative to economic conditions in one's homeland. For potential migrants, information about these conditions is often acquired from agents of American firms that recruit in Europe; from people who have already emigrated and write and send money to relatives overseas; from advertisements in the media; and simply by word of mouth.

The costs of immigration occur over a relatively short period of time and include transportation (steam driven vessels of the latter nineteenth century markedly decreased fares), establishment of a new household, and search for a job. Add to these the psychic costs of leaving one's relatives, friends, and culture, and the anxiety (often attended by discrimination) that attends residence in a new land. An excess of perceived benefits over perceived costs should elicit decisions to migrate.

Despite all these rather substantial costs, many considered them to be outweighed by potential benefits, and studies indicate that such calculations have tended by and large to be correct and immigrant decisions to be economically rational. Starting off with the disadvantages of language and other cultural barriers, immigrants earn, on average, somewhat less than native born Americans of the same age and education level. Over a period of time, however, sometimes as early as twenty years, the average income of these immigrants tends to exceed the average of comparable natives. One likely reason, of course, is that people who assume the risks and costs of immigration tend to be more self-confident, industrious, ambitious, and motivated than the average person and are more apt to undertake human capital investments in themselves by migrating from another country, learning the English language, acquiring knowledge about American culture, and developing marketable skills. As a result, immigrants tend to become more productive, a fact reflected in the relatively rapid growth of their wages.[5] Whether this pattern will repeat itself with recent immigrants remains to be seen.

There is already some evidence that more recent arrivals may in general have lower productivity characteristics than their counterparts of the past, and once again human capital theory can help to explain this phenomenon by focusing on the distribution of wages. Skilled workers who live in countries where the average earnings differential between skilled and unskilled workers is relatively small have a greater incentive to migrate to nations where the financial return on the skill or skills in question is higher, as evidenced by the relatively higher wage differential accorded to such workers in the country of destination. The accuracy of this human capital projection is borne out on the one hand by the disproportional migration of skilled workers, including professionals, from developed nations of northern Europe and on the other hand, by the fact that unskilled workers in countries where there is greater equality in the dispersion of wages show less incentive to migrate: they are doing rather well compared to skilled workers at home.

In countries exhibiting a wide dispersion in the average wages paid to skilled and unskilled workers, it is the unskilled who have the greatest incentive to move. The skilled workers are faring quite well and they probably have erected barriers (directly or indirectly) which prevent their unskilled countrymen from acquiring similar skills and thereby reaping higher financial returns. Such conditions provide significant motivation to undertake a human capital investment, and the disproportionate influx of poor, uneducated, unskilled third world immigrants since the 1965 changes in immigration law is consistent with economic theory. These facts imply that these more recent arrivals may not do as well (on the average), when compared to native workers as did previous immigrants from northwestern Europe. However, recent third world immigrants are still likely to receive greater financial rewards here than in their old country, and so for them, the return on their human capital investment should indeed be positive.[6]

Now let us examine some of the economic effects of immigration. Initially, immigration may depress wages and cause some generally temporary unemployment as labor markets adjust in the impacted occupations. Adjustments take the forms of wage changes; movement of some of the labor force to other jobs and geographic areas; transportation of goods to different areas of the nation; and capital flows seeking situations where labor costs have been lowered.

These adjustments, however, can have painful outcomes. According to a major study prepared by the National Academy of Sciences' National Research Council (NRC), there has been a significant negative effect on native born Americans without a high school degree. In fact, the NRC study estimates that some 44 percent of the decline in wages experienced by high school dropouts from 1980 to 1994 can be attributed to immigration.[7] Other sectors adversely effected include the welfare population (usually lacking high school diplomas) and earlier immigrants now competing with more recent arrivals. Also, only six states account for three quarters of the immigrant population and unskilled workers in these states most feel the impact as do taxpayers, because the costs of recent immigration (use of schools, hospitals, welfare expenses) exceeds the revenues (low taxes paid by low income people).[8]

In a given geographic area, an increase in the supply of low skilled workers may depress the wages of low skilled people already employed. But contrary to assertions from officials of labor unions and the Department of Labor, it is not the case that such an influx will cost Americans their jobs on a one to one basis. A lower wage may induce some to drop out of the labor force (especially if welfare payments are relatively attractive and available), and these workers may be replaced by immigrants. However, not all prior workers will drop out. Neither is it true as businessmen lament that without immigrants many firms could not operate because Americans simply refuse to engage in unskilled activities. Think of it this way: a mass deportation of aliens would by definition reduce the supply of labor, but such a diminished supply, all things being equal, would cause wages to rise and in turn would lead more native workers to take on jobs until the labor market "shortage" had evaporated.

Despite some adverse effects, immigration does mean that employment will be higher, that more work will be undertaken than otherwise would have been the case, and that all of this makes for a larger Gross Domestic Product (although not necessarily for growth on a per capita basis). Also, restraints on wages and increased production exert downward pressure on prices. Recipients of the national benefits bestowed by immigration also include employers who experience lower business costs and increased profitability, which lead to more capital investment, and expanded operations and employment. Of course, above normal profits will tend to erode over time as new entrants to the industries in question compete them away. Historically, immigrants have in general paid more in taxes then they received in public subsidies.[9] Given the immensity of the American economy, the NRC study found the immediate impact of immigration on various sectors of the economy to be miniscule although positive overall.[10]

The long run general contribution of immigrants to U. S. economic growth has been monumental. Their general willingness to work hard at almost any job is legendary. Although their expenditures on goods and services serve to keep the economy humming, new Americans tend to be thrifty and we know that saving is a vital component of capital formation. Many arrive here uneducated and unskilled but this is by no means always the case. Scientists, medical doctors, engineers, artisans, entrepreneurs, and indeed, representatives of virtually every occupation come to these shores.

It is also interesting to note that our immigrants' homelands bore some of the cost of rearing and educating them, and, in effect, those other nations bestow an enormous human capital gift upon the United States. This donation, among other things, allows the release of more of this nations labor force to build physical capital and thereby further contribute to economic development.[11]

Whether the immigrant experience of the past is repeated is an important and interesting question.[12] Again, an historical perspective can be helpful in predicting what the future may hold. Earlier waves of immigrants came to America poor although usually literate (they tended not to be the bottom of the barrel), often entered a world of slums, paupers, broken homes, high crime rates, overcrowding, filth, high mortality rates, inadequate public services and corruption.[13] Facing these obstacles, some groups made faster and greater progress than did others. The key question, then, is what explains this difference in success stories? And the answer revolves around the acquisition of the traits--virtues, if you will--that produce success in a commercial society. Once again we are talking about human capital investments: positive attitudes toward schooling and knowledge; the development of skills; business and work experience; and habits of thrift, self-reliance, dependability, planning ahead, and pride in achievement. These future oriented human qualities are not learned overnight, may be, in fact, slow in developing, and often take generations to acquire. Especially has this been true for immigrants arriving in an industrialized market economy from a premodern, rural, agricultural one.[14]

Assimilation is another issue. Early on, Americans displayed a desire to share their good fortune with others. One of the grievances against the King presented in the Declaration of Independence is that, "He has endeavored to prevent the population of these states; for that purpose of obstructing the Laws for Naturalization of Foreigners; refusing to pass others to encourage their migration hither..." In 1785 George Washington wrote, "let the poor, the needy and oppressed of the Earth, and those who want Land, resort to the fertile plains of our western country, the Second Land of Promise, and there dwell in peace, fulfilling the first and great commandment."[15] Washington also wrote that, "The bosom of America is open to receive not only the opulent and respectable stranger but the oppressed and persecuted of all Nations and Religions; whom we shall welcome to a participation of all our rights and privileges if, by decency and propriety of conduct, they appear to merit the enjoyment."[16] In other words, Washington, as well as Jefferson, Hamilton and other leaders of the time, would welcome immigrants on the condition that they assimilate and that meant the acquisition of American ways, customs virtues, and manners, that would define an American character. Included among these are love of freedom, virtuous behavior, respect for republican principles of government, and patriotism.

Nonetheless, a wary eye cast upon new arrivals and skepticism about their prospects for success and assimilation comprise an old American tradition. Benjamin Franklin, for instance, observing German immigrants in mid eighteenth century, asked, "Why should the Palatine boors be suffered to swarm into our settlements, and, by herding together, establish their language and manners, to the exclusion of ours? Why should Pennsylvania, founded by the English, become a colony of aliens, who will shortly be so numerous as to Germanize us, instead of our Anglifying them?"[17] In the first half of the nineteenth century, the mayor of Boston referred to the Irish as "a race that will never be infused into our own, but on the contrary will always remain distinct and hostile."[18] The second half of that century witnessed the arrival of Jews fleeing the from the pogroms of Eastern Europe, Jews whom other Jews already well-settled in America, considered an embarrassment.[19] American history is full of similar stories of disdain toward newcomers seeking to make their way in this land of opportunity.

But over the decades the various immigrant groups (some progressing more rapidly than others) have altered their attitudes and developed the traits necessary for success. They change and America changes them. Determination along with the assistance of ethnic self-help organizations, including those of a religious nature--and precious little assistance from government--allow them to make often outstanding contributions in the fields of science, education, the fine arts, literature, music, dance, sports, business, finance, fashion, food, entertainment, and public service. Their creation of wealth brings them acceptance and the respect of others, and instead of being viewed solely in terms of their ethnic background, they and their achievements are now considered part of the American heritage.[20] It is of more than passing interest that by the mid 1980's, more than thirty percent of all living American winners of the Nobel Prize were immigrants.[21] Given time and the proper environment for nurturing skills, the historic pattern described above should continue to repeat itself. Nonetheless, there are reasons for apprehension.

Nineteenth and early twentieth century immigrants came to the United States intending to assimilate and expecting little in the way of help from the government, and their expectations proved accurate. There were some private charities, ethnic self-help organizations, and public assistance programs--although nothing compared to the benefits of today's welfare state--of which quite a few immigrants did avail themselves.[22] Basically, however, it was a sink or swim atmosphere, harsh but effective as a stimulus to hard work. And not all succeeded. During the 1880-1920 period, for instance, many "birds of passage" came here and then returned to their native homes. Today's immigrants encounter different set of circumstances.

The welfare system is much more generous and available than in previous eras, even extending to illegal aliens and their children. Aged parents of third world immigrants who have become citizens often avail themselves of federal Supplemental Security Income benefits. In general, more recent arrivals (many of them are unskilled) have been making greater use of welfare, especially after they have been here for a while. Apparently, there is a learning process at work.[23] Receiving assistance in 1998 were 21 percent of immigrant households and 15 percent of nonimmigrant households.[24] Generally, the welfare system in America has done little to promote the ingredients that make for success (including family stability). Not only does it diminish work incentives, but it provides a source of income for those immigrants who fail in the United States and who would return to their native lands if welfare was not available. It would be ironic indeed if the costs of American welfare (about which the citizenry has become quite disenchanted) were to have the effect of reducing immigration quotas and thereby of depriving many of the American dream.

There is also our contemporary problem of assimilation. Immigrant groups have by no means been completely homogenized into a "melting pot" of society but have retained some of their ethnic heritage while still embracing the idea of America. Different immigrant groups and the native-born were molded into one people by the idea of citizenship. They were not hyphenated Americans--Irish-Americans or Jewish-Americans or Hispanic-Americans--but, with due respect for the heritage of their ancestors, were Americans who primarily identified with and owed allegiance to the United States.[25]

Today, however, the idea of assimilation has come under attack by those sometimes known as the "new class"[26] who advocate a radical brand of multiculturalism, and who consider cultural and linguistic unity as ethnic and racial oppression. Now an earnest attempt to understand another culture is surely a noble endeavor and, in fact, a mark of an educated person. Also worthy of praise are well thought out efforts to secure peaceful and harmonious relationships among different groups. All too often, however, those trumpeting multiculturalism are of a radical egalitarian bent.

Previous radical efforts to achieve equality and brotherhood in France during its revolutionary era and in communist countries in the twentieth century have all been first class disasters. Nonetheless, vocal and effective elites continue to view the institutions of western civilization as hopelessly corrupted with sexism, racism, and (wouldn't you know it), elitism and fervently believe these institutions to be worthy only of destruction.

Radicals like to direct things, which helps to explain why they loath free markets and the nation-state, both of which can get along fine without their input. (There is a significant Marxist influence in much of this.) Large scale immigration and its attendant problems provide them with a handy excuse for government intervention.[27] From the radical perspective the fragmentation of society which their programs set in motion will lead to the destruction of the nation-state and capitalism. These would be replaced by a socialist world government in which they (along with "new class" members of other countries) will be in charge.

Eschewing the relatively slow but sure work of free market institutions in developing prosperity while simultaneously promoting diversity, the new class elites, obsessed with utopian visions of equality, have turned their attention to the idea of multiculturalism. Under its banner, they have been able to enlarge the power of the state and to redistribute benefits among racial and ethnic groups. It is their intention to promote an equality of outcomes rather than an equality of opportunities.

As a result, various levels of government in the United States have ordered discrimination to be practiced in favor of a multiplicity of protected groups and have mandated preferential treatment for them in economic activities. And this anti-American idea of group rights, in contrast to individual rights, extends far. Ethnic groups are no longer encouraged to assimilate but rather to exert claims as "victims" for protected status in the political arena as well. This has come to include bilingual ballots and bilingual education in the schools along with a multicultural curriculum in which texts are rewritten not only to acknowledge hitherto neglected ethnic contributions, but to make the accomplishments and cultures of just about all ethnic groups worthy of equal praise. Exceptions to this principle are accorded to the canon of western civilization which tends to be viewed with distaste.

In some quarters, this has led to an aggressive assertion of ethnicity; tribalism accompanied by isolation which hardly makes one sanguine about the prospects of at least some recent immigrants for successful integration into the mainstream American economy and society. Also, this Balkanization may produce very unpleasant consequences for the nation. Recall the words of Abraham Lincoln in his address to the

1858 Republican Convention: "A house divided against itself cannot stand." One may wish to contemplate the horrors currently taking place in the Balkan area previously known as Yugoslavia as well as the aggressive hostility among ethnic groups in such countries as Spain, Iraq, Burma, India, and the former Soviet Union.[28] Happily, it does not seem that most immigrants have bought this menu offered by new class elites and have focused less on securing this notion of justice than on assimilating and getting ahead. Still, the very force of this tribalism does give cause for concern.[29] We will return to this topic in Chapter 14.

Finally, there is the issue of the size of the new immigrant groups which rival those at the turn of the century. Now, it is true that the population size of the United States was smaller in that era, thereby making the sum of immigrants a much larger percentage of total population than is the case today. However, the quota laws of the nineteen twenties, the great depression of the nineteen thirties, and World War II served to reduce immigration rates. This facilitated labor market adjustments which gave those new arrivals a better chance to make their way and assimilate. A "time out," if you will, was provided.[30] Today there does not appear to be any "time out" in sight, and given the birth rates of third world countries, pressures to emigrate from them should remain strong.

All this has dramatic implications for our lower economic classes, especially for many blacks. Although the latter have taken enormous strides, there remain a disproportionate number with poor labor market skills. Continuing large scale immigration of people with low education levels and minimal skill levels is just the type and degree of competition that might retard future progress. These industrious immigrants, who also are tying desperately to obtain a little more from this life, may unwittingly aggravate the conditions of those at or near the bottom of the social structure.

Although a tight labor market is not the only variable accounting for success, it does induce employers to search harder for workers, to reach down to less favored groups, and to provide them with jobs and training. It is possible that the large scale immigration after the American Civil War impeded the progress of recently freed slaves, and it is possible that the immigration lull after the 1920's facilitated the progress of many blacks who had migrated to the North to improve their economic chances. In this context, current immigration policy may not be conducive to economic progress for low income black Americans.

As we know, the native born citizenry dominates, by overwhelming amounts, the population structure of the United States. However, this nation is in many ways a nation of immigrants (and if you go back far enough so are virtually all nations), and should be proud of it. By and large, their contributions have been magnificent, and one can hope that new arrivals from around the globe will enjoy a repetition of the successes of their predecessors. However, the United States now takes in twice as many immigrants as the combined amount of the rest of the world (many countries take a dim view of any immigration), and does not "need" great quantities of immigrants to insure the growth of real per capita income. (Japan, for instance, has done quite well for itself with a relatively small population.) It is skills, ideas, attitudes toward work, and political and economic institutions rather than just numbers that account for prosperity.

Needless to say, numerous changes in immigration policy have been proposed. That you can enter the United States with AIDS but not with fruit for example, has caused consternation to at least some and there have been all kinds of suggestions about this and other aspects of current policy. Because of limitations of space only three ideas will be mentioned. First, it has been suggested that the current policy of providing for political refugees be continued, but that the policy of reuniting immediate family members be restricted to those comprising the nuclear family. Second, that America should admit more workers with special occupational skills and gifts and fewer of the unskilled.[31] Third that significant reductions be made in both legal and illegal immigration.

While labor markets do adjust, it takes time to do so. It is in America's interest that they do so quickly and that public policy not further exacerbate the conditions and hopes of those currently on the lower rungs of the economic and social structure. In the 1990's unemployment rates have been quite low. However, it is questionable whether year after year the economy will create and sustain the many new jobs needed to accommodate mass immigration and be willing to pay the steep welfare costs that would accompany a recession. History suggests that a *reduced* overall inflow--another "time out"--might be appropriate.[32] And there is evidence that every demographic group supports reductions in illegal and legal immigration.[33]

THE HUMAN FACTOR II: FREE MARKETS

Land and capital surely make their contributions to economic growth, but it is labor, the human factor, operating in a free market economy that remains the one vital and indispensable component. Some, however believe it to be otherwise.[34]

One understanding, especially dear to those enamoured with the writings of Marx and Lenin,[35] considers much economic growth in the West to be the result of imperialism, by which is meant the extension of sovereignty or control over areas beyond one's previous borders. Without doubt, the early colonists engaged in imperialistic activities toward the Indians, as did later Americans while they settled this vast continent. We shall have more to say about this sordid aspect of American history in the next chapter. Yes, they took the Indian's land, but, as will be explained below, land is only one of the factors that make for economic growth.

After independence, the United States acquired additional lands by purchase, treaty, or conquest, and this expansion represented a continuation of the "Old Imperialism," defined as the acquisition of land which is settled by those who acquire it.[36] Starting in the 1870's, economically developed nations--Great Britain, France, Belgium, the Netherlands, Germany and Japan--embarked on another phase of imperialism and began to carve up territories for themselves in various parts of the world, especially in Africa and Asia. The United States was a latecomer to this era of imperialism but did join in during the 1890's albeit on a more modest scale than other nations. As a result of the Spanish American War ("A splendid little war" as Secretary of State John Hay referred to it),[37] the U.S. gained control over Puerto Rico, Cuba, Guam, and the Philippines. The Republic of Panama was intimidated into permitting construction of a canal, and the

Roosevelt Corollary asserted the right to interfere in South America whenever necessary to enforce the Monroe Doctrine. The U.S. also sought and obtained influence in Asia.

What explains all this?[38] One argument cites the need for markets to provide an outlet for "surplus" goods resulting from capitalist "overproduction." However this is not an airtight argument. The United States at this time was a high income country more than capable of absorbing what was produced, and these foreign markets often sent more exports to the U.S. then they imported from it. Moreover, the imperialistic activities themselves hardly induced the native populations to want to buy American goods.

Then there is the assertion that foreign areas provided needed raw materials that were not available within "advanced" capitalist nations. This argument also falls flat. At the time, some of these areas were not known to possess raw materials unavailable in the United States and the raw materials acquired from such ventures were insignificant compared to the vast resources already under the U. S. domain. Moreover, the amount of raw materials that the U.S. exported exceeded the amount of raw materials that it imported. And, of course, we know that trade can and does take place without conquest.

Finally, there is the argument that imperialism was based on a "need" for investment outlets for advanced capitalistic nations experiencing declining rates of profit. However, the areas under consideration during the 1870-1914 period offered little in the way of investment opportunities compared to what was available in more developed nations, and there is no clear evidence that rates of profit were declining. Prominent businessmen in the United States--J.P. Morgan and Mark Hanna, for example--spoke vigorously *against* imperialist activities; in fact, during this period the U.S. received more foreign investment than any other country.

"Overproduction," "needed" raw materials, "falling rates of profit" do little to explain the imperialism of the United States or Western Europe.[39] What then were the real causes of imperialism during this era? First, imperialism does not necessarily develop out of capitalism. In fact, imperialism extends backward over millennia, and was practiced by numerous countries with a variety of different cultures and economic systems. In the time frame under consideration, imperialism developed out of a belief that the culture, political freedoms, standards of living, and economic systems of the United States and Western Europe were markedly superior to those in other areas. Therefore, the western way of doing things should be imposed on others. Political instability, slavery, the murder of a missionary etc. provided handy excuses for such incursions, ("savage wars of peace" as Kipling called them), and at times religion was used to justify imperialistic incursions. The disparities in political and economic conditions could be relied on to ensure victory.

Of course, there was more to Western imperialism than the conviction of Western superiority. Some businessmen did want to open up markets, and some nations did wish to insure an adequate supply of raw materials. And some nations desired to become great powers at a time when strong navies provided military prowess. Geographically scattered naval bases would help to secure expansion. Finally, nations considered foreign possessions as a source of prestige.

In the case of the United States, the desire for a strong military presence in Central America and strong feelings of nationalism inflamed by political oratory and sensational journalism overcame the resistance of many businessmen and others and led to the aforementioned imperialistic policies. Successful attempts to intimidate foreign powers into granting concessions did indeed make some individuals and business firms winners. However, there were also tremendous costs to the United States which in the aggregate dwarfed the gains that had found their way into the pockets of a limited few. These costs took the form of military buildup at the taxpayers' expense, and of greater importance, continuing resentment and distrust on the part of the native populations toward the United States. Especially was this true in South America. And when all is said and done, these activities did precious little to advance economic development.

Imperialism does not automatically confer significant lasting economic benefits. Spain and Portugal in earlier centuries, and the Soviet Union more recently exemplify imperialist nations whose aggressive behavior left little in the form of economic progress, while Switzerland, with such propensities virtually nonexistent, has maintained a strong economic record.

Some attribute American affluence to its vast natural resources. This argument bears a relationship to what has been just discussed. Of course, the extent of a natural resource base may well place some constraints on development (think of the man stranded on a desert island), and it is true that the United States had been blessed with an abundance of fertile soil, mineral resources, fuels, as well as a climate generally favorable to economic activity. However, other nations, not nearly so amply endowed--the Venetian republic, the Netherlands, Switzerland, Japan, and Hong Kong--have experienced considerable economic success at one time or another. Conversely, Brazil, Indonesia, and the Soviet Union, all in possession of enormous natural resources, and none have enjoyed spectacular economic success. One might note again that West Germany-- devastated at the end of World War II and without colonies--has provided us with a remarkable example of economic success. America became relatively wealthy when it was itself a colony and well before most of its natural resources were put into use or even made available. So, natural resources, while not unimportant, are not key to successful long run economic development.[40]

How to organize an economy so that resources may be best used to create wealth? This is the basic question, to which a free market economy still remains the best answer.

Free markets enable factor owners to try to maximize their own welfare as they perceive it. The forces of supply and demand determine resource prices which, in turn, become income for their owners. Consumer demand decides what will be produced, the profit motive induces production, and competition sees to it that cost is minimized and monopoly pricing eliminated, at least in the long run. Goods and services and the factors of production are allocated to their most economically valued uses, and this wealth creating market system promotes a greater volume of exchange, specialization, and the utilization of many different skills and talents. The government's role is restricted to insuring the observation of the system's rules, i.e. enforcing contracts, protecting life and property, correcting market imperfections where appropriate, and offering a safety net for the poor.

This system permits individuals to make independent decisions and to reap the gains or suffer the losses associated with them. It encourages cooperation and self-improvement among men, women, and families, and it inspires people to be industrious, to invest in their education and health, to save, to bear risk, to innovate, and to engage in capital formation--in short, to be responsible for their own destiny. Where free markets dominate, human effort and ingenuity flourish.

Attitudes are vital and the United States population surely has demonstrated an outlook favorable to economic growth. Material improvement ("getting ahead") has always been highly held, upward social mobility--in contrast to the outlook of the aristocracy--considered something to be proud of, and economically successful people are generally viewed with admiration. With commercial activities no longer stigmatized as they once were, and hard work considered a virtue, idleness (especially, among the gentry) was disrespected.[41] Moreover, the U.S. Constitution permitted citizens to pursue their own self-interests as they saw fit, and in so doing they generally looked to themselves for solutions to their problems and achievement of their goals.

Voluntary associations frequently developed to meet public needs including those of fire protection, defense, education and care of the sick, the injured, and the insane. Private associations helped to suppress vice, abolish slavery, advance the arts and sciences, and diffuse information about farming.[42]

Acceptance of change and the willingness to experiment, so evident in colonial times, also characterized the new nation. Instead of tradition, the best way to get the job done was what counted, and ones abilities rather than who one knew (although the use of "contacts" has never disappeared and never will), was more apt to determine success.

The words of de Tocqueville underscore the American character.

> I accost an American sailor and inquire why the ships of his country are built so as to last for only a short time; he answers without hesitation that the art of navigation is every day making such rapid progress that the finest vessel would become almost useless if it lasted beyond a few years. In these words, which fell accidentally, and on a particular subject, from an uninstructed man, I recognize the general and systematic idea upon which a great people direct all their concerns.[43]

Before the public school movement, schools in New England were ubiquitous. Education stressed the basics--reading, writing, and arithmetic --because this approach enabled the labor force to use technology and adopt to its many changes.[44] John Adams contemplating with some sadness the magnificent structures and public gardens in Paris, notes in a letter to Abigail that,

> The mechanic arts are those which we have occasion for in a young country as yet simple and not far advanced in luxury. I must study politics and war, that my sons may have liberty to study mathematics and philosophy, geography, natural history, and naval architecture, navigation, commerce and agriculture, in order to give their children a right to study painting, poetry, music, architecture, statuary, tapestry and porcelain.[45]

In both de Tocqueville and Adams we recognize that invincible American pragmatism which has informed our national economic activity from the first. There follow some examples of rational practicality flourishing in nineteenth century America's free market economy.

* Capital equipment was often resourcefully substituted for scarce labor. In the 1780's, Oliver Evans constructed a flour mill that used a continuous process "assembly line" technique which replaced some unskilled labor with capital but enhanced the productivity of the workers still employed. Although the principle of "uniformity" was already known, Eli Whitney (of cotton gin fame) implemented the principles of standardized (interchangeable) parts and division of labor. Receiving a contract from Congress to produce 10,000 rifles, Whitney first produced the machines to make the rifle parts, and then the parts themselves. With this method of "tooling up" before production, these weapons could be rapidly assembled and repaired by unskilled labor. Before this, rifles were laboriously constructed by a skilled gunsmith.[46]

* Such principles were applied to other industries and American unskilled labor became markedly more productive than its European counterpart. Not only did the American worker receive a higher wage, but there was greater equality within the American labor force as the skilled to unskilled ratio was lower than in other nations.[47]

* Successful farming required cleared land, fences, barns, and other types of agricultural capital. Immigrants were usually unable to meet these capital entry requirements and rationally sought jobs in urban areas.[48]

* So that scarce farm labor could be more effectively devoted to agricultural activities, farmers demanded and obtained factory produced (rather than home made) clothing and tools.[49]

* The mid-west concentration in the production of corn, wheat, and beef cattle exemplifies evolving regional specialization: when the Eastern states could no longer compete in producing these products, they turned to dairy farming. There was no central planning to interfere and keep inefficient operations alive.[50]

* The structure of nineteenth century American commercial banking--many small independent banks--reflected both individualism and fear of centralized power. In Great Britain, by contrast, there were only a few large banks, each with numerous branches throughout the country, and an entrepreneur could obtain money capital from a local branch which would draw upon the financial resources of its parent. American business firms, often unable to secure adequate credit from local banks developed a different system of finance. Smaller business firms were amalgamated into larger ones and this made attractive the stocks and bonds which they issued. Investment banking firms (J. P. Morgan's being the most famous) directed this process.[51]

These few nineteenth century examples, barely scratch the surface of American ingenuity; nevertheless, they demonstrate the dynamics of free markets. Allowing people to use their own resources as they see fit makes it likely that new ideas will receive a hearing in the market place, that new products and methods of production will be discovered, and that the status quo will be upset. At the heart of this process is the entrepreneur.

THE HUMAN FACTOR III: ENTREPRENEURSHIP[52]

As American as apple pie, the entrepreneur has been and remains the vital driving force in this nation's economic experience. Assuming uninsurable risk, he or she organizes land, labor, and capital into enterprises. Although risk inheres in virtually all activity (driving a car, changing a light bulb), entrepreneurs tend to be more self-confident and less risk averse than the average citizen. It is not, however, the assumption of risk that epitomizes the nature of entrepreneurship--rather it lies in the ability to innovate

Not only does the entrepreneur search for change and view it as opportunity to be exploited, he may actually create the opportunities himself. By introducing new products, different production methods, or a novel approach to organization, he generates new markets and sources of consumer satisfaction.

Ultimately, of course, it is the consumer who assigns value and determines economic worth. A baseball player's ability to hit fifty home runs in a season may command millions of dollars today but would have been considered worthless in the Middle Ages. By the same token, the skill necessary to kill a lion with a spear might elicit handsome rewards in a primitive society, but be regarded merely as a curiosity (a spectacular one to be sure) on Wall Street. At one time oil and bauxite were seen principally as contributors to soil infertility and penicillin mold was considered to be just a nuisance. The words of baseball umpire Bill Klem about a pitched ball, "It ain't nothing till I call it," might well be applied to the consumer in his role as sovereign.

Although personality types abound, the characteristics generally attributable to entrepreneurs include: enormous energy (they tend to be morning people); a desire for autonomy and adventure; curiosity; a sense that change is normal; commitment to a goal; inventiveness; daring; imagination; belief that a problem can be solved; determination in the face of adversity; and faith in one's work. Winston Churchill used to say that success was often nothing more than moving enthusiastically from one failure to the next. In a similar vein, Malcolm S. Forbes, Jr. noted that "Edison invented the light bulb on, roughly, his ten-thousandth attempt. If we had depended on central planners to direct his experiments, we would all be sitting around in the dark today."[53] These qualities and this spirit, constituting what George Gilder has called the "metaphysical capital" of a free enterprise system, play a crucial role in national economic development. One has only to look at the experience of West Germany after World War II for inescapable evidence of the value of this special type of human capital when it is allowed to operate in a market economy.

Entrepreneurs may work as employees or as employers, and sometimes they work alone. Contrary to popular belief, entrepreneurship may occur within the large corporation. General Electric has a history of starting new types of businesses and nurturing them into larger entities. To keep more creative workers and the profits they generate from leaving, some firms--Control Data, Hewlett Packard, and Texas Instruments--have permitted and facilitated entrepreneurship within the firm. The 3M Company has allowed its scientists to work as much as fifteen percent of their time on their own ideas.

Broadly construed, the category of entrepreneurship might include all who start up a business and thereby generate economic activity and employment. Our concern, however, is with the more innovative entrepreneurs whose dynamic ventures have had a more significant effect on the way we live. Although examples from the seventeenth through the twentieth centuries are plentiful, space allows mention of only a few of the more important and/or interesting entrepreneurs and their undertakings.

William Penn and Lord Baltimore epitomize an early colonial entrepreneurial spirit while the eighteenth century witnessed the ideas and deeds of Benjamin Franklin and Thomas Jefferson. Included among the famous names of the nineteenth century are John D. Rockefeller (petroleum refining), Andrew Carnegie (steel), J. P. Morgan (finance) and Cornelius Vanderbilt (steamships and railroads). Then there was Alexander Graham Bell, a compassionate entrepreneur whose work with the deaf (his mother and his wife were deaf) led him to the invention of the telephone.[54]

Notable entrepreneurs in the twentieth century include the following:

* Henry Ford: developed an inexpensive and easy to drive automobile.
* Wilbur and Orville Wright: the airplane.
* Frederick W. Taylor: "father" of scientific management.
* Theodore N. Vail: established a national telephone network known as AT&T.
* F. W. Woolworth: introduced fixed price merchandise.
* George Eastman: a sturdy lightweight camera.
* Edward Land: the Polaroid complete camera system (his three year old daughter asked him why she couldn't see her picture immediately after he took it with his camera).
* Thomas Edison: the phonograph.
* John and Will Kellogg: corn flakes breakfast cereal (they hated each other).
* The Hartford Family: the A&P supermarket chain.
* Milton Hershey: the Hershey Bar.
* H. J. Heinz : "57 Varieties" of processed food (he just liked the number).
* Henry Luce: *Time* magazine.
* Walt Disney: cartoon movies and recreational facilities.
* Clarence Birdseye; quick, palatable frozen food.
* Clarke and Gilbert Swanson: frozen dinner (designed for women who remained in the labor force after World War II; the package showed a TV set).
* William Levitt: affordable mass produced homes that enabled middle class families to move to the suburbs.
* Estee Lauder: cosmetics.
* Thomas Watson: pioneered the development of the computer at IBM.
* Arthur Murray: social dancing.
* Kemmons Wilson: clean reasonably priced motel rooms known as Holiday Inn (he took the name from a Bing Crosby movie).
* Thomas Carvel: soft ice cream chain.

* Peter Goldmark of CBS: the long playing record
* Ray Kroc: quick low cost meals in clean restaurants known as McDonalds. By the mid 1990's about one of every eight Americans who work have been employed at one time in this organization.[55] Within the fast food industry, McDonalds possessed the best record for advancing blacks.[56]
* Dave Thomas: abandoned as a child and epitomizing the self-reliance of entrepreneurship, his Wendy's successfully bucked the dominant competition of McDonalds, Kentucky Fried Chicken, and Burger King to establish itself as a major player in the fast food market.
* Earl Graves: founder and publisher of the *Ebony* magazine.
* William McGowan: founded MCI which successfully challenged AT&T's monopoly of long distance telecommunications.
* Josie Cruz Natori: with her knowledge of design brought from her native Philippines, she and her husband Ken (of Japanese ancestry) established a business producing elegant lingerie. In a short time, NATORI became a major name in the world of fashion.
* Fredrick Smith: Federal Express
* Vic Mills, Robert Duncan, and Norma Baker, of Proctor and Gamble: the disposable diaper.
* Willard and Forrest Walker: the automatic dishwasher.
* Willis Carrier: the air conditioner.
* Employees at the DuPont Corporation: nylon stockings.

One could go on and on with the zipper, pantyhose, television, radio, the VCR, and ballpoint pen, all of which have altered in various degrees the ways in which we live.

And often did entrepreneurship confound the experts. Before the automatic switchboard, Bell engineers predicted that by 1925, the services of *all* American women aged seventeen to sixty would be needed to meet the switchboard requirements of the growing telephone industry. At one time it was considered common knowledge that the computer would be of little use to business. IBM in the 1940's thought that at most, they might sell 100 of their big, bulky machines worldwide. Marconi's "wireless" was initially believed to be applicable only as a ship to shore communications device. The idea that radio could reach millions of people was developed by David Sarnoff.

Predicting the outcomes of entrepreneurial activities may not always be a very fruitful undertaking. The evolution and implications of the airplane surely would have strained the imaginations of the Wright Brothers, and who could foresee the effects that the automobile would have on the steel, rubber, glass, and petroleum industries, highway construction, the location of homes and businesses, not to mention the mating habits of teenagers.

Entrepreneurship can also be of a social nature.

* The Mayo Brothers developed the health clinic bearing their name.

* A. Phillip Randolph organized the Brotherhood of Sleeping Car Porters and led a long battle against racial discrimination.
* General George C. Marshall, Jr. offered his "Marshall Plan" at the 1947 Harvard University commencement. This became the blueprint for the redevelopment of the European economies devastated by World War II.
* The American clergy have established primary and secondary schools and colleges throughout the nation. The Society of Jesus (Jesuits), for instance, provide an outstanding example of franchising at the college level.
* In the post World War II era, Pace University and Farleigh Dickinson University established programs for nontraditional (mid-career) students who commuted to class, and often did so at nontraditional hours.
* Henry J. Kaiser pioneered Health Maintenance Organizations (HMO's). His World War II "Liberty Ships" and post war automobiles had made him a household name.
* Architectural firms have been formed to specialize in the preservation of historic buildings.
* After Candy Lightner's daughter was killed by a drunk driver, she founded Mothers Against Drunk Driving (MADD) which was instrumental in passing tougher laws against drunk drivers.
* Eddie Edwards, a black minister in Detroit organized a self-help program in the drug infested ghetto named "Ravendale." Community efforts include surveys of what residents want (jobs, places to shop, fewer crimes) a newsletter, houses painted and renovated, shrubs planted, security lighting, a little league, a health clinic, close of crack houses, and training for the unemployed. Although, far from a complete success, such activities indicate that entrepreneurial self-help has the potential to play a significant role in alleviating poverty.
* Robert L. Woodson, Sr. is the founder and president of the National Center for Neighborhood Enterprise which promotes inner-city, self-help projects.
* Former football star Jim Brown founded Amer-I-Can which recruits gang members off the streets and successfully redirects them into more positive endeavors.[57]
* Peter Cove and Lee Bowes founded America Works, an employment agency that contracts with state welfare agencies and provides brief training in basic skills as well as counseling to former welfare recipients. Its novel approach has placed thousands of clients in jobs and, "Employers have been overwhelmingly satisfied."[58]
* Profit making enterprises such as Work Family Direction of Watertown Massachusetts, Partnership Group in Landsdale Pennsylvania, and Pathfinder/ Eldercare in Scarsdale, N.Y. focus on the needs of older Americans and for a fee provide consultation, advice, and assistance. These organizations also have made their services available to the adult children of the elderly, and business firms which include IBM, AT&T, Travelers Corporation, Johnson and Johnson, Aetna Life, and Colgate-Palmolive.

* Former high school teacher Steve Mariotti established The National Foundation For Teaching Entrepreneurship (NFTE). This organization teaches entrepreneurial skills to handicapped and disadvantaged youth. Founded in 1987, NFTE has trained thousands of inner-city youth.
* Silas Purnell developed a program which has enabled over 40,000 black Chicago inner-city high school graduates to attend college.[59]

Starting a new business is hardly risk free. About one out of five new ventures fail within two years, and most of those that survive will experience but modest growth, and only a few will make it big.

Although the rewards of entrepreneurship are many, they are, perhaps, most apparent in the area of job creation. For instance, during the trying years 1974 to 1984, jobs in the U. S. economy grew by twenty-four million (at a rate markedly greater than in Japan), while Western Europe experienced a job loss of nearly three million. The dynamics of the American economy enabled it to absorb a tremendous influx of youngsters from the baby boom, accommodate the rapidly expanding female labor force, and provide work for millions of immigrants. All this took place at a time when traditional sources of employment--big business, education, and government--were in decline. This remarkable achievement was brought about primarily by small and medium sized businesses most of which had not existed a couple of decades ago. These positive trends associated with job creation have continued into the 21st century.

Small business is an important growth sector in the economy. In the early 1990's according to Dun & Bradstreet, small businesses (employing from one to five hundred people) accounted for two thirds of new jobs created and half of national output.[60] By 1996, there were 24.7 million small businesses, and while minorities accounted for only 2.9 million of that total, the growth of new starts for minorities (especially minority women) has recently grown significantly.[61]

Smaller scale enterprises create all types of employment opportunities. Contrary to popular belief, the managerial/technical/professional job classification accounts for nearly half of the jobs although many others represent entry level positions. The latter provide income and regular employment to the less skilled, particularly the young, thereby giving them access to basic work experience, and some training which later on may be parlayed into better jobs. Smaller business also tends to be more appreciative of and receptive to the skills of the older worker. Also, with over a third of U. S. companies owned by women, entrepreneurship has proven to be a very valuable source of income for females. Especially interesting, however, is the immigrant-entrepreneurship connection.

Entrepreneurship, broadly construed, has always served as an outlet for the economic energies of immigrants--even before the nation was formed. It has been more important to some groups than others; occurring more frequently among Jews, Italians, Chinese, Koreans, Japanese, Cubans, and people from the Middle East and less for Irish, Mexicans, and blacks (with the exception of those from the West Indies), and Puerto Ricans.

Capital to initiate a venture can come from one's own resources as well as from family, friends, and ethnic credit associations that offer loans on a rotating basis. But at least as important as money in accounting for success has been the willingness to work long hours; to practice thrift; to involve family and other ethnic group members in the business; to share information (networking, as they say today); to buy from one another; to concentrate in particular receptive industries; and throughout many, many hardships, to put on a happy face.

The effects of immigrant entrepreneurs have reverberated throughout the economy, especially in the food, clothing, and hairdressing, funeral, and insurance services. Sometimes an immigrant business becomes so successful that it expands beyond the principal ethnic group it was originally designed to serve: Italian and Chinese restaurants come to mind. Faced with a less than favorable business climate, immigrant entrepreneurship has mobilized capital, created jobs, and enlarged income. It has offered goods, services, and ambiance to low income communities which often endure rampant discrimination from the larger society.[62]

The great economist Joseph Schumpeter (1883-1950), believed entrepreneurship to be a vital dynamic force of capitalism. And it is the entrepreneur who spearheads the process of what he called "creative destruction" wherein free markets are constantly evolving as new products, new markets, and new methods of organization, distribution, and production revolutionize the economy. Old and inferior products and ways of doing things are discarded as the new ones appear and in this manner does capitalism efficiently use the factors of production to maximize wealth. Creative destruction is a long run competitive process that alters the economic structure "from within." It keeps businessmen on the alert and is a constant threat. "It disciplines before it attacks."[63]

Focusing on the deeds of great generals and politicians, historians are apt to ignore the importance of entrepreneurship when they characterize our national experience. The foibles of academic disciplines not withstanding, this nation's economic path has indeed been charted by entrepreneurs, and their endeavors have mobilized resources, accumulated capital, advanced technology, altered organizational structures, enriched our lives with an incredible variety of goods and services, and created all kinds of jobs for all kinds of people. It is by insisting on change that entrepreneurs keep stagnation at bay in both the private and public sectors and offer self-renewal to society. As George Gilder had observed, it is not the politicians, generals, or socialist intellectuals who create wealth or even know how wealth is created. Rather, "It is the entrepreneurs who know the rules of the world and the laws of God. Thus they sustain the world.... They are the heroes of economic life."[64]

---

[1]For a discussion of this decision-making process see Richard B. McKenzie and Gordon Tulllock, *The New World Of Economics*, 3rd. ed., (Homewood, Illinois: Richard D. Irwin, Inc., 1981), pp. 88-105.

For a more comprehensive presentation see Randall J. Olsen, "Fertility and the Size of the U.S. Labor Force" The Journal of Economic Literature (March 1994). pp.60-100.

[2]Steven A. Camarota, "Does Immigration Harm The Poor?," The Public Interest, Fall 1998, p.23.

[3]Roy Beck, "Overriding Elites." National Review June 16, 1997.

⁴Ronald G. Ehrenberg and Robert S. Smith, *Modern Labor Economics*, 5th ed.. New York: Harper Collins Publishers, 1994), pp.326-359.

⁵Ibid., pp. 333-338.

⁶Ibid., pp. 333,334.

⁷Steven A. Camarota, "Does Immigration Harm The Poor."

⁸Ibid., pp.27,28.

⁹Ibid., pp.349-356. Also see George J. Borjas, "The Economic Benefits From Immigration", *Journal of Economic Perspectives*, Spring 1995 and Steven A. Camarota, "Does Immigration Harm The Poor?"

¹⁰ Steven A. Camarota, "Does Immigration Hurt The Poor."p.24, 25 28.

¹¹Jonathan Hughes, *American Economic History*, 2nd ed. (Glenview, Illinois: Scott, Foresman and Company, 1987), p.106.

¹²For a robust discussion of the pros and cons of immigration policy see George J. Borjas, *Friends or Strangers: The Impact of Immigrants on the U.S. Economy* (New York: Basic Books, 1990) and Julian L. Simon, *The Economic Consequences of Immigration* (Cambridge: Basil Blackwell, 1990). and Peter Brimelow, *Alien Nation* (New York: Random House,1995). A sophisticated review of the literature can be found in George J. Borjas, "The Economics of Immigration," *Journal Of Economic Literature*, December, 1994, pp.1667-1717.

¹³Thomas Sowell, *Race and Economics* (New York: David McKay Company, Inc. 1975), pp.61,62, 143.

¹⁴Ibid., pp. 142-149, 238.

¹⁵Matthew Spalding, "From Pluribus to Unum," *Policy Review.*, Winter 1994,p35.

¹⁶Ibid., p.38.

¹⁷Lance Morrow, "Immigrants," *Time*, July 8, 1985, p.25.

¹⁸Lance Morrow, "Immigrants," p. 25.

¹⁹Thomas Sowell, *Race and Economics*, pp. 66-71.

²⁰Thomas Sowell, *Ethnic America* (New York: Basic Books, Inc. Publishers, 1981), p.14.

²¹Lawrence H. Fuchs, "The Search for a Sound Immigration Policy: A Personal View," in *Clamor At The Gates*, ed. Nathan Glazer (San Francisco: Institute for Contemporary Studies 1985), p.18.

²²Frederick Rose, "Muddled Masses," *The Wall Street Journal*, April 26, 1995.

²³Ronald G. Ehrenberg and Robert S. Smith, *Modern Labor Economics*, p.355.

²⁴George J. Borjas, "Immigration, the Issue-in-Waiting, "*The New York Times OP-ED* April 2, 1999.

²⁵Matthew Spalding, " From Pluribus to Unum," p.41.

²⁶The composition, ideas, and influence of the "new class" are discussed in more detail in Chapter 14.

²⁷Peter Brimelow, *Alien Nation*, pp.222-233.

²⁸For a forceful discussion of this issue, see Arthur M. Schlesinger, Jr., *The Disuniting Of America* (New York: W.W. Norton & Company, 1992).

²⁹Lawrence A. Uzzell and Donald Devine, "The Pros and Cons of Immigration," *Chronicles*, July, 1990, pp. 14-19.

³⁰Lawrence Auster, "The Forbidden Topic," *National Review*, April 27, 1992, pp.42-44.

³¹Barry R. Chiswick, "Immigration Policy for a Post-Industrial Economy," *The American Enterprise*, March/April 1995.

³²Peter Brimelow, "Time To Rethink Immigration?", *National Review*, June 22, 1992, pp. 30-46.

³³Steven A. Cararota, "Does Immigration Harm The Poor," p.32. Also, see Roy Beck, "Overriding Elites," *National Review*, June 16, 1997.

[34] Nathan Rosenberg and L. E. Birdzwll, Jr., *How the West Grew Rich* (New York: Basic Books, Inc., Publishers, 1986), pp.3-36.

[35] Thomas Sowell, *Marxism* (New York: William Morrow and Company, Inc., 1985), pp.213-215.

[36] Harold Underwood Faulkner, *American Economic History*, 8th ed. (New York: Harper & Brothers Publishers, 1960), p. 553.

[37] Samuel Eliot Morison, *The Oxford History of The American People* (New York: Oxford University Press, 1965), p.801.

[38] Robert C. Puth, *American Economic History*, 3rd ed. (New York,1993), pp.7,8,463-470. Also see, Strart Bruchey, *Enterprise: The Dynamic Economy of a Free People* (Cambridge: Harvard University Press, 1990), pp.381-390 and Gary M. Walton and Hugh Rockoff, *History of the American Economy*, 7th ed., (New York: The Dryden Press, 1994), pp.468-471.and Nathan Rosenberg & L. E. Birdsell, Jr., *How the West Grew Rich* (New York, Basic Books, Inc., Publishers,1986), pp.16-18.

[39] Thomas Sowell, *Marxism* (New York: William Morrow and Company Inc., 1985), pp. 213-215.

[40] Robert C. Puth, *American Economic History*, 3rd ed., pp.6,7.

[41] Gordon S. Wood, The Radicalism of The American Revolution (New York: Alfred A. Knopf, 1992), pp. 271-286

[42] Oscar Handlin and Mary Handlin, *Liberty in Expansion 1760-1850* (New York: Harper & Row, Publishers, 1989),pp.219-244.

[43] Alexis de Toqueville, *Democracy In America*, vol. II (New York: Vintage Books, 1957),p.35.

[44] Jonathan Hughes, *American Economic History*, 2nd ed., pp.112-113.

[45] Catherine Drinker Boowen, *Miracle at Philadelphia* (Boston: Little, Brown And Company, 1986))p. 165.

[46] Jonathan Hughes, *American Economic History*, 2nd ed., p.138.

[47] Ibid., pp. 139-141.

[48] Ibid., pp. 109, 185,186.

[49] Ibid., p. 141.

[50] Ibid., pp. 185-190.

[51] Ibid., pp. 355,356.

[52] The following books have provided the basis for the discussion of entrepreneurship: Peter Drucker, *Innovation and Entrepreneurship* (New York: Harper & Row, Publishers, 1985). George Gilder, *The Spirit Of Enterprise* (New York: Simon and Schuster, 1984). Jonathan Hughes, *The Vital Few*, expanded edition (New York: Oxford University Press, 1986).

[53] Malcolm S. Forbes, Jr., "Three Cheers for Capitalism," *Imprimis,* September, 1993.

[54] Dick De Voss, "Compassionate Capitalism," in Michael Bauman, *Morality And The Markerplace* (Hillsdale: Hillsdale College Press: 1994), p.116.

[55] Barnaby J. Feder, "Dead-End Jobs? Not for These Three," *The New York Times*, July 4, 1995.

[56] Jonathan Kaufman, "A Break Today," *The Wall Street Journal,* August 23,1995.

[57] Richard Price, "Jim Brown's Rebellion," *USA WEEKEND*, July 31-August 2, 1992.

[58] Sol Stern, "Back to Work," *The Wall Street* Journal, September 7, 1993.

[59] Ben Gose, "How a Resourceful Counselor Has Sent 40,000 Black Students to College," *The Chronicle Of Higher Education*, August 14, 1998.

[60] Steve Lohr, "Signs of Thaw for Small Business," *The New York Times*, November 4, 1992.

[61] David Judson, "Minority Enterprise On Rise," *Business: Gannett Newspapers*, Sunday, September 6, 1998. Also see Jeffrey A. Tannenbaum, "Enterprise: U.S. Firms Owned by Minority Women Grew by 153% in 9 Years, Report Says," *The Wall Street Journal*, June 25, 1997.

[62] Thomas Sowell, *Markets and Minorities* (New York: Basic Books, Inc., Publishers, 1981), pp.60-65. and Ivan Light, "Immigrant Entrepreneurs in America: Koreans in Los Angeles" in *Clamor At The Gates*, Nathan Glazer ed. pp. 161-178.

[63] Joseph A. Schumpeter, *Capitalism, Socialism, and Democracy*, 3rd ed. (New York: Harper & Brothers, Publishers, 1950), pp. 82-85.

[64] George Gilder, *The Spirit Of Enterprise*, pp. 18,19.

CHAPTER 10

FREE MARKETS IN ACTION: THE RESULTS

SOME SUCCESSES

"Respectable Professors of the Dismal Science" is the well-deserved appellation bestowed upon economists by the nineteenth century essayist Thomas Carlyle. For, prominent among what Karl Marx called the British classical school were the Reverend Thomas Malthus and David Ricardo, authors who indeed offered dismal predictions.

In 1798, Parson Malthus, as economists refer to him, penned his famous *Essay On The Principle of Population as It Affects the Future Improvement of Society* in which he posits the tendency for a nation's population to grow in geometric fashion (2,4,8,16...) while the food supply rises arithmetically (1,2,3...). This propensity for the population to outstrip the means of subsistence will lead, unless checked, to lives of poverty and misery for the masses. Malthus does, however, conjure two checks to population growth. Positive checks such as pestilence, war, and famine will produce the less than joyous effect of raising the death rate, while preventive checks--including postponement of marriage, abstinence from sex outside of marriage, and moral restraint--serve to reduce the birth rate. Malthus considers the former checks a much more likely occurrence than the latter, although either way, doom and gloom fill his vision.

David Ricardo, stockbroker, member of Parliament, and friend of Malthus, developed the ideas of the latter in his *Principles of Political Economy and Taxation* (1817). In this brilliant but rather complicated and badly written book, Ricardo sets forth his concept of the "iron law of wages," the proposition that the lot of the worker is, in the long run, a real wage hovering around subsistence. Wage increases above subsistence induce people to breed more, notes Ricardo, and, as the increased population enters the labor force (entry in those days was at a tender age), wages are competed back down to subsistence. A population increase of sufficient magnitude can force real wages below subsistence--that is, until enough people die off and restore "equilibrium".

Happily, these diagnoses, at least with regard to the industrialized nations, have proven to be erroneous. Although population growth was characteristic of both the nineteenth and twentieth centuries, (its rate declining for reasons already presented), so, too, was real output, and the latter (because free markets promoted productivity gains) exceeded the former by a significant margin. This margin was greater in America than in any other nation.

As we know, there are but two ways a nation can increase its real output and income; by augmenting the quantity of its factor inputs (labor, land, capital and entrepreneurship) and by making these inputs more productive. There is evidence that increases in productivity (the ratio of output to input) have been responsible for over half of American growth; the remainder has derived from an expansion of resources.[1]

Productivity advances enable us to enjoy higher levels of output while the schedule of hours worked diminishes. Using fewer resources per unit of output helps to conserve these scarce factors and holds down unit costs of production, and this in turn permits money wages and real wages (what you can actually buy with your money wage) to rise without the need for increases in product prices. Productivity gains restrain inflation and keep the economy internationally competitive. Finally, differences in productivity increases among industries help to explain changes in their relative importance. For instance, substantial productivity gains in one industry may result in a reduction of unit costs and a decline in relative prices (prices relative to the prices of products of other industries), which, *ceteris paribus* (all things being equal), should cause a rise in consumer demand, output, and employment. Industries where productivity is stagnant, might well experience, ceteris paribus, opposite effects.

Starting with the presidency of George Washington, the United States of America settled and developed much of a continent plus Hawaii. This democratic nation, governed under a rule of law, eventually became the world's leader in manufacturing and service industries, and although much diminished in relative importance, success in the agricultural sector enabled the United States not only to produce what it consumed (unlike other great nations such as China, India, and the former Soviet Union), but to be a major exporter of foodstuffs. Millions of immigrants have been absorbed into America's economy and culture, and every race, ethnic, and national group is represented in this country. Cities have been built, a sophisticated communications network constructed, educational, charitable, and artistic institutions established while government provided a dazzling variety of services, implemented a spectacular space program, and compiled an outstanding record of military defense. More than once in this century has government helped to preserve the liberties of the very countries from which our immigrants once embarked.

Real economic growth, uneven to be sure and interrupted by panics, recessions, and depressions was characteristic of both the nineteenth and twentieth centuries. By 1997, real Gross Domestic Product had reached an amazing 7.1 trillion dollars. This and per capita income were judged to be the highest in the world.[2]

Despite unending criticisms from those hostile to the market economy (especially their contempt toward downsizing), the U.S. has continued to display an outstanding record in providing work: there is evidence, for instance, that during the 1980-1998 period, net job creation was about 2 million jobs per year.[3] "From 1989 to 1995, total employment increased by 6.7 million to 124.9 million." And "...from an occupational perspective, growth in the managerial specialty groups (high paying occupations) accounted for 75 percent of the employment change." Moreover, "About four-fifths of that increase was in occupational-industry cells for which the median weekly earnings were above the median for all workers ($394)."[4] Remember that downsizing is an old story and reflects the reallocation of resources according to changing consumer demand, as expressed by dollar votes in the marketplace. A free enterprise system greatly facilitates this task and the reader will find it fruitful to compare this dynamic U.S. performance with performances of the rather stagnant welfare states in Europe.

Studies of national wealth tend to be made infrequently, but one analysis estimates per capita wealth in 1966 at about $11,000 or roughly ten times greater than that of colonial America in 1774.[5] Moreover, when standards of living (which include national income levels as well as costs for inhabitants) are calculated for different countries, the United States stands right at the top.[6]

While national income is unevenly distributed throughout the U.S. population, the benefits of long run development have (in varying degrees) spilled over to all income groups. Indeed, mobility has proved to be a very striking characteristic of income classes. Between 1975 to 1991 the incomes of the poor generally increased. Of those in the bottom 20 percent of the income distribution in 1975, only 5 percent remained there in 1991, and nearly a third moved up to the top 20 percent. In that same time period, the bottom 20 percent (by definition, there always has to be a bottom twenty percent) experienced a growth in average real purchasing power that exceeded that of the average gain of the top 20 percent. In addition, the poor today are much better off than in the past. While in 1920 the poor used about 75 percent of consumption expenditures to buy necessities, by 1993 that number had declined to 45 percent.[7] Employing today's poverty definitions, the percentage of families in poverty has declined form about 47 percent in 1900 to approximately 13 percent by 1967 (before the great expansion of the U.S. welfare state) and that is the number which it has hovered about until today.[8] As noted by Joseph Schumpeter, "The capitalist achievement does not typically consist in providing more silk stockings for queens but in bringing them within reach of factory girls in return for steadily decreasing amounts of effort."[9]

And what a cornucopia free markets have turned out to be. On the average, today a smaller percentage of the family budget goes to food and clothing (a sure sign of wealth) than it did in the past, and the quality of diet has much improved. People dine out more frequently, and wardrobes have become more elaborate. Housing typically includes more and larger rooms, indoor plumbing, air conditioning, and better furnishings. An assortment of cleaning machines, frozen foods, and disposable diapers have markedly diminished the burden of housework and markets have taken over the chores of caring for the sick and waking the dead. Televisions, stereos, video cassettes, VCR's, movies, theaters, and sporting events provide entertainment while telephones, computers, fax machines, automobiles, trains, buses, and airplanes facilitate communication and opportunities to travel. Moreover, a New York Stock exchange survey reveals that about 21 percent of the population directly owns stock or shares of equity mutual funds--a five hundred percent increase since 1952.[10] And roughly fifty percent of Americans either directly or indirectly own financial securities.

Although there is still a long way to go (and lately there has been a very long way to go), educational achievements nonetheless have been impressive. Currently, the average

American receives slightly more than 12 years of schooling, approximately 75 percent of the population has been graduated from high school, about 20 percent have obtained college degrees, and over half of those of college age are engaged in some type of higher education. Many graduate programs are the best in the world. In addition, business firms spend over $30 billion a year on employee training programs.[11]

Philanthropy has always been important in America. Currently, the citizenry gives to approximately one million nonprofit institutions operating within the United States. Included in this total are schools, hospitals, religious organizations, and some 550,000 charities.[12] About a billion hours of time are volunteered by almost 80 million Americans.[13] In 1993, nearly 92 percent of households with incomes in excess of $100,000 donated money to nonprofits, and it is interesting to note that the amount of household income and church attendance each correlate positively with the size of the donation.[14]

Nor have Americans neglected the arts. Billions of dollars allocated to the construction, maintenance, and operation of museums, theatres, opera houses, and concert halls have enabled millions of people each year to enjoy exhibitions and cultural performances. Book clubs and publishing houses are thriving. Despite the ubiquitous popular culture, more and more Americans increasingly wealthy and better educated pursue activities relating to the fine arts, and this thrust toward higher culture has spread throughout most of the United States. Thus, during the 1997-98 season 27 million people attended theatrical shows of which almost 60 % of them were outside New York. More than 110 symphony orchestras have been founded since 1980. Opera attendance rose to 7.5 million in the 1996-1997 season, an increase of 34 % since 1980. And 430 million more books were purchased in 1995 than in 1982. Tastes in food, drink, and clothing have also become more sophisticated.[15] All of which is to say that contrary to the complaints of social critics, American cultural achievements have been laudable.

Tremendous changes in the world of work have accompanied the relative decline in primary (agriculture and mining) and secondary (manufacturing) industries, and rise in tertiary sectors (such as communication, trade, finance, insurance, real estate, education, and government). Employment in white collar occupations has increased while the blue collar counterpart has experienced stagnation or decline. Today the assembly line is a far from typical American work site, and jobs generally are safer, cleaner, quieter, physically less demanding, pleasanter, better paying, and more likely to be chosen than in earlier periods.

Although in the Book of Genesis God directs man to work six days and rest on the seventh, we have come a long way from this first personnel policy. Today the work week averages around five days although there is evidence of a trend since the 1970's of more hours being allocated to the work place.[16] The quantity of paid vacations, holidays, sick leave etc. has increased substantially, and people have more free time to enjoy their families as well as for travel, entertainment, cultural or recreational activities, and just taking it easy.

Improved diet, sanitation, and medical care along with less physically strenuous work has allowed average life expectancy to rise to 74 years, contrasted to less than 50 years in 1900.[17] According to former Surgeon General C. Everett Koop, "Of all the people that ever turned 65 in the U.S., half of them are still alive. We expect by the year 2020 we will have 100,000 people who are 100 years old."[18]

And contrary to the conventional wisdom, overall U.S. productivity--the fount of these remarkable achievements--remains highest among all nations according to recent studies.[19] America's relative success can be traced, in part, to less severe government regulations with the result that firms can operate more efficiently and more competitively, which in turn forces them to follow and adopt to changing technologies, production methods, and other circumstances. Although the U.S. has long held the lead, there is little room for complacency. This is because the U.S. has lagged behind some other nations in *annual* rates of productivity increase which is to say that if such trends continue, these nations may surpass the overall productivity achievements in America.

SOME FAILURES AND SHORTCOMINGS

> Out of the Crooked Timber of Humanity No Straight Thing Was Ever Made.
> Emmanuel Kant

(A) Native Americans: The Indians

In 1492, thinking he had come upon the group of islands off the coast of Asia known as Indies, Christopher Columbus called the inhabitants *los Indios* or Indians. These were people who had traveled from Asia to Alaska perhaps over 15,000 years before by crossing a land mass later covered by the Bering Strait.[20]

Although no consensus exists, the number of Indians living within present United States borders may have exceeded five million at the end of the fifteenth century.[21] The Indian population consisted of numerous tribes, the names of which are familiar in one way or another to many Americans today, and include the Iroquois, Algonquin, Apache, Massachusetts, Mohegan, Delaware, Shawnee, Huron, Susquehannock, Conestoga, Mohawk, Seneca, Ottawa, Kickapoo, Winnebago, Peoria, Miami, Wichita, Mobile, Cherokee, Canarsie, Illinois, Dakota, Sioux, Missouri, Kansas, and Seminole.

De Toqueville thought them to be poor and ignorant but equal and free.

> Mild and hospitable when at peace, though merciless in war beyond any known degree of human ferocity, the Indian would expose himself to die of hunger in order to succor the stranger who asked admittance by night at the door of his hut; yet he could tear in pieces with his hands the still quivering limbs of his prisoner. The famous republics of antiquity never gave examples of more unshaken courage, more haughty spirit, or more intractable love of independence than were hidden in former times among the wild forests of the New World. The Europeans produced no great impression when they landed upon the shores of North America; their presence engendered neither envy nor fear. What influence could they possess over such men as I have described? The Indian could live without wants, suffer without complaint, and pour out his death-song at the stake. Like all the other members of the great human family, these savages believed in the existence of a better world, and adored, under different names, God, the Creator of the universe. Their notions of the great intellectual truths were in general simple and philosophical.[22]

Of course, not all tribes were alike and diversity was to be found not only in physical appearance, language and religion. There were tribes that exhibited bellicose tendencies and a ferocity that led to the torture and cruel execution of enemies which might include other tribes as well as white soldiers and civilians--both young and old and male and female. Some tribes enslaved their captured enemies. Sometimes, cannibalism was practiced. Others abhorred warfare; the Hopis, for instance, were among the most peaceful on earth.[23] Some tribes were authoritarian and there were those that employed democratic political institutions.

However, generalizations can be made and, by and large, Indians tended to be deeply spiritual people who believed that supernatural forces linked them to all other living things. They also held the land in profound respect. An Indian might believe it necessary to ask a tree's permission before cutting it down-although not for reasons closely connected to environmental concerns.[24] Willa Cather has explained how the Indian way (in contrast to that of the white man), "...was to pass through a country without disturbing anything; to pass and leave no trace, like fish through the water, or birds through the air." She also observes, "They seemed to have none of the European's desire to 'master' nature, to arrange and re-create. They spent their ingenuity in the other direction, in accommodating themselves to the scene in which they found themselves."[25] While a tribe might claim a particular territory as its own for hunting, fishing and dwelling, that land would be held and used in a communal manner and no one able to claim land as his personal property and to deny access to another member.[26] Finally, a "Belief in the freedom and dignity of the individual was deeply ingrained in many Indian societies."[27]

Vast differences emerged when Indian and European cultures collided. The former, while efficient at farming, did require extensive land for hunting and fishing. They were more present oriented than the Europeans and gave little thought to measuring time in terms of hours and days--the vocabulary of the Plains Indians, for example, contains no word for time.[28] Theirs was an unacquisitive society which sought not capital formation nor wealth augmentation but rather emphasized the status quo--something like the vision of Europeans during the Middle Ages. Illiteracy often characterized the Indians in North America and absent were the great civilizations and monumental buildings found among the Aztecs or Incas.[29] Surrounded by fertile soil and an abundance of resources, by today's standards they could be considered as impoverished.[30] Women gathered food while males acted as hunters and warriors and beyond the rigors associated with such roles, hard work was not only abhorred but looked upon as degrading.[31]

By contrast, the European settlers harbored sharp acquisitive instincts and placed a high premium on work. While the colonists' diet did not require nearly as much land as that of the Indians, the Europeans believed the land should be put to immediate use-- farmed, lived upon, built upon or held for speculation. In other words, they craved the Indians' land and tried to obtain it.[32] Thus, was the stage set for conflict, and arrive it did in copious amounts.

According to Adam Smith,

> Folly and injustice seem to have been the principles which presided over and directed the first project of establishing those colonies; the folly of hunting after gold and silver mines, and the injustice of coveting the possessions of a country whose harmless natives, far from having ever injured the people of Europe, had received the first adventurers with every mark of kindness and hospitality.[33]

And, indeed, from the very beginning the Indian taught the white settler methods of fishing, hunting, and planting; showed the way along trails, and introduced him to new implements and foods. It is doubtful whether the earliest settlements would have survived without the Indians' assistance. In 1621 the Pilgrims acknowledged at their first Thanksgiving dinner that without the advice of their Indian friend Squanto, they would not have had a harvest to celebrate.[34] Moreover, before the English settlement at Jamestown, the Indians had had a lengthy period of contact with the French which evolved into amicable trade relations. Peaceful coexistence through alliance, treaties, and mutual trade was in fact the case in the early years of Indian/English relations. William Penn's business dealings with the Indians, for example, were scrupulous.[35] However misunderstandings based on ignorance of different cultures, growing suspicions, corporate retaliation for perceived injuries (Indians might hold any white responsible for the transgressions of another white--a policy Indian tribes also might pursue with one another), along with a heady dose of English arrogance brought irreparable harm to the cause of peace.[36]

In a message to Congress, President Washington asserted that "We are more enlightened and more powerful than the Indian nations; we are therefore bound in honor to treat them with kindness, and even with generosity."[37] Alas, that was not to be. Rather, the folly and injustice inflicted on the Indians took not only the form of warfare and massacre (both sides were guilty in these activities), but forced removal from traditional hunting grounds, and confinement to reservations.

Alexis de Toqueville has provided us with the following sorry picture.

> The expulsion of the Indians often takes place at the present day in a regular and, as it were, a legal manner. When the European population begins to approach the limit of the desert inhabited by a savage tribe, the government of the United States usually sends forward envoys who assemble the Indians in a large plain and, having first eaten and drunk with them, address them thus: "What have you to do in the land of your fathers? Before long, you must dig up their bones in order to live. In what respect is the country you inhabit better than another? Are their no woods, marshes, or prairies except where you dwell? And can you live nowhere but under your own sun? Beyond those mountains which you see at the horizon, beyond the lake which bounds your territory on the west, there lie vast countries where beasts of the chase are yet found in great abundance; sell us your lands, then, and go to live happily in those solitudes." After holding this language, they spread before the eyes of the Indians firearms, woolen garments, kegs of brandy, glass necklaces, bracelets of tinsel, ear-rings, and looking-glasses. If, when they have beheld all these riches, they still hesitate it is insinuated that they cannot refuse the required consent and that the government itself will not long have the power of protecting them in their rights. What are they to do? Half convinced and half compelled, they go to inhabit new deserts, where the importune whites will not let them remain ten years in

peace. In this manner do the Americans obtain, at a very low price, whole provinces which the richest sovereigns of Europe could not purchase.[38]

Especially pernicious were the policies of Presidents Andrew Jackson and Martin Van Buren during the 1830's whereby tens of thousands of Indians were forcibly moved to various parts of Oklahoma. In 1838 and 1839, in what has become known as "The Trail Of Tears," almost a quarter of Cherokees who were being pushed from Georgia into Oklahoma died of "disease, starvation, and hardship.[39]

In matters of real estate, fraud became the rule rather that the exception when the Indian encountered the white man and his government.

> Sitting Bull, for example, stated that he would be glad to make a treaty with white men if the government would send him a white man who would tell the truth. The Cherokee tribe took a voluntary vow of poverty, because they believed that as long as they possessed anything worth taking, white men would keep after them until they got it.[40]

These nefarious activities were, of course, rationalized in various ways: that the Indian was too savage and dangerous to civilization; that he must be assimilated into white culture or separated from it; and that the existence of other nations and tribes on this continent were inconsistent to the idea of a United States of America. Then, there was the ever present problem of who should own and control the land. As President James Monroe wrote in 1817, "The hunter or savage state requires a greater extent of territory to sustain it than is compatible with the progress and just claims of civilized life...and must yield to it."[41]

While many Indians acquiesced to these policies with shame, resignation and confusion, many others under the leadership of such people as Tecumseh, Chief Joseph, Geronimo, Sitting Bull, and Crazy Horse put up resistance. In 1879 Chief Joseph was permitted to visit Washington where he eloquently pleaded for justice.

> If the white man wants to live in peace with the Indians he can live in peace....Treat all men alike. Give them all the same law. Give them all an even chance to live and grow. All men were made by the same Great Spirit Chief. They are all brothers. The earth is the mother of all people, and all people should have equal rights upon it.... Let me be a free man--free to travel, free to stop, free to work, free to trade, where I choose, free to choose my own teachers, free to follow the religion of my fathers, free to think and talk and act for myself--and I will obey every law, or submit to the penalty.[42]

However, such equal rights were not to be and the physical conquest of the Indian continued during the nineteenth century, reaching its completion during its last decade with the massacre at Wounded Knee in South Dakota in 1890, and then in the 1898 battle at Leech Lake, Minnesota.[43]

Nor is this the end of the story. For accompanying the coercion, violence, and chicanery inflicted on the Indian tribes was no small amount of paternalism. Those in charge of Indian reservations often attempted (when they were not actively engaged in cheating their subjects), to force assimilation by undermining the Indians' traditional methods of self-government, persecution, and other harsh modes of intimidation.

One of the effects of all this was a tremendous decline in the Indian population. By 1910 the Indian population in the United States had declined to but a couple of hundred thousand. Moreover, many Indians, stripped of responsibility for their own success or failure, found themselves poverty stricken with little motivation, and high rates of alcoholism and other pathologies.[44]

Although problems continue to abound, the twentieth century has been witness to at least some positive change. Many Indians volunteered for service in World War I and in 1924 a grateful nation conferred citizenship on all Indians who are free to move about within the 50 states just like any other citizen. Their lives, however, are influenced by treaties and special agreements which make them a unique minority. Many, but by no means all, have been assimilated into the larger society (without necessarily losing their Indian culture), and today one finds college trained Indian men and women in business, politics, and a wide variety of professions.[45] Some success has been achieved through increased militancy over the rights to ancestral lands (including the natural resources contained within them), as well as the right to self-determination including that of being different--also known as "the white man's problem." The Hopis, for example, urge their people to avoid the competitiveness of the non-Indian world, and retrain the customs of their ancestors and seek harmony with the universe.[46]

Because of self-definition, it is difficult to obtain exact statistics on the number of Indians in the United States. However, during the twentieth century, the Indian population has experienced significant growth. By the decade of the 1990's it is estimated to approximate 2 million with about 300,000 living on reservations.[47] A few tribes have struck it rich with financial windfalls from oil and other energy sources, and other tribes are successful in agricultural, mining, manufacturing, service and recreational endeavors including casino gambling.[48] There is evidence of growing entrepreneurship in these areas, and since 1968, 26 tribal colleges (giving associate, bachelor's, and/or master's degrees) have been established.[49] Founded recently and modeled after elite boarding schools that prepare students for Ivy League colleges, the Native American Preparatory School in New Mexico is successful in preparing Indian youth for elite institutions of higher learning, as well as for participation in tribal life.[50] More Indians are becoming assimilated while at the same time a reinvigorated pride in their Indian heritage is emerging. Nonetheless, Indian unemployment rates as well as mortality rates are above the national average and their average incomes below it. Poverty and its accompanying ills remain ubiquitous. Many of these cultural and economic problems can with ease be traced to what Thomas Jefferson in a somewhat different context once called a "long train of abuses and usurpations."

(B) Slavery

As we know, not everyone who came to these shores did so voluntarily, and the enslavement of Africans provides another example of less than virtuous behavior in American history.

Early in the seventeenth century these unfortunate souls began to arrive here in chains. Now the property of Europeans and Americans they were, "Marched in chains to points of embarkation, sold to strange-looking men who spoke an incomprehensible language, branded, dragged struggling, into long canoes that took them to ships waiting offshore...Some had never before seen giant ships, the ocean, or white men."[51] Then came the infamous "Middle Passage": Africans were crammed into filthy vessels and in pain and terror made to suffer the voyage to America. Upon arrival in America more trouble awaited. "Whether subjected to a "scramble," whereby prospective purchasers rushed on board seeking the likeliest slaves at a fixed price, or to a public auction, the Africans found themselves examined, poked, and prodded by eager customers."[52] Eventually, they were sold off to a master. New slaves often resisted and these "savages" were "broken in" by close supervision and physical punishment.[53]

Government proved a willing accomplice to the slave trade through legislation which limited slaves' personal, economic, and civil liberties. They could not travel freely, vote, marry white women (and this applied to free blacks as well), or carry arms. Prohibitions were vigorously and often cruelly enforced. Moreover, it was illegal to teach slaves or free negroes to read, which markedly reduced their ability to learn ways to gain freedom and thus reduced their incentive to escape.[54]

Slaves worked at quite a variety of occupations, and this was true from the very beginning. They were employed as hunters, guides, lumbermen, as well as in skilled trades (such as carpenter, blacksmith), and as domestics.[55] However, the agricultural sector (especially those parts of it that embraced tobacco, cotton, and rice) was the principal one to which they were allocated, and it was here that they engaged in long, arduous labor cultivating crops on farms (large in number but relatively small in size) or on plantations (small in number but large in size). Most slaves did not work on plantations.[56]

The treatment slaves received from their owners ranged from the kind and gentle to the psychopathic. Masters often claimed that they knew and loved their slaves and occasionally there was some truth to these assertions. However, they must be interpreted in the context of the extreme paternalism and the violence that characterized the master/slave relationship. Yes, many masters knew the names of their slaves, looked after them and on the average provided an ample, if not well balanced, diet and adequate, albeit, crude living quarters. Time off was awarded, holidays celebrated, and parties held to mark an event.[57] Of course, slaves were an expensive investment (the price of a prime field hand approximated $1,800 in 1860), and the treatment of slaves reflected, in part, the owner's desire to keep them healthy and productive. In fact, high slave prices would often lead owners to use them in tasks considered physically safe.[58] Positive incentives such as gifts, bonuses, more leisure, and the possibility of rising in status to be the driver of a work gang or an overseer, were widely employed to achieve efficiency.[59]

Yet at no time could slavery be considered painless or benign. Without doubt, slaves suffered exploitation. They received less than they produced and they were forced to work under conditions that free workers would reject.[60] Moreover, a slave could not only be bought or sold or rented or moved but the inherent paternalism meant substantial interference in his or her life. Abundant rules determined the time the slave was to rise, to get to work, and to take breaks. Permission was required to visit neighbors or to marry.[61] Treated as a child, the slave had much of his independence as well as his ambition destroyed.

Punishment, another aspect of paternalism also contributed to the molding of slave behavior. Punishment could range from withholding privileges such as visiting neighbors or having one's own vegetable garden, to the physical which included whippings, amputations, incarceration in private jails, use of the stockade, torture and for women, exploitation and rape and even death. Although there were laws against cruelty to slaves, violations rarely made it to the courtroom.[62]

Slaves, in turn, shaped their own lives as best they could and away from their labors they lived in a world little known to the master. Slave families, with remarkable resilience, acted as a vital bulwark in resisting the dehumanizing forces surrounding them. Slave marriages were usually long lasting, and the children received love and care.[63] "When the master's work was done, they ate, sang, prayed, talked, quarreled, made love, hunted, fished, named babies, cleaned house, tended their garden plots, and rested. They strove to fill their lives with pleasurable activities that would help them to transcend their status as slaves."[64] We can only try to understand the fear which slaves harbored that members of their families might be sold off to another master who might take them far away. For slaves in the upper south, the possibility of being "sold down the river" (in this case the Mississippi River) to areas where slavery was especially harsh, was an ever present source of fear and anxiety.[65]

Religion assumed great significance in the lives of American slaves. Religious belief generally combined Christianity and the practice of faith the slaves brought with them from Africa. Rituals from the latter might be employed to harm enemies or prevent punishment to oneself, whereas Christianity offered comfort to the oppressed and raised the prospects of deliverance to freedom--perhaps in this world, and, if not, in the next.[66]

Although slave insurrections were few, there was no small amount of resistance to it. What might be called "silent sabotage" included stealing, feigning illness, "accidentally" breaking equipment, and working at a deliberately slow pace. Thousands of slaves ran away, and some masters were murdered.[67]

As we have already seen, various justifications for slavery had been offered during the seventeenth and eighteenth centuries in defense of this inhumane system. During the nineteenth century, defenders of slavery in the south asserted that under their paternalistic system slaves were better off than peasant populations in various parts of the world or than were the free "wage slaves" in England and in the northern states which were experiencing the turbulence associated with industrialization. Pro-slavery spokesmen also denounced the exploitation of labor in a free market which they linked to excesses of liberty and democracy. For them (unlike the socialists who also focused upon exploitation) the sound foundation for a civilized society comprised hierarchy, order, and inequality, and slavery was a proper component. There were also religious arguments, the most prominent stressing the desirability of bringing Christianity to the heathen.[68]

However, not everybody bought the old assortment of justifications for slavery. From the beginning there were Americans who despised the institution. Most of them never held slaves and many of those who did, eventually set them free and the system became an important social issue in the latter part of the eighteenth century. The ideology of the Enlightenment, emphasized equality, freedom, and liberty and questioned the alleged depravity and inferiority of the slave and the inhumanity of the slave system. Moreover, this was a system contrary to the ideology and institutions of free market capitalism with its emphasis on economic liberties and incentives for self-improvement.[69]

Some states began to provide for manumission, some slaveholders set their slaves free and the abolitionists surely dramatized the issue. By the time of the Emancipation Proclamation there were perhaps 500,000 "free people of color" and much prosperity was to be found in this group thanks to hard work and the assistance of churches and various mutual aid organizations.[70] However, the South stood its ground, and it was not until the midst of the Civil War that the central government saw fit to abolish the institution of slavery.

A majority of the framers of the U. S, Constitution successfully fought to terminate the importation of slaves and hoped that over time it would just fade away and die. This, however, was before the invention of the cotton gin which accelerated the demand for cotton and slaves. Obviously, slavery neither died (eight of the first twelve presidents were owners of slaves), nor showed any sign of doing so by 1860. In that year, approximately twenty-five percent of southern whites owned slaves, and there were many others who hoped to do so.[71] Slavery was a profitable business,[72] and slave owners were disproportionately represented in southern political structures. The potential abolition of southern slavery would mean not just a tremendous economic loss but the death of a social system--a way of life--and the destruction of southern "liberty."[73] In other societies, such as ancient Greece and Rome, slaves were a relatively unimportant component of the population, and they could and often did purchase their own freedom. However, this possibility was denied to slaves in the South. As Thomas Sowell has observed, such a course of action would have imposed substantial costs on the white citizenry, "...including (1) increased costs of holding and controlling the remaining slaves, and (2) political costs from the presence of freedmen emerging from a slavery in which they had been kept ignorant and demoralized."[74] Thus in 1860 was the South led to war with the North.

Employing his powers as Commander-in-Chief of the armed forces, President Lincoln, acted in a manner that he thought would help to win the war and on January 1, 1863 issued the Emancipation Proclamation which brought a legal end to slavery in rebel territory. It did not extend to states loyal to the union where slavery still existed. However, two years later, the Thirteenth Amendment prohibited slavery anywhere in the United States. Subsequently, the Civil Rights Act (1866) and the Fourteenth and Fifteenth Amendments (1868 and 1870) gave blacks all the rights accorded to other citizens of the United States.

Reconstruction legislation did not include any big welfare programs or affirmative action. Many blacks shared the view of Frederick Douglass, an influential American leader who had escaped from slavery, edited an anti-slavery journal, advised President Lincoln, became Marshall of the District of Columbia, and General Consul to Haiti. When it came to ex-slaves, Douglass thought it best that they be left alone; "our duty is done better by not hindering than by helping our fellow-men," and "the best way to help them is just to let them help themselves."[75]

And these newly freed people did help themselves. They moved into cities, sought to own their own land, established their own churches, displayed a passion for education, and exercised limited political power. And this in spite of the forced labor system from which they had emerged, a system which did little to prepare them for success in a free market economy. Despite their consequent lack of experience in budgeting, planning, taking the initiative, and despite their initial illiteracy, their efforts to take advantage of new opportunities met with some success.[76] However, high expectations were dashed as states enacted laws designed to restrict the freedoms of blacks. Accompanied by violence and threats of violence, state legislation effectively negated the voting franchise, mandated segregation for education, transportation and entertainment facilities, hotels, and drinking fountains and in defiance of the very tenets of economic freedom, erected a variety of other impediments to economic progress.[77]

Remarkably, in face of these obstacles, blacks through their families, churches, educational institutions, and self-help associations[78] have fought over the decades to dismantle the more virulent forms of racism--whether de jure or de facto--and courageously have continued to improve themselves. As a group, American blacks have advanced in terms of land ownership, business enterprise, union membership, occupational mobility, real income, and participation in the political process. Their contributions to this nation are manifest in every occupation and industry, and bravely have they fought in every war including the American Revolution. Sadly, however, the legacy of slavery continues to take its toll in many ways and for a disproportionate number of blacks, realization of the "American dream" is very far away.

(C) Women

While the treatment generally accorded to women as a group did not approach the harshness directed at Indians and slaves, they nonetheless have not always enjoyed full personal, political, and economic freedoms. Denied the right to vote in the new republic and legally subsumed in their husbands identity (married women frequently had no right to own or control property independently),[79] both married and unmarried women often found ways to become entrepreneurs and to organize and participate in a wide assortment of voluntary associations. Female interests were expressed not just in church sponsored sewing circles, but in raising funds and building charitable and educational institutions, in fostering the temperance movement and anti-slave societies, in organizing aid societies during the Civil War, and in establishing settlement houses and reform associations to help the downtrodden.[80]

In the political arena, the desire of some women to challenge the ideology of separate spheres for men and women became the subject of a meeting at Senaca Falls, New York in 1848. Led by Elizabeth Cady Stanton and Lucretia Mott, over two hundred women and nearly forty men (including the abolitionist Frederick Douglass) assembled. As Mrs. Stanton put it, others, including "Drunkards, idiots, horse-racing, rum-selling rowdies, ignorant foreigners, and silly boys," had privileges denied to women.[81] Recalling how their great grandmothers and grandmothers had boycotted tea and made clothing for soldiers of the Revolutionary Army, and how their mothers had been a prime factor in the "Great Awakening" a generation before, and holding themselves "born for liberty," they issued a Declaration of Sentiments which began, "We hold these truths to be self-evident, that all men and women are created equal..."[82] In such manner did women claim their rights as autonomous individuals of full citizenship, including the right to suffrage.

The right to suffrage found resistance in many quarters. Grover Cleveland believed that female voting might disrupt "a natural equilibrium so nicely adjusted to the attributes and limitations of both {women and men} that it can not be disturbed without social confusion and peril." Despite obstacles, the women's perseverance and continued protest finally resulted in the Nineteenth Amendment, which provided women the right to vote and was signed into law in 1920.

Tennessee became the 36th state to approve the Nineteenth Amendment, which put it over the top. The deciding vote in that state was cast by Henry Thomas Burn, a formerly anti-suffrage legislator. Admonished by his mother to vote in the affirmative ("Hurray and vote for suffrage--Don't forget to be a good boy", she wrote to him), young Henry explained his vote in a speech from the floor: "I know that a mother's advice is safest for her boy to follow and my mother wanted me to vote for ratification.... But I appreciate the fact that an opportunity as does seldom come to mortal man to free 17 million from political slavery was mine. I do it not for any personal glory but for the glory of my party."[83]

Besides the issues already mentioned, one must note that the majority of adult American women engage in economically productive work. This is as true today as it has been in the past. Historically, the work performed by women of a direct economic nature can be separated into three categories: production of goods and services for consumption by their own families; production of goods at home for sale in the market; and market work outside the home for money.

In preindustrial colonial America, women performed the traditional household tasks of cooking, cleaning, and caring for children. In addition, they engaged in some light manufacturing at home, producing goods that were difficult to obtain from outside sources such as soap, candles, cloth and clothing. Also, the shortage of labor characteristic of this society facilitated the entry of women into occupations such as store manager, tavernkeeper, domestic servant, and seamstress. At harvest time, women assisted the men in the fields.

Although most of the spinning and weaving output in the seventeenth century was for home consumption, women sold some of their yarn and cloth to local shopkeepers. By the latter half of the eighteenth century, women found work spinning yarn for merchants who either sold it or put it out to be woven into cloth. In the nineteenth century, factories had begun to produce textiles and women sought employment in this and other growing industries. They were finding ways to supplement family income while they continued to engage in agricultural activity in an economy still characterized by labor shortages.

During the nineteenth century, market work continued to be important for many women. Usually employment was (and often still is) a necessity for women who were widowed or divorced. Wives of immigrants typically sought employment, and often in the factories where their husbands and children worked. This not only increased family income at a time when wage rates were low, but it allowed them to watch over their children. In the latter part of the century, women found increasing opportunities in teaching, nursing, and clerical work.

In addition to work outside the home, women earned money by taking in boarders, doing laundry, and homework for the needle trades. Also, the production of goods at home for family consumption continued to be important. Women were growing vegetables, raised poultry, preserved food, baked, and made clothing, curtains, and other home furnishings.

The twentieth century has witnessed a substantial increase in the participation rates of women in market work. In 1890, when official data first were collected, the Female Labor Force Participation Rate (FLFPR) was 18.2, and 17 percent of all workers were women. The FLFPR grew slowly in ensuing decades, and by 1940 it stood at 28.9. There was a sharp increase in female employment during World War II, as women were needed to overcome labor shortages. And work they did at all kinds of jobs including ship construction, ferrying airplanes, and railroad track maintenance. *"Rosie The Riveter"* was a popular song. By 1945, the FLFPR had reached 38.1 but after the war, many women returned to the home, and by 1947, the FLFPR had declined to 30.8. Shortly thereafter it began to rise again, and by 1994 it stood at 58.8, with females accounting for 45.9 percent of all workers.[84]

Prior to 1940, the "typical" female worker was in the 20-24 age cohort and single. During the 1940's, older married women began to enter or reenter the labor force in increasing numbers. This trend continued into the 1950's so that by 1960, the number of women over 34 years old represented a much higher percentage of the female labor force than it had in 1940. Especially was this true for the 45-54 age cohort. In subsequent decades increasing numbers of married women have sought market employment and the most significant growth had been in the 20-34 age cohort. Many women in this category are mothers with preschool children.

These changes have made the profile of the female labor force more representative of the total female population of working age in terms of age and marital status. Today the working women is no longer atypical. Moreover, women work in a much broader variety of occupations than they did in the not too distant past when sex segregation was more pronounced. In fact, women regularly make contributions in medicine, theatre, politics education, publishing, management, and just about all other professions.

As previously indicated, entrepreneurship has been an exceptionally valuable route for women who wish to participate in the national economy. Female owned firms employ more workers than do the Fortune 500 companies.[85] In the early 1990's over half of new businesses were started by women.[86] American women also have reached top executive levels in the corporate world.[87]

Of course we know that market work for females has never received universal male approval. In the post revolutionary era, the proper role for a young, middle class woman was to marry and then to channel her energies into domestic activities and children. This profile was an outgrowth of the idea that an enlightened society should treat women not as not as beasts of burden or virtual slaves, but rather with delicacy and love. She was thought to have the power to civilize and refine man and thus to promote public virtue. Especially was it important--in fact, patriotic--to assume the responsibility of raising her children to be moral and virtuous citizens.[88] As de Toqueville noted, "No free communities ever existed without morals, and...morals are the work of woman."[89] And, by the way, not having to work was considered a freedom.[90] De Toqueville also believed that women had played a role vital to American success:

> As for myself, I do not hesitate to avow that although the women of the United States are confined within the narrow circle of domestic life, and their situation is in some respects one of extreme dependence, I have nowhere seen woman occupying a loftier position; and if I were asked, now that I am drawing to the close of this work, in which I have spoken of so many important things done by the Americans, to what the singular prosperity and growing strength of that people ought to be attributed, I should reply: To the superiority of their women.[91]

Because it led to female financial independence, factory work was considered especially dangerous to this ideal. According to Friedrich Engels, the revolutionary comrade of Karl Marx, "The fact that a married women is working...{leads} to a reversal of the normal division of labor within the family. The wife is the breadwinner while the husband stays home {when unemployed} to look after the children and do the cleaning and cooking....It deprives the husband of his manhood and the wife of all womanly qualities."[92]

These attitudes were reinforced in the second half of the nineteenth century when a substantial increase in the quantity of immigrants induced society to emphasize the need to find employment for men. Market employment for a white middle class wife was held to be inconsistent with her social status. "A women who works degrades her husband." Employment, however, continued to be acceptable for wives of Blacks and poor immigrants.

While the Knights of Labor welcomed women, other labor unions, especially the more successful American Federation of Labor, excluded them from membership. Labor laws in the twentieth century (more on this in Chapter 11), regulated minimum wages, maximum hours, night work and physically hazardous work. Although they were supposed to protect women, they also had the effect of excluding women from higher paying positions, and not all women supported these measures.

Among the major factors accounting for the rise in FLFPR during the twentieth century were the productivity increases in a growing economy, which not only made more jobs available to choose from, but also created more service jobs that were less physically demanding and hazardous and these had wide appeal to women. Another vital force was the secular increase of real wages for women in the labor market. This meant that a woman who refrained from market work incurred a significant opportunity cost (what one gives up as a result of a course of action). Higher levels of education (which women have very much been a part of) tend to be positively correlated with higher wages and thus with higher opportunity costs. Other incentives for women to work include the desire to enhance family living standards, the rising divorce rates which reinforce women's desire for financial independence and security, and a more favorable societal attitude toward market work for women that has been accompanied by an outlook that denigrates the roles of housewife and mother. The proper role for women in the family, in the workplace and as individuals; discrimination against women in the workplace; and the proper role of government in such matters have been, are, and without doubt will continue to be highly contentious issues. They are issues with profound economic, political, personal, and societal implications. As this section draws to a close, let us simply note that the choices and opportunities available to women in the United States have become, in a relatively short period of time, truly phenomenal.

(D) Other Problems

While other minority groups in America have escaped the harsh treatment accorded to Indians and African Americans, most have experienced the pain of discrimination. Irish, Italians, Jews, Poles, Chinese, Japanese, Hispanics, and others have been ridiculed for their cultural habits and religious practices; have been regarded with suspicion, fear, and hostility; and have had opportunities denied them on the basis of race or ethnicity. Especially has this been true for the first waves of an ethnic group. Within a couple of generations, however, immigrants tend to be assimilated into the American mainstream, at which point they themselves often did the discriminating. Economic discrimination (such as blocking the entry of an ethnic group into an occupation or paying an equally skilled ethnic group a lower average wage than other groups) continues, along with other forms of discrimination, to be part of the American scene.

The behavior of the participants in a free market economy is sometimes lacking in ethical dimension, and on this subject, juicy tales may be told.

* In the first half of the nineteenth century, commercial banks issued their own bank notes, and this paper money (which the banks promised to redeem in gold or silver) served as an important component of the money supply. At one time, over 10,000 *different* types of bank notes circulated in the economy, and one can only imagine the chicanery. To guard against any loss of specie, a less than consumer friendly Georgia bank required anyone bent on redeeming one of its notes to swear before a justice of the peace and in the presence of five bank directors that the notes belonged to him and not to another bank. In Michigan, only the main office of a bank with branches would redeem its notes, and that office located perhaps in the woods (where the wildcats lived), might be somewhat inaccessible. Again in Michigan, bank officials outwitted the bank examiners by quickly transferring the same gold and silver to another bank and then to another, always one jump away from the examiners.
* Bribes to legislators and other public officials (who often took them) was hardly unknown and railroading in the second half of the nineteenth century proved a particularly fertile ground for this activity. Vice President of the United States Schuyler Colfax and Congressman (later to become President) James Garfield were among other high officials who used their political influence to cover up financial shenanigans related to the construction of the Union Pacific Railroad.
* The triumvirate of Jay Gould, Daniel Drew, and "Jubilee Jim" Fisk fleeced the stockholders of New York's Erie Railroad and left that line in financial shambles.

* Market cornering, kickbacks, price manipulation, and monopolistic practices, although hardly dominant, are nonetheless part of the mosaic of economic growth. There is a story about a hard driving businessman who rather indignantly said to the financier J. P. Morgan, "Mr. Morgan, you engage in the same practices as I do only you conduct them behind closed doors." To which Morgan replied, "and that is what doors are for."
* Unethical behavior, obviously has not remained the exclusive province of the nineteenth century and our own era has had its share of objectionable conduct by business, political, and labor leaders as well as by the lesser folk. Scandals associated with the Reconstruction Finance Company in the 1930's and more recently Savings and Loan Banks as well as the brokerage industry and the Teamsters union easily come to mind.

And there exists a multiplicity of problems awaiting the design and/or implementation of more effective solutions. These problems include inflation, recession, poverty, drug abuse, crime, shoddy education and those associated with old age, ill health, and pollution. Deeper and, perhaps, more significantly it would seem that increasing numbers of Americans lack a sense of direction for their lives. Many appear lost. We will return to these topics in subsequent chapters.

SOME PERSPECTIVES AND OBSERVATIONS

Do the accomplishments of free market capitalism in the United States outweigh the problems associated with it? Although personal answers flow from the weight one assigns to each of many issues, this writer chooses to vote overwhelmingly in the affirmative. Nonetheless, arguments for and against free market capitalism need to be put into a perspective. Following are perspectives on some of the issues associated with an evaluation of American capitalism.

* *POLLUTION* Smoke fouling the air, chemicals and debris discarded into bodies of water (a river declared a fire hazard), toxic waste buried in the soil, noise assaulting the ears, and modernization erasing picturesque views--these are some of the many kinds of pollution which accompany industrialization. Methods of dealing with these spillovers, or externalities as economists refer to them, include fines, taxes, subsidies, and the establishment of markets through which rights to pollute can be bought and sold. Although the anti-pollution track record is less than perfect, these devices have been incorporated into legislation and much has been accomplished.

In assessing the condition of today's environment, however, one might harken back to the nineteenth century, when horses served as the principle means of transportation and when refuse was thrown into unpaved streets. So much garbage accumulated that some streets actually rose several feet in height. Large families crowded into small rooms of jerry-built tenements, and the use of privies and wells was the norm. One should also remember that an affluent society is likely to be more willing to deal with its environmental problems then a poor country which might well hesitate to reallocate its scarce resources away from more basic and pressing problems--or even listen to its environmentalists.

* *INFLATION* This rise in the general level of prices erodes savings, complicates planning, distorts economic behavior, and arbitrarily redistributes income, all of which harms creditors, savers, and fixed income groups in particular. In post World War I Germany, inflation was so extreme that the price of a street car ticket exceeded the national debt and the value of the mark changed so rapidly that workers were paid several times *a day*. People resorted to barter, a mode of exchange hardly compatible with efficiency. In the twentieth century, several other nations including Hungary, Bolivia, Brazil, and Israel also have been inflicted with the devastating effects of hyperinflation.

Although the United States has escaped the ravages of this extreme form of price behavior, inflation has made its appearance more than once. It arrived on the scene with some vigor during the 1960's and reached annual rates of double digits in the next decade. Since the 1980's the rate of inflation has been significantly reduced. Inflation reflects the national government's unwillingness to exercise monetary and fiscal discipline: it has by no means disappeared and remains a constant threat.

* *UNEMPLOYMENT* That most of us at some time or other have probably been asked by a virtual stranger at a social gathering what we do for a living is indicative of the pervading importance of work in modern society. A response to the virtual stranger of "I do nothing" might elicit an interesting reaction. The jobs we hold not only generate the lion's share of income to purchase basics as well as the good things of life, but also confer social status. Long spells of unemployment can be devastating to a persons self-esteem, to his or her family, and to the nation.

The United States has had its share of economic contractions, the largest during the Great Depression of the 1930's: the civilian unemployment rate averaged 24.9 percent in 1933. Since that debacle, many public and private programs and policies have reduced the severity of recession and the sting of unemployment. Nonetheless, these problems have not been eliminated and still retain the potential to do much harm.

**WORK AND LEISURE* In the early days of factory production, the familiar, traditional agricultural model--sunup to sundown--served to establish the hours of factory work. Even in the first decades of the twentieth century, some firms required employees to put in a twelve hour day, with work on Saturdays considered standard. Today, thanks to productivity gains, a typical work week is less than 40 hours from Monday to Friday, along with many paid sick days, holidays and paid vacations. However, in counting the hours Americans devote to labor market activity, one must also include moonlighting and overtime work. Moreover, travel to and from the work site often takes considerable time. Yes, our free market economy has generated an abundance of goods and services and simultaneously reduced the amount of time producing them, thereby affording more leisure time to more people. However, economic growth has also quickened the pace of our lives.

The inscription on an ancient Roman sundial reads HORAS NON NUMERO NISE SERENS--the hours do not count unless they are serene.[93] And consider the words of Jesus Christ as He speaks about the birds: "They sow not, neither do they reap nor gather into barns; yet your Heavenly Father feedeth them. Are ye not much better then they?" And "Consider the lilies of the fields, how they grow; they toil not, neither do they spin." All of which signifies that ancient philosophers and early religious authorities while granting the necessity of labor for survival, held work itself (not to mention the quest for riches) in rather low esteem.[94]

During the Renaissance human accomplishments were more highly regarded and later during the Reformation came the secular conviction that work was not only good but that in it inhered an ethical significance--a calling. The number of holidays decline (there were approximately 160 holidays during some stages of the Middle Ages), and a more serious attitude toward work developed.[95] Time assumed more significance. Max Weber has summarized the thoughts of one of the Puritan authors.

> Waste of time is thus the first and in principle the deadliest of sins. The span of human life is infinitely short and precious to make sure of one's own election. Loss of time through sociability, idle talk, luxury, even more sleep than is necessary for health, six to at most eight hours, is worthy of absolute moral condemnation.[96]

The practical equation of time and money was alive and well in colonial America, as the words of Benjamin Franklin attest:

> Remember, that *time* is money. He that can earn ten shillings a day in his labour, and goes abroad, or sits idle, one half of that day, though he spends but sixpence during his diversion or idleness, ought not to reckon that the only expense; he has really spent, or rather thrown away, five shillings besides.[97]

According to Lewis Mumford, "The clock, not the steam engine, is the key machine of the modern industrial age."[98] But as late as the eighteenth century, the clock was still considered something of a play thing for the rich. "Marie Antoinette received fifty-one watches as engagement gifts. The new watches, all of them encrusted with diamonds, pearls, gold, silver, enamel, and miniature portraits..."[99] In the next century, however, these mechanical measurers of time became indispensable.

Until the industrial revolution, agriculture dominated economic activity and peoples lives were shaped with life guided not by exact divisions of time, but by farming tasks associated with different parts of the day or with the different seasons. Manufacturing tended to be small scale--the word itself means "make by hand"--and usually took place in a less hectic manner. The nineteenth century, however, brought with it large scale operations located inside factories where scores of people arrived and departed at specific times, and in between performed rigidly scheduled tasks. The clock became a crucial element in this environment. As Daniel Bell has observed, "...modern industrialization became possible only after the mass production of clocks and watches."[100]

As industrialization proceeded, specialization developed apace as did the need for precision. In the late nineteenth century, Frederick Taylor, the father of scientific management, developed a method called time and motion study whereby (with the use of a stop-watch) various parts of a task were broken into smaller segments and the most efficient procedure determined. Taylor was intent on improving productivity as well as wages, and the success of his efforts might be gauged by this tribute of Nicholai Lenin who advocated "...the study and teaching of the Taylor system and its systematic trial and adoption."[101] Taylorism laid the foundation for the assembly line, industrial engineering and sophisticated personnel policies which all made accurate measures of time indispensable.

Today, life has become increasingly subject to scheduling. We wear time pieces on our wrists so we can "watch" the time and the aptly named alarm clock wakes us to days so busy that the time to perform chores and satisfy wants appears much too brief.

An underlying factor here has been productivity gains which have made for a vast array of goods and services available and financially feasible for much of the population. Less obvious is the fact that the consumption and maintenance of these goods and services take time. Listening to an opera, playing a game of tennis, or attending a ballet or movie use up time, as does the upkeep of goods such as houses, automobiles, and swimming pools. Note also that time cannot be stored, and that individuals who are most productive with in a given time frame tend to be highly valued in the marketplace.

Reason (at least the economist's sense of reason) dictates that time be allocated to its highest yielding use. Thus, well paid (highly productive) business executives fly on the Concorde, while those retired from the labor force and college students who have yet to enter it (both with productivity characteristics valued lowly by labor markets), may be found taking stand-by discount flights en route to leisurely tours of Europe. Fast food restaurants have developed a market niche for those who consider their time too precious to allocate on unhurried, tranquil luncheons, and a news magazine--*Time*--is published for those who want a quick digest of the week's news.

This "so much to do, so little time to do it in" attitude has led some to conflate their consumption of products: People have read newspapers while watching television, or watch two or more television programs at once, or drive and talk on the telephone, or drive, eat, and (God help us) read a magazine. Steffan Linder has rather nicely summarized what he refers to as "simultaneous consumption" in his engaging work *The Harried Leisure Class*. Here is a consumer who "...after dinner, he may find himself drinking Brazilian coffee, smoking a Dutch cigar, sipping French cognac, reading The New York Times, listening to a Brandenburg Concerto, and entertaining his Swedish wife-all at the same time, with varying degrees of success."[102]

Thus we find in economically advanced countries an abundance of goods and a paucity of time. Less developed, economically poor nations experience the reverse. In the industrial world one is supposed to better himself or his property. As Sebastian de Grazia notes: "In some parts of the world, sitting or standing still, whether thinking or not, is considered an activity. In the United States it is not." Even our literal references to time--"Be here in half an hour"--"Come here this second."--indicate how different we are from other cultures.[103] Again, de Grazia observes that, "Wherever timesaving appliances, communications, and transport abound, time-harried faces appear at every turn."[104] Leisure means to be free from the demands of work and duty and leisure activities are undertaken for their own sake. The abundance of goods and services we enjoy has meant some sacrifice of unhurried leisure.

* *POVERTY* The distribution and absolute level of real income have much improved since the eighteenth century, when indentured servitude and slavery were widespread. Although poverty as defined by the standards of a twentieth century affluent nation still exists, a great deal has been done through private and public programs to eradicate it, or at least to lessen its impact. Economic growth, the principal force responsible for what has so far been eradicated, has also raised the standard of living of those still technically classified as poor. This is not to minimize the hardship, frustration, and despair of the less fortunate, but simply to draw a broader picture. One suspects that the vast majority of the readers of this volume would not wish to change places with the American poor, nor would the latter wish to occupy a somewhat higher rung on the relative income scale of most other nations. According to the sociologist Orlando Patterson, "The sociological truths are that America, while still flawed in its race relations...is now the least racist white-majority society in the world; has a better record of legal protection of minorities than any other society, white or black; offers more opportunities to a greater number of black persons than any other society, including all those of Africa..." [105]

* Finally, let us note that change, dislocation, insecurity, and uncertainty are more the problems of modernization (industrialization and urbanization) than any one type of economic system. This is true of many of the problems that have been presented briefly in this chapter. Moreover, inflation and unemployment make themselves known in other systems although sometimes under camouflage. In the history of humanity, discrimination, at times in most virulent and violent forms, appears to have been ubiquitous. In that same time frame, some of the cultural practices of other nations have been far from admirable.

With these accomplishments, shortcomings, and perspectives setting the stage, we now turn to a discussion of the historical economic role of the state in America's free market system.

---

[1] Campbell R. McConnell and Stanley L. Brue, *Economics: Principles, Problems, and Policies*, 12th ed. New York: McGraw-Hill Inc. 1999), pp. 373-376.

[2] This statement is based on purchasing power parity exchange rates which take into account price levels of different countries.

[3] Christopher Lee, "Sizing Up Downsizing, *"The Freeman*, October 1998.

[4] Randy E. ILg, "The Nature of Employment Growth 1989-95," *Monthly Labor Review* June 1996.

[5] Barry W. Poulson, *Economic History of the United States* (New York: Macmillan Publishing Co, Inc., 1981), pp. 113-115, 633,634.

[6] Dr. Paul W. Boltz, "A Weak Dollar Belies High U. S. Living Standards," *The T. Rowe Price Report*, Summer 1995.

[7] Christopher Lee, "Sizing Up Downsizing," *The Freeman*, October 1998.

[8] Don Mathews, " The Free Market: Lifting All Boats," *The Freeman*, April 1997.

[9] Joseph A. Schumpeter, *Capitalism, Socialism and Democracy*, 3rd. ed. (New York: Harper and Brothers Publishers, 1950),p. 67.

[10] Louis Rukeyser, "Stock Ownership Lures More People," *Reporter Dispatch*-a Gannett Suburban Newspaper, June 16, 1991.

[11] *Louis Rukeyser's Business Almanac* (New York: Simon and Schuster Inc.,1988)p.476.

[12] William Tucker, "Sweet Charity," *The American Spectator*, February 1995.

[13] John H. Fund, "A Spiritual Manifesto for a New Political Age," *The Wall Street Journal*, July 13, 1994.

[14] Ed Rubenstein, "Right Data: Policy or Hypocrisy?," *National Review*, September 11, 1995.

[15] Douglas A., Blackmon, "Forget the Stereotype: America Is Becoming A Nation of Culture" *The Wall Street Journal*, September 17, 1998.

[16] See Juliet B. Schor, *The Overworked American: The Unexpected Decline of Leisure* (New York: Basic Books, 1992). Also see Sue Shellenbager, "Work & Family," *The Wall Street Journal*, July 30, 1997 and the excellent and sophisticated review article by F. Thomas Juster and Frank P. Stafford, "The Allocation of Time: Empirical Findings, Behavioral Models, and Problems of Measurement, "*Journal Of Economic Literature*, June 1991.

[17] Robert C. Puth, *American Economic History*, 2nd. ed. (New York: The Dryden Press, 1988), p.615.

[18] "Age & Yogurt, "*Forbes*, May 30, 1988.

[19] Sylvia Nasar, "U.S. OUTPUT PER WORKER CALLED BEST," *The New York Times*, October 13, 1992.

[20] Alvin M. Josephy, Jr., *The Indian Heritage of America*, rev. ed. (Boston: Houghton Mifflin Company, 1991), pp. 37-48.

[21] Ibid., p.53.

[22] Alexis de Tocqueville, *Democracy In America*, vol. 1(New York: Vintage Books, 1957),pp.24,25.

[23] Alvin M. Josephy, Jr., *The Indian Heritage of America*, rev. ed., p.28.

[24] Robert Royal, *1492 And All That*, (Washington, D.C.: *Ethics And Public Policy Center*, 1992), p.90.

[25] Willa Cather, *Death Comes For The Archbishop* (New York: Alfred A. Knopf, 1927), pp. 236, 237.

[26] Alvin M. Josephy, Jr., *The Indian Heritage of America*, rev. ed., pp.23-35.

[27] Ibid., p.35.

[28] Paul A. Brinker, *Economic Insecurity and Social Security* (New York: Appleton-Century Crofts, 1968), p.439.

[29] J. M. Roberts, *The Triumph of the West* (Boston: Little, Brown and Company, 1985), pp.147-150.

[30] P.T. Bauer, *Equality, the Third World, and Economic Delusion* (Cambridge, Mass: Harvard University Press, 1981, p.45.

[31] Paul A. Brinker, *Economic Insecurity and Social Security*, pp.439, 440.

[32] Stanley Lebergott, *The Americans: An Economic Record* (New York: W.W. Norton and Company, 1984), pp. 12-21.

[33] Adam Smith, *An Inquiry Into The Nature And Causes Of The Wealth Of Nations*, ed. and with an introduction by Edwin Cannon and an introduction by Max Lerner (New York: The Modern Library, Random House, 1937), p.555.

[34] Arthur Quinn, "The Miracle Harvest," *The New York Times*, November, 24, 1994.

[35] J. M. Roberts, *The Triumph of the West*, p.150.

[36] Robert Royal, *1492 And All That*, pp.160-162.
[37] Alexis de Toqueville, *Democracy In America,* vol.1,p. 364.
[38] Alexis de Toqueville, *Democracy In America*, vol.1, pp.353, 354.
[39] Alvin M. Josephy, Jr., *The Indian Heritage of America*, rev. ed., pp.323, 324.
[40] Paul A. Brinker, *Economic Insecurity And Social Security*, p.437.
[41] Alvin M. Josephy, Jr., *The Indian Heritage of America*, rev ed. p.334.
[42] Alvin M. Josephy, Jr., *The Indian Heritage of America*, rev.ed.,329,330.
[43] Roger Pinckney, "Old Bug's Necklace," *American History*, Vol. XXIX, No.5.
[44] Ibid., p.349.
[45] Ibid.,pp.8,9.
[46] Ibid., p.347.
[47] Ibid.,p.378.
[48] Ibid., p.377,378.
[49] Dirk Johnson, "Economies Come to Life On Indian Reservations," *The New York Times*, July 3, 1994. Also see Doug Bandow, "Native American Success Stories," *The Freeman*, April 1998
[50] Jane Salodof, "A New School Bridges Two Worlds," *The New York Times National Sunday* November 29, 1998
[51] Peter Kolchin, *American Slavery 1619-1877* (New York: Hill and Wang, 1993), p.20.
[52] Ibid., p.21.
[53] Ibid., p.57.
[54] Thomas Sowell, *Markets and Minorities* (New York: Basic Books, Inc., Publishers, 1981), pp.84-88.
[55] Peter Kolchin, *American Slavery 1619-1877*,. pp. 50-52. Detailing the variations of slavery and the ways in which it influenced the economy and society see Ira Berlin, *Many Thousands Gone* (Cambridge, Mass.: The Bellnap Press? Harvard University Press) 1998.
[56] Ibid., p.32.
[57] Ibid., pp.110-118.
[58] Thomas Sowell, *Markets and Minorities*, p. 92.
[59] Robert C. Puth, *American Economic History,* 3rd ed. (New York: The Dryden Press, 1993), pp.194-196.
[60] Ibid., p.196.
[61] Peter Kolchin, *American Slavery 1619-1877*, pp.118-120.
[62] Ibid., pp. 120-132.
[63] Ibid., pp. 134-143.
[64] Ibid., p.149.
[65] Ibid., pp. 97,98.
[66] Ibid., pp.143-148.
[67] Ibid., pp. 155-156.
[68] Ibid., pp. 189-197. Also see, Oscar Handlin and Mary Handlin, *Liberty in Expansion 1760-1850*. (New York: Harper & Row Publishers, 1989), pp. 323-326.
[69] Peter Kolchin, *American Slavery* 1619-1877, pp. 63-70.
[70] Thomas Sowell, *Race and Economics* (New York: David McKay Company, Inc., 1975), pp.39-41.
[71] Peter Kolchin, *American Slavery 1619-1877*, p.180.
[72] Robert C. Puth, *American Economic History*, 3rd ed., pp. 191-194. Also see Gary M. Walton and Hugh Rockoff, History of the American Economy 7th ed. (New York: The Dryden Press, 1994), pp.280-288 and Robert Fogel and Stanley Engerman, *Time on The Cross: The Economics of American Negro Slavery* (Boston: Little Brown, 1974).

[73] Peter Kolchin, *American Slavery 1619-1877*, pp. 197, 198.
[74] Thomas Sowell, *Markets and Minorities*, p. 98.
[75] Peter Kolchin, American Slavery *1619-1877*, p.211.
[76] Thomas Sowell, *Ethnic America* (New York: Basic Books, Inc., Publishers, 1981), pp.199,200.
[77] Peter Kolchin, *American Slavery* 1619-1877, pp. 209-237.
[78] John Hope Franklin, *From Slavery to Freedom,* 3rd. ed. (New York: Alfred A. Knopf,1967), pp.382-412.
[79] Sara M. Evans, *Born for Liberty* (New York: The Free Press, A division of Macmillan, Inc., 1989), p.64.
[80] Ibid., pp.67-173,passim.
[81] "When Women Got The Vote," *Good Housekeeping*, March 1995.
[82] Sara M. Evans, *Born for Liberty*, p.95.
[83] Ronald Smothers, "One Small Vote for a Man Brought One Giant Leap for Women," *The New York Times*, August,16,1995.
[84] These figures are taken from *Employment and Earnings*, United States Department of Labor, Bureau of Labor Statistics.
[85] Deborah Walker, "The Women's Agenda," *The Freeman*, April 1994.
[86] A. David Silver, "The New American Hero," *The Wall Street Journal*, April 9, 1994.
[87] Judith H. Dobrzynski, "Way Beyond the Glass Ceiling," *The New York Times*, May11, 1995.
[88] Gordon S. Wood, *The Radicalism of the American Revolution* (New York: Alfred A. Knopf, 1992), pp.356,357.
[89] Alexis de Toqueville, *Democracy In America,* vol. 2, p.209.
[90] Peter F. Drucker, "The Continuing Feminist Experiment," *The Wall Street Journal*, October 17,1994.
[91] Alexis de Toqueville, *Democracy In America,* vol. 2, p.225.
[92] John Chodes, "Are Women Exploited By the Free Market?, "*The Freeman*, September 1994, p.510.
[93] Sebastian de Grazia, *Of Time, Work, and Leisure* (New York: Anchor Books, Doubleday & Company, Inc., 1964)Ibid., p.3.
[94] Ibid., p. 23.
[95] Ibid., pp.82,83.
[96] Max Weber, *The Protestant Ethic and the Spirit of Capitalism* (New York: Charles Scribner's Sons, 1958) Ibid., pp..157, 158.
[97] Ibid., p.48.
[98] Daniel Bell, "The Clock Watchers: Americans at Work, "*Time Magazine*, September 8, 1975.
[99] Sebastian de Grazia, *Of Time, Work, and Leisure*, p.290.
[100] Daniel Bell, "The Clock Watchers: Americans at Work," Time. Magazine. September 8, 1975.
[101] Ibid.
[102] Steffan Linder, *The Harried Leisure Class*, (New York: Columbia University Press, 1970), p79.
[103] Sebastian de Grazia, *Of Time, Work, and Leisure*, pp.292-295.
[104] Ibid., p. 314,315.
[105] Orlando Patterson quoted in Arthur Schlesinger Jr., "A New Era Begins-But History Remains," *The Wall Street Journal*, December 11, 1991.

CHAPTER 11

ECONOMIC FREEDOM AND THE STATE: I

Although always of importance, the scope and influence of public economic policy has changed markedly during the history of the United States. For most of this nation's history, it was relegated to a vital but subservient position, with local and state authorities usually dominant. In the late nineteenth century, however, the federal government began to assume a more active role which during the twentieth century reached leviathan proportions. This evolution makes for a fascinating tale.

1790-1865

From the beginning lower levels of government frequently influenced economic activity. John Adams, for instance, borrowing the Puritan designation, considered the State of Massachusetts to be a Common Wealth--a society in which men with diverse interests would, nonetheless, operate within a framework of the common good. The state would have interests of its own. This view, shared by others in Massachusetts and those in other states as well, induced governments to assist the economy in ways which civic leaders believed would redound to the benefit of their respective communities.[1]

For what was believed to be the common good, governments supported education and provided loans, bounties (in Massachusetts, "four pounds for the head of each crop-destroying wolf"), and even released young men from service with the militia.[2] On the national scene, Hamilton, ever the activist, gave credence in his *Report On Manufacturers* to the argument that "infant Industries" warranted protection and so, from the outset, indirect subsidies in the form of tariffs were erected. Popular in the North but detested in the South, these barriers to free trade have always been with us and at times during the nineteenth century averaged as much as sixty percent of the value of durable goods.

Government played a very important role in the development of the corporation. This collective entity, known in Europe and colonial America, grew in volume before the Civil War, and after that conflict it became the dominant legal form of business for many industries. Referred to by Justice John Marshall in the Dartmouth College case as "an artificial being, invisible, intangible, and existing only in contemplation of law," the corporation with its characteristics of limited owner liability and perpetual life (if it remained profitable), greatly facilitated the ability of many people to pool their financial resources, engage in economic ventures, and realize the efficiencies of large scale enterprise.

Although corporate charters were issued by both the federal government and state governments, the latter proved more significant. Often the charters were granted for endeavors thought to contribute to the common good. This was especially the case where high risk or large capital requirements might prevent a project from being undertaken without some type of monopoly privilege. Thus we find charters awarded to engage in various internal improvements--the construction of canals and bridges and the establishment of banks, insurance companies and medical societies. Typically the state issued charter specified the sort of business to be conducted, the location of the venture, and the amount of capital to be used and initially, each charter required a special act of the state legislature. However, general rules of incorporation could be found early on (New York in 1811), although they did not enjoy widespread use in the states until the 1870's.[3]

Well before the Civil War state chartering policies, often with monopolistic attributes, came under attack from potential competitors. The latter received an assist from the United States Supreme Court when in Charles River Bridge v. Warren Bridge (1837), it accepted the argument that competition rather than monopoly best served the public.

The Court ruled that a state's grant of a chartered franchise neither implied a monopoly for the recipient nor a barrier to the award of additional state charters to enterprises intent on engaging in similar economic activity.[4] With few legal barriers, free markets grew and as industrialization proceeded, they became more complex. Compared to government regulation, free markets came to be viewed as more efficient methods of control and this led governments to forsake the commonwealth ideal and along with it much regulation and other paternalistic economic direction.[5]

Government also assumed the task of getting acreage into the hands of its citizenry. Under Jefferson's land ordinances of 1785 and 1787, surveys were made, boundaries established, and secure tenure awarded to holders of real property in the northwest territories. These ordinances mitigated a most fertile source of conflict, furnished a tax basis for the states, and served to diminish the power of the federal sector. Later on, the Homestead Act of 1862 also facilitated land settlement although its impact was less significant.

The Latin word credere means "to believe" and inducing a person to lend money usually means that the creditor believes the borrower to be of good character and have a sense of responsibility. By the time of Washington's inauguration, the states and the national government had incurred enormous debt and both were accurately perceived to lack such character. Then along came Alexander Hamilton. Appointed by Washington as first Secretary of the Treasury at age 34, this wizard of finance believed strongly in the sanctity of contract. With a staff of five he formulated and implemented policies through which the war debts of both state and central government were paid off at face value.

This went far to advance the credit worthiness, both home and abroad, of the young nation. Referring to American Treasury bonds, the French Minister Tallyrand observed that, "They have been funded in such a sound manner and the prosperity of the country is growing so rapidly that there can be no doubt of their solvency."[6] In addition Hamilton advocated, and was instrumental in the establishment of the First Bank of the United States which provided currency for the country, capital for industry, and served as a fiscal agent for the federal government.

Four counties in western Pennsylvania refused to pay a tax on whiskey and it was Alexander Hamilton who put down this Whiskey Rebellion. This action gave notice that the U. S. government possessed the authority and ability to collect taxes. However, it is also the case that no one paid the hated tax in the back country or in the frontier sections of Maryland, Virginia, Kentucky, Georgia, and the Carolinas In fact, so widespread was the sentiment against the tax on whiskey that the national government chose not to use force in those areas. Taxes definitely were not popular in America. A few years later Thomas Jefferson abolished *all* federal domestic taxes.

Hamilton, unlike Jefferson, believed that the central government should have an active role in the economy and this stance was reflected in the *Report on Manufactures* which he submitted to the House of Representatives in 1791. Hamilton rejected the ideas of the French Physiocrats who believed that only agriculture is productive and that laissez faire is the route to economic growth. He felt that manufacturing was more productive than agriculture and provided a "spirit of enterprise." To stimulate American manufacturing, he proposed protective tariffs, bounties for new industries, "judicious regulation" to insure high quality manufactures and pecuniary awards for inventions, discoveries, and improvements.[7] Funds for his plan would come from surplus Treasury revenues and private contributions.[8] The scheme, however, was deemed too revolutionary to pass through Congress and failed to obtain the support of Washington who thought it extended beyond "the powers of the general Government" and "the temper of the times."[9]

The battle between the philosophies of Jefferson and Hamilton was not a struggle between those who favored the rich and those who would help the poor. Neither Jefferson nor Hamilton was a "leveler" and each would have been appalled at the idea of a "welfare state." Rather, what was at stake here was the issue of the proper role of government in the economy of the United States.[10] Standing at 5'7" and known as "the Little Lion," Hamilton was principled and incorruptible (this Secretary of the Treasury died poor). He presented his point of view with vigor and during his career made more than his share of enemies. The animosities that developed between him and Aaron Burr led to his tragic death in a duel at the exact spot where his eldest son had also died while dueling a few years earlier.

Throughout the nineteenth century, with times of war excepted, federal budgets were of a small scale. From 1790 to 1860 federal outlays grew from $5.1 million to $56.1 million and on a per capita basis from $1.31 to $2.01. Customs duties, supplemented at times with excise taxes, property taxes, and public land sales provided, by far, the most important source of federal revenue. Budgets were in surplus during forty-eight of the seventy year time span. Starting from about $75 million in 1789 (this large sum reflected revolutionary war finance), the national debt reached a high of $127.3 million in 1816 and 1860 had fallen to $64.8 million. Surplus revenues were used to retire the debt and in 1835 Andrew Jackson announced to Congress that the national debt had been paid off--eliminated--for the first and last time.[11]

During the first half of the nineteenth century, well before demand deposits (checkbook money) became important, state banks rather chaotically issued their own notes. Americans, hardly enamoured in this era with the idea of federal regulation, nonetheless did witness the establishment of two nationally charted central banks which acted as fiscal agents for the government and exercised some control over the state banks. However, after the charter of the Second Bank of the United States elapsed, central banking did not reappear until 1914. Despite this void, a national banking system instituted during the Civil War to meet the financial needs of the U. S. Treasury had some success in promoting sound practices and a uniform currency.[12]

Court decisions managed to stay within the general boundaries of the Constitution and provided the flexibility needed for entrepreneurship to flourish. Old common law doctrines protecting such property amenities as scenery, clean air, and quiet, gave way to judicial interpretations which allowed the companions of economic development--pollution and turmoil--to appear and often did so without compensation to the injured parties. Stated differently, the property rights of some people received more favored treatment than those of others, and what economists call spillovers failed to receive proper attention. Nonetheless, court interpretations of federal and state constitutions buttressed with such concepts as "natural rights," "fundamental rights," and "the law of the land," generally restrained those who would infringe on the rights of property.[13]

Of course, economic rights were never absolute. The police power of government is an attribute of sovereignty and through it government can insure orderly and peaceful conditions that reflect standards of behavior and morality. This police power has made economic freedom, especially when it came to business property, less than total. It was used in colonial America and found many outlets in the new republic. Exercised on state and local levels (the federal government being unimportant in this realm until the twentieth century), it served as a basis for regulation and might be used to determine who could form a business (licensure); the terms of exchange (price ceilings); the conditions of trade and manufacturing; the inspection of produce; and the hours of operation.[14]

However, as business entities multiplied within a growing and complex economy, the detailed controls associated with public micromanagement became increasingly cumbersome. By the middle of the nineteenth century, regulation, with the exception of public utilities (such as canals), tended to take more general forms. And as we noted previously, a sentiment favoring the free competitive market system as a superior method of control reinforced this trend.[15]

The power of eminent domain further qualified property rights. The fifth amendment permits property to be taken for public use and such "takings" are to be restricted to projects beneficial to the general society. In practice, however, this power was sometimes used to benefit private undertakings such as the construction of canals, railroads, and residential buildings. More than a few have deemed their compensation inadequate.[16]

Given the above exceptions, property rights, held in high regard by the populace, generally received similar respect from the courts. Thus in the matter of contracts, the U.S. Supreme Court in Fletcher v. Peck (1810) ruled that a state attempt to negate a contract it had entered was in violation of the contract clause (1-10-1) of the Constitution. Of even greater importance was the case of Dartmouth College v. Woodward (1819). Here the New Hampshire legislature after a dispute of a religious nature attempted to overthrow the trustees of Dartmouth College (a private institution established in 1769 by a charter from King George III), and turn it into a public college with a different set of trustees. Although the state's highest court ruled in favor of the New Hampshire legislature's enactment, the United States Supreme Court took a different stance. With Daniel Webster arguing for the defense ("it is a small college but there are those who love it well"), the Court ruled that the charter which had been passed to New Hampshire after the Revolution was essentially a contract which state law might not impair. Chief Justice Marshall's observation that "...all contracts, respecting property, remained unchanged by the revolution," makes an interesting contrast to the perspectives of the leaders of the French Revolution, the 1917 Bolsheviks, and current world tyrants.[17]

Sometimes court protection of property rights went too far. Illustrative was the infamous Dred Scott decision which occurred at a time when slavery was being hotly debated. In the background was a series of compromises which stipulated where slavery would be permitted and where it was prohibited. These compromises had provided a degree of some stability for this young nation, torn as it was between factions in the north and south.

The slave Dred Scott had brought suit for his freedom after his owner, Doctor Emerson of Missouri, had taken him to the free state of Illinois and to the Minnesota Territory (in which the Missouri Compromise had forbidden slavery), and then back to Missouri. Scott's claim to freedom ("Heap o' trouble" said Scott about his law suit), based on the fact that he had been taken to free soil, was initially upheld in Missouri, but then overturned by the Missouri Supreme Court. The case then came to the federal courts after Scott was sold by Doctor Emerson's widow to J. Sandford, a New York abolitionist, intent on making this a federal test. In Dred Scott v. Sanford (1857) Chief Justice Roger Taney of Maryland, spoke for a tribunal dominated by Southerners and proclaimed in a highly politicized situation that Scott was not a citizen, that he remained a slave, that he could be brought anywhere, and that he possessed no right to sue. In effect, Taney proclaimed slavery to be a constitutional right, a ruling that propelled the nation toward civil war.[18]

A judiciary which allowed the corporate form to be used in business found much of labor union activity inimical to the public interest. After a group of journeyman cordwainers (shoemakers) struck to obtain higher wages, a Philadelphia court in 1806 ruled that this combination of workers against master craftsman was a conspiracy against the public and in violation of the common law. This and similar court decisions in other locations did little to stimulate trade union growth.[19]

However, organized labor received a mighty assist in 1842 when Chief Justice Lemuel Shaw, speaking for the Massachusetts Supreme Court in Commonwealth v.

Hunt, declared that a union of workers designed to improve wages or working conditions should not be considered illegal per se. Rather, he maintained that the legality of an organization depended upon the means used to realize its goal and on this basis he upheld the right of a union to strike in order to secure a closed shop. While not a guarantee of success, this opinion, emanating from a distinguished jurist, provided an important precedent in labor law and a firmer legal basis for workers to organize into labor unions.[20] One should be aware that while all this was going on, employers were free to use scabs (strikebreakers) and spies and to induce potential employees to sign "yellow dog" contracts in which, as a condition of employment, an individual was required to swear that he was not a union member and promise that he would not join a union.

In other labor matters, the courts upheld mechanics lien laws to protect worker earnings but relied upon the assumption of risk and/or contributory negligence of a fellow servant doctrines to relieve employers of liability where an employee suffered industrial injury or death. Also, the law of contracts evolved in a manner which overturned traditional notions of equity--that parties should be roughly equal--and allowed women and minors, hitherto considered incompetent in commercial matters, to enter into valid contracts.[21]

Beyond what has already been mentioned, some notable U.S. Supreme Court decisions also helped to establish the sovereignty of the federal government, and to promote the cause of nationalism. In Marbury v. Madison (1803) the Court established its power to interpret the Constitution. By declaring a section of the Judiciary Act of 1789 (an act of Congress) unconstitutional, the Court instituted the process of judicial review of national legislation.

Relying on the "necessary and proper" clause (1-8-18) of the Constitution, the Court in McCulloch v. Maryland (1819) upheld the authority of the national government to establish a bank (not specifically mentioned in the Constitution), and to use its implied powers to carry out its lawful functions. Noting the supremacy of the Constitution and federal laws (Article VI), and that "the power to tax involves the power to destroy," the Court overturned the Maryland statute which had allowed that state to tax the notes of the Second Bank of the United States.

Then in Gibbons v. Ogden (1824), the Court, advanced a broad definition of commerce. It declared that a New York law which awarded a transportation monopoly over the waters of that state was in conflict (unconstitutional) with a federal statute that allowed the national government authority over the coastal trade. Adam Smith in 1776 had observed that the division of labor was limited by the extent of the market. This Supreme Court decision helped to widen the American market and to secure the benefits of a large free trade area.[22]

In summary, the American system of government during this antebellum period generally served to facilitate the development of capitalism. Lower levels of government played the key roles but all branches evolved in a manner that tended to be permissive toward the tenets of economic freedom. The U.S. Supreme Court in particular established the legal basis for a market economy and kept other branches of government in check. The words of Chief Justice John Marshall are indicative of the importance that he and many others of that era attached to the principle of limited government:

> That the people have an original right to establish for their future government such principles as, in their opinion, shall most conduce to their own happiness, is the basis on which the whole American fabric has been erected. The exercise of this original right is a very great exertion, nor can it, nor ought it to be frequently repeated. The principles therefore so established are deemed fundamental. The powers of the legislature are defined and limited; and that those limits may not be mistaken or forgotten, the Constitution is written. To what purpose are powers limited, and to what purpose is that limitation committed to writing, if these limits may, at any time, be passed by those intended to be restrained? The distinction between a government with limited and unlimited powers is abolished if those limits do not confine the persons on whom they are imposed.[23]

1865-1917

Dynamic economic and social change characterized America's development from the end of the Civil War until entry into World War I. Population growth, the rise of the big business corporation, mass production manufacturing, the relative decline of agriculture, new and improved methods of transportation and communication, and expanding urbanization--all of these were components in the mosaic of economic growth. In addition, substantial productivity gains brought forth falling prices, rising wages and growing profits. However, with the voting franchise extended, interest groups increasingly tried to protect themselves, to advance themselves, and to redress their grievances--in other words to influence economic outcomes--by using the political process. This was especially true in agriculture.

In the agricultural sector, technological progress and mechanization helped to promote commercial farming and enlarge output, and government played an important role in this process. The Morrill Act (1862) awarded land grants to states in order to finance colleges specializing in agriculture and the mechanical arts while state and federal agencies (particularly the Department of Agriculture) pioneered new methods of breeding and disease control. Established in 1875, and designed for the purpose of assisting colleges to study farm problems and disseminate information, agricultural experimentation stations received financial support via the Hatch Act (1887).

However, despite a record of outstanding progress, the agricultural sector was far from serene. To purchase agricultural equipment, farmers had gone into debt and then shouldered the resulting burden of fixed costs and other costs beyond their control at a time when prices for farm output were descending. That this was part of a national trend of general price decline did not matter. In truth, real farm income was growing, but--and here was the problem--at a slower pace than in other sectors of the economy. Moreover, markets, large scale commercial farming, manufacturing, and urbanization were becoming more important. Thus, the perception of a deteriorating economic and social position became the prime mover for an increasingly unhappy agrarian population. The distress felt by these recipients of a relatively smaller slice of a larger economic pie generated a good deal of suspicion and a host of conspiracy theories.

Especially vocal and influential was the Patrons of Husbandry, also known as the Grange. Founded in 1867 by some members of the Department of Agriculture, this organization (in keeping with the societies of the day it maintained a "secret work and ritual service") engaged in social, educational, economic, and political activities.

The Grange launched a powerful assault against "monopolies" with railroads as the prime target. Railroading, a big business to be sure, had received great notoriety not only for its importance in linking sections of the population and the economy together, but also because of the government subsidies it received, its unsavory practices (rate discrimination, pools, bribery, interlocking directorates), and the juicy scandals which accompanied all of this. The Grange was a vital force in the establishment of state commissions which were charged with insuring that the rates charged by railroads and the rates charged by warehouses were "just, reasonable and uniform," (whatever that might mean).

The U.S. Supreme Court in Munn v. Illinois (1877) upheld this power to regulate. The Court ruled that because the grain elevators owned by Munn (the plaintiff) were located in Illinois, this warehouse operation was intrastate in nature and therefore under the authority of the state of Illinois which could regulate its rates. According to Chief Justice Morrison Waite, "...when private property is devoted to a public use, it is subject to public regulation."[24] However, Associate Justice Field, in a less than sanguine dissenting opinion noted that with Munn, "...all property and all business in the state are held at the mercy of a majority of its legislature."[25]

A few years later, however, in Wahbash, St. Louis and Pacific Railroad Company v. Illinois (1886), the U.S. Supreme Court determined that an Illinois court had overstepped its bounds when it found a railroad guilty of rate discrimination. Goods, reasoned the nation's highest tribunal, had moved across state lines and any regulation governing such activity came under the commerce clause of the Constitution (1-8-3) and therefore during this antebellum period was the sole province of Congress.[26]

In consequence of this ruling, Congress in 1887 passed legislation which established the first of the federal regulatory authorities--the Interstate Commerce Commission (ICC). The legislation applied to railroads acting as common carriers across state lines and mandated that the ICC outlaw price discrimination and insure that all rates "...be reasonable and just." To accomplish such fascinating and elusive objectives, the ICC was empowered to force railroads to publish rate schedules from which they might not deviate without ten days public notice; to scrutinize railroad management including its records and accounts; and to investigate complaints and issue cease and desist orders (enforced by Federal Courts) where such complaints were thought to be legitimate.

The Elkins Antirebate Act (1903) provided penalties for those who gave rebates and those who received them, while the Hepburn Act of 1906 brought express companies, sleeping car companies, and pipelines under the jurisdiction of the ICC, and awarded that agency the authority to establish maximum rates. In Smith v. Ames (1898) the Supreme Court ruled that railroads were entitled to a fair return on their investment. To comply with this ruling, Congress passed the Valuation Act of 1913 which charged the ICC with the task of determining the "fair value" of railroad property.[27]

With the industry now politicized, railroad rates lagged behind the general price level and there developed a serious deterioration of that industry's capital stock. By World War I the financial and physical position of the railroads had become precarious. The less than felicitous results of government micromanagement, apparent even then, continue to this day to plague the railroads.[28]

Founded during the latter part of the nineteenth century, the short lived "People's" or "Populist Party" offers another interesting example of the attitudes which emerged from agrarian discontent. With numerous leaders and speakers including such colorful figures as "Sockless Jerry" Simpson, Mary Ellen ("Mary Yellin") Lease ("raise less corn and more hell"), and the evangelical orator "pin-headed" William Peffer, this party embraced such economic goals as free coinage of silver (easy money), an eight hour day, immigration restriction, nationalization of railroads and telegraph lines, and the elimination of tariffs and other business subsidies. Although not immediately successful in realizing their objectives, advocates of populist ideas would be joined over the ensuing decades by numerous others with diverse interests--all clamoring for government to satisfy their aspirations.

Many firms in nonagricultural industries were now enjoying significant economies of scale. They grew in size and increasingly they conducted their businesses across state lines. In this era of brass knuckles competition ("the public be damned" said Vanderbilt), market manipulation through bribery, kickbacks, collusion, and the formation of trusts had become public knowledge. Unsavory practices and the unfounded belief that monopolies were rampant led Congress to extend its reach beyond the ICC. The result, aimed at the large trusts, was the Sherman Act of 1890.[29]

But there was more to come and quickly did it arrive during the period dating roughly from 1900 to 1916 which historians refer to as the Progressive Era. "Progressiveness" was a crusade against "inhumane" social conditions, political corruption, and upper income groups. Its goal was to realize "the promise of American life."

The novels of Frank Norris--*The Octopus* and *The Pit*--portrayed the wickedness of monopoly, while Upton Sinclair's *The Jungle* described unsanitary conditions in the meat packing industry. *McClure's* magazine presented articles by Ida Tarbell about the monopolistic practices of the Standard Oil Company, and a series by Lincoln Steffens depicted incompetent government and widespread fraud at the voting polls. Other writers exposed the adulteration of medicine, degrading conditions of slums (Hells Kitchen, Bottle Alley), and the long work schedules of women and children. Some of these charges contained truth while others of an even more sensational nature often lacked accuracy. Government was selected as the prime vehicle for reform. Let us count the ways.

Beyond early twentieth century political reforms (direct primaries, the initiative, recall, popular voting for the election of U.S. Senators, and female suffrage), a Department of Labor and Commerce was established in 1903. Ostensibly it was supposed to promote the interests of both labor and commerce, but the primary reason for its establishment was to keep an eye on big business. As President Theodore Roosevelt said when addressing Congress, "The first essential in determining how to deal with the great industrial combines is knowledge of the facts--publicity. In the interests of the public, the Government should have the right to inspect and examine the workings of the great corporations."[30]

Then in 1906 Congress passed the Meat Inspection Act and the Pure Food and Drug Act.[31] In addition to the previously mentioned common carrier legislation, government also prosecuted business under the Sherman Act and tried to strengthen antitrust legislation with the Clayton Act (1914). In that same year Congress created the Federal Trade Commission to stop "unfair" methods of competition. and thereby check monopoly at its source.[32]

During this era the lifestyles of the rich and famous had succeeded in generating indignation among the envious who occupied lower rungs on the income ladder. The social efforts of these men of property on behalf of what the economist Thorstein Veblen called conspicuous consumption (and conspicuous waste) at times assumed forms not only ostentatious but bizarre. According to John Kenneth Galbraith,

> Mrs. William K. Vanderbilt gave her $250,000 ball in 1883. That of Bradley Martin in 1897 was rather more lavish. For this the ballroom of the old Waldorf-Astoria was transformed into a replica of Versailles. One guest appeared in a suit of gold inlaid armor valued at an estimated $10,000. A little earlier at Delmonico's-where Spencer had been entertained-guests were given cigarettes wrapped in hundred-dollar bills which they lighted with a legitimate sense of affluence.[33]

The concerns of the labor force also received attention. A shorter work day had long been a goal and by the first decade of the new century several states had passed laws curtailing hours of employment in private industry for women or children or both. However, attempts to make such restrictions a part of federal law ran afoul of the courts. Nonetheless, local and state governments were able to impose limits of the work day for male workers on public projects and in 1907 the national government did the same for railroad engineers, telegraphers, and dispatchers.[34]

Less successful were attempts to establish wage floors. State minimum wage laws first appeared in Massachusetts in 1912 and later were adopted by a few other states. Loosely drawn, badly enforced, and designed primarily to protect women, the Supreme Court found this legislation unconstitutional in 1923.[35]

Safety on the job was another problem. Complex machinery, swift transportation, high noise levels, and toxic materials all presented dangers which could cause injury, disease, disability, and death. Late in the nineteenth century some states began to require businesses to provide safeguards against these hazards and laws were passed which prohibited the employment of women and children in certain hazardous industries.

To secure financial support and medical care for victims of industrial accidents, states also began to pass workmen's compensation laws. The first, a 1902 Maryland statute was declared unconstitutional, but gradually laws were framed that the courts found acceptable. In 1908, the federal government assumed liability for some of its employees and made railroads liable for their employees.[36]

Labor and management relations--capital and labor as they used to say--supplied another source of controversy. Although Commonwealth v. Hunt had gone far to legitimatize labor unions in the legal sense, for most employers that legitimacy remained absent. In the words of Charles Baer, the head of a coal mining company, "The rights and interests of the laboring man will be protected and cared for--not by the labor agitators, but by the Christian men to whom God in his infinite wisdom has given control of the property interests of this country."[37]

With this or a similar philosophy deeply imbedded, employers maintained their prerogatives by using scabs, lockouts, blacklists, spies, and their private police. Nor were they shy about asking for help from the state militia or from the courts to enforce yellow dog contracts. Often employers were able to stop union enterprise in its tracks by successfully petitioning the courts to issue an injunction--an order which prohibits certain actions and demands immediate compliance. Organized labor suffered a major setback when, in Loewe v. Lawlor (1908)--the Danbury Hatter's case--a union's actions were judged to come under the provisions of the Sherman Act. For conducting a boycott, the union's members were fined an amount large enough to force some of them to sell their houses and substantially deplete their savings.[38]

In summary, direct government contributions toward the objectives of the American labor movement (high wages, shorter hours, improved working conditions) were less than gigantic. In what may be called the plus side for organized labor, a federal Bureau of Labor, charged with the duty of collecting information about labor and capital appeared in 1884 and a Department of Labor was added to the presidential cabinet in 1913.

A commission here and there and some minor pieces of legislation pretty much exhausted government efforts in the collective bargaining arena. Then in 1914 came the Clayton Act. While the primary focus of this legislation was big business, it also touched upon the problems of organized labor. According to this law, "...the labor of a human being is not a commodity or an article of commerce....Nothing contained in the anti-trust laws shall be construed to forbid the existence and operation of labor...organization..." Also it prohibited the use of the hated injunction, "...unless necessary to prevent irreparable injury to property...."[39] Although Samuel Gompers, the American Federation of Labor chieftain, referred to this the Clayton Act as the Magna Carta of labor, subsequent U.S. Supreme Court decisions substantially diluted its impact.

Between 1866 and 1893--twenty eight straight years--the federal budget showed a surplus. A reduction in military spending and interest payments to service the national debt more than offset increased allotments for internal improvements. The same period saw the abolition of the Civil War levies on inheritance and income while government land sales and high tariffs accounted for most of federal revenues. Surpluses were used to pay off the national debt, the total of which had by 1893 declined to $585 million--a level not pierced for the remainder of this narrative.[40]

Even a cursory examination of federal budgets near the end of the nineteenth century gives evidence of an expanding economic role for that sector. In fact, deficits were in evidence for twelve of the twenty-three years spanning 1894-1916 (the last year before the U.S. entered World War I), and financing this enlarged authority posed a significant problem.⁴¹ Since 1789, Article 1, Section 8 of the U.S. Constitution ("...all duties, imposts, and excises shall be uniform throughout the United States") had effectively negated an income tax, especially a progressive one. This restraint on the taxing power of the federal government caused it to rely upon land sales, and excise taxes (primarily on whiskey and tobacco), as well as customs duties to underwrite its limited activities.

An exception did occur during the Civil War when insufficient revenues led to the enactment of a progressive income tax--a levy repealed in 1872. It is interesting to note that the Supreme Court in 1881 held that tax to be not direct and therefore constitutional. Three years later, however, Congress legislated another income tax whereupon the Court reversed its position, and in Pollock v. Farmers Loan and Trust Company (1895) declared both a tax on land and a tax on the income of land to be direct, which meant that it had to be equally apportioned. Because the tax did not, it was declared unconstitutional.⁴² On the subject of an income tax, the remarks of Justice Field are insightful. "The present assault upon capital is but the beginning. It will be but the stepping-stone to others, larger and more sweeping, till our political contests will become a war of the poor against the rich; a war constantly growing in intensity and bitterness."⁴³

An amendment to the Constitution appeared to be the only avenue around the barrier of unequal income taxation, and efforts in this direction began to pick up steam. Congress in 1909 agreed to an income tax amendment offered by President William Howard Taft, and by 1913 a sufficient number of states had approved the Sixteenth Amendment:

> The Congress shall have power to lay and collect taxes on income, from whatever source derived, without apportionment among the several states, and without regard to any census or enumeration.

In that same year, the Underwood-Simmons Act contained provisions for a tax of one percent on corporate income and a personal income tax of one percent on income over $3000 for a single person ($4000 for a couple) plus a surtax as high as six percent on incomes above $20,000.⁴⁴

Support for the tax not only came from populist sentiment against the rich but also from the belief that this levy would only be imposed upon the rich. Some, however, proved to be better forecasters. For example, Richard E. Byrd, who was the Speaker of Virginia's House of Delegates predicted that,

> a hand from Washington will be stretched out and placed upon every man's business; the eye of the federal inspector will be in everyman's counting house....The law will of necessity have inquisitorial features, it will provide penalties, it will create complicated machinery. Under it men will be haled into courts distant from their homes. Heavy fines imposed by distant and unfamiliar tribunals will constantly menace the taxpayer. An army of federal inspectors, spies, and detectives will descend upon the state. ⁴⁵

Momentous changes also occurred in the banking sector. Since the Civil War, several financial crises had occurred and after the panic of 1907, a congressional investigation and the efforts of reform leaders produced the Federal Reserve Act (1913). Operative in the following year, the purposes of this quasi-public quasi-private Federal

Reserve system were to improve the supervision of commercial banks, to offer services such as check clearing facilities to them, and most important to insure that the nation's money supply possessed the elasticity (the key word) to meet the demands of the economy.[46] Easy money here we come!

During this long era, the courts generally assumed an economically conservative position and vital to such a stance was their interpretation of the Fourteenth Amendment. One may recall the three great reconstruction amendments associated with slavery: The Thirteenth abolished that institution; the Fourteenth made former slaves citizens and also protected their civil rights from encroachment by the states; and the Fifteenth established the right of freed slaves to vote: The Fourteenth Amendment which is our concern reads in part:

> Section 1. All persons born or naturalized in the United States and subject to the jurisdiction thereof, are citizens of the United States and of the State wherein they reside. No State shall make or enforce any law which shall abridge the privileges or immunities of citizens of the United States; nor shall any State deprive any person of life, liberty, or property, without due process of law, nor deny to any person within its jurisdiction the equal protection of the laws.

The second sentence became the basis for the evolution of constitutional law and the concept of "economic due process" held dominance until the nineteen thirties. The key words of the Fourteenth Amendment (lifted from the Fifth Amendment) "...nor shall any state deprive any person of life, liberty, or property, without due process of law...," received an interpretation which put property rights on a pedestal.

Thus, a corporation was considered a "person"; "liberty" embraced the right to enter into a voluntary contract; "property" included income from that property; and "due process of law" meant that such property could not be taken without reference to legal tradition which, of course, protected property rights. Although this "substantive" interpretation of the "due process" clause (by both the state and federal courts) failed to confer an absolute status on property rights, it did mean that government interference (usually via the police power) in economic affairs (particularly contracts) had to be justified by special conditions. As Bernard Siegan has observed, "*Substantive due process* usually refers to a judicial policy that substantially protects, under the due process clauses of the Fifth and Fourteenth Amendments, activities that are not elsewhere secured in the constitution. A more precise term for the doctrine protecting economic endeavors is *economic due process.*"[47]

The sanctity of freedom of contract advanced by the judiciary in this period reflected a desire to uphold the Civil War objectives of establishing and defending individual rights. It also embodied an antiunion posture that derived from the collective nature and practices of these organizations along with the belief that free markets including free labor markets presented the most effective road to national prosperity. It was a point of view of a propertied class of corporate lawyers and judges who believed it to be in keeping with the intentions of the founding fathers and the framers of the Constitution.[48]

While not always consistent in their approach, state courts generally embraced the economic substantive due process doctrine and did so before their federal counterparts.

They struck down laws which regulated terms of employment (unless clearly warranted by adverse effects on the health of minors or women); laws which blocked entry into an occupation; laws which prohibited the practice of a trade on certain days; and laws which arbitrarily denied the right to manufacture and sell a particular product. [49]

The following two cases provide some understanding of this judicial perspective. The first decision is that of a New York court and concerns a law that prohibited the manufacture of cigars in tenements located in large urban areas.

> It is plain that this is not a health law, and that it has no relation whatever to the public health. Under the guise of promoting the public health the legislature might as well have banished cigarmaking from all the cities of the state, or confined it to a single city or town, or have placed under a similar ban the trade of a baker, of a tailor, of a shoemaker, of a woodcarver, or of any other of innocuous trades carried on by artisans in their homes. The power would have been the same, and its exercise, so far as it contains fundamental, constitutional rights, could have been justified by the same arguments. Such legislation may invade one class of rights to-day and another to-morrow, and if it can be sanctioned under the Constitution, while far removed in time we will not be far away in practical statesmanship from those ages when government prefects supervised the building of houses, the rearing of cattle, the sowing of seed, the reaping of grain, and governmental ordinances regulated the movements and labor of artisans, the rate of wages, the price of food, the diet and clothing of the people, and a large range of other affairs, long since in all civilized lands, regarded as outside of governmental functions. Such governmental interferences disturb the normal adjustments of the social fabric, and usually derange the delicate and complicated machinery of industry and cause a score of ills while attempting the removal of one.[50]

The observations below are those of the Arkansas Supreme Court. They stress the importance of private property, freedom of contract and occupational choice.

> The right to acquire and possess property necessarily includes the right to contract; for it is the principal mode of acquisition, and is the only way by which a person can rightly acquire property by his own exertion. Of all the "rights of persons" it is the most essential to human happiness....A person living under the protection of this government has the right to adopt and follow any lawful industrial pursuit, not injurious to the community, which he may see fit; and, as incident to this, is the right to labor, make contracts in respect thereto upon such terms as may be agreed upon by the parties, to enforce all lawful contracts, to sue and give evidence, and to inherit, purchase, lease, sell or convey property of any kind. The enjoyment or deprivation of these rights and privileges constitutes the essential distinction between freedom and slavery; between liberty and oppression.[51]

The acceptance of substantive due process by the federal judiciary evolved at a slower pace. The foundation was erected upon four cases: Allgeyer v. Louisiana (1897), Lochner v. New York (1905), Adair v. United States (1908), and Coppage v. Kansas (1915).

Allgeyer v. Louisiana focused upon a Louisiana statute which required any person or business firm needing marine insurance to obtain it from an insurance company licensed by the state of Louisiana. The Allgeyer company was found by the Louisiana Supreme Court to have violated that law by purchasing insurance from a New York firm.

However, the U. S. Supreme Court overruled that decision and held that Allgeyer's deprivation of the freedom to contract for insurance had violated its Fourteenth Amendment rights. As Justice Peckham observed:

> The liberty mentioned in that amendment means not only the right of the citizen to be free from the mere physical restraint of his person, as by incarceration, but the term is deemed to embrace the right of the citizen to be free in the enjoyment of all his faculties; to be free to use them in all lawful ways; to live and work where he will; to earn his livelihood by any lawful calling; to pursue any livelihood or avocation, and for that purpose to enter into all contracts which may be proper, necessary and essential to his carrying out to a successful conclusion the purposes above mentioned.[52]

In Lochner v. New York (1905), perhaps the most famous in this set of cases, the U. S. Supreme Court, by a narrow margin, overturned a New York statute which required bakeries to limit the number of hours that an employee could work to sixty a week with a maximum of ten per day. The state contended that its police power enabled it to establish laws designed to protect worker health. However the Court in rebuttal proclaimed that the freedom of contract inherent in the due process clause could be overthrown only under clearly warranted conditions which in this case had not been proven.

In support of its position, the Court not only asserted that baking was an industry insufficiently hazardous to justify such regulation, but went on to note that a mandatory reduction of hours might bring harm to employees in the form of reduced total earnings (in an industry already characterized by low pay), and might even cause unemployment. Moreover, small bakeries would find it more difficult to comply with the law and therefore would be likely to suffer disproportionately.[53]

In addition to upholding the sanctity of contract, the Court expressed concern for a government which might intervene in more and more sectors of the economy. According to the Lochner Court,

> It might be safely affirmed that almost all occupations more or less affect the health. There must be more than the mere fact of the possible existence of some small amount of unhealthiness to warrant legislative interference with liberty. It is unfortunately true that labor, even in any department, may possibly carry with it the seeds of unhealthiness. But are we all, on that account, at the mercy of legislative majorities? A printer, a tinsmith, a locksmith, a carpenter, a cabinetmaker, a dry goods clerk, a bank's, a lawyer's or a physician's clerk, or a clerk in almost any kind of business, would all come under the power of the legislature, on this assumption. No trade, no occupation, no mode of earning one's living, could escape this all-pervading power, and the acts of the legislature in limiting the hours of labor in all employments would be valid, although such limitation might seriously cripple the ability of the laborer to support himself and his family....

> It also urged, pursuing the same line of argument, that it is to the interest of the State that its population should be strong and robust, and therefore any legislation which may be said to tend to make people healthy must be valid as health laws, enacted under the police power. If this be a valid argument and a justification for this kind of legislation, it follows that the protection of the Federal Constitution from undue interference with liberty of person and freedom of contract is visionary, wherever the law is sought to be justified as a valid exercise of the police power. Scarcely any law but might find a shelter

under such assumptions, and conduct, properly so called, as well as contract, would come under the restrictive sway of the legislature.[54]

The train of thought embodied in Lochner continued in two historic cases concerning labor unions. In Adair v. United States (1908), the United States Supreme Court, citing the rights of property contained in the Fifth Amendment, overturned a federal law which banned the yellow dog contract. Then, referring to the Fourteenth Amendment, the Court in Coppage v. Kansas (1915) negated a similar law on the state level.[55] Justice Harlan explained the Court's position in Adair.

> The right of a person to sell his labor upon such terms as he deems proper is, in its essence, the same as the right of the purchaser of labor to prescribe the conditions upon which he will accept such labor from the person offering to sell it. So the right of the employee to quit the service of the employer, for whatever reason, is the same as the right of the employer, for whatever reason, to dispense with the service of such employee.[56]

Despite its fondness for economic due process, the embrace given to that doctrine by the U. S. Supreme Court was not total. In Holden v. Hardy (1898) the Court upheld a Utah enactment designed to protect the health of miners by limiting their work hours. It also upheld workmen's compensation laws, and even a statute which permitted the national government to affect the wages and hours in the railroad industry.[57]

An ominous example of government intervention arrived in 1916 with the Adamson Act. Intended to deal with the inability of the railroad unions and management to reach an agreement, this federal legislation mandated a basic work day of eight hours and required that overtime pay be calculated at 150 percent of the base wage. In this era, railroads were relatively more important than is true today, and the reform and politically oriented administration of Woodrow Wilson feared the economic and political consequences of a long strike.[58] The U. S Supreme Court, by a 5 to 4 vote in Wilson v. New (1917) upheld the Adamson Act. The majority, which relied upon a broad interpretation of the commerce clause, advanced the idea that the threatened railroad strike would inflict serious harm on both commerce and the public. Among the dissenters was Justice Mahlon Pitney.

> Rights of property include something more than mere ownership and the privilege of receiving a limited return from its use. The right to control, to manage, and to dispose of it, the right to put it as risk in business, and by legitimate skill and enterprise to make gains beyond the fixed rates of interest, the right to hire employees, to bargain freely with them about the rate of wages, and from their labors to make lawful gains-these are among the essential rights of property, that pertain to owners of railroads as to others. The devotion of their property to the public use does not give to the public an interest in the property, but only in its use.
> This act, in my judgement, usurps the right of the owners of the railroads to manage their own properties, and is an attempt to control and manage the properties rather than to regulate their use in commerce. In particular, it deprives the carriers of their right to agree with their employees as to the terms of employment.[59]

The importance of this case derives not only from the implications stated by Justice Pitney, but also because it helped to establish a precedent for government intervention whenever the "people" perceive an "emergency." Needless to say, the future would witness many more "emergencies."

---

[1] Oscar Handlin and Mary Flug Handlin, *Commonwealth*, rev. ed. (Cambridge: The Belknap Press of Harvard University Press, 1969), p.28,29.

[2] Ibid., pp. 78,79.

[3] Gary M. Walton and Hugh Rockoff, *History of the American Economy*, 6th ed. (Harcourt Brace Jovanovich, Publishers, 1990), pp. 210-212.

[4] Oscar Handlin and Mary Flug Handlin, *Commonwealth*, rev. ed., pp. 196-198.

[5] Jonathan Hughes, *American Economic History*, 2nd ed. (Glenville: Scott, Foresman and Company, 1987), p. 124.

[6] Robert A. Hendrickson," A Monument for Hamilton...Finally," *The Wall Street Journal*, November 7, 1990.

[7] Daniel J. Boorstin, ed. *An American Primer* (New York: A Meridian Classic, Penguin Books USA, 1985), pp. 197-209.

[8] Donald F. Swanson and Andrew P. Trout, "Alexander Hamilton's Invisible Hand," *Policy Review*, Winter 1992.

[9] James Thomas Flexner, *Washington: The Indispensable Man* (Boston: Little, Brown and Company, 1974),p.248.

[10] Ibid., p.241.

[11] Barry W. Poulson, *Economic History of the United States* (New York: Macmillan Publishing Co., Inc., 1981), pp. 335-339.

[12] Ibid., pp. 335-366.

[13] Jonathan Hughes, *American Economic History*, 2nd ed., pp. 126,127.

[14] Forest McDonald, *Novus Ordo Seclorum* (Kansas: University Press of Kansas, 1985), p.288.

[15] Ibid., pp. 123-125.

[16] Ibid., p.129.

[17] Ibid., pp. 131-133.

[18] Robert H. Bork, *The Tempting of America* (New York: The Free Press, 1990), pp. 28--34. Also see Mary Ann Harrell, *Equal Justice Under Law*, rev. ed. (Washington, D. C., The Supreme Court Historical Society, 1988), pp. 41-48.

[19] Jonathan Hughes, *American Economic History*, 2nd ed., pp. 111,112.

[20] Gary M. Walton and Hugh Rockoff, *History of the American Economy*, 6th ed., pp. 231,232.

[21] Jonathan Hughes, *American Economic History*, 2nd ed. 127-129.

[22] Ibid., p. 131.--Also see Mary Ann Harrell, *Equal Justice Under Law*, rev. ed., pp. 21-42.

[23] Barry W. Poulson, *Economic History of the United States*, p. 141.

[24] Donald L. Kemmerer and C. Clyde Jones, *American Economic History* (New York: McGraw-Hill Book Company, inc., 1959), p..302.

[25] Jonathan Hughes, *American Economic History*, 2nd ed., p.337.

[26] Gary M. Walton and Hugh Rockoff, *History of the American Economy*, 6th ed., pp. 334-336.

[27] Ibid., pp. 336-338.

[28] Ibid., p. 338,339.

[29] Ibid., pp. 344-366.

[30] Arthur Cecil Bining and Philip Schriver Klein, *A History Of The United States*, vol. II (New York: Charles Scribner's Sons, 1951), p. 270.

[31] Gary M. Walton and Hugh Rockoff, *History of the American Economy*, 6th ed., pp. 424,425.
[32] Ibid., pp. 366-368.
[33] John Kenneth Galbraith, *The Affluent Society*-p.59.
[34] Arthur Cecil Bining and Philip Shriver Klein, *A History Of The United States*, vol. II, pp. 264,265.
[35] Clair Wilcox, *Toward Social Welfare* (Homewood: Richard D. Irwin, Inc., 1969), pp. 212,213.
[36] Arthur Cecil Bining and Philip Shriver Klein, *A History Of The United States*, vol. II, pp. 265,266.
[37] Ibid., p.274.
[38] Sanford Cohen, *Labor Law* Columbus: Charles Merrill Publishing Company, 1964),pp. 117-119.
[39] Ibid., pp. 119,120.
[40] Barry W. Poulson, *Economic History of the United States*, pp. 352-355.
[41] Ibid., pp. 593-598.
[42] Robert Higgs, *Crisis and Leviathan* (New York: Oxford University Press, 1987), pp. 97-103.
[43] Paul Craig Roberts and Lawrence M. Stratton Jr., "The Roots of the Income Tax," *National Review*, April 17, 1995.
[44] Barry W. Poulson, *Economic History of the United States*, p. 595.
[45] Paul Craig Roberts and Lawrence M. Stratton, "The Roots of the Income Tax."
[46] Ibid., pp. 597-608.
[47] Bernard H. Siegan, *Economic Liberties and the Constitution* (Chicago: University of Chicago Press, 1980), p.16.
[48] Ibid., pp. 123-125.
[49] Ibid., pp. 55-59.
[50] Ibid., p.56.
[51] Ibid., p.57.
[52] Ibid., p.111.
[53] Ibid., pp. 113-121.
[54] Ibid., p. 120.
[55] Ibid., pp. 121-125.
[56] Ibid.,, p.122.
[57] Ibid., pp. 150-155.
[58] Robert Higgs, *Crisis and Leviathan*, pp. 116-121.
[59] Ibid., p.120.

CHAPTER 12

ECONOMIC FREEDOM AND THE STATE: II

WORLD WAR I AND THE 1920'S

The United States participation in World War I entailed a massive reallocation of resources from civilian to military uses and federal spending increased from $1.9 billion in 1917 to $18 billion in 1919. Despite the new income tax and a host of other levies, revenues proved insufficient to run the war economy and borrowing took place on a scale so massive that the national debt which was $1 billion in 1914 stood at over $25 billion by 1919.[1] But more important, the crisis atmosphere spawned by the conflict, permitted government intervention into the private economy to a degree that was unprecedented.

Patriotic exhortations, a draft, the threat of imprisonment for those who refused to heed the summons to arms, all helped to mobilize human resources. Also, legislation established a multiplicity of federal organizations which fixed prices, licensed business activity, supplied housing, requisitioned resources, controlled production, kept the peace between labor and management, and took over factories, the telegraph system, and the railroads. Bernard Baruch, in charge of the powerful War Industries Board, described his program as a "weapon of offense or defense more potent than anything the world has ever seen, more terrible, I think, than the mind of man has ever imagined."[2]

Washington's enlistment of business leaders in order to help plan and administer the war effort resulted in an unusual combination of the military, business, and government. But just as interesting was the attitude of the Supreme Court which upheld (in cases decided for the most part after hostilities had ended), on the basis of the war powers and necessary and proper clauses of the Constitution, these numerous intrusions into private sector activities. That not just economic liberties were at risk was made clear when the Court ruled against those who opposed government policy in speeches or in print. Justice Oliver Wendell Homes, for example, believed the citizenry should exercise restraint in time of emergency.

> When a nation is at war, many things that might be said in time of peace are such a hindrance to its effort that their utterance will not be endured so long as men fight and no Court could regard them as protected by any constitutional right.[3]

After the armistice, the U. S. government began to demobilize the armed forces, and at the instigation of President Wilson the government also withdrew from its extensive and intensive direction of the economy, and dismantled much of the attendant bureaucracy. Although most of the wartime institutions died, the idea of public sector--private sector cooperation and planning refused burial, and similar programs reappeared under different titles during the depression of the 1930's and World War ll.

However, one should not assume that the economic activities of the national government disappeared during the roaring twenties. Although the railroads were returned to private hands, an enlarged and more powerful ICC continued to influence policy, and the 1926 Railway Labor Act provided federal machinery to iron out labor disputes. Funds were allocated for veterans' bonuses, as well as for public works, educational purposes, subsidies to the merchant marine, and several programs to help the farmer. Higher tariffs protected much of industry and the Eighteenth Amendment prohibited the manufacture, transportation, or sale of intoxicating beverages. On a more positive note, the Nineteenth Amendment proclaimed suffrage for women, and an expanding economy brought substantial revenue increases which were used to lower tax rates and reduce the debt. Standing at $24 billion in 1920, the national debt declined to $16.6 billion in 1929. The federal budget was in surplus for nine years in a row.[4]

In this post war era, the Supreme Court proceeded to take away the gains that organized labor thought it had won. In Duplex Printing v. Deering (1921) the Court upheld the use of an injunction against a boycott and directed the union to assume litigation costs. That same year, in Truax v. Corrigan the Court overturned an anti-injunction statute in Arizona. In United Mine Workers of America v. Coronodo Coal Company (1922), the Court ruled that a union could be sued for any damage it caused and that union activities could be enjoined if even the threat of damage was present. Then, harkening back to the early nineteenth century when an action deemed legal if undertaken by one person became a conspiracy against the public when joined by others, the Court in Bedford Cut Stone v. Journeymen Stone Cutters of North America (1929) upheld an injunction against a union's attempt to gain employer recognition by advertising that the company was unfair.[5]

Various liberal efforts to secure social change also came under attack. For a long time, reformers had tried to eliminate child labor and Congress, eventually accommodated them with the Keating-Owen Act (1916). This legislation forbade the sale of goods that had been produced in factories employing children under fourteen years of age if the goods were traded in interstate commerce. However, the Court, reasoned that manufacturing was not commerce, and found in Hammer v. Dagenhart (1918) the law to be unconstitutional. Congress responded by placing a tax on articles produced by child labor, but this strategy was negated in Bailey v. Drexel Furniture (1922) when the Court labeled the maneuver an unwarranted attempt by Congress to force its will on the states in violation of the Tenth Amendment.[6]

Other efforts to intervene in labor markets also received little judicial sympathy. The Court in Adkins v. Children's Hospital (1923) declared unconstitutional a 1918 Congressional enactment for the District of Columbia which established minimum wages for women and children--a court decision strongly supported by feminists who opposed such "protective" legislation.[7] The Court argued that the law violated freedom of contract and due process. It also noted that the Nineteenth Amendment had markedly reduced female inferiority and thereby placed men and women on an equal footing when it came to matters of contract. In dissent, Justice Holmes remarked that, "It will need more that the Nineteenth Amendment to convince me that there are no differences between men and women," and that legislation should be able to "take those differences into account."[8]

In this era, the Court nonetheless, refused to adhere rigidly to substantive due process and upheld laws which regulated rents, insurance rates, and gambling; laws which permitted zoning; and laws which prohibited adulterated products and uses of real property considered unhealthful or dangerous. Nonetheless, economic liberty generally received a high level of support from both society and the courts and a much higher level than these parties would accord in the future.[9]

THE 1930'S

The Great Depression was not misnamed. In the brief period between the stock market crash of 1929 and 1932, banks failed by the thousands, manufacturing output declined by almost fifty percent and real income by nearly thirty percent. In 1933 (the trough of the business cycle) the civilian unemployment rate hovered around twenty-five percent and as late as 1939 stood at 17.2 percent.

Pity Herbert Hoover. For in a 1928 campaign speech he had uttered the following prophesy:

> Our American experiment in human welfare has yielded a degree of well-being unparalleled in all the world. It has come nearer to the abolition of poverty, to the abolition of fear of want, than humanity has ever reached before.[10]

Macroeconomic forecaster he was not. He did, however, sincerely try to grapple with the disaster, but sometimes his policies aggravated the problem. Herbert Hoover's "program" included protective tariffs, expenditures on public works, expanded federal credit for farmers and homeowners, and sponsorship of the Reconstruction Finance Corporation which made loans to business, and the Emergency Relief and Construction Act that allowed federal loans to be made to the states. By 1932, the national deficit had exceeded $1 billion--a sum that Democratic presidential challenger Franklin Delano Roosevelt called, "a Deficit so great that it makes us catch our breath." The Hoover administration responded to this deficit with the Revenue Act of 1932 which lifted the top income tax rate from 25 percent to 63 percent, and raised the rate applicable to the lowest income bracket from 1 percent to 4 percent.[11]

These and other efforts failed to halt the economic debacle and thus made the 1932 presidential election a shoo-in for Roosevelt. As his Vice-Presidential running mate John Nance Garner observed, "All you have got to do is to stay alive until election day."[12] And so the Democratic contender, with the music of *Happy Days Are Here Again* (the composers, Milton Ager and Jack Yellen also wrote *Ain't She Sweet*) ringing in the background, handily conquered his opponent whose supporters went to defeat amidst dirge-like tunes containing such lyrics as "let's get behind Herbert Hoover"--a task in itself considering the extent to which he trailed FDR.

With this strong election mandate, Roosevelt and his "brain trust" (many of whom were drawn from the private sector) proceeded to formulate and implement a "New Deal." This consisted of relief programs and policies intended to promote recovery and reform measures to insure that economic calamity would never be repeated.[13]

Popular in the 1930's (and by no means dead today) was the belief that competition caused unnecessary risk, depressed prices, harmed the national economy, and thereby stood in the way of recovery. Therefore, from the beginning, the New Deal sought to suppress competition, and one of its first pieces of legislation, the Agricultural Adjustment Act of 1933, attempted through a variety of coercive measures to raise farm prices. Also in 1933 the National Industrial Recovery Act (NIRA) allowed business firms to band into industry groups which could plan profitable price and output levels--in other words they were permitted to form cartels. A National Recovery Administration (NRA) led by General Hugh Johnson administered the act, and stood ready to approve these collusive "codes of fair practices" and disapprove of "unfair" competitive practices.

To protect small grocery stores threatened by more efficient chains, the 1936 Robinson-Patman Act limited the discounts which the latter could extract from its suppliers. (One should note that these discounts would have been passed on to consumers in the form of lower prices.) A year later the Miller-Tydings Act permitted manufacturers to set prices which retailers could not reduce.

The New Deal awarded the financial sector immediate attention and in March 1933 the President declared a "bank holiday" during which the nation's banks closed their doors. A couple of days later most reopened under the watchful eye of the government, although close to four thousand were ultimately declared insolvent and went out of business.

Many New Dealers believed that inflation promoted full employment, and the United States Treasury was influenced by a theory concocted by a Professor Warren of Cornell University. According to this theory, a rise in the price of gold would lift the prices of other commodities. With this in mind, the Treasury using the authority given to it by the Gold Reserve Act (1934), proceeded to raise the price that it would pay for this precious metal. This legislation also forbade the citizenry to hold or export gold, and abrogated contracts requiring gold for payment. By other enactments, the Federal Reserve obtained new powers to control the money supply, and in 1935 a Federal Deposit Insurance Corporation (FDIC) was authorized to levy premiums on commercial bank deposits and to insure these deposits. Also in 1935 a Securities Exchange Commission (SEC) was established to regulate securities markets.

High on the list of New Deal priorities were the problems of unemployment and poverty. Established in 1933, the Federal Emergency Relief Agency (FERA) granted funds to states so that they might give emergency relief. The year 1933 also witnessed the establishment of other agencies: a Civilian Conservation Corps (CCC) offered work on conservation projects to young men; a National Employment Service provided information about job opportunities; and the Public Works Administration (PWA)--replaced by a broader Works Progress Administration (WPA) in 1935--promoted construction projects. To facilitate slum clearance and build low rent housing, a United States Housing Authority began to operate in 1937. Last, but by no means least, the Social Security Act of 1935 provided annuities funded by payroll taxes for the aged; established incentives to develop state administered unemployment insurance systems; and gave aid to special categories of people such as needy children or aged who failed to qualify for the annuities.

The national government also injected itself directly into labor market activities. Prior to the New Deal, the Davis Bacon Act of 1931 had mandated that workers on federal government construction projects be paid at least the minimum wage which prevailed in the area where the construction was taking place. In effect, the prevailing minimum wage was the union minimum wage. To this legislation was added the Walsh-Healy Government Contracts Act (1936), which required employers with federal contracts to pay no less than the prevailing wage levels (also interpreted as the union scale) for the skills being utilized. Two years later, the Fair Labor Standards Act stipulated a minimum wage for the wide range of jobs covered by this law, and mandated a standard work week of forty hours with additional hours of work paid at premium rates.

A new and solid basis for labor union power and growth arrived with the 1935 National Labor Relations Act (Wagner Act). Extending beyond the 1932 Norris-La Guardia Act which had limited the use of the injunction, and made yellow dog contracts unenforceable, the new legislation accorded workers the right to form into unions of their own choosing, and made illegal certain practices deemed unfair to labor. An employer could be charged with an unfair labor practice if he refused to bargain with a union, attempted to dominate a union, or fired a person for joining a union. In addition, the Act created National Labor Relations Board (NLRB) which had the power to supervise union elections, to certify a particular union as the exclusive bargaining agent of the workers, to hear complaints of unfair labor practices, and to issue cease and desist orders when violations of the law occurred.

In order to restore confidence, Hoover's response to the economic onslaught had focused on balancing the budget, and initially Roosevelt upheld the desirability of fiscal prudence. As he proclaimed in his first radio address,

> Revenues must cover expenditures by one means or another. Any government, like any family, can for a year, spend a little more than it earns. But you and I know that a continuation of that habit means the poorhouse.[14]

The rhetoric not withstanding, deficits were in evidence throughout the 1930's and reached a high point of $3.5 billion in 1936. Toward the end of the decade, Roosevelt ceased talking about the virtues of orthodox fiscal policy. Perhaps his faith in what originally were conceived as "pump priming" measures and the regenerative power of free enterprise had dimmed. Perhaps, also, he had noticed the relationship between getting reelected and spending money and doing favors for special interest groups.

Although the judiciary eventually embraced New Deal activism wholeheartedly, its initial response was one of hostility. By 1936 Federal judges had issued approximately

1,600 injunctions which prohibited the implementation of various Congressional enactments, and numerous state laws were held to be unconstitutional.[15]

However, Roosevelt did experience some success with the judiciary in his programs to effect recovery and reform. The following significant cases illustrate both the success and the controversy surrounding it.

In Homebuilding and Loan Association v. Blaisdell et al (1934) the Supreme Court upheld a Minnesota law which temporarily extended the time in which creditors could foreclose on property and sell that property when the mortgage payments of a debtor were delinquent. In this case, the Court perceived the existence of an emergency, and ruled that the police power could be invoked to protect the public by negating the obligations of private contracts. In a vigorous dissent from this 5 to 4 decision, Justice Southerland proclaimed that the framers intended the contracts clause of the Constitution to be "primarily and especially" applicable during a crisis. "If the provisions of the Constitution be not upheld when they pinch as well as they comfort, they may as well be abandoned."[16]

Shortly after the Blaisdell decision, the Court by another 5 to 4 vote in Nebbia v. New York upheld a state statute which permitted a board to fix the price of milk. Mr. Leo Nebbia, a small retailer of milk, had been charged with violating the law when he sold milk below the official price. The Court ruled that he had not been deprived of his rights under due process and equal protection clauses of the Fourteenth Amendment. With the police power as the basis for his argument, Justice Roberts asserted that, "...neither property rights nor contract rights are absolute."[17] And with Munn v. Illinois in the background, he proclaimed that ":...there is no closed class or category of business affected with the public interest."[18] Moreover, "...a state is free to adopt whatever economic policy may reasonably be deemed to promote public welfare...,"[19] and "with the wisdom of the policy adopted...the courts are both incompetent and unauthorized to deal."[20]

In contrast, Justice McReynolds who wrote for the minority maintained that the,"...Court must have regard to the wisdom of the enactment."[21] He found the implications of this judicial philosophy most disturbing: "If here we have an emergency sufficient to empower the Legislature to fix sales prices, then whenever there is too much or too little of an essential thing--whether milk or pork or coal or shoes or clothes--constitutional provisions may be declared "inoperative"[22]..." Nor did the fact that dairy farmers and large milk dealers comprised the "general interest" in this controversy go unnoticed in the dissent:

> Not only does the statute interfere arbitrarily with the rights of the little grocer to conduct his business according to standards long accepted--complete destruction may follow; but it takes away the liberty of twelve million consumers to buy a necessity of life in an open market. It imposes direct and arbitrary burdens upon those already seriously impoverished with the alleged immediate design of affording special benefits to others. To him with less than nine cents it says--You cannot procure a quart of milk from the grocer although he is anxious to accept what you can pay and the demands of your household are urgent! A superabundance; but no child can purchase from a willing storekeeper below the figure appointed by three men at headquarters! And this is true although the storekeeper himself may have brought from a willing producer at half that

> rate and must sell quickly or lose his stock through deterioration. The fanciful scheme is to protect the farmer against undue exactions by prescribing the price at which milk disposed by him at will may be resold![23]
>
> The Legislature cannot lawfully destroy guaranteed rights of one man with the prime purpose of enriching another, even if for the moment, this may seem advantageous to the public....Grave concern for embarrassed farmers is everywhere; but this should neither obscure the rights of others nor obstruct judicial appraisement of measures proposed for relief. The ultimate welfare of the producer, like that of every other class, requires dominance of the Constitution and zealously to uphold this in all its parts is the highest duty entrusted to the courts.[24]

The importance of Nebbia derives from the fact that many New Deal as well as state enactments were designed to fix prices and limit competition. The decision also struck a major below to the doctrine of substantive due process.

Overall, however, the judiciary remained an enormous obstacle to New Deal policy. That the administration lost 14 of 17 key Supreme Court cases is indicative of the general pattern of hostility from this sector. Especially devastating were the Court's decisions which overthrew the NIRA and the AAA.

In 1935, an exceptionally important dispute came before the Supreme Court--A.L.A. Schecter Poultry Corporation v. United States. This controversy revolved around provisions of the NIRA which authorized the President of the United States to develop a code of fair competition for an industry if the industry failed to do so on its own. These codes included such matters as prices to be charged, minimum wages to be paid and maximum hours of work. President Roosevelt had promulgated a Live Poultry Code which the defendant had been convicted of violating. Ruling that the NIRA had neglected to set standards and had delegated an unwarranted amount of power to the President, the Court unanimously declared the legislation unconstitutional.

In defense, the administration had maintained that intrastate labor markets indirectly affected interstate commerce and therefore could be brought under federal regulatory authority. However, the Court asserted that the wage and hour provisions of the code unjustifiably intruded into interstate commerce. As Chief Justice Hughes observed, "Otherwise...there would be virtually no limit to the Federal power, and for all practical purposes we should have a completely centralized government."[25] Justice Cardozo also expressed his concern rather bluntly: "I find no authority in the commerce clause for the regulation of wages and hours in intrastate transactions that make up the defendant's business."[26]

Then, in U.S. v. William M. Butler et al (1936) the Court by a 6 to 3 vote held the Agricultural Adjustment Act of 1933 to be unconstitutional. It found the Act's tax on processors to be unjustifiable and the regulation of agricultural produce an invasion of states' rights. It also expressed concern that policies such as this might eventually result in "...the regulation of all industry throughout the United States."[27] That taxes were being used to benefit of privileged class also received notice (the federal budget was in surplus for nine years in a row).

President Roosevelt was infuriated by these decisions. He was also aware that Congress in its history had seen fit to change the number of Supreme Court judges six times. Emboldened by his 1936 landslide victory, he attempted to overcome the judicial obstacle by asking Congress to expand the membership of the Supreme Court, which of course would enable him to make appointments of individuals who favored New Deal policies. However, President Roosevelt (not the first or last chief executive to play fast and loose with the law) greatly underestimated the vigor of the opposition from the general public, the Republicans and even members of his own party.

Shortly after Roosevelt's message to Congress, the Supreme Court surprisingly began to uphold New Deal enactments. Two Justices, Roberts and Hughes, hitherto considered uncertain or swing votes (the "roving judges"), began to side consistently with the three liberals, Brandeis, Cardozo, and Stone. And this made for a liberal majority ("A switch in time saves nine"). Roosevelt's attempt to reorganize ("pack"), the Court suffered defeat in the Senate by a 70 to 20 vote. However, when Justices Southerland, VanDevanter, McReynolds, and Butler (the conservative "four horsemen") retired, the President was able to remake this tribunal more to his liking.[28]

Standing out among the key decisions emanating from that now friendlier body were those which upheld the National Labor Relations Act, the Fair Labor Standards Act, and the Second Agricultural Adjustment Act.

In National Labor Relations Board v. Jones and Loughlin Steel Corporation (1937), a firm with various operations in different states had attempted to prevent its employees from organizing into a union and also had refused to abide by an NLRB order to do so. The Court reasoned that a company-wide dispute would adversely and severely affect interstate commerce. It therefore supported the provisions of the Wagner Act and the ability of Congress to regulate this labor market:

> When industries organize themselves on a national scale, making their relation to interstate commerce the dominant factor in their industries, how can it be maintained that their industrial labor relations constitute a forbidden field into which Congress cannot enter...[29]

This ruling not only overturned the philosophy of Addair and Coppage, but now allowed a broadly interpreted commerce clause to become the basis for regulation. By a vote of 5 to 4, the Court in West Coast Hotel v. Parish (1937) upheld a state of Washington minimum wage law which applied to men and women. Authorities consider this decision, which overturned Adkins v. Children's Hospital, to mark the end of substantive due process. Chief Justice Hughes spoke for the majority: "Liberty under the Constitution is thus necessarily subject to the restraints of due process, and regulation which is reasonable in relation to its subject and is adopted in the interests of the community is due process."[30] His prime concern was that the law be reasonable and not arbitrary: "Even if the wisdom of the policy be regarded as debatable and its effect uncertain, still the legislature is entitled to its judgement."[31]

In U.S. v. Darby Lumber Company (1941) the Court denied the argument that Congress lacked the power to regulate the wages and hours of a manufacturing firm operating within a state. In this test case of the Fair Labor Standards Act, the Court overturned Hammer v. Dagenhart. It decided that the Darby Company fell under the regulating authority of the federal government because it sold lumber across state lines.[32]

The court's liberal stance continued in Wickard v. Filburn (1942) when it upheld the second Agricultural Adjustment Act. In this case, Mr. Filburn raised more than his allotted quota of wheat and refused to pay a fine for violating an acreage restriction plan. Filmer maintained that he only used the excess wheat for domestic purposes such as feeding livestock and making flour. Nonetheless, the Court concluded that such consumption affected market price, and therefore brought the defendant via the commerce clause under the jurisdiction of Congress. This interpretation also bestowed upon Congress the authority to regulate a vast amount of economic activity taking place within states.[33]

From these and other cases decided in this era, a judicial philosophy emerged which became dominant. According to this philosophy, there are two classes of liberties: fundamental and nonfundamental and those of an economic nature belonged in the latter category. And as a correlative: an act by a legislature or executive which would take away a fundamental liberty should receive strict judicial scrutiny, while the scrutiny applied to the nullification of an economic freedom need only be of a minimal nature.[34]

Although our presentation fails to mention all the New Deal laws, policies, and court decisions, it more than suggests the scope and depth of the federal government's intrusion into the private economy. True, World War I had witnessed the spread of government tentacles deeply into the private domain, but this had been justified as a temporary response to emergency conditions. By contrast, the New Deal made the government a permanent "partner." Looking back to the Great War and then forward to the 1930's and even beyond that for the rest of the twentieth century, a clairvoyant in the 1920's might well be reminded of the signature words of the popular entertainer Al Jolson: "You ain't heard nothin' yet, folks."

WORLD WAR II

Shortly after America entered World War II, the demands placed upon the economy generated that which proved so elusive in the previous decade--full employment. Most of the New Deal make work agencies disappeared, only to be replaced by a host of organizations designed to stabilize prices, foster production, ration goods and commandeer human services. Planning as in World War I came back into style and once again, executives recruited from the private sector (often for a nominal fee) issued directives.[35]

New taxes and increased rates applied to existing taxes helped to finance this command economy. In addition, the Revenue Act of 1943 called for automatic payroll deductions (as had the social security program a few years earlier). This process led one to be less aware of the full magnitude of the income tax, and simultaneously made the tax more difficult to avoid. Alas, none of these measures proved sufficient to cover federal expenditures which rose from $14 billion in 1941 to $95 billion by 1945. There were large deficits in each of the war years (1943 held the record at $53.8 billion), and by 1945 the national debt had reached $260.1 billion.[36]

The restrictions on property rights brought about during the war were indeed numerous. Among other things, the government could condemn property, commandeer property, fix prices, wage scales, hours of work, control the flow of materials, establish priorities in transportation, and tell a manufacturer what to make.[37] And to all of this the Supreme Court said amen. Under the authority of the war powers of Congress and the President, virtually anything was allowed, including the placement of over 110,000 people of Japanese descent (about two thirds of whom were U.S. citizens) into internment camps.[38]

POST WORLD WAR II AMERICA

Full employment and the other economic achievements of the first half or the nineteen forties appeared to validate the ideas of John Maynard Keynes (1883-1946), whose 1936 volume *The General Theory of Employment, Interest, and Money* served as the theoretical basis for the use of government spending to cure a depression.[39] According to this most influential British economist, the free market adjustments propounded by mainstream neoclassical economists could no longer be counted upon either to maintain full employment or to restore it if there was a depression. In essence, Keynes believed that a "mature" capitalist economy was likely to be bedeviled by conditions wherein private spending would be insufficient to generate full employment.

His tonic for this malaise--government spending financed with deficits--appeared so successful in the early 1940's that it supplied a major reason for the national government to pass the Employment Act of 1946 (not the *full* employment act--not yet anyhow). Under this legislation the federal government assumed the responsibility of managing the macroeconomy "...to provide maximum employment, production, and purchasing power."[40] Other reasons for the passage of this precedent breaking law included the fear in the United States that the end of World War II might bring forth another economic debacle. Also Britain and other nations wished to insure that the U.S. economy would remain healthy, and thus provide a robust export market in order that they could obtain needed American dollars. Pressure from these nations to adopt this legislation also played a role.

Following the relatively painless conversion to a more civilian oriented economy, the Korean conflict which began in 1950 brought forth additional government activities although on a lesser scale than was true five years earlier. When hostilities ceased, these too receded into the background, and both the Eisenhower and Kennedy administrations, beyond cold war military expenditures, launched few major new social programs. However, starting with the Lyndon Johnson administration, public policy changed significantly (as did American behavioral patterns in general), and government assumed more and more authority in economic affairs.

Among the numerous factors which led to policy changes were the evidence of poverty amidst plenty, charges of discrimination, environmental concerns, an energy "crisis", the war in Vietnam, alienation of the young, the woman's liberation movement, disrespect for authority, renunciation of traditional values, and a desire--experienced so intensely by more than a few--not just for new lifestyles, but for novel approaches for much that mattered in their lives. Joining traditional actors such as union officials and business executives on the political stage were an assortment of new characters who sprang forward claiming and clamoring to speak for women, the environment, a variety of ethnic groups, and consumers. A common thread among these disparate bodies was the belief that government (especially the federal) should be the vehicle to realize their revolutionary aspirations.

From this political activism emerged a deluge of policies, enactments, programs and organizations which were intended to eradicate poverty, promote equality, protect the consumer, prevent discrimination, provide a clean environment, produce safer goods, eliminate hazards at the worksite, and solve the energy shortage. The following incomplete list (the titles usually express the hoped for results) conveys an indication of the extent to which federal government regulation grew during the 1960's and 1970's.[41]

1962--Food, Drug, and Cosmetic Act Amendments
1962--Air Pollution Control Act
1963--Equal Pay Act
1964--Civil Rights Act
1966--Cigarette Labeling and Advertising Act
1966--Child Protection Act
1966--Traffic Safety Act
1966--Coal Mine Safety Amendments
1967--Flammable Fabrics Act
1967--Age Discrimination in Employment Act
1968--Consumer Credit Protection Act
1968--Interstate Land Sales Full Disclosure Act
1969--National Environmental Policy Act
1970--Amendments to Federal Deposit Insurance Act
1970--Securities Investor Protection Act
1970--Poison Prevention Packaging Act
1970--Clean Air Amendments
1970--Occupational Safety and Health Act
1972--Consumer Product Safety Act
1972--Federal Water Pollution Control Act
1972--Noise Pollution and Control Act
1972--Equal Employment Opportunity Act
1973--Vocational Rehabilitation Act
1973--Highway Speed Limit Reduction
1973--Safe Drinking Water Act
1974--Campaign Finance Amendments
1974--Employment Retirement Income Security Act
1974--Hazardous Materials Transportation Act
1974--Magnuson-Moss Warranty Improvement Act
1975--Energy Policy and Conservation Act

1976--Hart-Scott- Rodino Antitrust Amendments
1976--Toxic Substances Control Act
1977--Department of Energy Organization Act
1977--Surface Mining Control and Reclamation Act
1977--Export Administration Act
1977--Business Payments Abroad Act
1978--Saccharin Study and Labeling Act
1978--Fair Debt Collection Practices Act
1978--Age Discrimination in Employment Act Amendments

In the decades following World War II, the judiciary generally exhibited a marked hostility toward economic liberties and awarded its imprimatur to the above legislation as well as to the regulatory legislation of the 1980's and 1990's.

With exceptions such as antitrust law, the federal sector had in the past usually established a regulatory agency to oversee a particular industry; for instance the ICC for the transportation industry or the SEC for the securities industry. Moreover, these authorities assumed among their other functions the responsibility for the health of the industry itself. In contrast, much of the new regulation established bodies such as the Environmental Protection Agency, the Occupational Safety and Health Administration, the Consumers Product Safety Commission, and the Equal Employment Opportunity Commission which cut across industry boundaries and, in fact, envelope much of the market economy. Further, these newer organizations tend to focus on a specific task-- elimination of job discrimination or the development of a "safe" worksite--and they exhibit little interest in the overall health of the great variety of firms and industries under their domain, the impact of their rulings on matters such as productivity, employment levels, and the cost of all this to the consumer.[42]

Many of these newer laws supercede state authority in ways different from earlier enactments. In the past, federal laws that pre-empted state authority concerned themselves with such matters as national standards for weights and measures, or copyrights, or railroad safety, and such laws cost the states little or nothing. However, the more recent federal pre-emptions focus upon health, the environment, and discrimination among other things, and impose costly mandates upon the states.[43]

Great inefficiencies (politely put), obvious to any knowledgeable person, accompanied this legislative avalanche and probably helped to explain the 1976 election of Jimmy Carter (who promised to streamline government operations), to the Presidency. Important steps in this direction were taken with the 1978 Airline Deregulaton Act and in 1980 the Motor Carrier Act, and the Depository Institutions Deregulation and Monetary Control Act. However, when this amiable engineer departed from office, he had created two new cabinet level departments (Energy and Education), and signed the 1978 Full Employment Balanced Growth Act (Humphrey-Hawkins Act). The latter, a piece of legislative fantasy, extended the goals of the 1946 Employment Act by mandating (like King Canute) that the national unemployment rate be reduced to 4 percent by 1983--the actual rate wound up at 10 percent in that year.

Then came the Great Communicator whose administration orchestrated a significant reduction in federal income tax rates (the top rate on the personal income tax fell from 90 to 28 percent), a more simplified income tax structure, a decrease in regulatory activity, and spending cutbacks in several programs. Although there were no new major social spending programs undertaken, and despite much talk about "getting government off our backs," Ronald Reagan departed from office with that back weight still substantial.

George Bush in quest of "a kinder and gentler nation" was next to assume the mantle of President and with his arrival came a host of new laws. Three enactments stand out: The Clean Air Act (over 800 pages long--enough said), the Americans With Disabilities Act of 1990, and the Civil Rights Act of 1991.

The Americans With Disabilities Act seeks to bring the disabled into society's mainstream by removing barriers and inducing employers to emphasize ability rather that disability. It bars discrimination against the disabled in areas of employment, public accommodation, transportation, and telecommunication service. A disabled person is one who has a "physical or mental impairment that substantially limits one or more of the major life actives." Examples of major life activities include, walking, speaking, breathing, sitting, hearing, seeing, lifting, learning, working, and reading. The legislation extends beyond people with traditionally defined disabilities (the deaf, blind, of paraplegic) and embraces those who suffer from drug addiction, alcoholism, and AIDS. The courts have generally supported this agenda.

While the precise long term effects of the law remain unclear, it does require private enterprise to make "reasonable accommodations" for the disabled. Also significantly affected is the job interview process. Before a job offer is made, an employer may not ask the applicant or the applicant's references about his or her medical history, prior insurance claims, absenteeism from work due to illness, or part-time treatment for mental illness, use of drugs, or alcoholism. We know that broad definitions of disability have resulted in substantial increases in the number of people filing claims for workmen's compensation benefits, and social security benefits, as well as for the special treatment of children.[44] Attention deficit disorder (ADD) is a rapidly growing disability category. Perhaps some of this growth can be attributed to the fact that those "diagnosed" with ADD are entitled to special privileges. For example, they may be given additional time when taking important exams such as the Scholastic Assessment Test or Law School Admission Test. Efforts to comply with this law can turn out to be quite costly and while some undoubtedly benefit from the Act, it may also channel individuals into positions for which they are ill-suited. Also, we know that the American with Disabilities Act has been a windfall for trial lawyers, and that this windfall is likely to continue as more and more people sue to have their "disabilities" (nearsightedness, hypertension,) covered by the law.[45] One surely must sympathize with the idea of making a nicer life for the truly disabled. Whether the heavy hand of government is the best approach to realize this goal is questionable.

The Civil Rights Act of 1991 permits the collection of punitive damages (hitherto available only to victims of racial discrimination), by those who also have been discriminated against because of gender or disability. Also, this legislation shifts the burden of proof that such discrimination was unintentional and the result of business necessity from the worker to the employer.

Finally we have William Jefferson Clinton, the forty-second President of the United States, who waged a successful campaign for this nations highest office with slogans such as "Putting People First" and "Reinventing Government." He did promise a more active federal government and in this respect he has delivered. The agenda of this "New Democrat" has embraced medical leave legislation, higher tax rates, extensive nutritional labeling on food products, and numerous other programs and regulations including universal health care under the direction of the federal government.

The preceding narrative has concentrated on the evolution of government institutions, laws, and judicial philosophies. However, there are other indicators of public sector activity. One of these is fiscal policy, the ingredients of which include government spending, taxing, and borrowing. While a "mine eyes glaze over" multiplicity of numbers can be indeed overwhelming, the presentation of a few of the more telling ones provides another useful perspective on the magnitude of government.

First to note is the immense growth in government expenditures from about one tenth of national output in 1929 to roughly a third of output today. Also, there has been a tremendous change in the relative importance of the federal sector. In 1929 the expenditures of the state and local governments were almost three times greater than those of the federal sector, while in the 1990's, the outlays of the national government were almost 50 percent higher than the outlays of the lower levels.

One might be surprised to discover that the source of the increase in total government spending as a percentage of national output is not to be found in the national defense sector--broadly defined to include the military, space, science, technology, and foreign affairs. Although national defense expenditures did rise markedly when expressed on an absolute basis, its share of gross domestic product, which was about 6 percent in 1950, declined to about half of that in the 1990's.

Rather, the relative growth in government spending can be attributed to a great increase in the previously mentioned activities performed at the federal, state, and local levels. It also can be attributed to the large rise in the amount of transfer payments: money expended for which no current service is performed or goods are received. Social security, Medicaid, unemployment compensation, aid to families with dependent children (AFDC) exemplify transfer payments. Many of these now bear the name "entitlement" which means that Congress has little direct control over the amounts expended. In fact, transfer payments grew from almost $4 billion in 1929 to $1,304 billion in 1996. And how, pray tell, was all this financed? Answer: through taxes and borrowing (accompanied by monetary expansion), all of which arrived big time in the U.S.A.

Just as one example, in 1994 total tax revenues received by all levels of government reached $2,078 billion of which the federal sector accounted for $1,453 billion. In contrast, the federal government received a paltry $3.9 billion in 1929, and in 1945 (the last year of World War II) obtained but $45.2 billion. By 1970, federal tax revenues had climbed to $192.8 billion, but even by 1980 had "only" reached $517.1 billion. Alas, these sums usually proved insufficient to match the onslaught of spending, and this necessitated substantial borrowing.

Here are more interesting statistics. For 1998, the Tax Foundation has estimated that beginning on January 1, if all earnings were sent to the tax collector, the average American would have to work until May 10 before his tax obligations to federal, state, and local governments were satisfied for the year. (In 1902 the date was January 31 and in 1940 it was March 8.) Also in 1998, the combined taxes of local, state, and federal government consumed 31.5 percent of Gross Domestic product--a sum exceeding that of World War ll.[46] In 1914, the year in which the federal income tax was first implemented, there were 360,000 filers, 14 pages of tax law, and 4 pages of IRS forms. In 1994, there were 113,829,000 filers, 9,400 pages of tax law, and 4000 pages of IRS forms. Taxation in America has become a major source of irritation.[47]

The growth of spending had continued to outpace the rise in tax revenues, and, oh, how those deficits did accumulate! A national debt of $16.9 billion in 1929 had soared to $5,369 billion by 1997. For each of those years respectively, the per capita debt was $134 and $20,044.[48] And for those same years, interest payments on the debt (which unlike other budget items cannot be cut without defaulting on debt obligations), grew from $0.7 billion to $244 billion.[49] Which is to say, that budgetary deficits have been the rule. In fact, the last year when the on-budget account showed a surplus was in 1960. The much heralded budget surplus of some $70 billion for 1998, for which both Democrats and Republicans have taken such pride, was really accomplished by including off-budget items (in the so called "unified budget"), especially the surplus revenues of about $130 billion that had accumulated in the Social Security Trust Fund. Absent this fiscal slight of hand, the 1998 budget would have displayed a deficit of over $30 billion. In fact, it was not until the fiscal year 1999 that a true federal surplus was realized.

Millions, Billions, Trillions! What fantastic sums. Many years ago, the late Senator Everett Dirksen jokingly remarked about the budget cutting process, "You save a billion dollars here, a billion dollars there and pretty soon you are talking about some real money." And this frequently is the perspective of members of our national legislature. However, the astronomical size of these numbers tends to escape us. To illustrate: Suppose that a firm starts with $1 billion in capital. Assume further that it loses $1,000 a day. After 2,000 years this firm would still be in business and could remain in business for another 800 years. A trillion is a million multiplied by a million. The money spent annually by Congress approximates the financial wealth of one and one half million millionaires.[50]

Employment statistics offer another view of the enlarged scope of government. Here we find that total government employment grew from around 3 million in 1929 to 18 million in 1990. State and local governments account for the lion's share of this increase which reflects in the growth of their educational, welfare and health services. However, the relative stability of federal sector employment is misleading. A great deal of federal work in contracted out, and individuals so employed do not appear in federal payroll data. Also worthy of note is the fact that by 1990 Congressional appointments awarded to personal and committee staff members was about triple the size of this group in the early 1970's. Finally, the composition of the federal workforce has changed from a blue collar to a white collar emphasis and the latter often possess immense power to regulate the private economy.[51]

Another revealing index of the extent of federal activity is the number of pages in the Federal Register, a publication which contains executive orders and the regulations issued by federal agencies. Approximating 10,000 pages in 1970, the number of pages soared during the Nixon, Ford, and Carter administrations and reached 87,000 pages by 1980. While President Reagan's tenure witnessed a decline to 55,000, the number of pages ascended to about 67,000 during the 1990's.[52] Related to this topic is the observation of Richard Darman, the Director of the Office of Management and Budget during the administration of President Bush. In his Director's Introduction to the 1990 federal budget, Darman noted that it embraced 190,000 accounts, and that the award of but a minute of reflection upon each of the accounts would take over a year of eight hour days.[53] And the annual real costs of federal regulations have been estimated to be at nearly $700 billion.[54]

During the 1990's regulations have continued to increase as have expenditures, the national debt, and taxation. As a result, we find government at all levels, but especially at the federal level deeply involved in the nation's economy. What can be produced, which firms can produce it, how much of it can be sold, how it can be marketed, and where it can it be produced are all subject to government supervision. Government agencies are concerned with the technology employed in the productive process, and who is hired, promoted, laid off, and discharged. The state influences the price of goods, services, labor, money capital, and rental property. How much money one makes, what one does with it, and the choice of one's medical doctor, the method of payment for medical bills, where the children go to school, what the children are taught, and the substance of retirement plans--all of these have become the business of a variety of political entities.

To the above should be added loan guarantees for government sponsored agencies that seek to borrow money at reduced rates to carry out their functions. Included among these are the Federal National Mortgage Association (Fannie Mae) which helps to provide liquidity in the mortgage market, the Student Loan Marketing Association (Sallie Mae) which resells student loans, and the Resolution Finance Corporation (Refcorp) which was charged with administering the Savings and Loan bailout. In addition, governments have awarded direct loans, tax concessions, tariff protection and other subsidies to various industries and groups. There have been numerous antipoverty, health, and environmental programs along with the endeavors which government runs by itself. The latter include gas, electric, and water companies, the post office, buses, trains, hospitals, police and fire departments, grade schools, high schools, colleges, and universities.

While some people benefit from government policies others are adversely affected. Which is to say that outstanding success is not always the mark of government activity. Farm programs elevate the prices of food, hurt the poor, and redistribute income to wealthy farmers; minimum wage laws benefit those who keep their jobs, but cost many, especially youngsters, employment opportunities; licensure laws raise the wages of individuals who possess the license to work, but keep thousands from entering chosen occupations; international trade barriers raise profits and wages in protected industries, but bring higher prices for consumers; rent controls may benefit those who have lived in a particular apartment for a long time, but they also generate housing shortages and discourage new construction; welfare programs have alleviated economic distress for some, but continue to leave too many people poor and disheartened; and public (government) education is far from satisfactory and in more than a few cases produces disastrous results.

The decline in economic freedom has elicited more than just adverse economic effects. For the increased politicization of the economic realm has been accompanied by a diminution of personal and civic tranquility and a less self-reliant populace. A thoughtful observer must draw the conclusion that this represents a major threat to each of our liberties and to a properly conceived concept of happiness.

Yes, on the subject of economic freedom, much has been presented and there is much upon which to ponder. Thus, it is time to sum up and to do so in a manner that reflects the relationships between liberty, virtue and happiness. The next section offers a detailed examination of these relationships.

---

[1] Barry W. Poulson, *Economic History of the United States* (New York: Macmillan Publishing Co., Inc., 1991), pp. 595,596.

[2] Arthur Cecil Bining and Philip Shriver Klein, *A History Of The United States*, Vol. II (New York: Charles Scribner's Sons, 1951) pp. 382,383.

[3] Robert Higgs, *Crisis and Leviathan* (New York: Oxford University Press, 1987), p. 149.

[4] Barry w. Poulson, *Economic History of the United States*, pp. 596--598.

[5] Jonathan Hughes, *American Economic History,* 2nd ed. (Glenville: Scott, Foresman and Company, 1987), pp. 390,391.

[6] Ibid., pp. 391,392.

[7] Bernard H. Siegan, *Economic Liberties and the Constitution* (Chicago: University of Chicago Press, 1980), p. 148.

[8] Robert H. Bork, *The Tempting of America* (New York: The Free Press, 1990), p.46.

[9] Bernard H. Siegan, *Economic Liberties and the Constitution*, pp. 152-155.

[10] Arthur Cecil Bining and Phiolip Shriver Klein, *A History Of The United States*, vol. II, p. 430.

[11] Editorial, *The Wall Street Journal*, October 27, 1992.

[12] Arthur M. Schlesinger, jr., *The Crisis of the Old Order* (Boston: Houghton Mifflin Company, 1957), p.416.

[13] For description and analysis of the New Deal and the Great Depression see the following:
Jonathon Hughes, *American Economic History*, 2nd ed. (Glenville: Scott, Foresman and Company, 1987), pp. 445-471.
Robert C. Puth, *American Economic History*, 3rd ed. (New York: The Dryden Press, 1993), pp. 546-577.
Gary M. Walton and Hugh Rockoff, *History of the American Economy*, 6th ed. (New York: Harcourt Brace Jovanovich Publishers, 1990), pp. 478-517.

[14] Arthur M. Schlesinger, jr., *The Crisis of the Old Order*, p.420.

[15] Robert Higgs, *Crisis and Leviathan*, p. 180.

[16] Ibid., 183,184.

[17] Ibid., p. 184.

[18] Ibid., p. 185.

[19] Ibid., p.185.

[20] Robert H. Bork, *The Tempting of America*, p. 57.
[21] Ibid., p. 57.
[22] Bernard H. Siegan, *Economic Liberties and the Constitution*, p. 140.
[23] Ibid., pp. 140,141.
[24] Ibid., p. 141.
[25] Robert Higgs, *Crisis and Leviathan*, p. 188.
[26] Raoul Berger, *Federalism: The Founders' Design*, (Norman: University of Oklahoma Press, 1987), p.121.
[27] Robert Higgs, *Crisis and Leviathan*, p.188.
[28] Arthur Cecil Bining and Philip Shriver Klein, *A History Of The United States*, vol. ll. pp. 502-506.
[29] Jonathan Hughes, *American Economic History*, 2nd ed., p. 458.
[30] Bernard H. Siegan, *Economic Liberties and the Constitution*, p.146.
[31] Ibid., p. 185.
[32] Jonathan H. Hughes, *American Economic History*, 2nd ed., p.458.
[33] Ibid., p. 459.
[34] Bernard H. Siegan, *Economic Liberties and the Constitution*, pp. 184-203.
[35] Robert Higgs, *Crisis and Leviathan*, pp. 196-236.
[36] Barry W. Poulson, *Economic History of the United States*, pp. 613-617.
[37] Robert Higgs, *Crisis and Leviathan*, p. 220.
[38] Ibid., p. 225.
[39] John Maynard Keynes, *The General Theory Of Employment, Interest, and Money*, (New York: Harcourt Brace Jovanovich, Inc., 1953)
[40] Jonathan Hughes, *American Economic History*, 2nd ed., p.505.
[41] For a more complete list see Murray L. Weidenbaum, *Business, Government, And The Public*, 2nd ed. (Englewood Cliffs: Prentice-Hall, inc., 1981), pp. 8-10.
[42] Ibid., p.20.
[43] Michael deCourcy Hinds, "U.S. Adds Programs With Little Review Of Local Burdens," *The New York Times*, March 24, 1992.
[44] Richard Vedder, "America the Disabled," *The Wall Street Journal*, September 4, 1996.
[45] Leslie Kaufman, "Adjusting the Legal Bar for Disability," *The New York Times: Week in Review*, April 18, 1999.
[46] Peter Brimelow, "The Reason Why," *Forbes*, August 26, 1996.
[47] Paul Craig Roberts and Lawrence M. Stratton Jr., "The Roots of the Income Tax," *National Review*, April 17,1995.
[48] Campbell R. McConnell and Stanley L. Brue, *Economics: Principles, Problems, and Policies* 12th ed. (New York: McGraw-Hill,Inc., 1999),p.388.
[49] Ibid., p.388.
[50] Stephen Moore, "If You Bought 2 Trillion Copies Of This Paper....," *The Wall Street Journal*, February 6, 1995.
[51] Brink Linsdsey, "System Overload," *Policy Review*, 1991.
[52] Edwin S. Rubenstein, *The Right Data* (New York: A National Review Book, 1994), p.172.
[53] Warren T. Brooks, "Dead Wrong Again," *National Review*, October 7, 1991.
[54] Raymond J. Keating, "An Optimist's View of the Entrepreneurship Explosion," *The Freeman*, March 1997.

PART THREE

ECONOMIC FREEDOM: HAPPINESS AND VIRTUE

CHAPTER 13

ECONOMIC FREEDOM: HAPPINESS AND VIRTUE I

PHILOSOPHY AND RELIGION

As well we are aware, Thomas Jefferson, in 1776, penned the assertions, radical for their time, that"... all men are created equal; that they are endowed by their Creator with certain inalienable rights; that among these are life, liberty, and the pursuit of happiness." This chapter focuses on the quest for happiness.

As a thought with which to begin, it somewhat recently has been estimated that the average American is roughly ten times wealthier today than was his counterpart during the Revolutionary era.[1] Enough wealth, according to Tom Wolfe, to make "the Sun King blink." That this typical American is ten times happier is questionable, to say the least. And although America has achieved some remarkable successes, there is a feeling in large sectors of the populace that things are not quite right, not as they should be in the United States; that we could be doing better. To develop a more profound understanding of American achievements and shortcomings, let us explore the meaning of the word "happiness," the various concepts of virtue, and the interrelationships of happiness and virtue with economic freedom.

HAPPINESS

One suspects that almost everyone not only wishes to be happy but considers it to be an important if not supreme goal. Moreover, happiness has vital implications for society. A happy person is likely to be kind and generous to others, whereas the unhappy individual tends to be preoccupied with himself and be less likely to perform good works.[2] With his judgement clouded, others may receive the blame for his woes (the Nazis blamed the Jews and the Communists indicted the capitalists). The unhappy person may well seek refuge for his personal problems in destructive social movements.[3]

An elusive concept to be sure, happiness nonetheless has for centuries been awarded the attention of philosophers, theologians, and others concerned with the human condition. Socrates, an advocate of the Delphic motto "know thyself," thought happiness is found not through material possessions, but by knowingly acting in a right manner. In his view, philosophy should concern itself with the proper care of the soul which in turn influences the physical, intellectual, and moral aspects of man: in other words, philosophy should develop man's capacity for virtue which leads to happiness. For Plato, Socrates' pupil, happiness is an inner peace that obtains when there is harmony among the parts of the soul and when there is harmony among the classes of citizens in the ideal state. Plato's pupil, Aristotle, believes happiness will be realized when an individual acquires that which is necessary to satisfy human needs and possesses that which is good for him. Happiness is the ultimate goal and is, unlike other goods, a good chosen for its own sake. The happy man has what he desires; what he desires is what he should desire, and he wants for nothing. Moreover, the highest form of happiness is contemplation, for contemplation accords with the highest and best in us, our ability to reason.

During the Middle Ages, theologians including Saint Thomas Aquinas, while in substantial agreement with Aristotle (Acquinas referred to him as "The Philosopher"), nonetheless considered the happiness possible in this life imperfect because perfect happiness is the immortal soul at rest in the beatific vision of God. Moreover, original sin has rendered man incapable of even the imperfect happiness of this world without God's grace: "... the free and undeserved help that God gives us to respond to his call to become children of God..."[4] Over the centuries, many notions of happiness have been propounded. The nineteenth century utilitarians, as we have seen, conceived of happiness as a condition in which the amount of pleasure exceeds the amount of pain. In more recent times, there are writers who believe happiness to consist of both a healthy body and a healthy mind. Peace for the latter arrives when inner conflict is conquered, when the individual becomes well adjusted to his environment and acts in a manner which feels good.

Although thinkers have expressed many views about happiness, there are some aspects of it upon which general agreement prevails. First, there are varying degrees of happiness, as in "I was happier this year than last year." Also, we move between states of happiness and unhappiness, or experience degrees of both at once: a person might believe himself to be a generally happy fellow and yet feel anxiety while studying for an exam or contemplating pending root canal surgery. The "high" experienced by a drug addict is not considered true happiness. Similarly dismissed from discussion of real happiness is the attainment of ephemeral or peripheral desires, such as the consumption of an ice cream soda, the purchase of a new television set, or the enjoyment that comes from having one's team win the Superbowl. In fact, one might be experiencing pleasure in all of these and yet, be a deeply troubled person at heart. In any case, happiness should not be considered as just a one time sensation but rather something which is pursued over a lifetime.[5]

Inscribed at the temple of Apollo at Delphi is the motto "nothing in excess," and philosophers favor the view that excess is contrary to happiness; that real happiness is an outcome (all else being equal) of an upright or virtuous life. From his own point of view, the authentically happy person has some understanding of his place in this world. He is generally satisfied with the pattern of his life and the components of it that he believes important. His outlook is positive, and the good aspects of his existence already have and/or are expected to outweigh its tragedies and disappointments. Peace is with him. But what is the path to this felicitous state? Why, the answer is a simple one to which most thoughtful people would assent: virtuous behavior.

VIRTUE

Although philosophers before and after Aristotle have concerned themselves with the link between happiness and virtue, it is the writings of The Philosopher that for centuries have proved so influential. Thus, it behooves us to explore the work of this great man who founded a school (the Lyceum), tutored Alexander the Great, and pursued numerous scholarly inquiries into logic, physics, metaphysics, biology, aesthetics, politics, and of course, ethics. We will focus upon *The Nicomachean Ethics* which takes its name after the editor of this work, Aristotle's son Nicomachus.[6]

Aristotle holds man to be a rational animal who, unlike brute animals beneath him, can ask questions, seek answers, and engage in philosophical thought. He believes because of these human attributes that we have an obligation to pursue 'happiness' or the 'good life--or 'well-being'--(these words are used interchangeably). To do so, we must have a plan that will lead us to happiness, an end sought not for the sake of anything else, but an end in itself. Such a plan indicates what one ought to try to acquire over a lifetime with happiness delivered in proportion to which this quest meets with success. Note, that the very word "plan" implies a some degree of freedom; if everything is determined for us, the idea of a plan is moot.

Now, we need certain types of "goods" to realize happiness. These goods include bodily goods, such as health and vitality, as well as pleasures of the body and the absence of pain. Also needed for the sake of the body are food, shelter and clothing--Aristotle refers to these goods as "wealth." Then there are the goods the soul needs including knowledge, skills (especially the skill of thinking), friendships (man is a social animal), the pleasures of the mind (such as viewing works of art or making something well), the reciprocated love of other human beings, and deserved self-esteem. All these comprise the goods which satisfy our natural needs, these Aristotle deems necessary for happiness.

Also necessary to the successful pursuit of this good life is the development of high moral character and this entails the acquisition of another type of "goods"--good habits. Habits may be of the sort through which a skill is developed so that a task can be performed with a degree of excellence--in sports, or perhaps music, or mathematics. However, there also are habits that concern themselves with making the right moral choice, and doing so rather easily and on a regular basis.

The Greek word for good habits has been translated to "excellence" in English. However, we are more apt to refer to these good habits with the English translation of the Latin translation--that is "virtue." Good habits reflecting skills are called "intellectual virtues," while those concerned with making right choices receive the appellation of "moral virtues." Both classes of virtue are necessary for the good life, although Aristotle awards the prime position to virtue of a moral nature, for it is moral virtue that enables us to make virtuous decisions and thereby to obtain the correct goods in their proper amounts, and to avoid that which is harmful. Moreover, the firmer the habit, which itself is acquired through repetition, especially of small acts, the easier it becomes to make the right choices. As Great Britain's King George V wrote, "The secret of happiness is not to do what you like to do, but to learn to like what you have to do."[7] Thus, morality can be considered as a state of character or perhaps in contemporary terms, what you do when no one is looking. There are also bad habits. Aristotle calls them vices--and here also, the more that bad habits are ingrained in us the easier the choice, but in this case in the wrong direction.

For Aristotle, then, happiness tends to flow from obtaining what one desires providing these desires are consistent with moral virtue. Through the rational powers of the mind, we develop and follow an appropriate plan for life. However, even here there is no guarantee, because even if we possess sterling moral virtues, there are some things in life over which we may have little or no control. We may be born with bad health or with an incurable physical defect, or into abject poverty, or the offspring of incompetent parents, or into a totalitarian society. In other words, chance, or luck or good and bad fortune play their roles in the quest for happiness. However, virtuous habits, such as courage may help us to bear up during hard times. One also is reminded of the aphorism of Branch Rickey, the former general manager of the Brooklyn Dodger's baseball team, "Good luck is the residue of design." In any case, misfortunes happen to all of us, so the fact that we are not enjoying a perfect state of happiness, does not necessarily mean that we are not in some degree happy. Aristotle put it this way:

> ...no blessed man can become miserable; for he will never do the acts that are hateful and mean. For the man who is truly good and wise, we think, bears all the chances of life becomingly and always makes the best of circumstances, as a good general makes the best military use of the army at his command, and a good shoemaker makes the best shoes out of the hides that are given him; and so with all other craftsmen. And if this be the case, the happy man can never become miserable....[8]

Aristotle was not the only Greek philosopher to concern himself with virtue. From the time of the ancients onward, many thinkers and moralists have cited virtues which they deem important for people to practice. Among these often overlapping virtues are courage, temperance, justice, prudence, faith, hope, charity, industry, honesty, responsibility, humility, perseverance, compassion, integrity, patriotism, and loyalty. Let us begin this discussion of moral excellence by attempting to sum up rather briefly the essence of what various authorities have to say about what are known as the "traditional" or "classical" virtues: courage, temperance, justice, and wisdom.

Courage can take many forms, but essentially it refers to strength of mind in the face of adversity. Aristotle conceives of this virtue (and others) as a "golden mean" lodged between two vices: the courageous person is neither rash nor a coward. Courage for the soldier or martyr can be the overcoming of fear of physical harm and death when confronting one's enemies. It can mean taking responsibility for your actions. and standing up for your convictions. In this regard, the names of Patrick Henry, Susan B. Anthony, Rosa Parks, and Martin Luther King, Jr. come quickly to mind. The civic official may need courage to uphold the law and the scholar may require it in his pursuit of the truth no matter where that journey takes him. American blacks displayed it abundantly when confronting the humiliation and rigors of slavery. It is the willingness to proclaim that the end does not justify the means as well as to admit a mistake (Once chided by a friend for changing his economic analysis, Lord Keynes replied, "When the facts change, I change my mind. What do you do, sir?"). Courage may be thought of as the habit of perseverance and of taking the steps necessary (the painful process of acquiring new skills, for instance), to secure the good life.

Temperance has the connotation of self-control or the mastery of oneself. We employ our reason and the habit of self-discipline to check the bodily appetites and passions for food, drink, sex, and wealth. Temperance implies an understanding that we are responsible for our actions: it does not mean abstinence, but rather balance or moderation. For the intemperate man not only is never satisfied but may bring harm to himself as well as to his family and society. Adam Smith, as we have seen, deemed self-control to be the basis for the other virtues.

We demonstrate the moral virtue of justice when we are fair and honest in our dealings with others, when we respect the rights and dignity of others, when we refrain from inflicting harm on others, when we keep promises, when we give others their just due, when we obey laws and consider the common good. Just acts promote our own well-being and the well-being of society.

Then, there is the intellectual virtue of wisdom. This word, often associated with the ancients had two meanings for them. One of these, speculative wisdom, is identified with contemplation of God and the highest levels of philosophical knowledge and may be called theology or metaphysics. The other aspect of wisdom is of a practical nature. Prudence, or practical wisdom, embraces the knowledge of how to deliberate and choose the proper means to a given goal--especially in matters relating to the good life and ultimate end of mankind. The prudent person may harbor worthy ambitions but is wise enough not to expect to realize all of them. Prudence is the mean between excessive caution and impetuosity. It is a virtue that we develop as we habitually weigh alternatives and make the right choices. Temperance provides the foundation and guide for the other three virtues. It is also known as *auriga virtutum*--the charioteer of the virtues.

Aristotle believes that we cannot attain perfection through only one moral virtue. Perfection would be the possession of all moral virtues. Although a thief might show courage and practical wisdom in his thievery, his goal hardly conforms with the dictates of justice. So we see that the virtues, properly conceived, overlap, complement and reinforce one another. Practical wisdom and the moral virtues feed upon each other.

These virtues or moral principles concern themselves with right or wrong in action or desire. They represent aspects of character that define the good man leading the good life. As Marcus Aurelius observed long ago, virtue is its own reward. Moreover, reward extends to both the political and economic realms, because a virtuous citizenry is likely to bring forth a prosperous and harmonious society as well as a government marked by the classical virtues.

Religion also has had a great deal to say about these matters, for virtue is nothing less than the health of the soul. The Old Testament sets forth what is essential to the love of God and neighbor and what is contrary to it. These moral precepts are in the Ten Commandments. Later in the Christian tradition (which coupled with the Judeo tradition, has played such a dominant role in the development of western civilization), the virtues of courage, temperance, justice, and prudence are designated as cardinal, (the Latin word for hinge), and it is upon these that all other virtues pivot. They are at the heart of human morality and can be known through our human nature. The objective of a virtuous life is be like God and these virtues play a foundational role. Courage, for instance, is important in resisting the temptations of this world and justice includes giving God as well as one's neighbor his due. But possession of the cardinal virtues are not enough to be saved, and for Christians, the road to paradise requires the three supernatural or theological virtues: faith, hope, and charity, and these are acquired by grace.[9]

Faith is the belief in God and in His teachings and revelations. Faith is also a freely made commitment to God and the understanding that grows out of that commitment. Through hope one desires heaven and eternal life. Hope is the certainty that God's promises will be kept, and during hard times hope keeps us from being discouraged. The theological virtue of charity is that, "... by which we love God above all things for his own sake, and our neighbor as ourselves for the love of God." Charity is held to be the first and greatest of the three supernatural virtues and its fruits are joy, peace, and mercy. In the words of Saint Thomas, "For there are two precepts of charity: one pertains to loving God, the other to loving our neighbor. These two precepts are mutually related; for what must be principally loved through charity is God, the supreme good and source of man's happiness. After God, we are obliged by charity to love our neighbor, to whom we are bound by special ties due to our common vocation to happiness."[10]

Further, the Sermon on the Mount offers the beatitudes, or modes of virtuous behavior--the actions and attitudes that characterize Christian life. They are Humility, Mercy, Mourning, Peacemaking, Hunger and Thirst for Righteousness, Purity, and Bearing Persecution for the Sake of Justice. To be avoided are the seven deadly vices or sins; Pride (the Greeks considered this a virtue), Avarice, Lust, Anger, Gluttony, Envy, and Sloth.

As any student of history knows, a wrongful interpretation of religious creeds can lead to bigotry, discrimination, persecution, physical cruelty, and even war. On the other hand, religious creeds are major repositories of codes for virtuous behavior. We will come back to this Judeo-Christian tradition shortly.

ECONOMIC FREEDOM AND VIRTUE

Virtuous behavior is a necessary component for the successful operation of free markets, and the latter go far in stimulating the former.

The classical virtue of courage enables the entrepreneur to launch a new business, to manage it during the difficult formative years and to persevere under adverse conditions. Nor is courage restricted to the higher realms of enterprise. For the employee, it may mean showing up for work and giving the boss his due, even when personal problems might lead one to be absent. It may entail remaining at an unpleasant job or working overtime in order to pay family medical bills or to insure an appropriate education for one's children.

The correct posture for an employer is a temperate one: intemperate behavior can bring harm to the firm and its employees. A worker also needs to be in sufficient control of his appetites so that he can put in a fair day's labor. One should neither be a miser nor a spendthrift but should exercise judicious frugality and thereby provide the proper goods for family members. Members of a thrifty society put aside funds (when possible) for the proverbial rainy day, and these savings make possible real capital formation. Temperate behavior is responsible behavior, and temperance and courage produce self-reliance.

Justice denotes honesty and fairness in one's dealings and applies to relationships among employers, employees, and customers. For an employer it means going about one's business in a truthful and forthright manner and with a sincere attempt to secure appropriate remuneration and working conditions for the firm's labor force. The latter should respond with an honest day's work.

Finally, practical wisdom, which may be gained through formal schooling as well as through experience, becomes a most important virtue in eliciting courageous, temperate, and just behavior among the participants in the national economy. Virtuous behavior promotes the successful performance of a free market economy. But we can also assert that economic freedom does in itself ordinarily foster the development of moral excellence.

The free market system has performed better than any other economic arrangement in history. Its characteristic negative freedom has proved to be the best way to obtain and secure positive freedom. In fact, it is the greatest instrument for the creation of wealth that the world has ever seen. However, for most of history, monarchs, dictators, feudal lords, mercantile authorities, theologians, saints, philosophers, princes of church and state, along with hosts of bureaucrats have helped to design and/or implement economic arrangements. They did so with the belief that economics is essentially a zero-sum game.

As a result, the vast majority of people throughout world history have lived in abject poverty. Although some--especially radicals--tend to romanticize pre-industrial society, it should not require deep thought to realize that a life lived out in involuntary, pitiful, degrading, miserable, and hopeless poverty, subject to exhausting work, prejudice, and arbitrary power is unlikely to be as happy as life can be. Even as late as the eighteenth century Adam Smith could observe, "It is not uncommon, I have been told, In the Highlands of Scotland for a mother who has borne twenty children not to have two alive."[11] Not one of Queen Anne's children survived her, and many women, pregnant from puberty to death, failed to see any of their offspring reach adulthood.[12] And recall how Thomas Jefferson was appalled at the widespread poverty that he encountered in European cities.

However, during the last couple of hundred years, in areas where free markets have dominated, the story has been different indeed. Not only has there been a tremendous amount of wealth *created*, but the distribution of the goods and services necessary not only to avoid hunger and plagues but to extend life expectancy and secure the "good life" has been ubiquitous. While poverty (the definition of which continues to expand), has by no means disappeared, the common man has gained a new dignity through an improved economic and social position, (including a proper name) and acquisition of assortment of legal rights.[13]

Economic freedom produces societies characterized by more harmony than is found in other economic systems. There are several reasons for this. First of all, a free market economy tends to induce moral behavior. Success greets those who produce what others wish to purchase (one serves his fellow man), and competition sees to it that firms which fail to meet the mandates of the sovereign consumer will depart from the economic scene. Thus, great incentives present themselves to participants in the national economy to engage in morally correct behavior. Courageous entrepreneurship may be rewarded with profits and prestige. Owners and managers are encouraged via the profit and monetary incentives to be fair and honest with customers and to foster trust, especially where the enterprise is based on repeat business and referrals. The same attitude directed toward employees encourages an industrious and loyal labor force. Intemperate or unjust personal behavior by management or labor can spell economic ruin for all concerned. Moreover, moral excellence in economic affairs, which through repetition becomes habitual, is likely to spill over to other realms of life, including family, friends, and community and political associations and undertakings.

Private property plays a vital role in the manner through which a free enterprise economy encourages moral excellence and societal harmony. Where property is relatively easy to acquire and where property rights are highly held, clearly defined and enforced by the courts, power tends to be diffused throughout society rather than concentrated in the hands of a few. In such circumstances it is difficult to undertake actions which impose costs on others (such as taking away some of their property or the rights attaching thereto for personal gain). When the justice system holds perpetrators responsible for the harm they inflict on others, people tend to be more careful of what they do and more respectful of the rights of fellow human beings. As we noted in Chapter One, private property serves as a foundation for other freedoms. It also promotes moral behavior because a free society lets people exercise choice, learn from mistakes, grow in wisdom, and practice and affirm virtuous behavior.

Critics of a free market system often focus their wrath on its competitive aspects. However, in evaluating the merits of competition, one does well to ponder the outcome of its polar opposite, monopoly (higher prices, less produced, and inferior quality). Moreover, competition has a long history of contests in fields such as sports, music, drama, chess, flower arrangement, and many, many others. In these competitions, competitors may even be friends, and this is true as well in a free market system. Many consider competition to be a natural aspect of human behavior that serves as a stimulus to excellence and progress. In the economic realm, this vital force not only provides opportunities and encourages ambition and the desire to excel, but it also insures that scarce resources are directed to satisfy human wants as people go about working to realize their varied aspirations.[14] Competition induces us to search for better ways of doing things, to improve the methods of production, and to develop new and superior products.

Nonetheless, despite the undeniable advantages it provides, competition may take unethical forms and is not always an activity that, at least directly, advances tranquillity. However, it also must be remembered that cooperation (a companion of competition, if you will) is another essential ingredient of a free enterprise system.

Surely more pleasant than the hostility engendered by coercion, cooperation develops out of differences in the interests and talents we possess and facilitates the development of business firms, labor unions, and other cooperative associations. Cooperation also leads to an elaborate division of labor whereby an enormous variety of employment opportunities present themselves. These, in turn, provide a basis for self-development, as well as enhanced production and productivity. The voluntary force of cooperation helps us to realize a great diversity of objectives and focuses us on getting along with each other rather than on the ways we disagree. Capitalism provides the liberty--the space--for people to join together in a variety of nonprofit arrangements that promote charitable, educational, and other worthy causes that build community. There is a conspicuous absence of such arrangements in collectivist nations, where the state dominates economic activity.

These statements hold true when economic intercourse takes place on an international level. Nations that emphasize commerce seek not to conquer each other but to secure economic rewards based on voluntary exchange, and thus, as Montesquieu observes, "The spirit of commerce unites nations."[15] He also notes, "it is almost a general rule that wherever manners are gentle there is commerce; and wherever there is commerce, manners are gentle."[16] The city of Amsterdam chose Commercium et Pax as its motto.[17] When David Hume compares commercial civilizations with those of a martial, aristocratic, or religious character, he notes that with the former, "Factions are then less inveterate, revolutions less tragic, authority less severe, and seditions less frequent."[18] And as James Q. Wilson observes, vendettas or dynastic wars upset the routines of commerce and those preoccupied with family honor will likely be less financially successful than those whose prime interest is commerce.[19]

Adam Smith, holds similar views. One might also note that when the opportunity presents itself, it is not to the socialist nations but rather to those that have embraced capitalism that the poor of this world flee.

Out of these influences, there tends to arise some regard for the tastes and opinions of others which enable people from different cultures and values to live together rather harmoniously. Moreover, a wealthy and educated society is likely to show more compassion toward the less fortunate, for as Adam Smith notes, "If our own misery pinches us very severely, we have no leisure to attend to that of our neighbor."[20]

These observations forcefully demonstrate that a free market economy not only is compatible with moral excellence but elicits the peaceful conditions within which virtue thrives and positive change can take place. Moreover, this is in keeping with the Judeo-Christian heritage, which upholds the importance of the individual, free will, choice, responsibility for ones actions, creativity, peace, harmony, love of one's neighbor, affluence, and compassion. And this heritage is a foundation for moral behavior. Although an extended analysis of this Judeo-Christian heritage is well beyond the scope of this volume, its relation to the subjects topics of wealth and compassion do warrant our investigation.

THE JUDEO-CHRISTIAN HERITAGE

The Bible is an appropriate place to begin. It seeks to offer answers to basic human questions about the origin and meaning of this world and of life, suffering, and death. In Genesis 1 and 2 we learn that God created the universe in six days and rested on the seventh. It was on the last day of His labors that He made man and woman in His image, placed them in the Garden of Eden, and was pleased with the results. He commanded them to be fertile and multiply, and gave them dominion over the earth. From these verses of Genesis, we learn that the earth and its wealth are good and that the creative powers of man and woman (both made in God's image), if used as God tells them, will be pleasing to Him.

After Adam and Eve eat the forbidden fruit of the tree of knowledge (through which they thought they might become gods themselves), God placed them under a curse forcing them to work hard to obtain anything--and thus was the need to economize born. God expelled them from the Garden of Eden. Later in Genesis, appalled by the wickedness on earth, the Lord destroyed its inhabitants with the forty day flood. Excepted was Noah, with whom He was pleased, along with Noah's family and the animals aboard the ark. God blessed Noah and his sons, gave them command of the earth and promised not to destroy it again with a flood (Genesis 8 and 9). In summary, Genesis 1 and 2 explains how the earth ought to be. Genesis 8 and 9 observes that God blessed the human race and promised not to put a curse on the earth even though man may harbor evil thoughts. In other words, good and evil might exist together.[21]

The book of Exodus describes the flight of the Israelites from Egypt, where they had been in bondage, and their journey to Sinai, where they enter into a covenant with God and are formed into a new nation under God's Law. This Law, which is contained in the first five books of the Jewish Bible (also known as the Torah), is deeply religious in nature and consists of a body of complex regulations concerned with the nation's moral, civic, social, and (of course), religious life. Best known is The Decalogue, or Ten Commandments, the basic Law of the covenant.

In the world of the Old Testament, material conditions were important, as was social justice, and a vital underlying theme is the command "...to love your neighbor as you love yourself" (Leviticus 19:18).[22] This obligation takes several forms, a few of which are presented below.

* Foreigners should not be mistreated. "Treat them as you would treat a fellow Israelite, and love them as you love yourselves. Remember that you were once foreigners in the land of Egypt" (Lev. 19:33,34).
* Do not cheat anyone. "Use honest scales, honest weights, and honest measures" (Lev. 19:35,36).

* When giving a loan, do not charge interest to the poor, and be sure to return any collateral they might have pledged (Exodus 22: 25-27).
* One should give generously and unselfishly to the poor (Deuteronomy 15:10,11).
* Every seventh year, money debts are to be canceled for fellow Israelites. This obligation does not apply to foreigners (Deuteronomy 15: 1-3).
* In the seventh year any Israelite that another Israelite has enslaved is to be set free. "Remember, that you were slaves in Egypt and the Lord your God set you free" (Deut. 15: 12-15).
* Every fiftieth or Jubilee year, the original owner shall have the right to buy back any property that has been sold (for the land belongs to God), and slaves shall be set free (Lev 25:8-55).

However, the Jubilee regulations do not suggest any equal division of land. The tribes of Israel do not receive equal shares in the Promised Land, first born sons receive a double share of land, and daughters receive nothing, which is also was the case for non-Israelites as well as the poorest of the poor. Nor are property rights to be abolished. After all the Commandments "Thou Shall Not Covet The Neighbor's Goods," and "Thou Shall Not Steal," do imply there is private property to steal and covet.

The extent to which these biblical mandates were put into practice is uncertain, and some of them--forgiving all your debts, for instance--are impractical and may be downright dangerous in a modern economy. Nonetheless, we see that the Old Testament gives considerable attention to the less fortunate. Delight, however, is by no means absent and coexists with compassion. For instance, God commands His people to, "Set aside a tithe"-- a tenth of their output each year and take it as tithe to the place chosen by the Lord and consume it to "learn reverence for the Lord..." If this is not possible, then "Sell your produce and take the money with you to the one place of worship. Spend it on whatever you want--beef, lamb, wine, beer--and there, in the presence of the Lord your God, you and your families are to eat and enjoy themselves." In addition, every third year the tithe is to be given to the "...Levites, since they own no property, and for the foreigners, orphans, and widows who live in your towns. They are to come and get all they need" (Deut 14: 22-29).

Moreover, if the people of Israel obey the Law of the God who liberated them, they will be blessed not with a bare minimum subsistence but with abundance: "...He will bless your fields, so that you will have grain, wine, and olive oil: and He will bless you by giving you many cattle and sheep....No people in the world will be as richly blessed as you." (Deut. 7:13,14). "The Lord your God is bringing you into a fertile land--a land that has rivers and springs, and underground streams gushing out into the valleys and hills: a land that produces wheat and barley, grapes, figs, pomegranates, olives, and honey. There you will never go hungry or ever be in need" (Deut. 8: 7-9).

The Book of Proverbs, which concerns itself with moral teaching on everyday practical matters, takes a favorable position toward wealth and at times positively correlates it with virtue and poverty with vice.

* "Being lazy will make you poor, but hard work will make you rich"(Proverbs: 9:4).
* No matter how much a lazy person may want something, he will never get it. A hard worker will get everything he wants" (Proverbs 13:4).
* "No one likes a poor man, not even his neighbors, but the rich have many friends" (Proverbs 14:20).
* "Have reverence for the Lord, be humble, and you will get riches, honors, and a long life" (Proverbs 22:4).

It is important to note that this abundance, this excess, this superfluity, this delight, this wealth is accompanied with stern warnings.

> Make certain that you do not forget the Lord your God; do not fail to obey any of his laws that I am giving you today. When you have all you want to eat and have built good houses to live in and when your cattle and sheep, your silver and gold, and all your possessions have increased, be sure that you do not become proud and forget the lord your God who rescued you from Egypt, where you were slaves.
> He led you through that vast and terrifying desert where there were poisonous snakes and scorpions. In that dry and waterless land he made water flow out of solid rock for you.
> In the desert he gave you manna to eat, food that your ancestors had never eaten. He sent hardships on you to test you, so that in the end he could bless you with good things.
> So then you must never think that you have made yourselves wealthy by your own power and strength.
> Remember that it is the Lord your God who gives you the power to become rich. He does this because he is still faithful to the covenant that he made with your ancestors.
> Never forget the Lord your God or turn to other gods to worship; and serve them. If you do, then I warn you today that you will certainly be destroyed. If you do not obey the Lord, then you will be destroyed just like those nations that he is going to destroy as you advance (Deut 8:11-20).

The theme of compassion coexisting amidst delight or affluence is developed in other Old Testament passages. The prophet Amos, for instance, attacks the prosperous who have secured their wealth by exploiting the weak.(Deut 2:6-8 and Deut 5:10-13). He also inveighs against the narcissism of those enjoying luxuries. who have failed to show compassion for the poor (Amos 3:15-4:3 and 6:4-7). Nations and individuals, especially those with power, must act in a moral manner: "...let justice flow like a stream, and righteousness like a river that never goes dry" (Amos: 5:24). And in Isaiah, the Lord says, "Remove the chains of oppression and the yoke of injustice, and let the oppressed go free. Share your food with the hungry and open your homes to the homeless poor. Give clothes to those who have nothing to wear, and do not refuse to help your own relatives"(Isaiah 58:6,7).

The rich, of course, are not always righteous although they may be; nor is poverty always the result of immoral behavior, although it also may be. Moreover the righteous as well as the oppressors do not always receive their just desserts in this world. In fact they might receive the opposite of what they deserve. As the Book of Job makes abundantly clear, horrible things happen for apparently no good reason, which is to say that only God knows the moral essence of a personal situation, and his justice may not be immediate but, as the economist would say "in the long run."[23]

One can make a strong case that God does not favor the rich or the poor, but the righteous. In this complex world with its complex economic dimensions, we should be faithful to God and His Law like Abraham and Job. This means that we may enjoy good fortune if it comes our way, but we also have a duty to follow the Lord, who in the Exodus liberated His people. We need to show compassion and give assistance to the poor and suffering.[24] Proverbs sums it up rather nicely:

* "If you make fun of poor people you insult the God who made them. You will be punished if you take pleasure in someone's misfortune" (Proverbs 17:5).
* "When you give to the poor, it is like lending to the Lord, and the Lord will pay you back" (Proverbs: 18-17).
* "Be generous and share your food with the poor. You will be blessed for it" (Proverbs 22:9).

The New Testament relates the story of Jesus, the promised Savior through whom God will fulfill His promises. For Christians, the New Law makes perfect the Law of the Old Testament. It does not devalue the Old Law, but rather adds to it, reforms the heart through which man chooses the pure or the impure, and orients the divine promises toward the Kingdom of God.[25] Jesus comes not just for the Jewish people but to redeem all humanity. His message is one of redemptive love. Here also we find extensive treatment of wealth, poverty, and compassion.

One of the themes developed by Jesus during his public ministry is of a radical and sorrowful nature. Earthly possessions and ties are to be renounced and disciples are even told to abandon their families in order to follow him. A vital message of Christ is to show compassion to the poor and suffering.[26]

The radical Jesus taught privileged people to help the poor and suffering. The rich were given stern warnings that earthly things are less important than eternal life and that they have an obligation to help the unfortunate of this world.

* "And so I tell you not to worry about the food you need to stay alive or about the clothes you need for your body. Life is much more important than food, and the body much more important than clothes. Look at the crows; they don't plant seeds or gather a harvest; they don't have storage rooms or barns; God feeds them! You are worthy so much more than birds" (Luke 12:22-25).
* "Sell all your belongings and give the money to the poor." (Luke 12:33). "...none of you can be my disciple unless he gives up everything he has" (Luke: 14:33).
* "How hard it is for rich people to enter the Kingdom of God! It is much harder for a rich person to enter the Kingdom of God than for a camel to go through the eye of a needle" (Luke: 18:24,25).
* "Well, religion does make a person very rich, if he is satisfied with what he has. What did we bring into the world? Nothing! What can we take out of the world? Nothing! So then, if we have food and clothes, that should be enough for us. But

those who want to get rich fall into temptation and are caught in the trap of many foolish desires, which pull them down to ruin and destruction. For the love of money is a source of all kinds of evil" (1 Timothy 6: 6-!0).

Yet we know that there was another side to Jesus that shows Him more favorably disposed to the delights of wealth. And not just wealth in an isolated context, but that in which the joys of affluence are surrounded by poverty.[27] Historically, this is an image that has received less attention.

* The Gospel according to Matthew (2:1-11) explains how at the birth of Christ, *rich* wise men from the East followed a star to the place of his birth and presented him with gifts of gold, frankincense and myrrh. His father was a carpenter, as was Christ himself. Although far from the affluence of twentieth century America, this occupation does suggest that he grew up not among the poorest of the poor but rather of what might today be called a middle class background. "The child grew and became strong; he was full of wisdom, and God's blessings were upon him" (Luke 2:40). Finally, after his crucifixion, a *rich* man, Joseph from Arimathea, took his body, "...wrapped it in a new linen sheet and placed it in his own tomb..." (Matthew 27: 57-61).

* Nor were his behavior and perspective always of a moderate nature. "The son of man came, and he ate and drank, and you said, 'Look at this man! He is a glutton and wine-drinker, a friend of tax collectors and other outcasts" (Luke 7:34). After the ordinary wine is finished off by the guests at the wedding feast at Cana, Jesus keeps the party going by changing water into superior wine (John 2:1-12). On another occasion, a woman pours a full jar of nard over Jesus. When some of the people criticize this action as a waste of very expensive perfume, Jesus replies, "Leave her alone! She has done a fine and beautiful thing for me. You will always have poor people with you, and any time you want to, you can help them. But you will not always have me" (Mark 14: 3-8).

We see Christ's attitude toward the rich in the excerpts below:

* Zacchaeus: The rich chief tax collector Zacchaeus (tax collectors tended to be a corrupt lot in those days), in response to public criticism, decides to "...give half my belongings to the poor, and if I have cheated anyone, I will pay him back four times as much." And Jesus says, "Salvation has come to this house today..." (Luke: 19:1-10). Note: he does not give all of his wealth to the poor but a substantial amount is used for righteous purposes.[28]

* The Rich Fool: This parable concerns a man who seeks to store up a multitude of possessions in order to give himself security: "Then I will say to myself, Lucky man! You have all the good things you need for many years. Take life easy, eat, drink and enjoy yourself! But God says to him, "You fool! This very night you will have to give up your life; then who will get all these things you have kept for yourself?" Then Jesus says, "This is how it is with those who pile up riches

for themselves but are not rich in God's sight" (Luke 12:13-21). Here we find not a criticism of riches per se, nor of the prudent behavior which this man exercises. What makes the rich man a fool is his making material possessions his sole goal and failing to store up treasure of redemptive love in God's Kingdom.[29]

* The Rich Man and Lazarus: In this parable an exceptionally rich man refuses assistance to Lazarus, an exceptionally poor man, who hoped to get food by waiting outside the door of the former's dwelling. Eventually, Lazarus goes to heaven and the rich man to hell, where God denies his anguished pleas for forgiveness and relief (Luke 16:19-31). Again, this parable is not a criticism of riches per se, nor of riches in an oppressive world, but of the failure of a rich person to assume his moral responsibilities and help the poor and suffering. Also, note the implication that the rich man is not condemned for failing to assume the mantle of a messiah and save the whole world, but for being unaware of and therefore neglecting conditions in his own realm, which in this case happens to be at his own doorstep.[30]

* The Parable of the Gold Coins: This is the tale of a nobleman who, before traveling to a distant land where he will be made a king, gives each of his servants a gold coin and instructs them to earn what they can with it in his absence. Upon the king's return, he finds that one servant has earned ten gold coins with the one entrusted to him, and as a reward the nobleman puts him in charge of ten cities. Another servant has earned five gold coins and the nobleman gives him command of five cities. However, a third servant has simply kept his gold coin hidden, and it has earned nothing. This servant tries to excuse his inaction by telling his master that he is a harsh man and is afraid of him. But the master will have none of it and informs the servant that at least he could have put the money in the bank and earned some interest. Then the master takes the one gold coin from him, gives it to the one who already has ten coins, and makes the following observation: "I tell you that to every person who has something, even more will be given; but the person who has nothing, even the little that he has will be taken away from him" (Luke 19:11-27).

This parable praises the courageous servants who took risks in the economic arena and enlarged the master's domain in his absence. Further, it honors the strong warrior king who would become even stronger and extend that earthly domain. On the other hand, punishment along with a warning are delivered to the timid who failed to assume their responsibilities and to take on the many trials and tribulations that inhere in the economic realm. The parable blesses the creation of wealth, an idea that we know extends all the way back to the Book of Genesis, and suggests that proper economic endeavors on earth will be rewarded in the hereafter. Also, we might infer that all of us in our different occupations--our various realms, be they large or small--have "gold coins" to work with in our own way, for our own good and that of our fellow human beings.[31]

Finally, let us turn to Saint Paul, who provides an interesting perspective on worldly matters. From his viewpoint, we are on this earth for but a brief time and the wealth that really matters flows from God. In a rather light hearted way he seems to taunt the world for its standards.[32] "What I mean, my brothers, is this: there is not much time left, and from now on married men should live as though they were not married; those who weep, as though they were not sad; those who laugh, as though they were not happy; those who buy, as though they did not own what they bought; those who deal in material goods, as though they were not fully occupied with them. For this world as it is now will not last much longer" (Paul 1 Corinthians: 7:29-32).

Paul also notes that we have responsibilities in this world and that those with plenty should help those in need (2 Corinthians: 1-15). Moreover, these gifts should come not through some legally mandated formula but out of love from the heart, and this will earn a liberal reward.[33]

> Remember that the person who plants few seeds will have a small crop; the one who plants many seeds will have a large crop. Each one should give, then, as he has decided, not with regret or out of a sense of duty; for god loves the one who gives gladly. And God is able to give you more than you need, so that you will always have all you need for yourselves and more than enough for every good cause. As the scripture says, "He gives generously to the needy; his kindness lasts forever." And God, who supplies seed for the sower and bread to eat, will also supply you with all the seed you need and will make it grow and produce a rich harvest from your generosity. He will make you rich enough to be generous at all times, so that many will thank God for your gifts which they receive from us (2 Corinthians 9:6-11).

In summary, we can say that in the Christian biblical heritage, wealth is not considered as evil *per se*, but it, like other aspects of human affairs, need be considered in the context of one's destiny with God. In other words, wealth should be viewed in eschatological terms--how we will be judged when life ends.[34] Indeed, providing that it was not obtained through exploitation or in another nefarious manner, wealth may indicate God's blessing. However, affluence must not be viewed as life's ultimate goal, and there is the danger that it might induce forgetfulness of God. Moreover, people who are able need to show compassion to the poor and suffering. Jesus, however, did not insist that everyone give up all his worldly possessions and become his disciple. Nor did he present a specific, detailed formula for doing his bidding. He did ask that we use our God given abilities--financial and otherwise--in ways appropriate to these abilities and in the realm in which we operate to enhance not only our own well-being but that of our brethren.

Over the centuries, many interpretations of both the Old and the New Testaments have been advanced. However, the interpretation presented above differs from two points of view that have received attention in modern times. One of these points of view perceives wealth as an unmistakable sign of godliness and divine favor. The more of it the better, with no strings--or hardly any--attached. The other extreme holds that personal wealth *per se* is suspect if not downright immoral. This point of view derives in part from emphasis on some of the biblical admonitions presented above (the difficulty of the camel going through a needle's eye, for instance), and this point of view reflects the fact that for long periods the major sources of wealth came from exploiting and plundering and looting. It also reflects the economic stagnation associated with the long dominance of agriculture in economic affairs, when the systematic creation of wealth was unknown, and economies were viewed as static pies to be sliced up. A larger slice for the rich meant a diminished one for the poor, and thus distribution rather than production received the emphasis.

In spite of massive evidence to the contrary, the latter brand of economic thinking has continued until today and has found favor with the radical left, which sees affluence--especially when it exists amidst poverty--as an unmitigated evil. Not surpassingly, given this perspective's Marxist origins, capitalism is portrayed as the evil system in which class conflict abounds (necessitating class warfare) and which is responsible for much of the poverty and evil in this world. Socialism, with its emphasis on distribution rather than creation, (and its tendency to separate effort from reward), is exalted as the proper remedy.

In contrast to each of these views, the present volume holds affluence to be a desirable goal and one compatible with our Judeo-Christian heritage which, as we have seen, emphasizes man's choices and decisions to create and to assume responsibility. Wealth derived through fair means, that does not become a narcissistic "be all and end all" is legitimate and a sign of God's blessing. Moreover, much of the "consumerism" so decried by the radical left is devoted to housing so that children will have decent homes and to good schools and to the purchase of such goods, as microwave ovens, that allow family members to spend more time together, or video cameras which record important family milestones.[35] The quest for financial security, for abundance, and for the delights of this world--a new automobile, nice clothing, a good vacation, dinner at a restaurant, a well-furnished home, theatre tickets, a stereo system, a personal library--is one of the things that separates us from the lower animals. Insightful are the words of William James:

> Man's chief difference from the brutes lies in the exuberant excess of his subjective propensities. His preeminence over them lies simply and solely in the fantastic and unnecessary character of his wants, physical, moral, aesthetic and intellectual. Had his whole life not been a quest for the superfluous, he would never have established himself so inexpungably in the necessary...Prune down his extravagances, sober him, and you undo him.[36]

However, there are dangers associated with wealth, and people of affluence have some responsibility--appropriately derived through grief and compassion--to be a force for good. They are charged with assisting others to enjoy a more pleasant and fruitful existence. Remember the Good Samaritan who not only cared for the injured man with his own hands but had money which he used to pay his bills at the inn (Luke 10: 25-37). And Oskar Schindler's success in business enabled him to save many people from the Nazis. Not all of us are called upon to save the entire world or even to become creative entrepreneurs. However, there is a mandate to offer compassion and benevolence in one's own way, in one's own realm--be that realm the family, town, job, civic association, or other institution or arrangement.

Beyond what has already been presented, one may entertain the following thoughts. Those who espouse the radical left position hold as immoral the enjoyment of wealth while others in this world have unmet basic needs. Taking this to heart means that every act of consumption by a person who is not poor will be looked upon with suspicion and need justification--perhaps to oneself or, more ominously, to some political body. Talk about taking the joy out of life! One is reminded of Henry Menken's definition of Puritanism as "the haunting fear that someone, somewhere is happy." On a somewhat different note, some have observed that the feeling of guilt induced by wealth has been for centuries a major fund raising strategy for churches, secular charities, and political parties.[37]

But what of the poor person who through his own energies, with perhaps the assistance of people of financial means, rises above the poverty level and now is able to find more enjoyment in life? Is he to be castigated? Does God really want everyone to be poor or to have a joyless existence that hovers about the poverty line? And who is to determine precisely what that line is? Note also that the economic system of socialism has compiled a less than stellar track record in alleviating earthly misery. Ernest van den Haag has remarked that "...merely being poor without having renounced anything is no virtue, any more than being rich without having deprived anybody is a vice."[38] And as Martin Luther King, Jr. observes, "Nothing in wealth is inherently vicious, and nothing in poverty is inherently virtuous."[39]

According to Jesus Christ, "You will always have poor people with you..." (Matthew 26:11). Under capitalism there are fewer poor people, at least proportionately, as more and more are afforded opportunities to exercise their free will, to assume responsibility, and to make choices as they attempt to improve their own material, cultural, and spiritual lives and those of their neighbors and their society. Spirituality is not at the core of a free market economy. However, like the Bible (which also focuses on rewards and punishments--a kind of inequality, if you will), that economic system may be used as a tool for self-improvement.

Finally, let us note that religion stipulates a sacred purpose for life, teaches gratitude, provides a family bond and thus informs and strengthens a proper sense of duty as well as an awareness of who you are, where you came from, and where you are or should be headed.[40] Philip Dimitrov, Prime Minister of Bulgaria, puts it this way: "Because it is our nature as humans that for true achievement, emotional fulfillment and spiritual attainment, we need higher intensity of purpose than everyday concerns can provide."[41]

Religion gives an intellectual basis for understanding the purpose of this world. It provides the solace; the inner peace, and the courage to endure its hardships and miseries, and it helps us in the pursuit of happiness. Saint Paul taunts death with these words, "Where, Death is your victory? Where Death, is your power to hurt?" (1 Corinthians 15:55). Thomas More believes that "The times are never so bad but that a good man can live in them."[42] Saint Teresa says that when we arrive in heaven, our earthly trials will seem like "...one night in an inconvenient hotel":[43] In a similar vein, Adam Smith writes:

> This universal benevolence, how noble and generous so ever, can be the source of no solid happiness to any man who is not thoroughly convinced that all the inhabitants of the universe, the meanest as well as the greatest, are under the immediate care and protection of that great, benevolent, and all-wise Being, who directs all the movements of nature;

and who is determined, by his own unalterable perfections, to maintain in it, at all times, the greatest possible quantity of happiness. To this universal benevolence, on the contrary, the very suspicion of a fatherless world, must be the most melancholy of all reflections; from the thought that all the unknown regions of infinite and incomprehensible space may be filled with nothing but endless misery and wretchedness. All the splendor of the highest prosperity can never enlighten the gloom with which so dreadful an idea must necessarily over-shadow the imagination; nor, in a wise and virtuous man, can all the sorrow of the most afflicting adversity ever dry up the joy which necessarily springs from the habitual and thorough conviction of the truth of the contrary system.[44]

The idea of that divine Being, whose benevolence and wisdom have, from all eternity, contrived and conducted the immense machine of the universe, so as at all times to produce the greatest possible quantity of happiness, is certainly of all the objects of human contemplation by far the most sublime. Every other thought necessarily appears mean in the comparison.[45]

THE POLITICAL AND CULTURAL/MORAL SYSTEMS

Its critics indict capitalism as a system based on greed, and its critics on the far left charge that greed is peculiar to capitalism. Max Weber thought the latter a "kindergarten notion."[46] He believes that all economic systems depend upon greed, but that capitalism with its profit motive is the one that disciplines it.[47] Also, the study of history indicates that Americans as well as people in other nations where free markets dominate are no more greedy than those living in nations with economic systems based on command or on tradition. Criticism of the self-interest component of a free market economy also is misdirected, for rightly understood, self-interest means more than a simple myopic selfish quest for more and more material possessions. Rather, it includes the pursuit of those activities and goals which different members of the population value. Thus, one may work to realize the goal of a good standard of living and still seek to provide aid to the less fortunate, contemplate God, teach religious lessons in Sunday school, protect the environment, and care for one's family, friends, neighbors, and afflicted strangers. All of these nonmaterialist goals and more are properly embraced by self-interest. A little reflection by most readers on their own goals and experiences with family, friends, neighbors, and others they know will likely confirm the veracity of this statement. One thinks of the remark attributed to the University of Chicago economist Frank Knight about the similarity of the individual who maximizes *every* monetary opportunity and the Christian who loves *all* of his neighbors as himself: "neither of them has any friends."

However, as Michael Novak reminds us, the success of this system in promoting well-being also depends upon the performance of two other systems--the political and the cultural/moral--each of which should serve to direct human behavior and to restrain it from improper activity.[48] The political system should protect individuals from harm, define and defend property rights, and go about fulfilling its legitimate duties (as discussed in Chapter One). Its proper role is narrow but indispensable for the citizenry to pursue happiness.

The moral/cultural system consists of a nation's institutions which are concerned with appropriate behavior--what is right and what is wrong. These institutions include those of a religious nature, and those of an educational nature, the media, an assortment of private associations, and most important of all, the family. While some of the functions of these institutions overlap, it is the family (which is strengthened through religion) that establishes and promotes virtuous standards of behavior among its members. It is the institution through which parents lovingly watch over their offspring and make judgements, coupled with appropriate rewards and punishments, about what is right and wrong. According to James Q. Wilson, the family with its reciprocal obligations provides moral instruction that is necessary if we are to live as happy people in a prosperous society.[49] He contends that morality is not learned by value clarification and repetition of maxims but by being regularly led by families and institutions to observe standards of right conduct.[50] And as Theodore Roosevelt observed: "To educate a person in mind and not in morals is to educate a menace to society."[51]

The moral/cultural system and the political system working together act to tame the human passions that can destroy individuals and societies. Also recall that competition tends to restrain human greed or at least to channel it into beneficial results. The reader may remember Adam Smith's observation that while the quest for power and riches tends to present an unsatisfactory trade-off to the individual, it nonetheless is responsible for the construction of houses and cities, for inventions and improvements in the sciences and arts, for developments in communications, and productivity of the land--"The pleasures of wealth and greatness..."[52] Thus we see that each of the three systems depends upon each of the others and in fact, they reinforce one another, thereby enhancing the wealth creating energies of free people working in free markets, promoting the tranquility of a just society, and easing the pursuit of happiness.

---

[1] Barry W. Poulson, *Economic History Of The United States* (New York: Macmillan Publishing Co. Inc., 1981), pp. 633,634.
[2] Daniel Goleman, Emotional Intelligence (New York: Bantam Books, 1995), pp. 285-287.
[3] Dennis Prager, *Happiness Is a Serious Problem*, (New York: Harper Collins Publishers, Inc. 1998), pp. 72-74.
[4] *Catechism of the Catholic Church*,(San Francisco: Ignatius Press, 1994), p.483.
[5] Some of the complexities associated with the concept of "happiness" are addressed in Robert Nozick, *The Examined Life* (New York: Simon and Schuster, 1989), pp. 99-117.
[6] Aristotle, *The Nichomachean Ethics*, Translated with an introduction by David Ross (New York: Oxford University Press; World Classics, 1991).
[7] Billy Graham, *The Secret of Happiness* (Dallas: Word Publishing, 1985), p. 201.
[8] Ibid., p.21.
[9] See Peter Kreeft, *Back to Virtue* (San Francisco: Ignatius Press, 1986),pp. 71-78 and the *Catechism of the Catholic Church*, pp. 446-450.
[10] Mary T. Clark, ed. *An Aquinas Reader* (New York: Fordham University Press, 1988), p.501.
[11] Adam Smith, *An Inquiry Into The Nature And Causes Of The Wealth Of Nations*, ed. with an introduction by Edwin Cannon and an introduction by Max Lerner (New York: The Modern Library. Random House, Inc., 1937), p.79.

[12] Harry Lee Smith, "The Environment Since the Industrial Revolution," Cato Policy Report, March/April 1991.

[13] Nathan Rosenberg & L. E. Birdzell, Jr., *How the West Grew Rich* (New York: Basic Books, Inc., Publishers, 1986), pp. 1-6.

[14] Michael Novak, *The Spirit of Democratic Capitalism* (New York: An American Enterprise Institute/Simon & Schuster Publication, 1982), pp. 347,348.

[15] Ibid., p. 119.

[16] Dwight R. Lee, "Celebrating the Economic System That Makes Diversity Worth Celebrating," Intercollegiate Review, Spring, 1994, p.19.

[17] Michael Novak, "Eight Arguments about the Morality of the Marketplace," in *God and the Marketplace*, Jon Davies, ed.,(London: IEA Health and Welfare Unit, 1993), p.16.

[18] Michael Novak, *The Spirit of Democratic Capitalism*, p.119.

[19] James Q. Wilson, *The Moral Sense* (New York: The Free Press-A Division of Macmillan, Inc., 1993), pp. 209, 210.

[20] Adam Smith, *The Theory Of Moral Sentiments*, ed. by D.D. Raphael and A. L. Macfie (Indianapolis: Liberty Classics, 1976), p.205.

[21] An extended treatment of the ideas presented in this section are contained in John Schneider, *Godly Materialism* (Downers Grove, Illinois: 1994),pp. 43-64. Also see, Lewis H. Haney, *History Of Economic Thought*, 4th ed. (New York: The Macmillan Company 1949), pp. 39-55.

[22] This and other biblical quotes are taken from the *Good News Bible* (New York: American Bible Society, 1978).

[23] John Schneider, *Godly Materialism*, pp. 65-99.

[24] Ibid., pp. 96-99.

[25] *Catechism of the Catholic Church*, (San Francisco: Ignatius Press, 1994),pp. 476-480.

[26] John Schneider, *Godly Materialism*, pp. 101-121.

[27] Ibid., pp. 123-144.

[28] Ibid., pp. 134-138.

[29] Ibid., pp. 146-150.

[30] Ibid., pp. 150-156.

[31] Ibid., pp. 160-164.

[32] Richard John Neuhaus, "Wealth and Whimsy: Being Rich, Producing Riches," in Peter L. Berger, ed., *The Capitalist Spirit* (San Francisco: ICS Press, 1990). pp. 135-136.

[33] John Schneider, *Godly Materialism*., pp. 79-184. Also see Doug Bandow, "God and the Economy: Is Capitalism Moral?," in Michael Bauman, ed., *Morality And The Marketplace* Hillsdale College Press, 1994), pp. 67-69.

[34] Bishop John Jukes, "Christianity and Wealth Creation-Competition and the Values Demanded by the Christian Gospel," in *God and the Marketplace*, John Davies ed., p.31.

[35] Jerry Z. Miller, "Minding Our Manners and Morals," *First Things*, April 1990.

[36] William James quoted in John Schneider, *Godly Materialism,* p.58.

[37] John Kennedy, "The Wolf, the Goat and the Lettuce-The Church and the European Model of Political Economy," in *God and the Marketplace,* Jon Davies ed., p.107.

[38] Ernest van den Haag, "The War Between Paleos and Neos," *National Review*, February 24, 1989, p.23.

[39] Martin Luther King, Jr., *I Have A Dream* ed. Lotte Hoskins (New York: Grosset & Dunlop, 1968), p.153.

[40] Dennis Prager, *Happiness Is A Serious Problem*, p.169.

[41] Philip Dimitrov, "Freeing the Soul From Communism," *The Wall Street Journal*, March 23,1992.

[42] Peter Kreeft, *Back to Virtue*, p.159.
[43] Ibid., p.186.
[44] Adam Smith, *The Theory of Moral Sentiments*, p.235.
[45] Ibid., p.236.
[46] Max Weber quoted in Michael Cromartie, "The Evangelical Kaleidoscope: Economics, Politics and Social Justice," in Michael Bauman, ed., *Morality And The Marketplace*, p.102.
[47] James Q. Wilson, "Capitalism and Morality," *The Public Interest*, Fall 1955.
[48] Michael Novak, *The Spirit of Democratic Capitalism*, pp. 55-58, 68, 160-170.
[49] James Q. Wilson, *The Moral Sense*, pp. 162,163.
[50] Ibid., p. 239.
[51] Stephen Bates, "A Textbook of Virtues," *The New York Times*, Section 4A January 8,1995.
[52] Adam Smith, *The Theory Of Moral Sentiments*, p.183.

CHAPTER 14

ECONOMIC FREEDOM: HAPPINESS AND VIRTUE II

THE AMERICAN EXPERIENCE

The preceding chapter established the relationships between virtue, religion, economic freedom, prosperity, and happiness. In America, these linkages have been of long standing and they have been most fruitful.

RELIGION

Religion, this major source of moral excellence, has had a long and influential history in America. San Salvador (Holy Savior) was the name that Christopher Columbus bestowed upon the island where he first landed in the New World. Missionaries bent on bringing Christianity to the native inhabitants (who, of course, had their own religions) began their efforts in the sixteenth century and established themselves throughout America. In fact, the first Bible printed on these shores was in the Algonquin language. From the earliest settlements, Americans proudly considered themselves a religious people. Worthy of recall are words about the colonists offered in 1620 by William Bradford, the governor of the Plymouth colony:

> For summer being done, all things stand upon them with a weather-beaten face, and the whole country, full of woods and thickets, represented a wild and savage hue. If they looked behind them, there was the mighty ocean which they had passed and was now as a main bar and gulf to separate them from all the civil parts of the world...What could now sustain them but the spirit of God and His grace?[1]

Many of the dissenters who had fled from persecution sought to create a new "Israel."[2] Puritans wished to make a "new Jerusalem" at "a city upon a hill" (Boston). They and other Americans considered themselves as God's chosen people--a belief that has survived among some Americans until this day.[3] Many of the nation's famous institutions of higher education were established to augment the supply of clergy: Congregationalist--Harvard and Yale; Anglican--Columbia University and William and

Mary; Baptist--The College of Rhode Island (Brown); Presbyterian--the College of New Jersey (Princeton); Dutch Reformed--Queen's College (Rutgers); and Catholic--St. Mary's Seminary and Georgetown University.[4]

Frequent appeals for divine assistance and other religious observances were common in the Continental Congress, and in 1774 a chaplain opened its proceedings. Taxes from the citizenry were used to pay chaplains in the armed forces during and after the Revolution and up until today. The promotion of "religion and morality" was one of the reasons advanced by Congress in passing the Northwest Ordinance.[5] The founding fathers and framers of the Constitution, including those who were deists, used biblical metaphors and saw fit to recognize and appeal to a Supreme Being. The Declaration Of Independence begins with a reference to God, notes that "...all men are created equal, that they are endowed by their Creator with certain unalienable Rights," and concludes with these words: "And for the support of this Declaration, with a firm reliance on the Protection of Divine Providence, we mutually pledge to each other our Lives, our Fortunes and our sacred Honor."

James Madison asserted that "We have staked the whole of our political institutions on the capacity of mankind to govern itself...according to the commandments of God."[6] Franklin wished the Great Seal of the United States to present a likeness of Moses leading the Israelites across the Red Sea, and Jefferson favored similar imagery.[7] George Washington stressed the importance of religion in his farewell address.

> Of all the dispositions and habits which lead to political prosperity, religion and morality are indispensable supports. In vain would that man claim the tribute of patriotism, who should labor to subvert these great pillars of human happiness, these firmest props of the duties of men and citizens. The mere politician, equally with the pious man, ought to respect and cherish them. A volume could not trace all their connections with private and public felicity. Let it simply be asked, where is the security for property, for reputation, for life, if the sense of religious obligation desert the oaths which are the instruments of investigation in courts of justice? And let us with caution indulge the supposition that morality can be maintained without religion. Whatever may be conceded to the influence of refined education on minds of peculiar structure, reason and experience both forbid us to expect that national morality can prevail in exclusion of religious principle.[8]

After requesting the indulgence of the citizenry in carrying out his duties, Thomas Jefferson concluded his second inaugural address as follows:

> I shall need, too, the favor of that Being in whose hands we are, who led our forefathers, as Israel of old, from their native land, and planted them in a country flowing with all the necessaries and comforts of life; who has covered our infancy with his providence, and our riper years with his wisdom and power; and to whose goodness I ask you to join with me in supplications, that he will so enlighten the minds of your servants, guide their councils, and prosper their measures, that whatsoever they do, shall result in your good, and shall secure to you the peace, friendship, and approbation of all nations.[9]

Throughout the nineteenth century, religion continued its hold on Americans. It served as a fount of inspiration to carry on; as a restraint on human vice and passion; as an important source of charity for those experiencing misfortune; and as an engine of reform movements. Although Americans might differ on theological creeds, there was widespread agreement on the overall moral outlook of these religions which stressed character building and virtuous behavior. And as Paul Johnson has noted, this religious enthusiasm provided the basis or the glue for the melting pot to do its job (slowly, to be sure), and for democracy to work for an almost incredibly diverse citizenry.[10] The Old World rivalries were replaced with a new nationalism that with an agreed moral code was at peace with itself.[11] And in contrast to Europe where religious authority was considered as a barrier to freedom, in America the two were intimately and positively related. According to de Tocqueville,

> Religion in America takes no direct part in the government of society, but it must be regarded as the first of their political institutions; for if it does not impart a taste for freedom, it facilitates the use of it. Indeed, it is in this same point of view that the inhabitants of the United States themselves look upon religious belief. I do not know whether all Americans have a sincere faith in their religion--for who can search the human heart?--but I am certain that they hold it to be indispensable to the maintenance of republican institutions. This opinion is not peculiar to a class of citizens or to a party, but it belongs to the whole nation and to every rank of society.[12]

Also, recall Lincoln's words in his 1863 address at the Cemetery at Gettysburg, words which relate the principles of democracy to freedom, equality, virtue, and God.

> It is rather for us to be here dedicated to the great task remaining before us--that from these honored dead we take increased devotion to that cause for which they give the last full measure of devotion--that we here highly resolve that these dead shall not have died in vain--that this nation under God, shall have a new birth of freedom--and that government of the people, by the people, for the people, shall not perish from the earth.[13]

Religion was an important institution among slaves who found strength in the themes of salvation and the kingdom of God, as well as a staunch belief that "God wants you free." As St. Paul said in his second letter to the Corinthians 3:17, "where the Spirit of the Lord is present, there is freedom." This dream received special eloquence in Martin Luther King Jr.'s 1963 Washington D.C. civil rights address: ""Free at last, free at last, thank God Almighty, we are free at last."[14] Religion proved a force in the abolition movement (although in the South, many church leaders and their congregations upheld slavery), as people marched to the *Battle Hymn of the Republic* that begins, "Mine eyes have seen the glory of the coming of the Lord," and ends with "As he died to make men holy, let us die to make men free, While God is marching on." The deeply religious Underground Railway member Harriet Tubman used the words and symbols afforded by religion to signal her arrival: "{T}ell my brothers to be always watching unto prayer, and when the good old ship of Zion comes along, to be ready to step onboard."[15] In the post Civil War era black churches proved to be a vital stabilizing institution for former slaves. The views of black clergymen paralleled those of the deeply religious Booker T. Washington who believed that success for blacks was to be found in participation in

American capitalism.[16] Even today, a disproportionate amount of black leaders have come from the ministry.

A godly spirit for all races has continued throughout the twentieth century. It helped to propel the civil rights crusade and serves as an important source of charity. Today, it remains vibrant despite the successful attempts to overturn the ideal of toleration and respect for different religions and to remove their many dimensions from public life. Americans believe religion is a force which promotes order and serves as, "... a unifying bond that cuts across ethnic, racial, and, to a certain extent, social divides."[17]

The First Amendment prohibits Congress from preventing the free exercise of religion. The sacred and secular intertwine during our national holidays of Thanksgiving, Memorial Day and Independence Day.[18] In 1789, for instance, George Washington, who had authorized the first Thanksgiving Day, thought it the duty of all Americans "to Acknowledge the Providence of Almighty God, to obey His will, to be grateful for His benefits, and humbly to implore His protection and favor."[19] Two of the nations most popular songs, "America The Beautiful" and "God Bless America," have religious themes. The former ends with the words "America! America! God shed His grace on thee, And crown thy good with brotherhood From sea to shining sea!" The very title of the latter makes the point. Each of these songs has been suggested as a replacement for the current national anthem. Forty-seven states have references to God in their constitutions.[20] And throughout its history, America has offered refuge for peoples around the world who suffer persecution for their religious beliefs.

According to the 1990 National Survey of Religious Identification (NSRI), "The vast majority of Americans consider themselves to be religious and are not afraid to admit it."[21] The NSRI indicates that 87 percent of American males and 92 percent of females belong to or believe in some religion.[22] A different survey offered the following responses: 95 percent of Americans believe in God; prayer is an important part of daily life for 79 percent; for 88 percent religion is very or fairly important; 64 percent believe that religion can answer all or most of today's problems and that religious values should play a role in everyday decisions; and 69 percent think religion is losing its influence on American life.[23] In still another survey, 92 percent of Americans believe that the motto "In God We Trust" should remain on our currency.[24] Moreover, religious beliefs in America continue to exceed those in other industrial democracies.[25] Perhaps the result of an attempt to bring order into a hectic lifestyle, or the contemplation of the approaching millennium, or as a way to counter a void in this materialist world, or as a method of protecting offspring from worldly evils, an increasing number of Americans (especially the baby boomers) seem to be searching for a spiritual dimension in their lives--a quest reflected in attendance at religious gatherings as well as in current literature, music, and television.[26] We will come back to the topic of religion shortly.

VIRTUE

During the colonial era, under the influence of religion and tradition, a respect for the classical virtues was much in evidence, both in economic and other aspects of life. Courage was needed to undertake the hazardous journey to these shores and then to take the initiative and undergo the rigors of developing a livelihood through numerous hardships and dangers. Nor was temperance foreign to colonists of the seventeenth and eighteenth centuries. Self-discipline, industry, frugality, delayed gratification, and self-reliance provided the foundation for survival and growth. Justice also tended to characterize America during these times with honesty and fairness awarded veneration, compassion ubiquitous, and individuals held responsible for their own actions. Practical wisdom was especially important to the colonists, who sought to learn from experience, to cast aside inappropriate Old World habits, and to make sound judgements based on highly pragmatic standards. Economic progress was deemed to be of great importance by these colonists. Recall that Benjamin Franklin perceived a close link between happiness and material progress. Moreover, his aphorisms which were widely known and frequently quoted, show the nexus between virtue and success.

The revolutionary era was one in which morality received great emphasis and when an introspective people sought to recall their history and examine just who they were and what was truly important in their lives. In contrast to what they perceived to be the dominant virtuous characteristics in America, the colonists saw an England steeped in corruption and vice; where in the realms of economics and politics, abuse of power prevailed; where greed provided prime motivation; and where the licentious behavior of the British, which had extended overseas, threatened the liberties of their fair land. It was in this context that the Americans sought to protect their independence through strategies which, when they proved insufficient led to war and then, to victory. And it was in this period (both before and during the war) that the classical virtues of courage, temperance, justice, and wisdom were relied upon heavily.

Virtuous behavior dominated the Constitutional Convention in Philadelphia, where the framers constructed a government which would go far to preserve freedom, to allow human energies to flourish, to provide basic stability yet permit change to take place, and to protect against despotism. This republican form of government would place great emphasis on such commercial virtues as self-reliance, moderation, frugality, delay of gratification, and honesty. It was on this foundation that the American people, including the immigrant component, strove to realize their material and nonmaterial aspirations in an atmosphere of limited government.

It is of interest to note that the revolutionary leaders--Adams, Jefferson, Washington--and others who lived into the nineteenth century expressed disappointment that their hopes of building a republic based on enlightened principles were not working out as completely as expected. Allegiance to political parties, the turmoil of democracy, self-interest, the pursuit of money, and "getting ahead" seemed to dominate the motives of the populace. In evidence were not the great-souled men, but rather the ordinary people with ordinary concerns (hitherto the despised common masses), now free to pursue happiness in their own ways. Of course, this simply meant that some revolutionary goals were being fulfilled, but with materialism rather than the lofty ideals of the founding fathers dominant.[27]

Worthy of a short digression is the virtue of compassion. In the post-revolutionary era, during the nineteenth century and into the twentieth, compassion and charity were delivered, for the most part, in the same spirit as had been true in colonial times. Religious beliefs informed it and personal involvement was considered vital. Help came from family, religious institutions, and neighborhoods. As cities grew, special institutions to assist the blind, the deaf and dumb, orphans and abandoned children, unwed mothers, and others suffering difficulties were established. Immigrants developed self-help organizations, such as Vincent de Paul Societies, and the Hebrew Benevolent Society. Food, clothing, shelter, fuel, reading rooms, schools, day-care nurseries, medical clinics, and summer camps were among the many goods and services provided.[28]

Charitable efforts sought to insure that people remained or became self-respecting and self-supporting citizens. Distinctions were made between those deserving and those unworthy of aid, with assistance denied to the latter and tailored to the needs and capacities of the former. Thus able-bodied men might be required to chop wood, and able-bodied women to sew clothing for their sustenance. A Free African Society, founded in 1787, required members to give one shilling a month for distribution to those in need with the stipulation that "this necessity is not brought on them by their own imprudence."[29] Moreover, demoralized men and women were thought to need more than just physical relief, so biblical precepts stressing love and fear of God along with the importance of commercial virtues were an integral part of charitable endeavors.

Not all, however, shared this vision--a vision that for most of America's history has been mainstream. A different perspective held man as naturally good and in possession of a right to salvation in the next world and prosperity in this one. From this premise it was deduced that any human fault should be attributed to other than personal irresponsibility: to the environment (especially the capitalistic environment). Further, government should see to it that via redistributive policies, all enjoy a decent standard of living. Society was responsible for the poverty within it, and society should pay for poverty's eradication.

Horace Greely, editor of the *New York Tribune*, offered this view in the 1840's. Later in the century it evolved into the Social Gospel movement, which stressed charity given without a challenge to do anything to improve one's position. At the other extreme were the social Darwinists, who would deny all aid on the grounds that once vice has seized an individual, he has no chance to escape a perpetual corruption. Mainstream purveyors of charity, rejecting both of these positions, held to the idea that any human created in God's image is worthy of help, and that he can be reformed: they continued to spend their energies in the tried and true traditional manner. Great, although never total, success marked their efforts.[30]

Although there was no national welfare system in the nineteenth century, cities did begin to provide relief to people in their homes. Attempts to construct such a system were in evidence early in the twentieth century, and as we have seen, blossomed during the New Deal. Professionalism was emphasized (you had to take an exam to help the poor), and monetary (rather than in-kind) benefits were distributed impersonally.

Paperwork was in, God was out, volunteers began to depart, many private charitable organizations went under, and a "give me" attitude, although far from universal, began to develop.[31]

However, even by the early 1960's, welfare was not yet considered a right and the dole still carried a stigma. That view did, of course, change during the radicalism of that decade as Great Society visionaries multiplied programs and uncoupled relief from shame. The court decisions which followed this philosophy were instrumental in expanding eligibility for relief and the consequent swelling of welfare rolls and expenditures. Welfare (farewell), was now a right--an "entitlement"--which could be obtained without challenge, responsibility, or acknowledgement of (God forbid) God. Although, matters of space preclude fuller treatment, we note that most Americans consider the nation's welfare system not just a mess (politely put), but an expensive tragedy. Moreover, "compassion fatigue" seems to be on the fast track.[32].

Of course, one need not be a professor of history to know that not every American has always adhered to virtuous norms in all facets of life including the economic. Self-interest, for instance, dominated the national interest during the War of 1812, when some Americans found ways to sell provisions to the British.[33] Not everyone was civil or personally disciplined, and social pathologies have always been manifest in this nation. Violence was in evidence not just during the colonial period, but throughout this nation's history.[34] The treatment of Indians and the practice of slavery stand out as diametrically opposed to virtue. Women were excluded from the political process and much of economic life. Prejudice and discrimination can be found in every era. In addition, business executives have been found more than once to have engaged in unethical activities including fraud, false and tasteless advertising, shoddy treatment of employees, attempts to monopolize, and the rigging of markets. Note also that the production and distribution of illegal drugs, pornography, excessively violent movies, and lewd and inflammatory recordings reflect profit seeking economic activities as does the wanton destruction of the environment. Nor have employees always given their all; nor have labor unions (both leaders and members) always acted as paragons of moral excellence.

However, less than perfectly virtuous behavior in the different dimensions of life has been the case for the populace of every other nation and in every other economic system. On a religious level, one finds acknowledgement of human imperfection and frailty in the Roman Catholic sacrament of Confession and in the Jewish Day of Atonement. A free market economy is and never will be a utopia--nor does it promise to be. That which an economy delivers reflects the morality of its participants. Nonetheless, one can make a strong case that during the seventeenth, eighteenth, nineteenth, and into the twentieth centuries, virtue (both of a classical and religious nature) in an atmosphere of limited government tended to dominate the moral/cultural system. In other words, this exemplification of moral excellence stood high in what generally was agreed upon, preferred, and prized in the American hierarchy of values. Virtues and values are part of the heritage of western civilization which Adam Smith, Thomas Jefferson, John Stuart Mill, and other advocates of economic, political, and individual freedom took for granted.

We also know that in the late nineteenth century government-- especially at the federal level--began to play a larger role and continued to grow during the twentieth century. The public sector (and of course those who run things) began to expand beyond traditional boundaries and eventually became deeply immersed in the economic as well as other aspects of our lives. Then, during the 1960's, the cultural/moral system started to experience revolutionary alterations, and more and more of what had once been personal decisions became politicized. These changes in the political system and in the cultural/moral system have caused increasing conflict and turmoil, which most of us now experience in our everyday lives. The tranquility appropriate to democratic capitalism has been on the wane, and-- almost needless to say--so has virtue.

THE ASSAULT ON THE VIRTUES AMERICANS VALUE

Why has it happened? The cause is not inherent in capitalism (although that system, as we know, has at times lent itself to abuse). Other forces (led, of course, by human beings) have been at work. Some of the growth of government and the subsequent politicization of so many issues can be traced to those who simply wish to feather their own nests. Also of importance have been the efforts of well-meaning souls who, unaware of some of the consequences of the public policies they advocated (and they may still be unaware), sought to improve the workings of the market economy by increasing amounts government intervention. "New Dealers" illustrate this category. However, each of these groups generally sought to achieve their objectives within the basic capitalistic framework. Not so the most influential of all; the radicals of the left who came of age (as it were) in the 1960's and whose assault on the traditional moral/cultural system, the political system, and the free market economy have grown in effectiveness during the ensuing decades and have made America so different in so very short a time. Although the extreme right is more that capable of causing trouble (the somewhat recent terrorist bombing in Oklahoma City a case in point) it is the left that is properly our concern, and the following paragraphs epitomize the more extreme radical positions embraced by this group.

This "new class" (or "knowledge class" or "adversary class") spawned by some university intellectuals is drawn from the ranks of teachers, artists, scientists, lawyers, judges, politicians, bureaucrats, psychiatrists, health-care providers, foundation executives, members of the clergy, journalists, editors, authors, film producers, directors, actors and an assortment of "professional rights activists" and self-proclaimed "public interest" advocates.[35] It is an elite group with a perspective from the political left and an influence greatly disproportionate to its numbers.

Originating as a dissenting culture with an emphasis on youth, and dismayed with the treatment of American blacks, the legal and social restrictions on women, income disparities, the war in Vietnam, and what it considered to be rampant hypocrisy in high places, it evolved into a counterculture and then found favor with the philosophy of nihilism, which views the universe as aimless, meaningless, trivial, and without value in itself. They and their ideas represent a formidable force with which to be reckoned.

With backs turned on the classical and religious virtues and Western institutions, the "new class" also embrace the doctrine of moral relativism. Rejecting the ideas of objective truth (how different from Jefferson's, "We hold these truths to be self-evident") and beauty, the transcendent virtues, notions of right and wrong, or genius, or progress, they believe that one culture or way of doing things should be judged no better or worse (it's all a matter of taste) than another. Excepted, of course, are the United States and capitalism. Contemporary (as well as historical) America, and, indeed, Western Civilization are all portrayed as thoroughly and hopelessly corrupt. They have sinned grievously and need to be redeemed. This is the perspective that provides justification for radical leaders to direct a wholesale transformation of society.

This viewpoint also represents an outgrowth of Marxist philosophy, which maintains that one's position in society and the economy is determined by the ruling class, and that therefore one possesses little if any ability to make real choices ("so long" to free will and responsibility for the consequences of one's decisions). Know also that Marxists desperately need victims to justify their radical elitist positions, pronouncements and programs. Therefore, this "new class" (the economic background of which tends not to be of the poverty stricken but rather of the middle and upper middle classes) not only sees exploitation and oppression (for Marxists, the very process of free market exchange whereby people transfer things that they value less for things that they value more represents oppression) of class, but of race, gender (including marriage and child bearing), and ethnic heritage, and seeks to liberate these and numerous other "disadvantaged" groups from the wicked institutions dominated by white male elites. Further, as devotees of Rousseau's idea that man is born good but is corrupted by society, they would alter earthly conditions in order to restore that which is "naturally" good. Realization of their utopian dream of a perfect society where happiness reigns and in which equality of results (radical egalitarianism) and self-fulfillment with few, if any, limits (radical individualism) are the overlapping goals, requires warfare against the nation's traditional hierarchies, institutions, and values. The attack has come on several fronts.

Like the mosquito at a nudist colony, one scarcely knows where to begin. However, a good starting point might be to examine the radical perspective of the classical virtues. Courage is generally looked upon as not very intelligent behavior, or as one more contemptible source of self-aggrandizement (entrepreneurship is equated with greed). Justice, they hold, is impossible in this oppressive country, and capitalism, which tends to reward people according to how the market values their productivity, is considered incompatible with the goal of equality of results. Differences in wealth that have emerged between various cultures (which are considered equal) must be attributed to oppression. The practical wisdom of the ages that has produced this horrendous society is denigrated and held as irrelevant, and wisdom of a speculative nature is awarded similar disrespect. It is the virtue of temperance, however, that receives special attention.

Eschewing Dostoyevsky's aphorism "to live is to suffer," the radical perspective holds happiness to be a right, and when this youthful culture wants something (and given its desire to release "the inner child," much is desired), it wants it now. Of course this position comes directly into conflict with temperate behavior. One may recall that the latter entails self-control (the basis of the other virtues), and this in turn implies restraint and the ability to defer gratification. Lack of restraint further conflicts with religious precepts and perfect happiness in this world hardly conforms to the Judeo-Christian tradition. However, for many of those who embrace this new definition of freedom, God is dead or, at best, out of touch. Religion and its companion moral certitude are perceived as bitter enemies of freedom. Those who continue to hold dear to traditional tenets of religious morality--that which was taken for granted in the past--may now be demonized.[36]

Deeply alienated from traditional American values and virtues, radicals ridicule and scorn the legal system, technological progress, rationalism, traditional canons of scholarship, traditional religion, the traditional family (the major source of inequality), national patriotism (The old West Point motto of "Duty, Honor, Country" is held beneath contempt), deferred gratification, the idea that hard work makes for success, and, of course, capitalism.

America's institutions and bourgeois values derive from experience and elicit awareness of the limits of human aspirations.[37] They have provided a foundation for a free market system to perform successfully and have enabled the average person to realize many of his goals, and in fact, have allowed families to leap from poverty to a degree of affluence in but one or two generations. Radicals, however, do not consider themselves to be ordinary people. For all the talk of equality, more than just a few of them have college degrees, are located in upper income levels, and possess upscale homes, automobiles, clothing and other accouterments of "the good life." Moreover, they hold themselves superior in knowledge, ability, taste, imagination, vision, and heroic purpose to the average mortal (with his boring virtues and values), whom they desire to influence and direct. As a result, they would replace moral restraint with instant gratification (which received significant impetus from modern effective methods of birth control) and self-expression and the notion that what one feels comfortable with--what feels good--what lets you get in touch with yourself--what leads to self-fulfillment--should guide behavior. This approach to life is also known as the "ethic of authenticity." Acceptable, unacceptable, appropriate, inappropriate, replace the words right and wrong-good and evil and shame.[38] Astute are the insights of Alan Bloom:

> This absoluteness of desire uninhibited by thoughts of virtue is what is found in a state of nature. It represents the turn in philosophy away from trying to tame or perfect desire by virtue, and toward finding out what one's desire is and living according to it. This is largely accomplished by criticizing virtue, which covers and corrupts desire. Our desire becomes a kind of oracle we consult; it is now the last word, while in the past it was the questionable and dangerous part of us.[39]

The radical ideas described have been influential in educational settings, in the arts, in books, in the theatre, in advertising, in religious organizations, in government policy, and in many American institutions. It is, perhaps, in the movies, however, that they are best reflected. Relegated to a rather minor niche are motion pictures that portray America's history or heroes in a positive light, or those about happy families or people working through tough times with virtuous behavior. Instead, a very different theme is now on the silver screen: tales of psychopathic murderers; insults and attacks heaped upon religion; the traditional family portrayed as an anachronism and the dysfunctional and/or alternative family awarded prominence (by the way, a 1993 federal education law defined a family as "a group of interdependent persons residing in the same household"), an unwed woman's intent to conceive a child looked upon as just one more "choice"; business leaders characteristically exploiting workers, or the environment or the consumer or all of these at once; and America, including its armed forces, foreign policies, and military and political leaders indicted as "The Great Satan." And all this amidst large and gratuitous doses of violence, sex, and foul language.

Television offers a similar perspective, but adds some sleazy advertisements (lawyers begging you to sue). Talk shows dominated by guests who proudly inform audiences about their deviant behavior and hard core porn are pumped via cable into the living room. Of course the audiences of these free market activities are not just in the studio, and the messages delivered to all, especially to those without a strong moral compass, have the potential to be personally devastating.

Along with the radical conviction that we have a right to be happy (a notion promoted with considerable success by that cutting edge of the "caring industry," the psychiatric profession) has developed the idea that fault always lies elsewhere when a felicitous state fails to materialize or even to be approximated. All kinds of excuses (sometimes called syndromes or disorders or phobias) are offered to absolve individuals of responsibility for troublesome or deviant behavior. The parental abuse syndrome, the chronic lateness syndrome, the fan obsession syndrome, the tobacco use disorder, social phobia (shyness), academic achievement disorder (poor grades), and codependency (being dependent on other people's moods, behavior, or love), serve as examples-- examples which deny free will.[40]

There is also some tendency to define misbehavior as a disease or an addiction and in response an assortment of groups have started up: Gamblers Anonymous, Pill Addicts Anonymous, Nicotine Anonymous, Unwed Parents Anonymous, Debtors Anonymous, Workaholics Anonymous, Dual Disorder Anonymous, Batterers Anonymous, and Victims Anonymous.[41]

Driven by self-pity (and a quick way to make a buck for attorney and client), this approach to life has become a fertile ground for blame placing. If one drinks too much and has an auto accident, one blames the bartender; if a baby is born with a defect, blame the doctor; if the boss tells you something that you object to, claim that he is causing mental stress; if you fail to get a job or promotion or raise, no matter what the real cause, blame racism or sexism or lookism or heightism. If you gamble excessively blame the casino; if you smoke too much, blame the tobacco companies, if you are a criminal, blame your parents or society. Then sue the hell out of whoever you are blaming. The following exemplify some of the more bizarre cases.

* An FBI agent, discharged for embezzling government money in order to gamble is reinstated by court order because his gambling is considered a handicap.[42]
* An employee fired for continual tardiness sued on the ground that he is a victim of the chronic lateness syndrome.[43]

* A man who has stolen a car is killed while driving it and his family sued the owner of the parking lot for not taking more effective precautions to prevent theft.[44]
* Men who are injured in a race carrying refrigerators on their backs sued the manufacturer for not putting adequate warnings on the appliances.[45]
* A man jumped in front of a subway train and suffered severe injuries. His family sued on the grounds that the train did not stop in time.[46]
* The San Francisco Giants were sued for giving father's day gifts to men only.[47]
* A psychic sued her doctor under the claim that the dye in a CAT Scan that he used had impaired her psychic powers.[48]
* A man sued his barber claiming that his haircut was so bad that he had a panic-anxiety attack.[49]
* A couple placed in the smoking section of a restaurant brought suit for a million dollars on the grounds that the smoke "upset their expected right to conjugal happiness."[50]
* After being ticketed by the police for not wearing a seatbelt, the driver of the car claimed himself to be claustrophobic and sued the city on the basis of this disability.[51]
* Fired from her job as a government clerk because of obnoxious behavior, a woman sued for reinstatement on the grounds of being a manic depressive. She believed that the employer had an obligation to remove all the stress associated with her position.[52]
* A high school guidance counselor was fired for using cocaine and sued because the school had discriminated because of his addiction disability.[53]
* A deaf lifeguard sued the YMCA over its insistence that the position required the ability to hear calls of distress.[54]
* A golfer received a $40,000 award by suing a country club after she accidentally hit herself in the face with her own ball.[55]
* Lawsuits among prisoners (which in 1965 reached 65,000 in federal courts alone) include the following: A one million dollar suit based on the contention that the inmate's civil right had been violated because his ice cream had melted; an assertion that being forced to listen to country and western music constituted cruel and unusual punishment; and a suit from a prisoner who objected to being served chunky instead of smooth peanut butter.[56]

Legal definitions of deviant behavior and crime have been altered and normalized, and guests on the TV talk shows gain momentary fame by displaying their dysfunctional behavioral traits and personal agonies to the public. Even candidates for political office, including those for the nation's presidential office, have replaced contrition with the mantle of victimhood--(they do, however, regret being caught). In the past it was usually thought improper and lacking in dignity for great statesmen to be subject to inquiry or to revel in the details of their personal lives. Whereas Franklin D. Roosevelt tried to hide his disability (today's advocates for the handicapped insist that the proposed FDR

Memorial statue portray him in a wheelchair), the new breed of office seekers do not hesitate to share personal burdens--past and present--with the whole nation.[57]

Courage to face the human problems of death, illness, disability, job loss, and so forth has been replaced by the lawsuit and the visit to the professional counselor. How different from the not too distant past. As one author has noted, "The list of synonyms for fortitude could be a list of names of British 19th-century Battleships: Bold; Determined; Endurance; Fearless; Forbearance; Intrepid; Resoluteness; Resolved; Self-controlled; Steadfast; Unwavering."[58] Also recall the "...names of one's grandmothers-Constance, Faith, Hope..."[59] All these are words that fail to appear in the vocabulary of the "victim." For the "victim," moral language has become "inappropriate," and the word "guilt" (which reflects moral truthfulness about oneself), lies at the very core of such language. Thus, the denial of guilt means the denial of responsibility for the consequences of human action, and, of course, for freedom itself.[60]

This victim mentality has become increasingly widespread (although precisely how widespread is not known), as many in society turn from common bonds and a shared culture and identify themselves by sex, race, or ethnic group. Aaron Wildavsky has noted that if one were to tally all the groups that consider themselves oppressed minorities, it would come to 374 percent of the population.[61]

A truly liberal society is one where the various types of freedom thrive, and openness, fairness, truth, and responsibility dominate. To survive, such a society requires ubiquitous acceptance of certain norms and standards of behavior. After all, that is what a nation is about. Rather than emphasizing a common culture (with respect for appropriate ties to various ethnic heritages), which would promote unity (E Pluribus Unum), stability, and peace, and thereby facilitate the pursuit of happiness, it is difference among groups (radicals consider a common culture to be oppressive) which receives attention and, as we see, attention of a most dramatic sort.[62]

The victim mentality in which grievances fester abandons the virtues of responsibility and self-reliance and may diminish the grief and assistance that genuine victims deserve: for if everyone is a victim, then no one is a victim. Also, the victim mentality has added to its quest for happiness the strident demand for rights: the right to have a perfectly safe workplace; the right to risk-free products including those of a medical nature; the right to a smoke-free environment; the right of drug addicts to have public housing; the right to be free from discrimination; the right to self-esteem (not necessarily acquired through hard work and accomplishment but awarded, especially in the academy, on the basis of group membership); the right to the best medical care; the right to express yourself fully (as long as it is in accord with the "politically correct" views of the "new class"); the right to unbounded self-realization; the right to a risk-free life; the right to a life that is not unfair; and as we have seen, the right not to be responsible for one's actions.

It is not difficult to see that happiness will prove elusive indeed for anyone with the primary identity of victim. Blaming the world for one's woes, the victim easily slips into anger--an emotion difficult to eradicate (for that would mean that he no longer is a victim).[63]

The unalienable rights rooted in the Constitution, including its Bill of Rights, flow from a Creator and a natural law. This is in contrast to those of the 1789 French Declaration of the Rights of Man, which were granted by an "enlightened government."[64] Moreover, they are universal in that they are timeless and apply to all human beings. They provide protection from unwarranted incursions by government and others into the lives of individual citizens as they engage in the pursuit of happiness and place minimal demands on others.

However, the new "rights" and "entitlements" and preferences and double standards are man made. They are to be conferred by government (which in fiscal and other policy matters displays remarkably little of the virtue of temperance), on absolutist terms without condition on the basis of group identity. There are numerous broadly (and at times rather vaguely) defined "disadvantaged" and "oppressed" groups which are "outraged" and "owed" restitution. (Of course the disadvantages and oppression never end--their demise would terminate the benefits.) Any society falling short of the absolute standard is considered fatally flawed and in the radical vocabulary is referred to as "tyrannical," "authoritarian," "hegemonic," and "totalizing."[65]

Obviously, these "rights" do not apply to all: they can change over time as fashion dictates and may extract substantial costs from others.[66] Also note how far these new "rights" differ from the rights intended by the framers of the Constitution (a document that insures neither happiness nor social acceptance) who were bent on establishing a system wherein each selfish faction would be neutralized by other selfish factions, thereby impeding a majority from using its power to overturn inalienable rights.[67]

Prominent among the numerous types of preferences are those relating to university admissions, the awarding of government contracts to business firms, and hiring, promotion, and discharge policies--all of which, one might add, have become major sources of resentment and conflict as different groups struggle over which is the biggest victim and for what is "owed them." Because of the belief that only a victim in a group can understand its victimization, criticism from people outside that group suffers swift rejection, and further turmoil flows from the balkanization of each group striving to insulate itself from the others.[68] All the while, radicals preach the wonders of "multicultural education."

In the radical perspective, feelings are vital, and among "oppressed" people the sensitive and hypersensitive abound. Therefore, in order to halt "oppression" and insure equality, speech codes of forbidden words and phrases are developed and implemented at educational institutions including colleges and universities. They also are found in other parts of both the private and public sectors.

Under "new class" influence, The Pennsylvania Association of Realtors, the Pennsylvania Newspaper Association, and the Pennsylvania Human Relations Commission have issued guidelines against using the following vocabulary in real estate ads: "bachelor pad," "landmark," "couples," "mature," "older seniors," "adults," "single," "children," "senior citizen," "setting up housekeeping," "traditional neighborhood," "mother-in-law suite," "traditional," "exclusive," "young," "newlyweds," "young family," "private," "integrated," "executive buyer," "established neighborhood," and "mature person."[69]

However, those calling the shots at education's highest levels have proved much more imaginative. A handbook at the University of Missouri lists words and phrases that should not be used. These include, *"burly"* ("too often associated with large black men, implying ignorance"); *"glamorous"* (sexist); gratuitous reference to fried chicken (stereotypical of a black cuisine); the exclamation *"Ugh!"* ("Highly offensive" as a stereotype of Native Americans); and the word *"white"* (a product of the "racist power structure.").... *"banana"* (offensive to Asian Americans); *"qualified minority"* (because it implies that some are not); *"white bread"* (offensive to whites and bland people); any descriptions that imply a standard of beauty; *"gyp"* (offensive to Gypsies); "Mafia" (offensive to Italians); *"Dutch treat"* (offensive to the Dutch); and *"community"* ("implies a monolithic culture in which people act, think, and vote in the same way.").[70]

Michigan State University forbids the use of terms such as *"culturally deprived," "black mood," "yellow coward,"* and the pronoun "he." It also tells staff members and students to "Be aware of seating patterns, eye contact, interruptions, and domination of the class by certain groups or individuals."[71]

Radicals believe that one's inner feelings, opinions, and beliefs should be subject to correction by some politicized authority (authoritarian personalities abound among extremists on both the left and the right). Some of those who have shown themselves to be politically incorrect at the college and university level have been fired, suspended or in other way disciplined, and forced to attend "sensitivity" sessions to be "re-educated." Nobel Laureate Saul Bellow has observed that these trends also have appeared in literature. "The literary press is in the hands of the politically correct, which means a sort of wilderness, a jungle of opinion on all questions and a kind of compulsive, enforced orthodoxy that I connect in my own mind with the period of Stalinism in the 1930's. It's very similar--put a toe out of line and you'll be clobbered."[72]

Under the banner of oppression, various types of antisocial behavior, including rioting, deserve to be excused. Similarly, the meaning of sexual harassment has been expanded and hoaxes and false accusations dismissed (by the accusers and their supporters) on the grounds that they help to raise consciousness. Amidst the decline in standards of truthfulness and fairness, conspiracy theories increase, and the cynicism that breeds among the victims who view America with contempt is matched by the cynicism harbored by those who witness the double standards of public policy.

Radicals believe that America's problems (which, to be sure, exist and some of which--such as crime, drug abuse, poverty, the growing disparity between rich and poor, and low quality education--assume serious dimensions) are exclusively of a social nature and thereby solely amenable to technical--social engineering--solutions. Not human choice and free will, but external forces have become the only culprits, and suggestions that behavioral patterns be altered tend to be met with derision.

Eschewing persuasion or virtuous behavior as the means of change, or the family as a vital component of reform and progress (it is perceived as a major cause of the problems), and oblivious to the incremental advances derived from the tried and true operation of free markets, radicals would assign a major role to the state for the task of solving almost any problem within their ken. This coercive body is thereby chosen to award, finance, implement, and guard these newly found "rights." From this it follows that the state should expand its regulatory authority, not just over the economy but over speech and personal conduct as well.

It should not go unnoticed that a practical value adheres to this philosophy: the radical onslaught provides a rationale for more jobs (and income and job security and upward job mobility) to be generated, especially by the government for "new class" members who believe they have the knowledge and ability to solve the problems they have just happened to uncover. In any event, two results have been a deluge of new laws, and a radical interpretation of both old and new laws. These have significantly influenced the economic system with a substantial reallocation of resources to the public sector as government administrates and regulates more and more activities, an imposing tax burden, and a most impressive national debt. The political system and attitudes and modes of behavior also have been effected. Jefferson's words in the Declaration of Independence come to mind: "He has erected a multitude of New Offices, and sent hither swarms of Officers to harass our People, and eat out their substance."

The above summarizes the main components of the more extreme radical position of virtually unlimited freedom for the individual within a controlled economy. Needless (or it should be needless) to say that not all members of occupations from which "new class" members are drawn subscribe to these doctrines, nor are all movies, television, news reporting, so terrible. On the contrary, there are outstanding positive examples in all of the categories we have been discussing (and by the way, many of the old movies and television shows, especially those portraying the dumb stereotypes of blacks and Indians, were not so very great). Moreover, "new class" members adhere to these ideas with varying degrees of intensity, and perhaps many would not agree to every one of the tenets presented--the radical clergy, for instance, would still believe in God (although a God of a rather therapeutic--feel good--nature). One also can embrace radical egalitarianism, without being a devotee of hedonistic radical individualism, and the reverse holds true as well.

Now, some degree of radicalism, including civil disobedience, may be a necessary force in the realization of worthy objectives. The eighteenth century American Revolution comes to mind as does the nineteenth century abolitionist movement, and the twentieth century suffragette and civil rights movements. However, radical ideas may be inappropriate or if on target may generate excesses by those who espouse and attempt to implement them--excesses which may prove destructive to much of the population and to the national well-being. A good argument can be made that this has been the experience in the United States during the latter half of this century, and there is evidence that most Americans not only fail to share the "new class" perspectives, but are appalled by the problems that have accompanied its influence. According to Saint Matthew, "By their fruits ye shall know them." Some of these fruits are noted below.

* A rise in the total number of crimes committed from 3.3 million in 1960 to about 14.4 million in 1992.[73] The violent crime rate (per 100,000) went from 16.1 in 1960 to 75.8 in 1992.[74] According to Justice Department estimates, "... one out of twenty black men can be expected to be murdered, a death rate double that of U. S. soldiers during World War ll." Meanwhile, the expected median prison

sentence for serious crimes dropped from 22.5 days in 1954 to 8.0 days in 1990.[75] From 1965 to 1990 the juvenile arrest rate for violent crimes has tripled.[76] The nation has grown accustomed to all this as more and more murder and other violent crimes permeate society. The quantity of such pathologies no longer seems surprising.

* The evolution of an "underclass" of mostly young people who have little idea of concepts of right and wrong, but who do possess a tendency toward violent behavior.
* Between 1990 and 1995, the number of black men in their twenties who are imprisoned or on probation or parole has risen from 1 in 4 to 1 in 3.[77]
* From the early 1980's until the early 1990's, the prison population in the United States has more than doubled. It now exceeds one million people.[78]
* Twenty percent of high school students regularly carry a weapon.[79] Compared to 25 years ago, almost twice the number of the best high school students believe that schools are unsafe.[80]
* Although the overall use of drugs has declined by more than 50 percent since the 1970's peak, there are still about 1.5 to 2.5 million cocaine and crack cocaine users.[81]
* In 1992, 87.5 percent of high school seniors were reported to have used alcohol, 32.6 percent to have used marijuana, and 6.1 percent to have used cocaine. In that same year, 11.2 percent of eighth graders were reported to have used marijuana.[82]
* A study by the Carnegie Corporation found "...one-third of 13-year-olds acknowledge that they have used illicit drugs, that educational achievement levels of eighth graders have remained stagnant while the educational needs of the workplace have increased, that the homicide rate for those 10 to 14 years of age more than doubled from 1985 to 1992 and that self-destructive violence, particularly the suicide rate more than doubled from 1980 to 1992."[83]
* Since 1960, the rate at which people get married declined by more than 25 percent.[84]
* The divorce rate per 1000 married women was 9.2 percent in 1960. It peaked in the early 1980's and by 1991 stood at 20.9 percent. Already the highest divorce rate in the world, if present rates continue, almost half of all marriages in the United States can be expected to terminate in divorce.[85] It is more difficult to terminate a mortgage than a marriage, for in the eyes of the law, this solemn contract or covenant can be ended with relative ease.[86]
* Between 1960 and 1990 single-parent families as a percentage of all families with children rose from 9.1 to 26.7 percent. In that same time span, the percentage of children living with both biological parents has declined by 22 points.[87] All this has frightening consequences. "Compared to children who are raised by their biological father and mother, those raised by mothers, black or white, who have never married are more likely to be poor, to acquire less schooling, to be expelled or suspended from school, to experience emotional or

behavioral problems, to display antisocial behavior, to have trouble getting along with their peers and to start their own single-parent families. These unhappy outcomes afflict both girls and boys, but they have a more adverse effect on boys."[88]

* There has been an astounding and deeply troubling increase in births out of wedlock. At one time "illegitimacy" was the descripted word. In 1960 about 5.3 percent of children were born to unmarried mothers, but by 1990, the figure had reached 28 percent. Among blacks the percentages rose from 23 in 1960 to 65.2 in 1990.[89] During those same years, the birth rate for unmarried teenagers increased almost 200 percent.[90] A study by the National Center for Health Statistics indicated a 94 percent rise in illegitimacy rates among whites between the years 1980 and 1992.[91] In 1991 the illegitimacy rate in ten major United States cities ranged from 71.0 in Detroit to 51.9 in Pittsburgh.[92] In the 1960's, at a Howard University commencement address, President Lyndon Johnson asserted that family is the cornerstone of society, and when it collapses, "it is the children who are usually damaged. When it happens on a massive scale, the community itself is crippled."[93]

* The percentage of children in the government program Aid To Families With Dependent Children rose from 3.5 percent in 1960 to 11.9 percent in 1990.[94] Note also that welfare programs sometimes award the parent of the illegitimate child more money than the combined income of an intact family with both parents working.

* Since 1960, the teenage suicide rate has tripled and has become the second leading cause of death for this age group.[95]

* There is evidence that juvenile arrest, sexual activity, and drug and alcohol use are becoming more frequent among sixth and seventh graders.[96]

* Educational institutions have tended to award self-esteem and "getting along" greater emphasis, while the attention accorded to reading, writing, and mathematical skills has declined. Only 12 percent of black high school seniors are classified as proficient readers.[97] Combined average SAT scores of all students dropped from 975 in 1960 to 900 in 1990.[98] More teenagers can identify the Three Stooges than they can the three branches of the federal government.[99] Approximately two thirds of high school seniors are not proficient readers.[100] Colleges and universities (including many of the most prestigious) are requiring remedial courses in reading, writing and arithmetic of students that they *already have admitted*. Trailing much of the developed world in academic achievement, American students, influenced by the self-esteem approach, rate their own abilities highly.

* America has become an increasingly litigious society. In 1991, with 281 lawyers per 100,000 U. S. population (comparable ratios for England and Japan were 82 and 11 respectively), this nation has some 70 percent of the worlds supply of lawyers. Nor did this group of lawyers remain idle. In 1990, 250,000 lawsuits were filed in federal courts compared to but 100,000 in 1960.[101] It is estimated that during the 1990's law schools will graduate some 40,000 attorneys a year![102]

* Free speech has been used successfully as a defense for maintaining public funding for lurid art.
* Some public schools have promoted the distribution of condoms and taught sexual techniques. Prayer is off limits.
* Then there are the daily instances of uncivil behavior: automobiles frequently driving through red lights; loud music played from boom boxes in the streets; obscene chants greeting unpopular decisions at sports events; the in-your-face posture and violence associated with professional sports; boorish behavior among college students and faculty who shout down guest speakers with whom they disagree; the degradation of traditional norms of scholarship; charges of sexism, racism, and insensitivity used to close debate on complex issues; daily doses of protests, complaints, demands, and threats; pop songs, laced with foul language, that encourage violence, sex, and disrespect for women; video cassettes promoting all manner of hedonism; the coarsening of public language; people being accosted by vagrants and the mentally unstable (having been "unfairly" labeled as mentally ill, they are released and allowed to sleep outdoors and now are redefined as individuals who lack "affordable housing"); a never ending invasion of the privacy of one's place of residence by telephone calls from people selling all kinds of goods and services; the ever-present threat of a law suit; increased tension among racial, ethnic, and religious groups, as well as between the sexes. And readers of this volume are well aware that this list of the decline in public morality which has so much diminished joy--one could say happiness--in this life, could with ease be extended. One is reminded of the music played at Yorktown in 1781, *"The World Turned Upside Down."*

Fortunately, there is recent evidence that some of America's pathologies have been halted and even experienced decline. The divorce rate has declined, welfare rolls have diminished, the marriage rate has stabilized, as has the rate of births by unwed mothers. Accompanying these trends is a rise in virginity among teenaged boys, and a decline in youth violence.[103] Yes, this is good news, but we still have a very long road to travel. Crime rates are still high as are births out of wedlock. A hardcore welfare group remains as does a violent underclass. The media and intellectuals continue to flout traditional norms of morality, and the positive influence of the mediating institutions of society-- family, religion and school--is far from what it was and should be. Daniel Moynihan's words "defining deviance down" are indeed appropriate. What once was held to be abnormal or illegitimate if not illegal is now normal and legal. A case can be made that a significant segment of society has adapted to this new culture. After all, "everybody does it"-- and--"what can you do about it?"[104]

Much that has been written about in this chapter has serious adverse implications for the quality of the labor force, national productivity, and economic freedom, not to mention domestic tranquility and the pursuit of happiness. No wonder so many are offended, afraid, aghast, and angry over these developments and the direction this nation has been taking. For as Edmund Burke observed, "Among a people generally corrupt, liberty cannot long exist."[105] Collectively, however, Americans are now and always have been an intelligent people, an ethical people, and a patriotic people. Historically, they also have accorded great respect to the traditional family and embraced the ultimate authority found in religion and a code of right and wrong. Moreover, the cultural themes which marked America, however imperfectly, over the centuries--those that have emphasized self-improvement, reward according to merit, tolerance, diversity, compassion, generosity, competition, and cooperation--are still alive.[106] However, the attack on so much of this, especially the family, religion, notions of right and wrong, meritocracy, and patriotism, as well as the unwarranted intrusion by the state into private economic decisions have been of such a magnitude as to bring alarm to much of the citizenry. Some recent surveys indicate this concern.

* According to a 1990 Associated Press Media General poll, "...80 percent of Americans objected to the amount of foul language in motion pictures; 82 percent objected to the amount of violence, 72 percent objected to the amount of explicit sexuality, and by a ratio of 3 to 1 they felt that movies today are worse than ever."[107]
* A 1995 USA WEEKEND survey about television found that 96 percent of those surveyed were very or somewhat concerned about sex on TV and 97 percent were very or somewhat concerned about vulgar language and violence on TV.[108]
* In a 1993 Wall Street Journal/NBC poll, 75 percent of Americans strongly agreed that traditional values have weakened and need to be strengthened.[109]
* According to a 1994 survey by the Times Mirror Center, 66 percent of the respondents thought government was almost always wasteful and inefficient. Optimistically, however, 68 percent thought that America's problems could be solved and 62 percent did not believe that there were limits to its growth.[110]
* In a 1964 poll conducted at the University of Michigan, 76 percent of the people answered "most of the time" or "all of the time" to the question, "How much of the time do you trust the Government in Washington to do what's right?" A 1994 New York Times/CBS poll found that only 13 percent of the public believed that members of Congress should be reelected.[111]
* Another survey revealed that 81 percent of Americans thought that people make too many excuses in their everyday lives.[112]
* A Reader's Digest poll, which surveyed four age groups labeled Xers (ages 18-30), Boomers (31-48), Silents (49-62), and Depression Era (63+) found the following beliefs:[113]

  - Across the four age groups, between 66 and 78 percent think that hard work is the key to getting ahead.
  - Between 69 and 78 percent believe that unlimited opportunity is more important than insuring greater equality of income. To the question, "Should there be a limit on incomes so that no one can earn more than a million dollars a year?" an average of 74 percent said no and 78 percent of the Xers felt this way.

- Between 73 and 85 percent think that America is the best place in the world to live.
- Between 45 and 59 percent did volunteer work.
- Given their talents and effort, an average of 70 percent thought that they were about where they should be at their jobs.
- On a scale from "wonderful "to "miserable," an average of 85 percent rated their home lives as "wonderful " or "pretty good."
- An average of two thirds were dissatisfied with "the way things are going in the United States at this time."
- An average of 67 percent thought that big government posed a greater threat to the nation's future than did big business or big labor. In 1954, government was selected by only 16 percent, in 1965, by 35 percent, and in 1985 by 50 percent.
- An average of 79 percent wanted to halt or decrease the influence of government.
- An average of 62 percent thought that the ethics of politicians had declined.
- An average of 89 percent believed that members of Congress were more interested in their political futures than they were in passing good legislation.

* According to a 1997 USA Weekend poll, 95 percent of the people polled believe that freedom must be tempered by responsibility; 89 percent believe that it is their responsibility to help those who are less fortunate; 83 percent believe the USA is the greatest nation on earth; 81 percent believe a spiritual or religious belief is essential to a fulfilling life; 80 percent believe personal responsibility has more to do with success in life than do personal circumstances; and 79 percent believe people who work hard in this nation are likely to succeed. However, 45 percent believe that generally the nation is not on the right track, and only 56 percent believe that the greatest days for the United States lie ahead.[114]

* A 1998 survey found Americans indicate "a letdown in moral values" as a major cause of today's problems.[115]

Although surveys do have their limitations, and although the results change slightly from year to year, it would appear that many if not most Americans have rejected or have serious qualms about "new class" points of view. Of course it is impossible to state the precise magnitude of the radical influence on each member of the nation's population. Nonetheless, it is important to put these surveys into perspective.

Thus, some of those who profess family values may nonetheless award parenting a lower priority than their job and/or believe that a less than satisfactory marriage which interferes with their quest for happiness warrants a divorce.[116] While there is statistical evidence of America's being a "religious" nation, a denial of moral absolutes can be found among those who proclaim the importance of religion in their lives. Many, are wont to look at their own consciences rather than to obediently follow dogma.

There is also some tendency--particularly, although by no means exclusively--among baby boomers to select a religion not on the basis of a denomination or abstract creed, but on the extent to which it offers ambiance, warmth, fellowship, nonjudgmentalism, and happiness in this world. For them, sermons about the hereafter or (God forbid) punishment after death are simply out.[117] As the NSRI report put it, "...in the latter part of the 20th century is the growing secularization of a self-described religious people."[118] At times polls say one thing, but people do another.[119] There are those who take extreme positions--far left and far right--but most people seem to be located along a continuum between the polar opposites on many issues.[120] In any event, it would seem that organized religion, as a force which restrains human passion, has diminished.

Ambivalence also obtains when more strictly economic matters are considered. One wants his taxes reduced but wishes his neighbor's taxes to be raised. He condemns the waste and inefficiency in government and the preferential treatment awarded to others, but fights tenaciously to maintain the programs, preferences, and double standards that benefit him--the interest deductions on his house, the government policies which keep out competition, the direct subsidies to his business, etc. He rails against an incompetent Congress yet supports his own representative who promotes the policies (inefficient and inequitable though they may be) which reward him so handsomely. And so on.

All in all, a mixture that endangers freedom and hardly seems the approach most conducive to happiness. A disturbing picture to be sure, but one not without solution.

---

[1] Marvin Olasky, *The Tragedy Of American Compassion* (Washington,, D.C.: Regnery Gateway, 1992), p.217.

[2] Barry A. Kosmin and Seymour P. Lachman, *One Nation Under God* (New York: Crown Trade Paperbacks, 1993), pp. 18,19.

[3] Ibid., pp. 20-23.

[4] Ibid., p.30.

[5] M. Stanton Evans, *The Theme Is Freedom* (Washington, D.C.: Regnery Publishing, Inc. 1994), pp. 278,279.

[6] Peter Marshall, "Recovering The Original American Vision," in Michael Bauman, ed. *Morality And The Marketplace* (Hillsdale: Hillsdale College Press), p.120.

[7] Ibid., p.21.

[8] Daniel Boorstin ed., *An American Primer* (New York: a Meridian Classic by the Penguin Group, 1985), p.221.

[9] Merrill D. Peterson ed., *Thomas Jefferson: Writings*, (New York: The Library Of America, 1984), p.523.

[10] Paul Johnson, *The Almost Chosen People* (San Francisco: Laissez Faire Books-Audio, 1995).

[11] Ibid.

[12] Alexis de Tocqueville, *Democracy In America*, vol. 1 (New York: Vintage Books, 1957), p.316.

[13] Abraham Lincoln, "Address at Gettysburg, Don E. Fehrenbacher, ed., *Selected Speeches and Writings by Abraham Lincoln* (New York: Vintage Books/The Library of America), p.405.

[14] Barry A. Kosmin and Seymour P. Lachman, *One Nation Under God*, p.32.

[15] Sara M. Evans, Born for Liberty (New York: The Free Press, A Division of Macmillan, Inc., 1989), pp. 111,112.
[16] Barry A. Kosmin and Seymour P. Lachman, One Nation Under God, p.32.
[17] Ibid., p12.
[18] Ibid., p.13.
[19] Ibid., p. 279.
[20] William F. Buckley Jr. "Are States Constitutions Unconstitutional?, "National Review, September 25, 1995.
[21] Ibid., p.1.
[22] Ibid., pp. 212,213.
[23] "Public Opinion and Demographic Report, "The American Enterprise, September/October 1994,p.90.
[24] "Public Opinion and Demographic Report," The American Enterprise, November/December 1994, p.107.
[25] Barry A. Kosmin and Seymour P. Lachmann, One Nation Under God, p.8.
[26] "In Search Of The Sacred", Newsweek, November 28, 1994.
[27] Gordon S. Wood, The Radicalism of the American Revolution (New York: Alfred A. Knopf, 1992), pp. 365-369.
[28] Marvin Olasky, The Tragedy Of American Compassion, pp. 12-41.
[29] Robert L. Woodson, Sr., "The Jailor Called Welfare", Imprimis, August, 1995.
[30] Ibid., pp. 42-98.
[31] Ibid., pp. 116-166.
[32] Ibid., pp. 167-233.
[33] Oscar Handlin and Mary Handlin, Liberty in Expansion 1760-1850 (New York: Harper & Row, Publishers, 1989), pp. 18,19.
[34] Ibid., pp. 50-91. passim.
[35] For two brief but excellent analyses of the "new class" philosophy and influence, see Irving Kristol, "The Cultural Revolution and the Capitalist Future," The American Enterprise, March/April, 1992. and Robert Bork, "Hard Truths About the Culture War," First Things, June/July, 1995.
[36] Paul Johnson, The Almost Chosen People (San Francisco: Laissez Faire Books-Audio, 1995).
[37] Christopher Lasch, "Conservatism against Itself, "First Things, April 1990.
[38] Ibid., p.183.
[39] Alan Bloom, The Closing of the American Mind (New York: Simon and Schuster, 1987),p.175.
[40] Charles J. Sykes, A Nation of Victims, pp. 39 and 140.
[41] Ibid. p.9.
[42] Ibid., p.3.
[43] Ibid., p.3.
[44] Ibid., p.3.
[45] Ibid., p.126.
[46] ibid., p.126.
[47] Ibid., p. 127.
[48] Ibid., p.127.
[49] Ibid., p.128.
[50] Bryan Miller, "Hey, Waiter! Now There's a Lawyer in My Soup," The New York Times, March 12, 1995,p.16.
[51] James Bovard, "The Disabilities Act's Parade of Absurdities," The Wall Street Journal, June 22, 1995. Also see, James Bovard, "The Lame Game," The American Spectator, July, 1995.

[52] Ibid.
[53] Ibid.
[54] George C. Leaf, "Terms of Impairment," *The Freeman*, October 1998.
[55] "Hooking a Tort," *The Wall Street Journal*, July 20, 1995.
[56] Review & Outlook: "Criminal Oversight," *The Wall Street Journal,* June 10, 1996.
[57] Stephen Bates, "Vote for the Victims," *The Wall Street Journal,* November 4, 1994.
[58] Adrian Furnham, "Fortitude," in Digby Anderson, ed., *The Loss Of Virtue*, pp. 138.
[59] Ibid., p. 143.
[60] David Martin, "Making People Good-Again," in Digby Anderson, ed. *The Loss Of Virtue*, p.237.
[61] Charles J. Sykes, *A Nation of Victims*, p.13.
[62] John Gray, "Toleration," in Digby Anderson, ed., *The Loss Of Virtue* (U.S.A.: A National Review Book, published by The Social Affairs Unit, pp. 40-43.
[63] Dennis Prager, *Happiness Is a Serious Problem* (New York: Harper Collins Publishers, 1998), p.78.
[64] Benjamin Hart, *Faith & Freedom* (Dallas: Lewis and Stanley, 1988), p.305.
[65] Gertrude Himmelfarb, "Liberty One Very Simple Principle?", *The American Scholar,* Autumn, 1993. p.549.
[66] Heather R. Higgins, "The Principles Behind the Policies," *The Wall Street Journal*, February 16,1995.
[67] Alan Bloom. *The Closing of the American Mind*, with a Forword by Saul Bellow (New York: Simon & Schuster, 1987), pp. 25-43.
[68] Ibid., p.164,165.
[69] R. Randy Lee, "Housing for the Non-Discriminating Buyer," *The Wall Street Journal*, November 30,1994.
[70] University of Missouri and University of Michigan publications are quoted in Charles J, Sykes, *A Nation of Victims* (New York: St. Martin's Press 1992) p. 6.
[71] Ibid., p.6.
[72] Saul Bellow, "Notable & Quotable," *The Wall Street Journal*, June 9,1995.
[73] William J. Bennett, *The Index of Leading Cultural Indicators* (New York: A Touchstone Book, Simon & Schuster, 1994),p18.
[74] Ibid., p.22.
[75] Ibid. p. 34. The "expected punishment" is calculated by multiplying four probabilities (of being arrested, of being prosecuted, of being convicted if prosecuted, and of going to prison if convicted) and then multiplying the product by the median time served for an offense. See footnote on page 34.
[76] Ibid., p. 29.
[77] Fox Butterfield, "More Blacks in Their 20's Have Trouble With the Law," *The New York Times*, October 5, 1995.
[78] Paul J. McNulty, "Who's in Jail, and Why They Belong There," *The Wall Street Journal*, November 9, 1994. p. A23.
[79] William J. Bennett, *The Index of Leading Cultural Indicators*, p.31.
[80] Reuters, "More Students, In a Study, See Unsafe Schools," *The New York Times*, June 15, 1995.
[81] Ibid., p.38,39.
[82] Ibid., pp. 40-42.
[83] Peter Applebome, "Study Says Society Fails 19 Million Youths," *The New York Times*, October 12, 1995.
[84] Ibid., p.55.
[85] Ibid., pp. 58,59.

[86] James Q. Wilson, *The Moral Sense*, p.249.
[87] William J. Bennett, *The Index of Leading Cultural Indicators*, pp. 50,51.
[88] James Q. Wilson, *The Moral Sense*, p. 176.
[89] Ibid., pp. 46-48.
[90] Ibid., p.72.
[91] "White Fright," *The Wall Street Journal*, June 19, 1995.
[92] Ibid., p.48.
[93] Bob Dole and J.C. Watts Jr., "A New Civil Rights Agenda," *The Wall Street Journal*, July 27,1995.
[94] Ibid., p.64.
[95] Ibid., p.78.
[96] Kay S. Hymowitz, "Kids Today Are Growing Up Way Too Fast," *The Wall Street Journal*, October 28, 1998.
[97] Bob Dole and J. C. Watts, "A New Civil Rights Agenda," *The Wall Street Journal*, July 27, 1995.
[98] Ibid., p.84.
[99] Nicholas Lemann, "The New American Consensus," *The New York Times Magazine,* November 1, 1998.
[100] "Decline Found in Reading Proficiency of High School Seniors," *The New York Times*, April 28, 1995, p.18.
[101] Charles J. Sykes, *A Nation of Victims*, p. 14
[102] Ibid., p.126.
[103] Richard Nadler, "Glum and Glummer," *National Review*, September 28, 1998. Also see "Is America Turning A Corner?," *The American Enterprise*, January/February 1999.
[104] Gertrude Himmelfarb, "The Panglosses of the Right Are Wrong," *The Wall Street Journal*, February 4, 1999.
[105] Burke quoted in E.Calvin Breisner, "Stewardwhip in a Free Society," in Michael Bauman, ed., *Morality And The Marketplace*, p.25.
[106] Michael Medved, "You Must Remember This," *Policy Review*, Winter 1995, pp. 45-53.
[107] Michael Medved, "Hollywood's Poison Factory: Making It the Dream Factory Again," *Imprimis*, November, 1992.
[108] Dan Olmsted and Gigi Anders, "Turned Off," *USA WEEKEND*, June 2-4,1995.
[109] Gerald F. Seib, "Americans Feel Families and Values Are Eroding But They Disagree Over the Causes and Solutions," *The Wall Street Journal*, June 11, 1993, p. A12.
[110] John Fund, "The Revolution of 1994," *The Wall Street Journal*, October 19, 1994.
[111] "The Anger: Ever Deeper, "*The New York Times Magazine*, October 16, 1994, p.37.
[112] "Public Opinion and Demographic Report," *The American Enterprise*, September/October 1994, p.100.
[113] Everett C. Ladd, "Exposing the Myth of the Generation Gap," *Readers Digest*, January 1995, pp. 49-54.
[114] Steven Covey, "The Beliefs We Share," *USA WEEKEND* July 4-6, 1997.
[115] "Is America Turning A Corner?," *The American Enterprise*, January/February 1999.
[116] Barry A. Kosmin and Seymour P. Lachman, *One Nation Under God*, pp. 224-228.
[117] Ibid., pp. 230-250.
[118] Ibid., p. 279.
[119] Ibid., p. 282.
[120] Ibid., pp. 249,250.

CHAPTER 15

CONCLUSIONS

So many eighteenth century skeptics said that it could not be done. A large nation with a diverse population could not govern itself for long according to republican principles. Well, history certainly proved them wrong and for over two hundred years, the United States has survived, grown, and prospered beyond the dreams of friend or foe. This compound republic of limited government, personal, political, and economic freedoms and a grounding in virtue has enabled millions upon millions of people to pursue their own dreams of happiness and has provided compassionate assistance to other Americans and to those in foreign countries, including those countries it has defeated in war. While far from perfect, America is the envy of most of the world.

However, it is not just America but all of Western civilization which has developed much of which to be proud. According to Michael Novak, "Most of the ideals now regnant throughout the world are ideals which first emerged under democratic capitalism in the West: development, modernization, social justice, national liberation, independence, self-reliance...."[1] Gunnar Myrdal asserts that the American values of freedom and equality were to be the greatest foes of racist exclusion.[2] Arthur Schlesinger reminds us that "The crimes of the West have produced their own antidotes. They have provoked great movements to end slavery, to raise the status of women, to abolish torture, to combat racism, to defend freedom of inquiry and expression, to advance personal liberty and human rights."[3] Orlando Patterson notes that, "...non-Western peoples have thought so little about freedom that most human languages did not even possess a word for the concept before contact with the West."[4] Moreover, as historian Donald Kagan observed, the West has distinguished itself from other civilizations by limiting the claims of the state against the individual, by separating church from state, thereby affording protection to each, by tolerating diversity, and by encouraging criticism of itself. "Only in the West can one imagine a movement to neglect the culture's own heritage in favor of some other's."[5]

The people of western culture have sometimes behaved with cruelty among themselves and toward peoples of other civilizations, despoiling the environments of the latter, plundering their wealth, and behaving with cultural arrogance.[6] Such misdeeds should never be excused, but one must remember that all civilizations have been guilty of shameful actions during some part of their histories.

Alas, the ideals as well as the economic and other accomplishments of the Western democracies--and of the United States in particular--appear not only insufficient but grossly deficient to radicals for whom utopian perfection is the bitter enemy of the good, the very good, and even the excellent. As we have seen, this radical stance elicits assault on the free market and traditional virtues. Ironically, it is the high productivity associated with capitalism that has given so many the ability to achieve a higher education and has thus allowed so many radicals to choose their occupations. One is reminded of Mark Twain's witticism: "If you pick up a starving dog and make him prosperous, he will not bite you, and that is the principal difference between a dog and a man."[7] There appears little doubt that radical individualism, which is responsible for the decline in standards of behavior and the collectivism of radical egalitarianism, has been influential in the recent rapid growth of so many social and economic problems.

The downward shift in behavioral standards means that people have to tolerate sounds, words, deeds, and sights that previous generations considered anathema. The intrusion of the state beyond traditional and appropriate bounds into the private economy has meant that market outcomes are changed, that many people are coerced into actions from which they would have refrained if left free to choose, and were also coerced into paying higher taxes to enforce their own coercion. Although some have received benefits from such public policies, many more have been harmed by their inefficiencies and redistributive nature. Moreover, as the results of these policies fail to conform to their stated objectives, frustration mounts, opponents are demonized, discourse is envenomed, the search for scapegoats accelerates, conspiracy theories abound, demagogues receive more attention, social authority deteriorates, and the sense of community, which radicals claim to crave, disintegrates. All this unfolds amidst an increasingly hedonistic culture.

Under such conditions the danger thrives that increasing numbers will come to believe that their own efforts are less important than external forces in determining their status. This state of affairs is hardly the ideal for pursuing happiness, but it is fertile soil for the strong man--perhaps the totalitarian--from either the right or the left who would sell them their dreams for the price of their liberties. Warnings about this danger extend back to biblical times.

> This is how your king will treat you. He will make soldiers of your sons; some of them will serve in his war chariots, others in his cavalry, and others will run before his chariots. He will make some of them officers in charge of a thousand men, and others in charge of fifty men. Your sons will have to plow his fields, harvest his crops, and make his weapons and the equipment for his chariots.
>
> Your daughters will have to make perfumes for him and work as his cooks and his bakers. He will take your best fields, vineyards and olive groves, and give them to his officials.
>
> He will take a tenth of your grain and of your grapes for his court officers and other officials. He will take your servants and your best cattle and donkeys, and make them work for him. He will take a tenth of your flocks. And you yourselves will become his slaves. When that time comes, you will complain bitterly because of your king, whom you yourselves chose, but the Lord will not listen to your complaints (1 Samuel 8:10-18).

It is not the state that is God's concern here but the individual whom He created in His image. "To the Lord, the nations are nothing, no more than a drop of water" (Isaiah

40:125). And As St. Paul reminds us, man was meant for freedom. "Freedom is what we have-Christ set us free! Stand, then, as free people, and do not allow yourselves to become slaves again" (Paul's Letter to the Gallatians: 5:1).

The following illustrate the thinking of the American founding fathers:
Samuel Adams:

"When once the people lose their virtue, they will be ready to surrender their liberties to the first external or internal invader."[8]

Alexander Hamilton:

"...of those men who have overturned the liberties of republics the greatest number have begun their career, by paying an obsequious court to the people, commencing Demagogues and ending Tyrants."[9]

John Dickenson:

Indeed, nations in general, are not apt to *think* until they feel; and therefore nations in general have lost their liberty: For as violations of the rights of the *governed,* are commonly not only specious, but small at the beginning, they spread over the multitude in such a manner, as to touch individuals but slightly. Thus they are disregarded....They regularly increase the first injuries, till at length the inattentive people are compelled to perceive the heaviness of their burdens-They begin to complain and inquire-but too late. They find their oppressors so strengthened by success, and themselves so entangled in examples of express authority on the part of their rulers, and of tacit recognition on their own part, that they are quite confounded...

From these reflections I conclude that every free state should incessantly watch, and instantly take alarm on any addition being made to the power exercised over them. Innumerable instances might be produced to show from what slight beginnings the most extensive consequences have flowed....[10]

In the twentieth century, Mr. Justice Louis Brandeis offers a warning appropriate to the times:

Experience should teach us to be most on our guard to protect liberty when the government's purposes are beneficent. Men born to freedom are naturally alert to repel invasion of their liberty by evil-minded rulers. The greatest dangers to liberty lurk in insidious encroachments by men of zeal, well-meaning but without understanding.[11]

It would not be unfair to conclude that the ideology of the Enlightenment has failed to realize all of its goals.[12] True, secular rationalism has helped to eliminate many of the tyrannies of church and state and has done much to pave the way for (among other things), the acceptance of the idea of natural rights, a host of freedoms, democratic institutions, the abolition of slavery, and the more humane treatment of criminals and the insane. Although Enlightenment thought considers never ending progress to be normal we know that war and violence remain, as do greed, ethnic hostilities, poverty, and crime. The twentieth century, in which generally the level of formal education was relatively high, gave us World Wars I and II along with the Gulag, Auschwitz, and other gross inhumanities. America and other western nations continue to have serious problems. We also know that the above have been accompanied by a decline in the power of religion and a diminution of self-control and duty.[13]

One might question whether man can develop a strong moral code without being informed by God. From Immanuel Kant through John Dewey, advocates of secular rationalism thought it possible. However, we are aware that human behavior leaves much to be desired, and many believe great dangers exist where ethics are divorced from religion.

Moral choices can be exceedingly complex (for instance, when the virtue of charity conflicts with that of justice) and thus difficult for the smartest and most religious of people. Worse, man may be unaware of the implications of his alternatives. Even with a godly foundation and recognition of a morally correct decision, one may choose falsely because of fear or weakness. However, such moral failure becomes less likely when a person loves and fears God.

Dostoevsky observed in *The Brothers Karamazov* that "If God is dead, all things are permissible." In other words, a sense of the sacred tends to restrain the darker human impulses. One might note that fascist and communist totalitarian dictatorships of the twentieth century whose leaders inflicted horrendous hardships including torture and murder on millions of people, sought to diminish greatly if not eliminate the influence of religion.[14]

According to de Toqueville,

> ...liberty cannot be established without morality, nor morality without faith[15]. Liberty regards religion as its companion in all its battles and its triumphs, as the cradle of its infancy and the divine source of its claims. It considers religion as the safeguard of morality, and morality as the best security of law and the surest pledge of the duration of freedom.[16]...There are no great men without virtue; and there are no great nations-it may almost be added, there would be no society-without respect for right; for what is a union of rational and intelligent beings who are held together only by the bond of force?[17]....Despots may govern without faith, but liberty cannot.[18]

The deist Voltaire observes that "If God does not exist, it becomes necessary to invent him," and "I want my attorney, my tailor, my servants, even my wife to believe in God" because "then I shall be robbed and cuckolded less often."[19] Also, G.K. Chesterton: " If I did not believe in God, I should still want my doctor, my lawyer, and my banker to do so."[20] Chesterton also notes "that when men and women cease to believe in God, they do not believe in nothing, but in anything."[21] This may explain the zealotry with which some "rights" advocates (environmental, animal, feminist, children, aged, handicapped, and an assortment of cults), have, in the late twentieth century, pursued their single issue goals. Even the secular rationalists Will and Ariel Durant conclude that "There is no significant example in history, before our time, of a society successfully maintaining moral life without the aid of religion."[22] On a lighter note, Doctor Johnson, upon learning that a dinner guest did not believe in morality, opined, "But if he does really think that there is no distinction between virtue and vice, why, Sir, when he leaves our house let us count our spoons."

Vaclav Havel, former President of the Czech Republic and recipient of the Philadelphia Liberty Medal, addresses the problems of what he calls the post modern age. For Havel a symbol of this era is"...a Bedouin mounted on a camel and clad in traditional robes under which he is wearing jeans, with a transistor radio in his hands and an ad for Coca-Cola on the camel's back." He notes that "Politicians at international forums may reiterate a thousand times that the basis of the new world order must be universal respect for human rights, but it will mean nothing as long as this imperative does not derive from the respect of the miracle of Being, the miracle of the universe, the miracle of nature, the miracle of our own existence."[23]

Finally, let us ponder the words of President William Clinton. Although we know that not all Americans consider him the epitome of virtue, his remarks on virtue and religion are insightful. "Don't you believe that if every kid in every difficult neighborhood in America were in a religious institution on weekends--a synagogue on Saturday, a church on Sunday, a mosque on Friday--don't you really believe that the drug rate, the crime rate, the violence rate, the sense of self-destruction would go way down and the quality and character of this country would go way up?"[24]

Of course one need not be a religious believer to have high moral standards and this surely is the case for multitudes of people. However, whether an entire nation or civilization can long continue without religious foundations, basing its principles on reason alone, is a question without an optimistic answer. Moreover, any society in which a large majority of people abhor distinctions between virtue and vice and view the world and life itself as meaningless, is headed for deep trouble, if not extinction. What basis could it have for protecting the weak, or questioning authority, or preserving natural rights, or evaluating institutions and policies?[25] And, of course, the success of capitalism depends upon virtuous behavior. When virtue disintegrates, freedom (both positive and negative) and happiness are indeed placed in jeopardy.

Edmund Burke once observed that all that is necessary for evil to prevail is for good men to do nothing. Agreed. But what can or should the good men (and women) do? We all recognize that there is room for improvement in the way we conduct our lives. In light of this recognition, one attack on evil is to trumpet the classical, religious and commercial virtues and to direct our energies to their rejuvenation. This approach would by no means imply the restoration of old restraints on women and blacks or other injustices. It would emphasize commercial virtues and individual worth rather than group rights. It would advocate temperance, courage, justice, and wisdom along with the religious virtues ("and the greatest of these is charity"). If applied to personal, cultural, political, and economic endeavors this approach would do much to protect freedom and pluralism, rescue tranquility, ease the pursuit of happiness, and evade the dangers of our present course. Perfection eludes this proposal, but it would go far to eliminate some of the strains and tensions in this diverse society and reduce others so that we might live more peacefully together.

Vital to this proposal is the restoration of economic freedom, for it has been both radical egalitarianism and radical individualism that have been responsible for many of America's woes. This means more private decision-making and a diminished but important role for the state. After all, providing for public safety, protecting property, and performing the other legitimate functions of government are necessary conditions to the pursuit of happiness. And we have noted that while government has involved itself in activities that extend well beyond those legitimate functions, protection of individuals and of their property have been less than satisfactory.

Make no mistake about virtue being vital. Israel, Greece and Rome all suffered decline when virtue decayed. Our own century provides the examples of Nazi Germany and the Soviet Union, totalitarian nations that knocked down the barriers between public and private spheres. As John Adams observed, "Public virtue cannot last in a nation without private, and public virtue is the only foundation of republics."[26]

Consider how virtue in nineteenth century England prevailed over the ills of that period.[27] Appalled by the extent of immorality, Queen Victoria, her husband Albert, and concerned middle class citizens sought social reform through moral excellence. During her reign (1837-1901), sobriety, thrift, patriotism, work, self-reliance, courage, duty, cleanliness, self-respect, self-help, neighborliness, and family came to be virtues publicly valued (and their opposites were publicly devalued), by members of all social classes (including the lowest) who perceived themselves as free and responsible for their actions. Institutions such as Sunday schools, temperance societies, and especially the family reinforced these Victorian virtues.

Public policy and the moral language of virtue stigmatized welfare for the able-bodied, "undeserving" poor and made harsh the conditions of its receipt. Simultaneously, philanthropic organizations for the "deserving" poor sought to educate them while providing temporary financial assistance. The result was a marked decline in the rates of illegitimacy, crime, prostitution, drunkenness, and welfare expenditures, and a rise in civility other nations envied. It is notable that this reformation of society was concurrent with increasing industrialization, urbanization, and the inevitable great dislocations that accompany these aspects of modernization. The Victorian era was marked by prejudice, restrictions on freedom, and great inequalities of income and social class. Morality was an ideal toward which one should strive. It helped to provide the courage and the light to do the right thing. Yes, there was hypocrisy, but Victorian society (in contrast to ours, which seeks to normalize immorality), upheld moral principles. Although it failed to eradicate all social ills, it did prove to be a very powerful force in rejuvenating society and for many, facilitated the pursuit of happiness.

Virtuous behavior (and remember its by-product is happiness), the behavior this volume emphasized and applauded is possible at almost all levels of income. One can be a caring parent and a good neighbor, bring pride and cheer to the workplace, comfort the afflicted, and meet life's other challenges without great sums of money at one's disposal. People as poor as church mice have conducted themselves with a strong sense of morality, and this true dignity often has characterized the behavior of poor people in America. For instance, "During the 1960's, one neighborhood in San Francisco had the lowest income, the highest unemployment rate, the highest proportion of families with incomes under $4,000 a year, the least educational attainment, the highest tuberculosis rate, and the highest proportion of substandard housing. That neighborhood was called Chinatown. Yet in 1965, there were only five persons of Chinese ancestry committed to prison in the entire state of California."[28] Or think of those unsung heroes of today; the black mothers and fathers who manage to instill the classical, commercial, and theological virtues in their offspring amidst the inner city violence and chaos around them.

Of course, the restoration of virtue in America will not come easily, even when people acknowledge it to be the proper path. Recall the *Confessions* of St. Augustine: "Give me chastity and continence but not yet."[29] Moreover, external forces also must be considered. Virtue by itself will not eradicate pollution, poverty, unemployment, or inflation. Moreover, virtue may be difficult to practice (Aristotle said that it comes through practice rather than by precept) in areas where broken marriages, children born out of wedlock, drug use, crime, terrible schools, and dilapidated dwellings are the rule. But, it is especially in these areas that a dynamic free market economy along with a virtuous citizenry and limited but appropriate public policies, best comes to grips with such problems. The same holds true for most other social and economic problems.

Religious precepts and philosophical wisdom are essential to sound public policy. From these sources we know that wealth is important in the pursuit of happiness (G. B. Shaw said that it was not money but rather lack of money that was the root of all evil), but that wealth *by itself* does not guarantee happiness. There are several dimensions to the relationship between wealth and happiness and these are summarized below.

There is evidence that an increase in national wealth in poor countries does bring with it a heightened sense of national well-being--one might say happiness. This is especially true for the previously poor people who now can buy the basic things that make for happiness. More money also leads to a reduction in the afflictions of the poor, such as high infant mortality rates (an important relief from sorrow). Also, an increase in the overall level of wealth tends to benefit all classes, and as people realize that they are better off this year than last, they have less cause to make counterproductive invidious comparisons.

However, there does not seem to be a strong positive correlation between wealth and happiness *within* a developed country. But, there is one important exception. Although people who avow happiness and those who avow unhappiness can be found at all income levels, fewer poor people say they are happy or very happy and more poor people say they are unhappy when compared to those at higher income levels. Thus it does appear that, to some degree, more money will buy more happiness for people on the lower income rungs in economically advanced nations. As the nightclub entertainer Sophie Tucker put it, "Let me tell you, honey, I've been rich and I've been poor, and believe me, rich is better."

Given the above exception, several reasons account for the general failure of higher levels of income to correlate proportionately with higher levels of happiness. Various aspects of life, such as skill mastery, work-satisfaction, love, friendships, family life, religion, noncommercial leisure activities, good health, self-esteem, and effectiveness in meeting challenges are important determinants of happiness, and generally, can be obtained at most income levels. As Thomas Jefferson remarked, "It is neither wealth nor splendor, but tranquility and occupations which give happiness."[30] One might also note that some researchers believe levels of happiness are partially determined by the genes. They assert that each of us has a genetically developed 'set point' for happiness, and movements up or down a range from such a point are affected by other factors.[31] Perhaps. But even here, the sources of happiness just mentioned still play vital roles.

Moreover, people who believe that a large increase in income will provide them with greater happiness over the long run may well be deceived. Actually receiving that income may initially bring greater levels of happiness, but this tends to be transitory as the novelties associated with greater affluence wear off. Also, if one measures success by the subjective standard of a new higher income level, there are almost always other individuals located on higher income rungs. Not so incidentally, it seems that about the same amount of worrying (although over different matters), beset most income levels.[32] That the rich have more options from which to choose does not insure that they will make superior choices. Think of the many who achieved fame and/or fortune: movie stars, rock stars, sports celebrities and politicians, who were deeply troubled people.

Nonetheless, the quest for riches does help to create jobs and work is an important component of happiness: work stimulates human creativity which may redound to the well-being of society and the elevation of civilization; and work facilitates the practice of charity which should bring joy to both donor and recipient. In addition, the commercial society which emphasizes the creation of wealth is one that stresses the rule of law and the protection of property, and tends to promote peace (warfare being an activity that most people do not associate positively with happiness), all of which contribute to national well-being. But again, wealth standing alone is not enough.

Come to mind as our narrative approaches its close is Samuel Johnson's observation on Milton's epic poem, *Paradise Lost*, that "None ever wished it to be longer." Yet, there is one final message. Our goal in assessing economic systems and public policies is to preserve the personal, civic and economic liberties which facilitate the pursuit of happiness, properly conceived. In this regard, virtue rather than rights is the key, and it is virtue practiced by all sectors of society. The Roman historian Tacitus noted that the more corrupt the state, the more numerous the laws, and the motto of the University of Pennsylvania reads Leges Sine Moribus Vanae (Laws Without Morals Are In Vain).

Richard John Neuhaus has rather succinctly set forth the virtuous duties of the concerned Christian; obligations that one ardently hopes members of other religions as well as nonbelievers will applaud. They are to strive "to build a world in which the strong are just, and power is tempered by mercy, in which the weak are nurtured and the marginal embraced, and those at the entrance gates and those at the exit gates of life are protected both by law and love."[33] Ah freedom.

---

[1] Michael Novak, *The Spirit of Democratic Capitalism*, (New York: An American Enterprise/ Simon Schuster Publication, 1982), p.130.

[2] Charles J. Sykes, *A Nation of Victims* (New York: St. Martin's Press, 1992), p.208.

[3] Arthur M. Schlesinger, Jr., *The Disuniting of America* (New York: W.W. Norton & Company, 1992),p.127.

[4] Orlando Patterson, *Freedom, vol. 1 Freedom In The Making Of Western Culture*, (New York: Basic Books,, 1991), p. x.

[5] Donald Kagan, "The Role of the West," *The Freeman*, May 1995, p.275.

[6] J. M. Roberts, *The Triumph of the West* (Boston: Little, Brown and Company, 1985), pp. 290-291.

[7] G. Warren Nutter, "Freedom In A Revolutionary Economy," in *The American Revolution: Three Views* (New York: American Brands, Inc., 1975),p115.

[8] Peter Marshall, " Recovering the Original American Vision," in Michael Bauman, *Morality And The Marketplace*, p. 119.

[9] Jacob E. Cooke, ed. *The Federalist*, (Middletown: Wesleyan University Press, 1982),p.6.

[10] Clarence B. Carson, *Basic American Government* (Wadley: American Textbook Committee, 1993), p. 43.

[11] Louis Brandeis quoted in Bernard H. Seigan, *Economic Liberties and the Constitution* (Chicago: The University of Chicago Press, 1980),p.172.

[12] For an analysis of enlightenment failures see, Alasdair MacIntyre, *After Virtue*, 2nd ed. (Indiana: University of Notre Dame Press, 1984).

[13] James Q. Wilson, *The Moral Sense* (New York: The Free Press--A Division of Macmillan, Inc., 1993),p.218.

[14] Barry A. Kosmin and Seymour p. Lachman, *One Nation Under God* (New York: Crown Trade Paperbacks, 1993), p.9.

[15] *Democracy In America*, vol. 1, Alexis de Toqueville (New York: Vantage Books, 1957), p.12.

[16] Ibid., p. 46.

[17] Ibid., p. 254.

[18] Ibid., p. 318.

[19] James Q. Wilson, *The Moral Sense*, p.219.

[20] Peter Kreeft, *Back to Virtue* (San Francisco: Ignatius Press, 1986), p. 194.

[21] Paul Johnson, *The Almost Chosen People* (San Francisco: Laissez Faire Books-Audio, 1995).

[22] Will and Ariel Durant, *The Lessons of History* (New York: Simon and Schuster, 1968),p.51.

[23] Vaclav Havel, "The New Measure of Man, "*The New York Times*, July 4, 1994.

[24] "Nihilism, Religion and the President," *The Wall Street Journal*, July 14, 1995.

[25] Donald Kagan, "Why Western History Matters," *The Wall Street Journal*, December 28, 1994.

[26] M. Stanton Evans, *The Theme Is Freedom* (Washington D.C. Regnery Publishing, Inc. 1994), p.35.

[27] The following statements on England's move toward virtue in the nineteenth century rely heavily on Gertrude Himmelfarb, *THE DE-MORALIZATION OF SOCIETY* (New York: Alfred A. Knopf, 1995).

[28] James Q. Wilson and Richard Herrnstein, *Crime and Human Nature* quoted in William J. Bennett, *The Index of Leading Cultural Indicators*, p.21.

[29] Mary T. Clark, *Augustine of Hippo, Selected Writings* (New York: Paulist Press, 1984), p.91.

[30] Bob Condor, *"Why are some people naturally upbeat?,"* The Journal News, January 3, 1999.

[31] Daniel Goleman, "Forget Money; Nothing Can Buy Happiness, Some Researchers Say," *The New York Times*, July 16, 1996.

[32] A summary on recent findings on this subject can be found in Robert E. Lane, "Does Money Buy Happiness?," *The Public Interest*, Fall, 1993.

[33] Richard John Neuhaus quoted in Michael Cromartie, "The Evangelical Kaleidoscope: Economics, Politics, and Social Justice," in Michael Baumann ed., *Morality And The Marketplace*, p.106.

INDEX

A

absolutism, 69
Adams, John, 46, 48, 49, 57, 66, 68, 69, 70, 73, 74, 75, 76, 96, 104, 113, 129, 133, 136, 155, 193, 284
AFDC, 224
affirmative action, 178
Africa, 23, 27, 78, 110, 152, 177, 188
aggression, 52
aggressive behavior, 154
agriculture, 24, 30, 134, 135, 142, 155, 170, 186, 195, 199, 200, 247
AIDS, 152, 223
alcoholism, 175, 223
American Revolution, 23, 27, 31, 35, 36, 39, 54, 73, 79, 80, 81, 83, 108, 125, 137, 143, 164, 179, 191, 268, 275, 287
antitrust, 202, 222
anxiety, xiii, 35, 44, 94, 98, 99, 145, 177, 232
Articles of Confederation, 107, 108, 111, 113, 114, 115, 116, 131, 135, 136
Asia, 19, 20, 145, 152, 171
Asian Americans, 267
attitudes, xi, xiii, 19, 21, 133, 148, 149, 151, 182, 201, 236, 268
automobiles, 160, 169, 187, 262, 271
autonomy, 49, 157

B

Bahamas, 20
balance of payments, 27
banking system, 196
banks, 184
banks, commercial, 183, 205
barter, 89, 185

Belgium, 152
Bill of Rights, 60, 66, 68, 119, 266
birth control, 262
Bolivia, 185
Brazil, 154, 185
Britain, 38, 40, 47, 48, 49, 50, 52, 53, 69, 71, 76, 88, 93, 103, 110, 120, 152, 220
Bulgaria, 248
bureaucracy, 212
Bush, George H.W., 223

C

capital, 156, 162
capital accumulation, 89
capital formation, 26, 147, 155, 172, 237
capital stock, 201
capitalism, 6, 136, 150, 153, 162, 178, 184, 198, 239, 247, 248, 249, 256, 260, 261, 262, 279, 280, 283
Caribbean, 23, 24
Central America, 20, 153
chaos, 285
child labor, 142, 212
China, 86, 168
Christianity, 20, 24, 177, 251, 253
Christians, 61, 236, 243
Churchill, Winston, 157
citizen participation, 83
citizenship, 11, 149, 175, 180
civic liberty, 5, 176
civil rights, 60, 205, 255, 256, 268
civil society, 64, 123, 129
Civil War, 1, 59, 60, 61, 62, 143, 151, 178, 179, 193, 194, 196, 197, 199, 203, 204, 205, 255
classes, middle, 261
classless society, 13, 14
clerical work, 181

Cleveland, Grover, 180
coherence, 83
cold war, 220
collective bargaining, 203
colonialism, 134
Columbus, Christopher, 19, 20, 171, 253
common sense, 75
communism, 11
communities, 28, 94, 117, 160, 162, 182, 193
compensation, 8, 32, 196, 202, 208, 223, 224
competitiveness, 175
compound, 120, 122, 136, 279
concession, 50
conflicts, 48, 67, 107, 123, 143, 262, 282
conformity, 3
confrontation, 45
Connecticut, 28, 49, 111, 116
conscription, 103
constitution, 13, 31, 38, 42, 45, 49, 54, 68, 69, 74, 106, 111, 115, 116, 117, 119, 120, 121, 129, 205
consumerism, 247
consumption, 43, 45, 49, 93, 95, 142, 169, 180, 181, 187, 202, 219, 232, 248
contraception, 142
cooperation, 10, 154, 212, 239
corruption, 58, 70, 71, 83, 86, 93, 148, 201, 257, 258
cotton, 156, 176, 178
credit, 221
Cuba, 152
cultural habits, 183
Cultural Revolution, 275
culture war, xiii, 1
Czech Republic, 283

D

debt, 35, 222
decay, 70
decision-making process, 162
Declaration of Independence, ix, 57, 66, 75, 76, 77, 78, 79, 80, 106, 148, 268
Delaware, 49, 111, 116, 171
democracy, 8, 12, 13, 59, 62, 66, 69, 77, 122, 123, 131, 177, 255, 257
democratic institutions, 281
determinism, 4
deviation, 13
diamonds, 186
diet, 142, 169, 170, 172, 176, 206

discrimination, 10, 25, 29, 123, 144, 145, 150, 159, 162, 182, 183, 188, 200, 220, 221, 222, 223, 236, 259, 265
distribution of wealth, 89
District of Columbia, 178, 212
divorce rates, 182
downsizing, 168
drug abuse, 184, 267
durable goods, 64, 193

E

earth, 24, 54, 61, 68, 99, 104, 172, 174, 240, 245, 255, 273
earthquake, 47, 86
economic benefits, 154
economic development, 20, 65, 97, 133, 134, 135, 136, 147, 154, 157, 196
economic freedom, xi, xii, xiii, xv, 5, 6, 11, 12, 15, 21, 24, 29, 31, 35, 37, 47, 57, 84, 96, 100, 125, 145, 179, 196, 198, 219, 227, 231, 237, 253, 271, 279, 283
economic growth, 5, 21, 31, 35, 89, 95, 134, 135, 136, 147, 152, 155, 168, 184, 186, 195, 199
economic intervention, 30
economic loss, 178
economic performance, 11
economic policy, 31, 96, 193, 216
economic system, 8, 9, 90, 141, 153, 188, 238, 248, 249, 259, 268, 286
education, xi, 8, 28, 51, 73, 77, 78, 92, 95, 117, 142, 145, 149, 150, 151, 155, 161, 164, 170, 179, 181, 182, 184, 193, 222, 227, 237, 253, 254, 263, 266, 267, 280, 281
egalitarianism, xii, 13, 72, 77, 261, 268, 280, 283
Egypt, 67, 240, 241, 242
elections, 60, 106, 116, 124, 215
electricity, 117
Emancipation Proclamation, 178
emergence, 118, 137
emigration, 31
eminent domain, 32, 196
employment, 138, 170, 182, 188, 191, 214, 220, 221, 222, 225, 228
England, 2, 20, 22, 23, 24, 25, 26, 27, 28, 29, 30, 31, 32, 34, 35, 39, 40, 41, 44, 45, 46, 47, 48, 50, 51, 52, 53, 54, 58, 59, 60, 63, 66, 67, 69, 71, 72, 74, 79, 88, 92, 108, 110, 111, 117, 155, 177, 257, 270, 284, 287
enlightenment, 12, 61, 66, 72, 73, 84, 106, 178, 281
entrepreneurship, 13, 21, 157, 158, 159, 161, 162, 164, 168, 175, 181, 196, 238, 261
ethnic groups, 150, 151, 221

ethnicity, 150, 183
Europe, 6, 19, 20, 21, 22, 24, 25, 26, 27, 29, 30, 31, 35, 39, 41, 51, 54, 70, 79, 86, 88, 96, 110, 117, 134, 143, 144, 145, 146, 153, 169, 173, 174, 187, 193, 255
Europe, Eastern, 11, 148
Europe, Western, 29, 153, 161
exchange rates, 188
exclusion, 148, 254, 279
excuse, 150, 153, 245, 263, 272
executive branch, 114, 116, 132
exercise, 4, 10, 48, 77, 86, 88, 91, 93, 114, 120, 123, 129, 141, 185, 199, 206, 207, 211, 237, 238, 248, 256
exploitation, 90, 176, 177, 246, 261

F

failure, 23, 24, 52, 104, 143, 157, 175, 245, 282, 285
fairness, 237, 257, 265, 267
family, xi, xv, 4, 6, 12, 22, 26, 28, 44, 46, 51, 61, 85, 88, 90, 97, 105, 131, 136, 142, 144, 145, 149, 152, 162, 169, 171, 180, 181, 182, 185, 207, 215, 235, 237, 238, 240, 247, 248, 249, 250, 258, 262, 263, 264, 266, 267, 270, 272, 273, 284, 285
Far East, 24
farm income, 199
farm labor, 156
farming, 26, 75, 155, 156, 172, 186, 199
Federal Reserve, 204, 214
federal spending, 211
Federal Trade Commission, 202
federalism, 228
fertility rate, 142
feudalism, 29, 88
financial crises, 204
financial resources, 104, 121, 156, 194
financial sector, 214
financial stability, 131
financial support, 199, 202
finite, 69
firearms, 173
First Continental Congress, 48, 50
fiscal policy, 215, 224
flexibility, 196
Florida, 20, 30
Ford, Henry, 57, 158
foreign investment, 153
foreign trade, 91
forgiveness, 245
Fourth Amendment, 129

France, 9, 20, 25, 30, 39, 52, 59, 60, 75, 84, 103, 117, 150, 152
Franklin, Benjamin, 26, 28, 34, 41, 46, 50, 51, 74, 75, 117, 134, 137, 148, 158, 186, 257
free market, xii, 6, 8, 9, 10, 11, 12, 13, 91, 96, 136, 137, 141, 150, 152, 154, 155, 156, 162, 167, 169, 177, 178, 179, 183, 184, 185, 188, 194, 205, 220, 236, 237, 238, 239, 248, 249, 250, 259, 260, 261, 262, 263, 267, 280, 285
free market capitalism, 184
free speech, 60
free trade, 90, 135, 193, 198
freedom of speech, 135
freedom of the press, 70
French and Indian War, 39
full employment, 214, 220

G

general revenue, 44, 45
geography, 155
Georgia, 30, 49, 75, 106, 116, 130, 174, 183, 195
Germany, 22, 23, 144, 152, 185, 284
good deeds, 1
goods and services, 6, 7, 8, 10, 12, 69, 95, 147, 162, 185, 187, 188, 237, 258, 271
government, xi, 3, 11, 30, 32, 63, 64, 65, 66, 68, 77, 79, 81, 106, 123, 125, 126, 128, 130, 132, 133, 138, 176, 193, 194, 195, 201, 202, 215, 224, 226, 228, 272, 287
government contracts, 266
government intervention, 131, 150, 208, 209, 211, 260
government policy, 14, 211, 262
government regulation, 63, 194, 221
government spending, 220, 224
gratitude, 105, 248
gravitation, 72
Great Britain, 11, 16, 37, 40, 60, 69, 74, 76, 92, 93, 105, 156, 234
Great Depression, 185, 213, 227
Greece, 19, 78, 178, 284
Gross Domestic Product, 29, 147, 168
group membership, 265
Guam, 152

H

happiness, ix, xii, 76, 84, 96, 229, 231, 232, 250, 251, 253, 276, 287
harming, 132
Harvard College, 28
hate, 86

Hawaii, 168
health care, 224
health services, 225
hedonism, 1, 271
Henry, Patrick, 39, 42, 49, 50, 66, 113, 115, 234
Hispanics, 183
Hollywood, 277
Hong Kong, 11, 16, 154
House of Representatives, 42, 116, 121, 125, 132, 195
housing, 211, 215, 227, 247, 265, 271, 284
human behavior, 31, 34, 61, 62, 63, 238, 249, 282
human capital, 22, 142, 145, 146, 147, 148, 157
human creativity, 286
human resources, 211
human rights, 66, 279, 283
Hungary, 185
hypertension, 223

I

illegal immigration, 152
Illinois, 162, 163, 171, 197, 200, 216, 251
illiteracy, 5, 179
immigrants, 156, 163, 258
immigration policy, 144, 145, 151, 152, 163
immorality, 284
imperialism, 152, 153
import duties, 131, 132
imports, 27, 29, 35, 41, 45, 46, 49, 91, 111
imprisonment, 59, 211
income, 27, 149, 210, 221, 228
income inequality, 93
independence, 37, 46, 50, 52, 54, 68, 70, 74, 75, 77, 78, 83, 100, 103, 105, 107, 110, 113, 117, 119, 129, 134, 152, 171, 177, 182, 257, 279
India, 11, 39, 44, 47, 48, 50, 151, 168
Indian affairs, 52, 107
Indiana, 287
individual rights, 65, 150, 205
individualism, xii, 3, 12, 13, 51, 156, 261, 268, 280, 283
Indonesia, 154
industrial revolution, 89, 186, 251
industrialization, 134, 177, 184, 186, 187, 188, 194, 284
industrialized nations, 167
infant mortality rates, 5, 285
infinite, 141, 203, 249
inflation, 109, 168, 184, 185, 188, 214, 285
injustice, 78, 87, 98, 173, 242
inputs, 168

integrity, 51, 234
intelligence, 72, 86, 137
interest groups, 35, 40, 122, 125, 199, 215
interest rates, 63
intervention, 9, 12, 52
interview, 223
intimidation, 58, 174
inventions, 75, 195, 250
investment, 13, 22, 23, 24, 31, 142, 146, 147, 153, 176, 200
investment opportunities, 153
Iraq, 151
Ireland, 19, 23, 25, 50, 145
Israel, 185, 241, 253, 254, 284

J

Jackson, William, 114
Japan, 151, 154, 161, 270
Jefferson, Thomas, 2, 48, 51, 57, 66, 73, 74, 75, 76, 96, 110, 111, 112, 113, 115, 116, 128, 131, 134, 137, 138, 158, 175, 195, 231, 237, 254, 259, 274, 285
Jerusalem, 253
job security, 268
judicial review, 121, 198
justification, 7, 207, 261

K

Kansas, 36, 81, 112, 125, 138, 171, 206, 208, 209
Kennedy, John F., 75
Kentucky, 159, 195
King George II, 37, 38, 69, 75, 197
knowledge, xi, 2, 11, 23, 25, 29, 58, 61, 62, 71, 73, 88, 125, 146, 148, 159, 201, 202, 233, 235, 240, 260, 262, 268

L

labor costs, 146
labor disputes, 212
labor force, 30, 143, 146, 147, 155, 156, 158, 161, 167, 181, 187, 202, 237, 238, 271
labor law, 198
labor market, 136, 146, 147, 151, 152, 182, 185, 187, 205, 212, 215, 217, 218
labor movement, 203
labor shortage, 23, 144, 180, 181
labor, organized, 145, 197, 203, 212
land ownership, 179

leadership, 50, 68, 105, 109, 174
legal rights, 238
legislation, 35, 38, 40, 41, 43, 47, 48, 64, 71, 106, 110, 121, 122, 129, 131, 142, 143, 144, 176, 178, 179, 184, 198, 200, 202, 203, 206, 207, 208, 211, 212, 213, 214, 215, 217, 220, 222, 223, 224, 273
legislative powers, 54
liberalism, 4
liberals, 79, 218
life expectancy, 170, 239
lifestyle, 69, 202, 221, 256
liquidity, 226
living standard, 69, 182
Livingston, Robert, 74
loans, 19, 27, 117, 162, 193, 213, 226
local government, 224, 225
Locke, John, 2, 39, 61, 63, 66, 73, 78, 79, 81, 127
Louisiana, 30, 206
loyalty, 53, 234

M

Madison, James, 15, 16, 78, 96, 110, 111, 114, 115, 116, 118, 119, 122, 125, 127, 131, 132, 254
Mafia, 267
Maine, 32, 52
mainland, 20
manners, 148, 239
manufactured goods, 26
manufacturing, 8, 26, 30, 103, 108, 123, 131, 134, 168, 170, 175, 180, 195, 196, 199, 212, 213, 218
manufacturing sector, 26
market economy, 6, 7, 8, 12, 13, 16, 96, 148, 157, 168, 179, 198, 222, 249, 260
market system, 7, 8, 9, 96, 154, 196, 238
marketplace, 97, 169, 187
marriage, xi, 131, 167, 261, 269, 271, 273
marriage rate, 271
Marshall Plan, 160
Marx, Karl, 167, 182
Marxism, 164
Maryland, 25, 30, 49, 111, 113, 116, 130, 195, 197, 198, 202
mass production, 186, 199
Massachusetts, 25, 28, 30, 31, 38, 42, 45, 46, 48, 49, 50, 71, 75, 109, 111, 113, 116, 160, 171, 193, 197, 202
materialism, 258
Mayflower, 30, 59

mediation, 69
Medicaid, xi, 224
mercantilism, 29, 31, 35, 88, 89, 108
metaphor, 91
metaphysics, 233, 235
Mexico, 145
Miami, 171
Michigan, 20, 183, 267, 272, 276
Middle East, 161
military conflict, 108
military force, 41, 52
military presence, 153
militias, 103
Mill, John Stuart, 2, 15, 16, 259
minimum wage, 182, 202, 212, 215, 217, 218, 226
mining, 170, 175, 203
Minnesota, 174, 197, 216
minority rights, 13
Mississippi, 41, 48, 177
Missouri, 171, 197, 267, 276
modernization, 184, 188, 279, 284
money, 7, 10, 19, 22, 26, 29, 32, 34, 43, 44, 59, 71, 88, 93, 107, 108, 109, 110, 124, 127, 128, 131, 132, 133, 134, 135, 142, 145, 156, 162, 168, 170, 180, 181, 183, 186, 194, 196, 201, 205, 214, 215, 224, 225, 226, 241, 243, 244, 245, 247, 257, 263, 270, 284, 285
money supply, 183, 205, 214
monopoly pricing, 154
Monroe Doctrine, 153
Monroe, James, 174
moral standards, 283
morality, 3, 5, 32, 49, 58, 62, 85, 115, 116, 196, 234, 236, 250, 254, 257, 259, 262, 271, 282, 284
mortality rates, 142, 148, 175
motivation, 20, 146, 175, 257
multiculturalism, 150

N

narcissism, 242
national debt, 93, 185, 196, 203, 211, 212, 219, 225, 226, 268
national income, 29
national interest, 259
National Labor Relations Act, 215, 218
National Research Council, 146
national wealth, 29, 133, 169, 285
nationalism, 153, 198, 255
nationalization, 201
nation-state, 150

Native Americans, 171, 267
natural resources, 5, 26, 142, 154, 175
negotiation, 132
Netherlands, 20, 27, 46, 152, 154
networking, 162
New Deal, 214, 215, 217, 218, 219, 227, 258, 260
New Hampshire, 32, 49, 116, 118, 197
New Jersey, 16, 28, 111, 116, 117, 254
New Mexico, 175
Newfoundland, 21, 50
nihilism, 260
Nobel Prize, 75, 149
North Carolina, 49, 116, 130
Nova Scotia, 50

O

offspring, 28, 30, 34, 234, 237, 250, 256, 285
Ohio, 48
Oklahoma, 174, 228, 260
opportunity costs, 182
oppression, 58, 79, 92, 121, 124, 150, 206, 242, 261, 266, 267
originality, 75
output, 5, 6, 8, 12, 21, 26, 28, 30, 36, 89, 161, 167, 168, 180, 199, 213, 214, 224, 241

P

Pacific, 183, 200
Paine, Thomas, 52, 55, 104, 112
Panama, 152
Parliament, 31, 32, 38, 40, 41, 42, 43, 44, 45, 46, 47, 48, 49, 58, 59, 60, 67, 68, 69, 71, 74, 119, 167
Pennsylvania, 23, 25, 28, 29, 30, 31, 43, 45, 49, 106, 111, 117, 125, 134, 148, 160, 195, 266, 286
personal liberty, 51, 128, 279
personal relations, 67
personal responsibility, xii, 51, 273
personality, 157
persuasion, 267
Philippines, 152, 159
physical capital, 147
pipelines, 200
pluralism, 283
police, 196, 203, 205, 207, 216, 226, 264
political freedom, 11, 24, 35, 153
political parties, 59, 60, 248, 257
political process, 179, 199, 259
political reform, 201

pollution, 8, 184, 285
population growth, 24, 141, 167
pornography, 259
Portugal, 11, 20, 25, 154
postal system, 107
poverty, xi, xii, 1, 13, 21, 31, 35, 69, 72, 78, 87, 88, 97, 115, 132, 160, 167, 169, 174, 175, 184, 188, 213, 214, 220, 221, 234, 237, 241, 242, 243, 244, 247, 248, 258, 261, 262, 267, 281, 285
pragmatism, 35, 155
prenatal care, 142
presidential veto, 122
price controls, 134
prison population, 269
private enterprise, 34, 223
private interests, 137
private property, xiii, 7, 64, 65, 71, 84, 127, 128, 129, 200, 206, 238, 241
probability of success, 91
productivity, 21, 22, 26, 64, 89, 146, 156, 167, 168, 171, 182, 185, 187, 199, 222, 239, 250, 261, 271, 280
property rights, 8, 10, 31, 32, 41, 62, 65, 77, 129, 196, 197, 205, 216, 220, 238, 241, 249
puberty, 237
public assistance, 149
public debt, 131
public funding, 271
public health, 206
public interest, 87, 90, 114, 131, 197, 216, 260
public life, 69, 105, 113, 256
public opinion, 3, 5, 87, 275, 277
public policy, xii, 3, 32, 35, 93, 152, 220, 267, 285
public realm, 3
public schools, 271
public sector, 162, 212, 224, 260, 266, 268
public services, 148
public welfare, 32, 84, 216
public works, 212, 213
Puerto Rico, 152

R

race relations, 188
racism, 150, 263, 271, 279
rate, birth, 24, 141, 142, 151, 167, 270
rate, death, 24, 25, 167, 268
rate, immigration, 145, 151
rational, 57
rationalism, 262, 281, 282
raw materials, 6, 153

reasoning, 45, 50, 58
recession, 152, 184, 185
reconstruction, 178, 184, 213
refugees, 152
relatives, 145, 242
religious life, 240
religious observance, 254
Renaissance, 19, 20, 61, 186
repetition, 151, 234, 238, 250
residential buildings, 196
resolution, 76, 226
resource allocation, 8
restitution, 48, 266
reunification, 144
Revere, Paul, 45, 51, 71
rhetoric, 67, 85, 215
Rhode Island, 29, 30, 47, 49, 110, 113, 116, 254
rice, 23, 176
rights of individuals, 128
rights, political, 121, 124
road construction, 34
Roman Empire, 67
Roosevelt, Franklin D., 264
Roosevelt, Theodore, 202, 250
Royal Society, 63
Russia, 144
Rutledge, John, 49

S

safety net, 154
scarce resources, 7, 89, 90, 142, 185, 238
scarcity, 5, 9
scientific method, 63
Scotland, 23, 58, 84, 85, 88, 237
secularization, 274
self-help organizations, 149, 258
self-interest, 14, 31, 62, 83, 84, 85, 90, 96, 97, 119, 124, 136, 249, 257
sexism, 150, 263, 271
sexual harassment, 267
Sherman B., 74, 201, 202, 203
Sherman, Roger, 49, 74
slavery, 11, 14, 23, 24, 26, 50, 72, 75, 77, 78, 105, 130, 134, 136, 153, 155, 176, 177, 178, 179, 180, 188, 190, 197, 205, 206, 235, 255, 259, 279, 281
slums, 148, 201
small business, 161
Smith, Adam, ix, xiii, xv, 2, 47, 55, 83, 84, 90, 92, 94, 96, 99, 100, 101, 119, 135, 173, 189, 198, 235, 237, 239, 248, 250, 251, 252, 259
smoking, 187, 264

social acceptance, 266
social change, 199, 212
social justice, 240, 279
social mobility, 34, 77, 155
social movements, 231
social security, xii, 219, 223
social spending, 223
social structure, 151, 152
socialism, 248
societal standards, 3, 9
South Africa, 11
South Carolina, 49, 71, 75, 116, 130
South Dakota, 174
sovereignty, 58, 65, 69, 107, 108, 152, 196, 198
Soviet Union, 6, 151, 154, 168, 284
Spain, 20, 25, 39, 110, 151, 154
specialization, 89, 135, 154, 156, 187
spectacle, 105
spheres of influence, 29
Stamp Act, 42, 43, 45, 71
standard of living, 5, 13, 21, 24, 27, 37, 83, 89, 145, 188, 249, 258
stars, 52, 286
state regulation, 31
Statue of Liberty, 144
steam engine, 186
suicide rate, 269, 270
superstition, 43
supply and demand, 38, 89, 142, 154
Supreme Court, 105, 121, 122, 194, 197, 198, 200, 202, 203, 204, 206, 207, 208, 209, 211, 212, 216, 217, 218, 220
Sweden, 11
Switzerland, 154
sympathy, 85, 97, 212

T

tax base, 71
tax burden, 43, 268
tax collection, 44
tax concessions, 226
tax revenues, 224, 225
taxes, 34, 35, 37, 40, 41, 42, 44, 45, 47, 49, 59, 60, 65, 71, 88, 106, 108, 109, 120, 132, 135, 137, 147, 184, 195, 204, 215, 217, 219, 224, 225, 274, 280
Technology, 142
telecommunications, 159
telegraph, 201, 211
Tennessee, 180
third world, 145, 146, 149, 151
tobacco industry, 23

totalitarianism, 14
trade barriers, 90, 226
trade imbalance, 20
trade union, 197
traditional values, 37, 220, 272
training programs, 170
traits, 73, 88, 149, 264
transportation, 21, 22, 23, 145, 146, 179, 184, 198, 199, 202, 212, 220, 222, 223
Treaty of Paris, 39, 41, 110
tribalism, 150
troops, 40, 44, 48, 50, 51, 54, 71, 103, 104, 105, 110, 129
truthfulness, 265, 267
tuberculosis, 284
turbulence, 124, 177

U

underclass, xi, 269, 271
unemployment, 33, 90, 146, 152, 175, 185, 188, 207, 213, 214, 222, 224, 284, 285
unemployment rate, 152, 175, 185, 213, 222, 284
unions, 147, 182, 198, 203, 208, 215, 239, 259
United States, ix, xi, xiii, 1, 6, 8, 11, 12, 13, 35, 36, 46, 66, 68, 75, 76, 78, 105, 107, 108, 110, 112, 113, 114, 115, 116, 121, 127, 128, 131, 132, 135, 136, 137, 141, 143, 144, 145, 147, 149, 150, 151, 152, 153, 154, 155, 168, 169, 170, 171, 173, 174, 175, 178, 182, 183, 184, 185, 187, 188, 191, 193, 194, 195, 196, 197, 198, 204, 205, 206, 208, 209, 210, 211, 214, 215, 217, 220, 224, 227, 228, 231, 250, 254, 255, 261, 268, 269, 270, 273, 279, 280
urbanization, 134, 188, 199, 284
Utah, 208

V

Vermont, 106
veto power, 49

Vietnam, 220, 260
violence, xiii, 14, 174, 176, 179, 263, 269, 271, 272, 281, 283, 285
violent crime, 268
virtue, xi, xii, xiii, 3, 4, 9, 15, 16, 49, 54, 62, 70, 71, 73, 84, 87, 96, 108, 115, 120, 129, 132, 133, 134, 136, 137, 155, 181, 227, 231, 232, 233, 234, 235, 236, 237, 239, 241, 248, 253, 255, 257, 258, 259, 260, 261, 262, 266, 279, 281, 282, 283, 284, 285, 286, 287
voting, 179, 180, 199, 201

W

Washington, George, 34, 41, 49, 51, 52, 104, 112, 113, 116, 118, 121, 131, 141, 143, 148, 168, 254, 256
wealth, ix, 27, 34, 55, 83, 85, 88, 94, 96, 100, 101, 189, 247, 250, 251
welfare state, xi, xii, 149, 169, 195
welfare system, 149, 258
West Germany, 154, 258, 259
Western civilization, 279
western culture, 279
Whitney, Eli, 156
Wilson, James, 48, 117
Wilson, Woodrow, 208
Wisconsin, 20
working conditions, 22, 198, 203, 237
World War II, 151, 154, 157, 158, 160, 181, 219, 220, 222, 224

Y

Yugoslavia, 151